UNDERSTANDING STUDENT LEARNING

NEW PATTERNS OF LEARNING SERIES
EDITED BY P.J. HILLS, UNIVERSITY OF LEICESTER

Understanding Student Learning

NOEL J. ENTWISTLE and PAUL RAMSDEN

CROOM HELM
London & Canberra
NICHOLS PUBLISHING COMPANY
New York

© 1983 N.J. Entwistle and P. Ramsden
Croom Helm Ltd, Provident House, Burrell Row,
Beckenham, Kent
Croom Helm Australia, P.O. Box 391, Manuka,
ACT 2603 Australia

British Library Cataloguing in Publication Data

Entwistle, N.J.
    Understanding student learning.
    1. Learning, Psychology of
    I. Title   II. Ramsden, P.
    370.15'23   LB1051
    ISBN 0-7099-0921-7

First published in the United States of America 1982
by Nichols Publishing Company, Post Office Box 96, New York,
NY 10024

Library of Congress Cataloging in Publication Data

Entwistle, Noel.
    Understanding student learning.

    Includes bibliographical references and index.
    1. Learning. 2. Study, Method of. I. Ramsden, Paul.
II. Title.
LB1060.E55 1983   370.15'23   83-11443
ISBN 0-89397-171-5

Printed and bound in Great Britain
by Billing & Sons Limited, Worcester.

CONTENTS

Foreword

Preface

Acknowledgements

FOREWORD

by William G. Perry Jr.
Professor of Education, Emeritus,
Harvard University

The authors of this book invite you to accompany them in the search for an understanding of how college students learn. Fifty years have proved that this understanding will be complex and hard to find. Yet the goal is worthy of such heroic strategies of search and subtle tactics of divination as this book reports. I share these authors' conviction that success in this search may enhance the quality of our civilization through the improvement of advanced teaching.

Professors of Arts and Sciences on both sides of the Atlantic long shared a conviction that all the arts are subject to intellectual analysis - all the arts but one: that of teaching in higher education. This art was held sacred to the individual. The good lecturer was one who knew his subject and gave a clear exposition of it enlivened by his own personal style. Though many a conscientious lecturer wondered how so many students managed not to learn what he explained so clearly, he had little to comfort him but the thought that students differ in their aptitude. For shaping his teaching, he had few resources to call upon beyond his own experiences of having been taught.

The recent economic necessity to attract students and 'retain' them - especially competitive in the United States - has forced the issues into the open. It is now legitimate to concede that some college teaching may be susceptible of improvement - even perhaps one's own. There has followed a wave of 'Faculty Development Programs', the assumption being that the way to improve teaching is to get in there and improve it. Much university teaching has been so impoverished that even these direct methods have brought some results and won the gratitude of teachers who had worried in secret.

But in these programs the TV camera and the 'teaching hints' have commonly focused solely on the teacher's presentation. The students have then been allowed to evaluate the results with scales that ask 'Are the lectures well organized?'

Rarely does the evaluation form ask the student 'Did this course give you an opportunity to organize your thoughts about the subject?' The very form of the evaluation itself therefore confirms the students in a Lockean assumption about education in which their responsibility is to be passive recipients of the teacher's art. Such teachers' arts as clarity, organization and illustration are indeed open to analysis and improvement in their own right with only implicit reference to students. But I was once on the staff of a war-time course in celestial navigation in which every improvement in the lucidity of our exposition, beyond a certain point, was accompanied by a deterioration in most students' capacity to solve navigational problems. When we cleverly pretended befuddlement at critical moments and asked the students to bail us out, the result gave us confidence that it would be safe to go to sea with them.

The present authors assume boldly that the sole purpose of teaching is to facilitate learning. They assume that learning, well organized or not, is done by the student. They state openly their hope that once we understand more about how different students learn, we can help them to learn better. But who are 'we'? 'Study-counsellors' or 'educationists' like myself? The authors trust, as I do, that as professors of Arts and Sciences come to understand more about students' ways of learning, they will the better assist the learning; in short, they will teach better.

We are back to a prior question. Do we not know how students learn, or should learn, already? We once thought so. In 1942 I composed a manual of 'Effective Study Methods' for freshmen in a small college. Years later I discovered that my great-grandfather had composed in 1842 an identical manual for students in an academy in his parish. His language differed from mine in being quaint, but otherwise the handbooks were identical from their emphasis on principle to the inclusion of a ruled calendar on the back for the students' convenience in designing a schedule of their time. It is a commentary on the slow growth of knowledge in the field that both of these manuals were ahead of their own day - my ancestor's because he was original,

mine because I had at hand a decade of a movement
called 'Guided Study' or 'Supervised Study'.
What was radical in both manuals was that each contained one small concession to the realities of
student experience: we both acknowledged that life
seldom conformed to the boundaries of a rigid
schedule, making the schedule a source of such overwhelming guilt that moral survival required its
consignment to the waste-basket. We each suggested,
instead, that the student keep a log-book of reality
and we offered fictitious and only slightly idealized
examples of how such schedules-in-the-past-tense
might read.

Apart from this small comfort, our manuals were
probably as useful, useless, and disruptive, as any
others.   In the forties and fifties researchers made
the stunning discovery that the explication of
'principles and procedures of effective study' was
largely redundant: most students knew them in
advance; they simply did not follow them.   Such a
negative finding of mere research was of course not
enough to stop established practitioners of study-
coaching like myself.   Some students seemed to
benefit from our efforts.   ,

But we could not quiet our curiosity.   In
what ways did these 'some' students differ from other
students?   Did other students learn best in ways othe
than those outlined in our catechism of principles?
These simple, fateful questions then multiplied, burst
the boundaries of the field and went questing in all
directions at once.   Relevant variables revealed
themselves to researchers in individual differences
in personality, motivation, styles of perception and
cognition, and manners of 'information processing',
all qualitative differences well-nigh dissolving
the global notion of 'aptitude'.

These variations of mind and temperament obser-
vable in individual learners were found to interact
(as the folklore had always known) with the character
of the several disciplines: qualitative vs. quantitative, concrete vs. abstract, analytic vs. synthetic,
ambiguous vs. unambiguous, hierarchical vs. con-
tiguous and so on.   Viewed as characteristics of
the several disciplines, however, these variables
proved to be unstable.   Not only did they vary
from department to department and course to course
within a discipline but they varied, as the students
well knew, with the way a given course was taught.
The search now entered the social and institutional
context in which the learning was carried on.   Here
differences appeared in level of performance demanded,

procedures of assessment, fixedness and flexibility
in the guidelines for action, degrees and quality
of personal attention in the relation of teacher
and learner. These variables, in turn, were found
to reflect assumptions about the nature of knowledge-
ability defining the context of a classroom or
institution. Here the search has led into realms
of epistemology and the sociology of knowledge.

It is into the matrix of these variations of
learners, subjects and contexts that the present
authors take you. That they work successfully with
all three kinds of variables at once is enough to
put them at the forefront of the field; but their
trail opens fresh vistas through their creative
synthesis of disparate methods of inquiry.

First of all they have combined both quantitative and qualitative modes of inquiry. They
modestly claim only to have 'alternated' these modes,
but you will probably feel that they have made a
productive synthesis through interweaving of quantitative analysis of questionnaires with the qualitative
assessment of interviews. (The latter assessments,
contributed by the Gothenburg researchers, had been
subjected to strict quantifiable discipline. I
would urge you to accord these data a status of
'objectivity' of their own quite comparable to that
of factor analysis of questionnaires. This is a
claim the authors are almost, but not quite, ready
to make).

In their assessment of social contexts, also,
the authors have built on the phenomenological foundations of the Gothenburg group by focusing on
students' perceptions rather than on the observations
of outside researchers in which relevance has so long
been sacrificed to the assumption of objectivity.
Here, too the range in different students' perceptions
of the same context has led back fruitfully to
individual differences.

In keeping with these modes of inquiry the
authors have subordinated the conventional input-
output model of research to focus on the delineation
of process. The old preoccupation with students'
ultimate performance following different methods of
instruction has too often obscured the rich variety
of the intervening learning behaviours and the
influence on these behaviours of the learner's antici-
pation of the very means by which performance will be
assessed.

The authors synthesize these modes of inquiry
and foci of attention in a way that provides heuristic
power beyond the sum of the parts. I shall not

venture to summarize the steps of their search or
their findings. You may find it helpful, however, if
I raise certain questions that will doubtless rise
of themselves as you read. By having them in mind
in advance, you may be prepared to appreciate from
the outset the challenges the authors have faced
and the skill they have brought to their tasks.

First of all, about nomenclature. It is
inevitable in so complex a field, drawing on research
findings suddenly emerging in diverse sources, that
terms and concepts should be unstable. Consider
such terms as 'cognitive style', 'perceptual style',
'learning style', 'learning strategies', 'approach',
'orientation', 'study pattern', 'learning skill',
'learning process','strategic approach' or simply
'way'. I find little consensus among researchers
about the conceptual referents of such terms or
about the relationships among them. The authors
of this book cannot be immune to these difficulties.
Indeed you may find their struggles to keep any
one of these terms in one place as illuminating as
their frequent successes.

Let us suppose now that the authors succeed in
keeping such terms as 'meaning orientation', 'deep
approach', 'surface orientation', 'holistic approach'
etc. in stable reference to distinguishable processes
characterizing the ways different students learn.
If we then assume that such learner-characteristics
(singly or in constellations) tend to remain stable
over time in individuals we will find it appropriate
to speak of different 'types' of students. The
preponderance of research on 'learning styles' to date
can be taken to justify the assumption of stability
of a large number of learner traits. These findings
provide the foundations of a number of typologies
classifying learners by various constellations of
traits posited as stable over time. This evidence
commends us to think in terms of types of students,
each type characterized by abiding preferences for
proceeding in a certain way in address to learning
tasks, even though these tasks may differ. Indeed
some recent studies have reported that when college
students specialize in subject-matter congruent with
their preferred styles, they intensify their preference and narrow their variability in response to
differing tasks.

We now face a serious dilemma. If we accept
the evidence for stability, we should simply add the
new findings about learner types to our historic
efforts to identify students' strengths and steer
them toward the specialties most congenial to them.

We could do no more.

On the other hand the authors of this book explicitly state their hope that the understandings of research into students' styles will help us to teach students to learn the better how to learn. Presumably, since all students must learn in more than a single discipline, they should learn to vary their learning strategies in keeping with the nature of various tasks. How can we support such a hope? Are we to imagine that learner 'type', though stable, is not, somehow, immutable? Or are we to suppose that stability and flexibility occur at different levels and that we can help students develop variations within their preferred learning mode without violating its integrity?

The authors of this book did not intend to address this dilemma directly. They live with the question as a tension pervading the field, and they offer their advances as contributions toward a later resolution. As reader, however, you may find yourself pondering the issue. I want therefore to share some questions about the assumptions that create the question.

First, a small technical concern regarding the measures from which the finding of 'stability' of 'type' or 'style' derives. How much time is the respondent allowed on each test? A leading researcher recently told me "The differences in the means of the types in our population were small and we could only get them if we put the students under heavy time pressure, stop-watch and all". Could it be that, denied the opportunity to survey the nature of the tasks, the students are artifically limited to some most frequently used 'best bet' approach? If so, the test may in fact reveal a student's 'best bet' way of learning, but it cannot demonstrate that this way remains invariant when the student perceives differences in tasks. Such a bias of measurement may be compounded when analysis is limited to students scoring at the extremes of a trait dimension. May not flexibility of style be greatest in the students scoring nearer the mean? You will be grateful to the authors for letting you know just how they designed each inquiry.

On a broader scale, most striking is the authors' inclusion in their opening chapter of descriptions of the intellectual development of students in the college years. One of these descriptions starts with tripartite typology on a dimension of impulsivity and rationality. It then traces the convergence over time of students at the extremes

toward the balanced ideal type at the mean.   The
second description of development traces the way
students evolve more complex forms of thought to
accommodate their perception of increased complexity,
uncertainty and ambiguity.   In this evolution the
students sequentially revise their conceptions of
knowledge, their sense of their role as learners,
and their expectations of teachers.   Both of
these descriptions were derived from longitudinal
studies of relatively small samples extending over
years.

The authors point out that their own undertaking,
remarkable for its scope and depth, provides neither
funds nor time for longitudinal research.   Yet they
were so generous as to give space to these descriptions
of student development, leaving it to the reader to
speculate on the relevance of such developmental
issues to conceptualizations of student types.   As
the author of one of these descriptions of development,
I join them in hoping that you will indeed speculate.
One question is unavoidable: "Could a certain con-
stellation of learner-characteristics represent less
an enduring student-type and more a moment of
evolution in a student's notion of what learning is
all about?"

You will of course find more issues to ponder
than those I am sketching.   What fascinates me is
the way they all seem to converge at each marker
the authors establish in their quest.   I end with
one example.

In their search for traits distinguishing 'deep'
learners and 'surface' learners, the authors discovered
a type of students who seemed to be game-players.
These seemed concerned first of all with out-guessing
the ultimate assessment, and they pumped their
instructors in the service of this goal.   The point
of it all seemed to be, for them, the score.   The
authors named this type 'strategic'.   I confess a
reservation regarding this use of the term to label
an address to social context since the authors also
use it in its usual sense to refer to approaches to
learning in address to subject matter.   In any case,
their first overall analysis showed that students
evincing this 'strategic approach' were among the
'surface' learners.   Characteristically, the authors
did not stop with this sensible observation but continued to test it with the interplay of factor analysis
and ratings of interviews.   This analysis differentiated
a sizable minority of the 'strategic' group who emerged
as deep learners.

This fine discrimination involves the very

foundations of education. Could it be that by
paying careful attention to what a good teacher has
on his mind some students can learn to read and learn
with deep comprehension? As teachers, this is our
only hope.

We have been hoping it for centuries. We know
from our daily experience with 'some' students that
the hope is well founded. These authors bring us
to the very brink of the scientific confirmation of
the hope with modern research tools. But they are
doing far more than confirming what we feel we know
already. They are delineating the ways those 'some'
students learn and how they learn to learn. So
also, then, for those 'other' students. Only from
such delineations we can hope to expand 'some'
students to 'most'.

Students sometimes speak for themselves about
this motion. In the later chapters of this book
the authors quote from students' interviews. In
these, some students report the excitement of
'realization' - the discovery that learning can be
more than memorization, even meaningful. We can feel
how near the authors have come to the goal of their
search.

They do not pretend to have found it. Indeed,
we may feel that they have been so dedicated in their
care for precise delineation of each clue in the
search that they have been reluctant to stand back,
as we can, to see how close they may have come to
the place where all the pieces will fall together.

Such modesty is appropriate to the difficulties;
the ultimate synthesis must include identification
of: those strategies or styles of learning so inte-
gral to persons that to learn other ways would be
inefficient or violating; those styles or strategies
which seem readily learnable; those aspects of
development that provide or accompany such readiness;
those instruments which best reveal these variables;
and finally, those conditions of institutional and
teaching context - as the various students perceive
them - that best facilitate the students' learning
and their learning how to learn.

When we thank these authors for advancing us so
far in this search, they will I am sure reiterate
their heavy debt to other researchers in Britain,
Sweden, Switzerland and North America. They offer
this book as an invitation to international collaboration in the search.

Watertown, Massachusetts
March 1983

PREFACE

        This book is an abridged and less technical
version of the Final Report on a five-year Social
Science Research Council research programme begun in
1976.   The full report on Research Grant HR 3881 has
been lodged with the British Library at Boston Spa.
The purpose of the research programme was to investigate students' approaches to learning, and to
determine the extent to which these reflected the
effects of teaching and assessment demands rather
than representing relatively stable characteristics
of the individual learners.
        The research programme was directed by Noel
Entwistle, then Professor of Educational Research at
the University of Lancaster.   The Senior Research
Officer working full-time on the programme throughout its duration was Paul Ramsden.   For the first
two years, Maureen Hanley (nee Robertson) worked on
the development of the questionnaire on reading
academic articles and on the development of the
inventory.   For the next two years this post was
filled by Sarah Morison (nee Burkinshaw).   The
programme also involved other members of the
Institute for Post-Compulsory Education at Lancaster,
and we are particularly grateful for the continuing
discussions we had with Dai Hounsell about our
emerging findings.   We are also grateful for the
interest and enthusiastic help given by Patrick
Thomas of Brisbane College of Advanced Education who
was visiting Research Fellow at Lancaster in 1978/79.
        The qualitative analysis of the interview data,
and the main survey of student approaches to learning and perceptions of courses, were carried out by
Paul Ramsden.   He has the main responsibility for
chapters 7 8 and 9, which have been written up more
fully as a doctoral thesis.
        Sarah Morison undertook the experiments and

produced the draft reports which formed the basis of chapters 5 and 6.

The camera-ready copy from which this book has been produced was typed by Jane Moore. Our gratitude for her accuracy and fortitude in coping with this extensive task, in addition to her normal secretarial duties, can be well imagined. Her forbearance in dealing with our last minute amendments and additions is much appreciated.

ACKNOWLEDGEMENTS

We are grateful to John Wiley and Sons Ltd. for permission to reproduce extracts from 'Styles of Learning and Teaching' by N.J. Entwistle published in 1981.

Chapter One

STUDENT LEARNING IN ITS CONTEXT

Higher education is a large and expensive undertaking. Its effects are felt by all of us.
There are currently over half a million full-time
students in the British system of education which
builds on, and goes beyond, sixth-form studies and
their equivalent. A sizeable proportion of the
country's wealth flows into the sixty-seven
universities and polytechnics which dominate this
sector. Many of the students who graduate from
these institutions will eventually occupy some of
the most powerful and prestigious positions in our
society. Whatever contractions the system may face
in the 1980s, no-one would wish to argue that an
understanding of what goes on in higher education
is unimportant.
    It comes as something of a surprise to realise
that, as recently as twenty years ago, there was
hardly any research into higher education in
Britain. Writing in 1972, the editors of a
symposium of articles on research in this field
could say that

> a decade ago, the universities and colleges of
> Britain were open to the accusation that they
> did research on almost every topic but them-
> selves ... If they were aware of the need for
> a better understanding both of fundamental
> principles in teaching and learning and of
> human relationships in the quadrangle, they
> did singularly little about it. Ten years
> ago a book of this kind would necessarily have
> been very thin. (Butcher and Rudd, 1972).

Research into higher education has since
established itself in this country, as the founding

1

of new journals and periodicals (such as The Times Higher Education Supplement and Studies in Higher Education) demonstrates. It is interesting to examine Butcher and Rudd's selection of papers; they give a flavour of the developing pattern of research. There are papers on the objectives and administration of higher education, including the academic profession and its role; discussions of economic and planning issues; articles on student protest; papers concerned with development and change in the student (including, for example, the effects of counselling); articles on experiment and change in teaching methods; and there is a section on the selection and academic performance of students. With the possible exception of the chapter on student protest, this list gives a good summary of the kinds of research which have taken place since, as well as before, 1972.

At the heart of higher education is the three-way transaction between the student, his teacher, and the material being studied. Students in higher education are expected to learn complex subject-matter and develop independence of judgment in the course of a dialogue with their teachers. But little direct attention has been given by researchers to the process of student learning and the effects of teaching on it. Although student performance - measured in terms of degree results - and student wastage have been examined, how the student learns has not, at least until very recently. Although research into teaching methods is well represented - and has expanded greatly since 1972 - inquiries relating the teaching to students' learning are much less common. The research tradition in the field of higher education has touched on its central triangle but has barely begun to enter it.

How are we to explain this lack of interest? One of the reasons may be the dominant view of lecturers in higher education that success and failure is the responsibility of the individual student. Up to a point, this idea is a very reasonable one. It stems partly from the concern for the individual which distinguishes the British higher education system from its counterparts in other countries. It also has its roots in the experiences of the lecturers themselves when they were undergraduates. They were, by definition, very successful students. The general view seems to be that there are few "good" students - students able to become deeply involved in a subject and evaluate it critically - and many weak or mediocre ones (see Entwistle and Percy, 1974,

2

for evidence of this view). Lecturers tend to
think that the context or environment of student
learning is not of great importance: they attribute
success or failure to the characteristics of the
student, not to their teaching.

As a consequence we know remarkably little
about the effects of lecturers' teaching, assessment,
and course organization on student learning.
Students in British universities and polytechnics
spend a good deal of their time in one or two
academic departments; it seems quite possible that
the way students approach studying is influenced by
the way the departments are run. What are the
differing demands made on the students by learning
tasks in both arts and science departments, and how
do students respond to these demands? What makes
one department a "better" place to learn than
another? Students themselves are clearly aware
that departments differ in their attitudes to them,
just as they recognize that some lecturers are more
effective at putting over their subject than others.
Is student learning genuinely not a function of how
well lecturers teach? (If not, the implications
require at least some thought.)

The emphasis on individual attributes of students in the explanation of academic success and
failure has been complemented by the research designs
which have typically been used. A rather simple input-output model of students entering university
with a bundle of characteristics and leaving it with
or without a good degree has been adopted. The
results of attempts to predict academic success by
this method cannot be said to be unequivocal.
Correlations between performance and student characteristics - personality traits, previous evidence of
ability, scores in intelligence tests - are often
disappointingly low. It seems that something
happens during the period of the student's university
experience which traditional research has not examined.

All this does not mean, of course, that individual differences between students should be ignored.
Students enter higher education with different
interests, expectations, motivations, and personalities. It would be surprising if the ways they
study were not related to their individual preferences. But it is quite another thing to argue that
there is one best combination of individual characteristics which leads to success, or that "good" and
"weak" students remain unchanged by the teaching and
courses they encounter. Individual differences and

3

the university environment interact subtly and con-
tinuously, and a proper understanding of student
learning needs to take both things into account.
    This book contains the findings of the largest
programme of research into student learning ever
carried out in Britain, in a form which we hope will
be accessible to students, lecturers, and all who
have an interest in higher education. We hope it
will be seen partly as a contribution towards a
changing emphasis in research into higher education.
Our focus is on the process of student learning itself, and on the way it is influenced for better or
worse by the environment in which it takes place.
The approach derives much of its impetus from the
seminal work of a group of researchers at Gothenburg
University in Sweden, whose research will be described in the next Chapter. Qualitative methods,
such as semi-structured interviews, are one of the
hallmarks of this perspective. More traditional
quantitative techniques can, as we shall see, also
be incorporated without losing sight of the main
strengths of the approach; indeed, they can enrich
it. This perspective cuts across disciplines: insights from sociology and anthropology complement
psychological viewpoints. The interest is not so
much in the conventional outcomes of higher education - degree performance and numbers of students
as a proportion of resources invested - as in what
learning means to the students. This kind of research examines different conceptions of subject-
matter and differences in how students tackle learning tasks, and looks at how these differences arise
and how they are related to the level of understanding reached. How do students approach every day
academic tasks like reading, problem solving, and
assessment? Why do they seem to prefer very
different approaches? How do students' ways of
learning in different subjects differ? How is their
learning influenced by personal preferences and the
tasks and teaching they encounter? Which ways of
studying are most likely to bring success and satisfaction?
    Many of these questions start from the point of
view of the student, rather than that of the teacher
or researcher. We shall argue that they offer an
understanding of the reality of student learning
which other perspectives cannot. The answers to
these issues also have some far-reaching practical
implications. Many of the findings of this research have immediate relevance to lecturers who
wish to improve their teaching, and for students who

4

want to improve how they study.   There are also
important implications for increasing the efficiency
of learning in the costly business of higher
education.

Chapter Two

INTELLECTUAL DEVELOPMENT AND APPROACHES TO STUDYING

The research programme at Lancaster grew out of
previous work there which had been funded by the
Joseph Rowntree Memorial Trust. The main purpose
of that six-year study, which began in 1968, was to
examine the objectives of lecturers in higher
education in relation to students' academic performance. The research on students divided into two
parts. One was a longitudinal survey designed to
identify student attributes which might predict
their subsequent degree performances. The other
was an interview study intended to explore students'
reasons for entering higher education and their experiences of it. The experience gained in this
study substantially influenced the planning of the
new research programme. On the one hand, it had
shown the importance of trying to marry qualitative
and quantitative methods of educational research.
On the other, it had shown clearly the limitations
of the input-output model in thinking about higher
education. Relatively stable psychological
characteristics of students proved to be only weakly
related to levels of academic performance. It became clear that greater attention would have to be
placed on study processes and on the context, or
academic environment, within which students learn.
These two directions of research have been
developed out of quite separate sets of literature.
In presenting this report, therefore, the conceptual
basis for the research is also presented separately.
In this chapter the literature relating to intellectual development and approaches to studying is discussed, while research into the academic context of
learning in higher education is introduced in
chapter 7.
The studies which have influenced the work of
the programme are presented largely in historical
6

order, although at least one of these studies was not in fact 'discovered' until quite recently.

LECTURERS' EXPECTATIONS[A]

Part of the previous work at Lancaster was concerned with lecturers' aims and objectives and with students' experiences of higher education. Lecturers in various academic departments were asked questions about what they expected from 'good' students and what they saw as the characteristics of weaker students. Although there were, of course, great differences in the specific comments of lecturers in contrasting departments, there was an important common thread running through most of the replies. While knowledge and technical skills were expected, students had to be able to use these effectively - to combine and interrelate ideas. Short extracts from the comments of three of the lecturers provide an impression of what, in one way or another, most lecturers were demanding. An English lecturer, for example, said:

"I would be expecting a kind of alertness and openness - that may sound very general. Alert to what? Alert to all the signs of interest or significance in passages of literature. We try to develop their evaluative skills ... to develop the sense of what is the first hand piece of writing and what is purely derivative. .. the prime moral outcome of a literature course (should be the) ability to enter into different individual and social conditions ... to be able to realise what it is like to be somebody else, so that we can properly interact with other people and not always expect them to be mutations of oneself or of one's own culture."**

---

*   This section, and parts of other sections, have been taken from Entwistle (1981) <u>Styles of Learning and Teaching</u>, published by Wiley, which contains fuller descriptions of previous research, together with discussions of its psychological bases.
**   These interviews were carried out by Keith Percy and have been reported in more detail elsewhere (Entwistle and Percy, 1971; 1974).

A history lecturer saw the need for using evidence effectively, again combined with a form of social awareness.

"History, typically, does involve the assembly of evidence, coming to conclusions about certain problems ... (you tend) to consider (an idea) from all angles with a critical eye. Basically if you're treating it non-academically you tend merely to accept it and then to file it ... (but) then there's going to be no progress or change. Things are not going to move if you merely accept. You've got to scrutinize what you're doing (to see) if the thing cannot be done better."

In the science departments there was, of course, more emphasis on knowledge of facts, but even so there was also a recognition that factual information, in itself, is a rapidly diminishing asset. 'Knowledge' has to be reinterpreted to include

"techniques of analysis, rather than knowledge of facts; knowledge of techniques for finding facts, rather than the facts themselves."

The unifying theme both in the interviews and in the general literature on the aims of university education is that of 'critical thinking', or as Ashby has described it - 'post-conventional thinking'.

"The student (moves) from the uncritical acceptance of orthodoxy to creative dissent over the values and standards of society... (In higher education) there must be opportunities for the intellect to be stretched to its capacity, the critical faculty sharpened to the point where it can change ideas" (Ashby, 1973, pages 147-9).

What evidence is there that students do develop towards the intellectual goal described by lecturers?

RELATIVISTIC REASONING AND THE "REASONABLE ADVENTURER"

Two American interview studies shed light on this question. William Perry (1970) interviewed students once in each of their four years at Harvard or Radcliffe. Through all the transcripts of the interviews there seemed to run a dimension describing the progress students made from dualistic thinking to "contextual relativistic reasoning". Initially some students expected simple 'black and white' explanations in both their courses and their everyday life. Their experience of higher education was in conflict with this expectation; they found inconclusive evidence, alternative theories, and competing value systems. The enormity of this uncertainty challenges fundamental beliefs and values and can be a traumatic shock for some students.

Perry was able to identify nine positions along the dimension of intellectual and ethical development. Independent judges checked his categorizations. His summary of the nine positions is given below.

Position 1: The student sees the world in polar terms of we-right-good vs. other-wrong-bad. Right Answers for everything exist in the Absolute, known to Authority whose role is to mediate (teach) them. Knowledge and goodness are perceived as quantitative accretions of discrete rightnesses to be collected by hard work and obedience (paradigm: a spelling test).

Position 2: The student perceives diversity of opinion, and uncertainty, and accounts for them as unwarranted confusion in poorly qualified Authorities or as mere exercises set by Authority 'so we can learn to find The Answer for ourselves'.

Position 3: The student accepts diversity and uncertainty as legitimate but still temporary in areas where Authority 'hasn't found the Answer yet'. He supposes Authority grades him in these areas on 'good expression' but remains puzzled as to standards.

Position 4: (a) The student perceives legitimate uncertainty (and therefore diversity of opinion) to be extensive and raises it to the status of an unstructured epistemological realm of its own in which 'anyone has a right to his own opinion', a realm which he sets over against Authority's realm where right-wrong still prevails, or (b) the student discovers qualitative contextual relativistic reasoning as a special case of 'what They want' within Authority's realm.

Position 5: The student perceives all knowledge

and values (including authority's) as contextual and relativistic and subordinates dualistic right-wrong functions to the status of a special case, in context.

Position 6: The student apprehends the necessity of orienting himself in a relativistic world through some form of personal Commitment (as distinct from unquestioned or unconsidered commitment to simple belief in certainty).

Position 7: The student makes an initial Commitment in some area.

Position 8: The student experiences the implications of Commitment, and explores the subjective and stylistic issues of responsibility.

Position 9: The student experiences the affirmation of identity among multiple responsibilities and realizes Commitment as an ongoing, unfolding, activity through which he expresses his life style." (Perry, 1970, pages 9 - 10).

Perry (1978) provides a humorous interpretation of his carefully articulated scheme, in terms of four 'discoveries of the obvious'.

"When we first come into this world, it is obvious that there are authorities and that they know what they are doing, or at least so it seems. They tell us what to do and what not to do, and so they know what they are doing. That is discovery 1.
Discovery 2 is that they do not know what they are doing after all. And since they do not seem to know what they are doing and do not have all the answers, we think, 'Hurray! As soon as I can get out from under their tyranny I'm free, and any opinion is as good as any other, mine included.'
Discovery 3 is that when I get out from under their tyranny I walk smack into a plate-glass wall and find that I am still subject to a tyranny, not of <u>they</u> but of <u>fact</u>. And in that tyranny of reality I discover that, although there are a lot of differences of opinion among reasonable people, not every opinion is as good as any other, including some which I have that are no good at all. And then I have to get to work and start thinking about

all these things ...
    Then I make one more discovery, another
obvious one, that I am faced with the challenge
of affirming myself and my life as a person.
Given so many differences of opinion among
reasonable people, differences which reason
alone cannot resolve, I see that I can never be
sure I am making the 'right' decisions in life.
And yet I must decide. Oh, I have been told
never to make a wrong decision lest I regret it
all my life, but now I see I have no protection
against regret. Unless I am going to weasel
out of really living, I must choose what I believe in and own the consequences, and never
know what lay down the roads I did not take.
I have discovered ... what it means to commit."
(pages 267-8).

    Perry is stressing how students move from the
simplistic acceptance of facts presented by authority, through a period of confusion about the nature
of knowledge and belief, to a recognition that we
need to establish a personal philosophy of life
which is built out of our own interpretation of
relevant evidence, but which recognizes, and is
tolerant of, other people's alternative, even con-
flicting, interpretations of 'reality'.
    A very similar dimension of intellectual devel-
opment emerged from Roy Heath's (1964) interviews at
Princeton. But he defined it in terms of an ideal
type - the 'reasonable adventurer' - and three distinctive personality types 'the non-committer', 'the
hustler', and 'the plunger'. The contrasting personalities moved along different paths towards the
intellectual pinnacle already scaled by the reasonable adventurer. These personalities were limited
both in their personal relationships and in their
thinking. For example, the non-committer is over-
cautious, while the plunger's "thoughts zip from one
idea to another without apparent connection". The
reasonable adventurer manges to integrate these
apparently contradictory attributes showing

    "the combination of two mental attitudes: the
    curious and the critical. They do not occur
    simultaneously but in alternation. (The
    reasonable adventurer) at times is a 'believer'
    but at other times he is a 'skeptic'. The less
    effective personalities may show tendencies to-
    ward one attitude or the other but may not ex-
    perience the full reach of either". (page 31)

In a moment we shall meet again this description of thinking which brings together competing tendencies to create a whole which is more than the sum of parts.

THEMATIZATION AND CUE CONSCIOUSNESS

One limitation in both Heath's and Perry's research is the lack of any systematic exploration of the ways in which their more intellectually mature students approach everyday learning tasks. The questions asked are general; both Perry and Heath were interested in a whole range of students' experiences, both personal and academic. In contrast a series of studies, carried out mainly at Gothenburg University in Sweden, has examined conceptions of learning and the way students tackle an academic task of central importance in higher education - reading an academic article. The first two investigations demonstrate a connection between approaches to learning and intellectual development.

Saljo (1979) conducted interviews with adults who had differing lengths of formal education. He was interested in their conceptions of learning. One of the main characteristics of people who had either had an extended education, or had taken up studying again in adulthood, was the recognition that there are different types of learning appropriate for different sorts of tasks. For the majority of unsophisticated learners in the sample, learning was 'taken for granted' as involving rote memorization. For those who had experience of higher education, learning had become <u>thematized</u>.

"Learning is something that can be explicitly talked about and discussed and can be the object of conscious planning and analysis. In learning, these people realize that there are, for instance, alternative strategies or approaches which may be useful or suitable in various situations depending on, for example, time available, interest, demands of teachers and anticipated tests." (page 446).

The main distinctions drawn by these more sophisticated learners, besides the importance of context on the approach adopted, were between learning for real life and learning in school or between learning and understanding.
The 'awareness' that these learners show about

12

the selection of appropriate strategies is similar
to the 'cue-consciousness' described by Miller and
Parlett (1974) in relation to students' preparation
for examinations.

> "One group of students talked about the need to
> be perceptive and receptive to 'cues' sent out
> by staff - things like picking up hints about
> exam topics, noticing which aspects of the
> subject the staff favoured, noticing whether
> they were making a good impression in a
> tutorial and so on".   (page 52).

The artificiality of the examination situation,
and its effects on learning strategies, is seen
clearly by one of the students interviewed in this
study.

> "What is the purpose of the examination game?
> It becomes purposeless except for you, because
> you know you want to get a certain class of
> degree within the system, but as far as
> assimilating knowledge properly is concerned,
> it just doesn't work, because if you play the
> game properly you're choosing all the time, and
> not getting an overview because you know there
> will be a certain question you have to answer"
> (page 61).

The authors of the study identified two more
groups of students. The "cue-deaf" were less
sophisticated strategists, not believing that the
impression made on staff could affect their results
and not picking up hints. The "cue-seekers" were
cue conscious in a very active fashion - they went
out of their way to make a favourable impression on
their lecturers and to buttonhole staff about the
exam questions. Miller and Parlett argue that the
three groups of students mirror Perry's three main
stages of intellectual development (dualistic, relativistic, personal commitment to relativistic
reasoning).

READING ACADEMIC ARTICLES

The main series of investigations at Gothenburg,
led by Ference Marton, has looked in detail at one
of the main types of learning demanded of students -
reading, and understanding, academic articles.
Marton criticises previous research on prose learning as being so preoccupied with the quantitative

outcome of learning (how many facts and ideas have
been remembered), that qualitative aspects of
students' understanding of what they have read have
been ignored, in spite of the pioneering research of
Bartlett (1932). The prose passages have also been
trivial in content, short or artificially contrived
to facilitate experimental control. Marton examines students' approaches to reading relatively long
(1500 words) passages from actual academic articles.
These passages are chosen to be intelligible without
prior technical knowledge of the subject areas, and
to contain a tight logical argument based on the use
of detailed supportive evidence. Students are
invited, individually, to read the article at their
own pace, and in the way they do normally while
studying,but they are told that questions about it
will be asked afterwards. When students have
finished reading, they are interviewed to discover
what they have learned and how they approached the
task.

During the interview, the students are first
asked a general question of the form, "Well now,
perhaps you can tell me about what you've been
reading". Students are encouraged, through neutral
questioning, to elaborate what they have remembered.
They are then asked more specific questions about
sections of the text, followed by another general
question, with probes, to discover how they had
interpreted the instruction to read the article,what
their intention was in approaching the task (what
they expected to get from the article), and how the
experimental situation had affected them (whether
they were anxious, for example). Finally, in some
of the studies, questions were asked about their
normal approach to studying.

The interviews were tape-recorded and transcribed. Analysis of the lengthy transcripts was
difficult and time-consuming. The interviews were
initially read through as a whole and then responses
to separate questions were examined carefully. In
a sense the approach to analysis is similar to the
development of 'grounded theory' (Glaser and Strauss,
1967). No explicit theoretical framework is imposed
on the data. The responses are examined looking for
important consistencies within each transcript on its
own, then patterns of response recurring across the
interviews are identified (Svensson, 1976). Finally,
explanatory constructs are hypothetized to facilitate
understanding of the students' approaches to learning
and levels of outcome (what they remembered).

This method of analysis puts an enormous

responsibility on the research worker to be guided by the data without imposing preconceived interpretations. It is, of course, crucial to check that similar constructs are identified by independent judges. It is extremely unlikely, faced with a relatively unstructured set of free responses, that different judges will identify <u>identical</u> explanatory constructs. In this research, however, there was a high level of agreement on the categories which were chosen to describe both the levels of outcome and the approaches to learning (Svensson, 1977).

There is also great difficulty in communicating the findings of this type of research. In most analyses of interview transcripts, the main categories which best describe recurring types of answer are reported with choice quotes to illustrate them (as in Perry's study). What Marton and his colleagues have done is to extend the process of qualitative analysis much further. Students' comments are examined more intensively to consider the implications of consistencies and variabilities within an individual transcript, as well as between transcripts. The categories within each explanatory construct that emerges are then delimited - the boundary of meaning surrounding each category is explored in terms of the differing emphases or aspects mentioned by individual students. The quotations included are thus very carefully selected to provide a definition of the various categories within each explanatory construct. The instances used to delimit the categories can then form the basis on which independent judges can assign transcripts to response categories (Marton, 1975). Of course, when it comes to publishing findings from such studies, there is rarely sufficient space available to make fully clear the detailed way in which categories are delimited, and there is a danger that the results will be treated as little more than impressionistic. In fact this form of qualitative analysis now has its own checks and balances, its own systematic procedures, to produce findings which have their own rigour and their own form of scientific objectivity.

Following this analytic procedure Marton and his colleagues were able to describe important regularities both in the qualitatively different outcomes of learning (what students were able to recall about the articles) and in their approaches to learning.

LEVELS OF UNDERSTANDING

The problem with categorizing the outcome of learning is that it necessarily depends on the particular article read. But as long as the article is appropriately difficult and presents a clear argument supported by evidence, it is possible to use a general classificatory scheme for describing differences in the levels of understanding reached by students in these experiments. It is usually possible to identify <u>four</u> types of response (Fransson, 1977; Säljö, 1975).

A. <u>Conclusion-orientated, detailed</u>

The student summarizes the author's main argument, shows how evidence is used to support the argument, and explains the thoughts and reflections used to reach personal understanding of that argument.

B. <u>Conclusion-orientated, mentioning</u>

Again there is an adequate summary of the main argument, but the use of evidence or personal ex-, perience to support that argument is not made clear.

C. <u>Description, detailed</u>

The student gives an adequate list of the main points presented in the article, but fails to show how these are developed into an argument.

D. <u>Description, mentioning</u>

A few isolated points are made, some relevant, others irrelevant. At the bottom end of this category an impression of confusion and misunderstanding is given by the student's comments.

When students talked about their <u>approach</u> to, and process of, reading the article, again a simple distinction occurred. Some students adopted a <u>deep approach</u>. They started with the intention of understanding the meaning of the article, interacted actively with the author's arguments (<u>relating them to previous knowledge and their own experience</u>) and tried to see to what extent the author's conclusions were justified by the evidence presented. Other students seemed to rely almost exclusively on a <u>surface approach</u>. Their intent was to memorize the parts of the information they considered to be important, guided by the type of questions they anticipated being asked subsequently. These students were thus constrained by the specific task requirements, and anxious about that constraint. While these descriptions are clearly ideal types and few students will show all the characteristics attributed to either type, when students were assigned to one or other category on the basis of one of the main defining features it proved possible to make such an allocation with high inter-rater reliability for most, and sometimes for all, students. This distinction between deep and surface approaches to learning thus appears to be a powerful form of categorization for differences in learning strategies. Svensson (1975) independently read the transcripts and although his categorization coincided closely with that of Marton, there were differences in emphasis and terminology which are worth noting. His categories were 'holistic' and 'atomistic' which represented different ways in which students organized or structured their responses in describing what they remembered. The 'holistic' approach involves integrating the main parts into a structured whole. The 'atomistic' approach concentrates on aggregating the parts without interrelating or integrating them. These initial categorizations allowed the relationships between approach and learning to be investigated. Marton used what he calls a disjunctive method of assigning students' responses to categories. He classified the approaches used by students as deep or surface if they showed at least one clear indication of either of these approaches. Where the approach was unclear a third category was used. The relationship Marton established can be seen in Table 2.1.

Table 2.1 RELATIONSHIP BETWEEN LEVEL OF OUTCOME AND APPROACH TO LEARNING (from Marton and Säljö, 1976a)

Level of Understanding	Approach to Learning		
	Deep	Not Clear	Surface
High	9	6	1
Low	0	1	13

A deep approach is thus, at least in this small sample, clearly related to a deep level of understanding. Marton also found that the deep approach was associated with better recall of detail, particularly after a five week interval. Svensson (1977) has argued that this relationship should be thought of not simply as statistically significant, but as to some extent inevitable. While it is possible for a student adopting a deep approach to fail to reach a deep level of understanding through lack of previous knowledge or lack of attention or effort, it is impossible for a student adopting a surface approach ever to reach a deep level of understanding, as long as he persists with that approach. If deep understanding depends on being able to relate evidence and conclusion, a student's approach must necessarily have included this activity if deep understanding has been reached.

FACTORS AFFECTING THE APPROACH TO STUDYING

The next step in the Gothenburg studies was to examine the link between a student's approach to learning in the experiment and the normal approach to studying, based on the final question in the interview. Svensson (1977) was able to detect deep and surface approaches to normal studying and to compare these both with the experiment and with the examination performance of the students at the end of their first year. Table 2.2 shows that there were close relationships in both these ways. 23 out of 30 students were categorized as taking the same approach in the experiment and in normal studying. Of the students classified as being deep in both, 90 per cent had passed in all their examinations, while only 23 per cent of the doubly 'surface' students had this level of success.

Table 2.2 RELATIONSHIP BETWEEN APPROACHES TO LEARNING
AND STUDYING, AND EXAMINATION PERFORMANCE
(FROM SVENSSON, 1977)

Cognitive Approach		Examination Performance		Total
Experiment	Normal Studies	Passed All	Some Failure	
Surface	Surface	3	10	13
Deep	Deep	9	1	10
Deep	Surface	4	2	6
Surface	Deep	1	0	1

Svensson went on to show that students adopting a deep approach also tended to spend longer in
studying. Again this relationship is almost inevitable. Students who study their subjects deeply
are likely to find the material more interesting and
easier to understand. Long hours of work become no
hardship then. Students who adopt a surface
approach are concentrating on an inappropriate
technique of learning - rote memorization. It takes
a long time to cover books in this way, and it is a
tedious and unrewarding activity. Thus, eventually,
students who persist with the surface approach are
likely to do less and less work and eventually fail
their examinations. Svensson (1977) reported the
results of one examination in which 9 out of 11
students adopting a deep approach to normal studying
also did three or more hours' independent work a day.
All 9 passed the examination. Nineteen students
adopted a surface approach and 8 of them, even in
the first year, admitted to working less than three
hours a day. All 8 failed the examination.
    In another study Säljö was interested in
whether students' approaches to studying were affected by the type of questions they were given in tests
(Marton and Säljö, 1976b). He used two comparable
groups of students and three separate passages of
prose. The students were asked to read each of
these passages, and after each passage they were
asked a series of questions. After each of the

first two passages one group was given questions
designed to encourage a deep approach - attention to
the underlying meaning. The other group was given
specific factual questions, intended to induce a
surface approach. After the third passage both
groups of students were given the same set of
questions containing both 'deep' and 'surface'
questions. Säljö found that students in the
'surface' group who had initially adopted a deep
approach tended to have shifted to a surface
approach by the time they read the third passage.
Although there was an effect on students in the
'deep' group, most of the students who had initially
adopted a surface approach apparently found it
difficult to move fully to a deep approach.
Instead they adopted what Säljö called a 'deep
technified' approach. These students were content
with summarizing the author's argument without
examining it actively or in detail. Säljö's conclusion that it is much easier to induce a surface
approach than a deep one could be important. We
shall refer back to it in subsequent chapters.

Another of Marton's colleagues examined the
level of understanding of basic concepts reached by
first-year students of economics. Dahlgren (1978,
Dahlgren and Marton, 1978) paid particular attention
to the naive concepts, such as that of 'price',
which students had at the beginning of the course
and to the technical meanings they should have
understood by the end. The layman's idea of price,
for example, can be expressed as what an article is
worth - what its value is. This implies that
'price' is a fixed attribute. The economist's concept of price brings in the idea of supply and
demand. The price of an article depends not just
on the production costs and raw materials, but also
on its popularity in relation to its availability.
Dahlgren was able to show that although the results
of a first-year examination implied that students
should have developed an understanding of the technical meaning of such basic concepts, in fact:

> "If a more thorough understanding is required
> in order to answer a question, the number of
> acceptable answers is very low ... In many
> cases ... it appeared that only a minority of
> students had apprehended basic concepts in
> economics in the way intended by teachers and
> text-book authors. Complex problems seem to
> be solved by application of memorized algo-
> rithmic procedures ... In order to cope with

overwhelming curricula, the students probably
have to abandon their ambitions to understand
what they read about and instead direct efforts
towards passing the examinations ... (which reflect) the view that knowledge is a quantity,
and that the higher the level of the educational system, the more pieces of knowledge should
be taught per time unit" (Dahlgren, 1978, pages
1, 11, 12).

Putting together Säljö's findings and
Dahlgren's comments we see that the type of question
given in a test can induce a surface approach to
studying and that the factual overburdening of
syllabuses and examinations may be responsible for
the low level of understanding exhibited by students
when prevented from reproducing answers by well-
rehearsed methods.

In many of the reports produced by the Gothenburg research group there is a repeated emphasis
on the importance of both content and context in
affecting a student's approach to learning. Thus
it is not possible to characterize a student as
'deep', only an approach to a particular academic
task. The effect of content and context is shown
elegantly in the last of these studies. Fransson
(1977) examined how levels of interest and anxiety
affected students' approaches to learning. Level
of interest was controlled by selecting an article
concerning examination procedures in the education
department. One group of students were in that
department; another group, from a different department, were expected to have much less interest in
the article. Two situations, or contexts for
learning, were created. In one condition students
were told that after reading the article, one
student would be chosen to explain out loud what he
had learnt. The explanation would be tape-recorded
for subsequent detailed analysis. A large tape-
recorder placed in a prominent position reinforced
what was intended to be an anxiety-provoking
situation. In the contrasting situation, attempts
were made to create a relaxed friendly atmosphere.

It was clear from the results that both interest
and anxiety did affect the students' approaches to
learning, but not in a simple way. It was not so
much that anxiety-provoking situations induced a
surface approach to learning, but that students who
felt the situation to be threatening, whether that
was intended or not, were more likely to adopt a
surface approach. Lack of interest or perceived

relevance also tended to evoke this mechanical rote-
learning approach.   Thus where a student feels
threatened, or under pressure to respond to examination demands or syllabuses which have little personal relevance, it is less likely that a deep
approach will be adopted.

HOLIST AND SERIALIST STRATEGIES OF LEARNING

Pask and his colleagues have carried out
several series of experiments in trying to discover
important differences between students in their
learning strategies.   Marton deliberately left his
instructions about reading the article vague.   The
students had to decide for themselves whether
reading for understanding or rote memorization would
be the best way of answering the subsequent
questions about the article.   Through this ambiguity it was possible to demonstrate the contrasting
approaches to learning that students considered
appropriate for this academic task.   In most of
Pask's experiments, however, the students are
required to reach a deep level of understanding, and
Pask is interested in the strategies they use in trying to carry out this instruction.

In the first series of experiments reported by
Pask (Pask and Scott, 1972) he asked students to try
to establish for themselves the principles of classification underlying the division of two imaginary
species of Martian animals - the Clobbits and the
Gandlemullers - into a series of sub-species.   In
the first experiments, information about Clobbits
was provided in the form of 50 cards.   These were
placed face down in ten columns (each column
representing a separate subspecies).   The five rows
contained separate categories of information about
the ten subspecies (e.g. habitat, physical characteristics, drawings of animals, etc.).   Students
could also write their own information cards if they
found this helpful.

Students were asked to turn over the cards to
obtain the information they wanted.   They were told
to turn the cards over one at a time and to give a
reason for the particular card they had chosen.
Each reason amounted to a hypothesis about the
nature of the classification system which the
information on the card was expected to test.   A
record was kept of the order in which the cards were
used and also of the hypothesis given at each step.
Finally students were required to 'teach back' to the
experimenter what they had learned about these

22

Martian animals.

Pask discovered interesting differences both in the types of hypothesis used by students and in the ways in which they explained the classification schemes. Some students concentrated on a step-by-step strategy in which they used simple hypotheses about, say, a single property of the animals

"Do Gandlemullers have sprongs?"

This strategy was described as <u>serialist</u>, indicating the linear progression from one hypothesis to the next. Other students used more complex hypotheses which combined several properties simultaneously.

"Are there more kinds of Gandlers with mounds (dorsal or cranial) than Plongers?"

This strategy was described as <u>holist</u>, (not to be confused with Svensson's different use of the same term), which indicates a more global approach to problem solving. Pask also identified an additional type of holist, <u>the redundant holist</u>, who depended on <u>individualistic ways of discriminating</u> between the sub-species.

"The ones that were discovered first are gentle; the other kinds, the aggressive beasts that were found later, well they are the ones with less mounds."

The important aspect of the redundant holist is that imaginary descriptive terms are used. In the above example, there was nothing in the information given to the student to suggest either an order of discovery or 'temperamental' differences between the sub-species. What seems to happen is that the redundant holist personalizes learning. The order of discovery is probably the order in which he turned up the cards, while an impression of gentleness or aggressiveness was perhaps created by the drawings. In the end the redundant holists understood the principles of classification just as well as the holists or serialists, but they relied on personal (redundant) 'props' to aid that understanding.

When students were asked to 'teach back' what they had learned, very similar differences were found between the two main types. The serialists described the principles of classification in a straightforward logical manner keeping to the bare essentials. For example:

> "Zoologists have classified the Gandlemuller on the basis of physical characteristics. The three main types are Gandlers, Plongers and Gandleplongers. Gandlers have no sprongs. Plongers have two sprongs. Gandleplongers have one sprong. There are four subspecies of Gandler: M1, M2, B1 and B2. The M's have one body, the B's have two bodies. The M1 and B1 have a single cranial mound. The M2 and B2 have a double cranial mound ..."etc.

In contrast a redundant holist set about the description in a very different way:

> "I want to tell you about a funny Martian animal which has been recently discovered and classified by scientists conducting surveys. They are funny sluglike things with various protruberances. These animals are called Gandlemullers, because they churn about in the swamps near the Equator and Gandle is the Martian for swampmud, hence the swampmudmiller (Muller is German for miller). These things churn through the mud eating it by some curious process which means they eat and excrete at the same time."

Only after a great deal of redundant elaboration does this holist describe the essential properties of the various sub-species, and even then they are presented in an idiosyncratic order. It is perhaps unfair to describe the holist as illogical; it may be that the order follows a different set of rules. There may well be understandable principles in his ordering of the information; if so, they seem to be more like those used by novelists or journalists than by scientists. The holist starts with what seems to be the most interesting or striking point and includes a good deal of human or personal interest. The holist thrives on anecdote, illustration, and analogy, while the serialist uses these sparingly, if at all.

In later series of experiments Pask and his colleagues have been able to extend the descriptions of holists and serialists. For example, holists tend to look further ahead when asked to work their way through a hierarchy of sub-topics towards an understanding of the topic as a whole (Pask, 1976b).

They also have a wide focus of attention, bringing together several sub-topics, right from the start (Robertson, 1977). Where students are given a choice between a series of abstract topics and an exactly parallel series of topics which are drawn from the 'real world', serialists work their way step-by-step through either the abstract topics or the real world topics, bringing them together only when forced to do so to achieve overall understanding of the main topic. The holists in contrast move from real world to abstract and back again, examining the analogies between the two sets of topics as well. In the end both groups of students can reach the same level of understanding, but their ways of reaching that understanding are very different. The serialists apparently put much more emphasis on the separate topics and the logical sequences connecting them, forming an overall picture of what is being learned only rather late in the process. The holists try to build up that overall picture, as a guide to learning, right from the start and see where the details fit into that picture much later on.

PATHOLOGIES OF LEARNING

Pask (1976a) has developed what he calls a conversational theory of learning which describes how a student works his way towards a full understanding of a topic by questioning, or trying out his ideas on, either a teacher or an 'alter-ego', another part of the mind which monitors and interacts with the learning process. Pask argues that a full understanding occurs only when the student can explain the topic by reconstructing it, and can also demonstrate that understanding by applying the principles learned to an entirely new situation. The theory also indicates that appropriate analogies are as important a part of understanding a 'teach-back' as the recognition of the logical steps and processes through which an understanding of the topic is built up. Pask argues that the two major pathologies commonly found in learning are the failure to examine the logical structure or the evidence in sufficient detail, and the failure to make use of appropriate analogies. The link between the holist and serialist strategies and learning pathologies, at least within Pask's theory, should now become clear.

The holist strategy involves looking at the whole area being learned, taking a broad perspective seeking interconnection with other topics and making use of personal and idiosyncratic analogies. The examination of the logical structure and of the supporting evidence comes later when understanding is demanded, but left to himself the holist is likely to put off what he may see as the more boring parts of learning. Heath describes his category of 'plunger' in similar terms:

> "His thoughts zip from one idea to another without apparent connection; ... characteristically (he) fails to clothe his ideas in a framework that would make sense to others ... He may beg permission to go ahead with a project ... only to lose interest later, particularly if hard uninteresting work looms ..."

Pask describes as globetrotting the tendency of the holist to make inappropriate or vacuous analogies. This pathology might also take the form of an over-readiness to generalize from insufficient evidence to form hasty, personal judgements.

The serialist falls into the opposite trap. He fails to make use of valid and important analogies and may not build up for himself any overall map to see how the various elements of the topic interrelate and how the topic fits into the subject area in general. Pask calls this pathology improvidence.

STYLES OF LEARNING

The strategies of learning described so far might be no more than reactions to a single task (the Clobbits) or to a particular piece of apparatus which controls learning in a somewhat atypical way. Pask accepts that his early experiments did artificially accentuate differences between students, but he argues that the holist and serialist strategies are manifestations of important underlying differences in the way people think and tackle problems. He argues that some students are disposed to act 'like holists' whenever they are given that opportunity, whereas others behave 'like serialists'. The general tendency to adopt a particular strategy is referred to as a learning style. The 'holist like' style is called comprehension learning which involves 'building descriptions of what is known'. The 'serialist like' style is called operation learning, which is 'the facet of the learning process concerned with mastering procedural details'.

Pask (personal communication) has likened these two aspects of thinking to the way an architect designs a building. He has to build up the overall plan (description building) and also to work out the detailed processes, and the logistics of those processes, (operation and procedure building) whereby the plan can be converted into an actual building. Any weakness either in the plan, or in the description of that plan, will prevent the building being satisfactorily completed (understanding being reached).

Students who show sufficient consistent bias in their learning strategies to be described as 'comprehension learners' or 'operation learners' are likely to show equally consistent pathologies of learning. But there are other students who are readily able to adapt their learning strategy to the requirements of the particular task, emphasizing either comprehension learning or operation learning as appropriate, and using both in tandem wherever possible. Pask describes these students as having a 'versatile' style of learning.

> "A student who is <u>versatile</u> is not prone to vacuous globetrotting; he does indeed build up descriptions of what may be known by a rich use of analogical reasoning, but subjects the hypotheses to test and operationally verifies the validity of an analogy and the limits of its applicability" (Pask et al., 1977, page 68).

Pask's description seems to echo Heath's ideal type - the reasonable adventurer. Versatility is also descriptively related to "cue-consciousness" (Miller and Parlett, 1974) and to "thematization" in learning.

MATCHING STYLES OF LEARNING AND TEACHING

Perhaps one of the most important of Pask's experiments was his investigation of the effects of matching and mismatching learning materials with students' learning strategies. On the basis of the Clobbit experiment students were identified as having adopted holist or serialist strategies. Pask then asked the students to work through a set of programmed learning materials and take a test to discover how much they had learned. There were two versions of this material. One version was designed to suit the comprehension learner, being rich in analogy and illustration. The other was presented in a logical, step-by-step sequence without 'enrichment'. Students were assigned either to a matched or a mismatched condition (holist with holist material; holist with serialist material; etc). The results were dramatic, although based on small samples; there was little overlap in the scores of the matched and mismatched groups. The students in the matched conditions were able to answer most of the questions about what they had learned, whereas the other students generally fell below half marks.

Pask's descriptions of styles and pathologies of learning seem to overlap, in places, with Marton's ideas about deep and surface approaches to learning. It was the intriguing possibilities raised by these apparent connections which provided some of the initial impetus for our own research programme. But our approach was deliberately different. Our main concern was to use both quantitative and qualitative methods of collecting and analysing data, as a progression from the earlier research at Lancaster, and to explore the effects of natural contextual differences - differences between academic departments - in their effects on approaches to learning.

This chapter has described the work of both Marton and Pask in detail as it is their concepts which form the main theoretical basis for our own work, and a full understanding of those concepts seems to be an essential prerequisite to the description of our research design and findings which follows.

Chapter Three

THE PROGRAMME OF RESEARCH

The main purpose in carrying out this programme of research was to extend, conceptually and empirically, the work of Marton and Pask described in the previous chapter, in relation to the previous research on students carried out at Lancaster. There were six main areas within the programme:

1. The measurement of approaches to and styles of studying, using an inventory.
2. The exploration of the cognitive skills, cognitive styles, and personality characteristics underlying different approaches to studying.
3. The extension of Marton's work on reading academic articles, using a questionnaire.
4. The identification, by questionnaire, of students' perceptions of the academic 'climate' of departments.
5. The use of interviews to investigate students' strategies in carrying out particular types of academic task.
6. An investigation of how contrasting academic contexts appear to affect the approaches to studying adopted by students in those departments.

Marton had limited his research methodology to qualitative analyses of small samples of mainly social science students. Pask had used lengthy experimental learning tasks, again restricted to small opportunity samples. The intention in this research programme was to obtain firmer evidence of the existence of contrasting learning styles or approaches to studying from a wider range of disciplines, and to explore the extent to which these approaches represented relatively stable characteristics of students, rooted in their abilities and personality, or in contrast were specific reactions

to the nature of particular academic tasks or learning contexts.
      Methodologically there was a deliberate attempt
to capitalise on the strengths of different
approaches to research. Thus interviews with
students were used both as a source of items for the
development of inventories and questionnaires, and
as the raw data for qualitative analyses. Data
from inventories were exposed to repeated, complex
statistical analyses to explore the nature of the
relationships both between the various dimensions of
approaches to studying, and between approaches to
studying and students' perceptions of academic
departments. The patterns of relationships emerging
from these quantitative analyses were reassessed in
the light of students' comments in the interviews,
and new items or sub-scales were then produced for
the inventories. Over a period of four years it
was thus possible to make substantial advances in
understanding students' approaches to learning and
to produce carefully constructed instruments for
further research or evaluation studies in higher
education.
      The general work on the programme can be des-
cribed in three phases. In the first phase there
was exploratory work on five fronts. A questionnaire variant of Marton's interview procedure on
reading academic articles was given to three
separate samples. Results from two pilot studies
enabled improvements to be embodied in a questionnaire given to 248 first-year students. Secondly,
a pilot version of an inventory to identify distinctive approaches to studying was developed from
an existing Lancaster inventory supplemented with
items suggested by the ideas of Perry, Marton and
Pask. Thirdly, exploratory interviews were held in
which students were asked to describe their approaches
to specific academic tasks, and more generally to
discuss their experiences of studying and their perceptions of the courses and the teaching they had
encountered. Fourthly, interviews with staff were
carried out to explore the possibility of defining
'academic climate' through lecturers' perceptions of
the departments in which they worked. This last
approach was not pursued, as a focus on <u>students'</u>
perceptions seemed to be more fruitful with the
limited time and resources available. Thus the
final activity in this phase of the programme was
the development from the interview data of a
questionnaire to assess quantitatively students'
perceptions of their courses and their main

academic department.

In the second phase of the programme, the inventory of approaches to studying and the course perceptions questionnaire were given to 767 first-year students. Analyses of these data led to final research versions of the inventory and questionnaire being produced. From students' responses to the inventory it was possible to identify a group of 60 students with extreme scores on approaches to studying who agreed to spend some ten hours, spread over a period of over a year, taking tests of convergent and divergent thinking, cognitive and learning styles, and personality, and also taking part in a learning experiment involving the reading of three short articles. The main round of interviews with students from six contrasting departments was also carried out during this phase.

The final phase of the programme involved qualitative analysis of the interview data, which proved a formidable task. Statistical analyses were also carried out on the test scores of the 60 volunteers. Finally there was a major survey of 66 university and polytechnic departments throughout Britain. 2208 students completed the approaches to studying inventory and the course perceptions questionnaire, from which it was possible, in conjunction with the interview data, to assess the effects of academic departments on students' approaches to learning.

Details of each of these areas of research are presented in the following chapters. First there is a report on identifying distinctive approaches to studying through the development of the inventory. Chapter 5 describes the extent to which it was possible to find underlying differences in ability, cognitive style or personality between students with contrasting scores on the inventory. In Chapter 6 results of a series of learning experiments are presented in which students were asked to read academic articles, recall what they had learned, and comment on their reading and learning strategies.

Chapter 7 begins the exploration into the effects of academic context or environment on how students learn, with a description of the course perceptions questionnaire. Chapter 8 is a report on students' experiences of learning and studying in higher education, while Chapter 9 presents the results of bringing together the approaches to studying inventory with the course perceptions questionnaire. The final chapter is an attempt to take stock of the progress made during the programme in trying to understand how students learn. It also presents indications of the practical utility of the research in relation to teaching and learning in higher education.

Chapter Four

IDENTIFYING DISTINCTIVE APPROACHES TO STUDYING*

EARLIER RESEARCH AT LANCASTER

In earlier research at Lancaster (Entwistle and
Wilson, 1970; Entwistle and Entwistle, 1970;
Entwistle, Thompson and Wilson, 1974; Entwistle
and Wilson, 1977) a series of inventories had been
developed, initially for the specific purpose of pre-
dicting subsequent levels of academic performance.
In the main study an inventory with two scales was
used - motivation and study methods. 1087 first-
year students from seven English universities completed these scales and correlations with subsequent
degree class were calculated. The highest correlation reported was 0.39 (study methods in engineering), but overall levels were around 0.20. Although
these values seem low, it must be remembered that
they are about the same as correlations between 'A'
levels and degree class.
     One of the versions of the inventory contained
items indicative of extraversion and neuroticism
(Eysenck, 1970). In higher education it has been
consistently found that introverts in most subject
areas tend to be more successful than extraverts,
but an interesting study by Wilson, (1969; Entwistle
and Wilson, 1977) showed that extraverts who had
high scores on motivation and study methods were
equally successful as introverts with comparable
scores. However few extraverts, compared with introverts, had high motivation or good study methods -

---

* Much of the work on the first two versions of the
inventory was carried out by Maureen Hanley (née Robin-
son). Later versions were developed in association
with Sarah Morison (née Burkinshaw), Dai Hounsell and
Patrick Thomas.

hence the overall relationship between introversion and degree class. Although this earlier work was not designed to examine study processes, nevertheless it did indicate that students of differing personality types might approach studying in contrasting ways. This possibility was explored further by the use of cluster analysis, which identifies students with similar profiles of scores. This method was used to define groups of successful students who seemed to have followed different paths to success. Three successful groups and one which was unsuccessful were described (Entwistle and Wilson, 1977). The first group was outstandingly successful and was apparently motivated by ambition or 'hope for success' (Atkinson and Feather, 1966).

> "Cluster 1 contained students with high 'A' level grades who were satisfied with their courses. These students had not had a particularly active social or sporting life, nor had they concentrated on developing aesthetic interests ... They were highly motivated and had good study methods. In personality they were emotionally stable and had high scores on theoretical and economic values, linked with a tendency towards toughminded conservatism. This combination of characteristics suggests a rather cold and ruthless individual, governed by rationality and spurred on by competition to repeated demonstrations of intellectual mastery."

The second group was in many ways the opposite of the first, yet students still obtained fairly good degree results.

> "The main defining features ... were high scores on neuroticism and syllabus-boundness, and low scores on both extraversion, (study methods), and motivation. Their self-ratings were uniformly negative. They saw themselves as neither likeable nor self-confident. They had no active social life and few aesthetic interests; (they worked long hours) ... It is tempting to see these students as motivated by 'fear of failure' (Birney, Burdick, and Teevan, 1969)... The possibility that neurotic introverts with low motivation and poor study methods might (still) be almost as successful as highly motivated students was noted in a preliminary analysis of the interview data. (Entwistle,

Thompson, and Wilson, 1974)" (op. cit, page 130).

The third group of students was also successful. It contained mainly arts and humanities
students with high aesthetic and low economic
values who espoused radical ideals. They were
highly motivated, had good study methods, worked
long hours, but were distinctly syllabus-free in
their attitudes to studying.

The final group contained the least successful
students. This group had active social or sporting
interests combined with very low motivation, poor
study methods, and few hours spent studying. Some,
but by no means all of the students, came to
university with poor 'A' level grades and had low
scores on a verbal aptitude test.

Another way of drawing attention to differing
attitudes to studying was to use factor analyses to
identify groups of items which were closely interrelated. In this way the initial two dimensions
of motivation and study methods were broken down into
five sub-scales which paralleled the cluster analyses,
but produced two factors associated with poor degree
results. The five factors were labelled competitive
and efficient, fear of failure, syllabus-free,
cynical and disenchanted, and disorganized and
dilatory. The four most distinctive items from each
factor are shown in Table 4.1, and these items formed
the first part of the pool of items used to develop
the 'Approaches to Studying Inventory' for this
research programme.

DEVELOPMENT OF PILOT INVENTORIES

The purpose in developing a new inventory was
not to improve levels of prediction of academic
success; it was instead an attempt to understand
students' approaches to learning. In particular,
the intention was to measure, and to investigate the
inter-relationships between, the explanatory concepts identified by Marton and Pask. Thus
additional items were written which were based on
Marton's descriptions of 'deep' and 'surface' processing and on Pask's indications of the varying
learning strategies used by 'holists' and 'serialists'.
In addition the ideas of Miller and Parlett (1974) on
'cue consciousness', as modified by Ramsden (1979)
into a more general dimension of 'strategic
approach to assessment', created an additional set of
items.

As the interviews with students progressed

(see Chapter 8) additional items were suggested. Eventually a pool of 120 items was used in the first pilot inventory. Alpha factor analysis with rotation to oblique simple structure (Nie et al, 1975) was used to identify groups of items which were consistently linked together. The items were also subjected to conceptual analysis in relation to the constructs found in the literature. It was soon clear that the 'deep approach to studying' and 'organized, motivated study methods' were major dimensions, and that a third factor brought together surface processing with fear of failure and syllabus-boundness.

Table 4.1   STUDENTS' ATTITUDES TO STUDYING

DISORGANIZED AND DILATORY   (Poor degree results)

My habit of putting off work leaves me with far too much to do at the end of term.

I'm rather slow at starting work in the evening.

It's rather difficult for me to organise my study time: at school this was done for me.

It is unusual for me to be late handing in work (Disagree).

CYNICAL AND DISENCHANTED   (Poor degree results)

I can't see any relevance to most of the work we do here.

There seems to be little point in following up the references we are given in lectures.

There are very few of the recommended text-books which are really worth buying.

I sometimes wish I had gone straight into work after school.

SYLLABUS-FREE   (Above average degree results)

I tend to learn more effectively by studying along my own lines than through set work.

I am often involved in following up my own ideas when I am supposed to be doing set work.

Often I try to think of a better way of doing something than is described in a lecture or book.

I should prefer the set work to be less structured and organised.

Table 4.1   STUDENTS' ATTITUDES TO STUDYING (continued)

FEAR OF FAILURE   (Above average degree results)

My friends always seem to be able to do things better than me.

Worrying about an exam or about work which is overdue often prevents me from sleeping.

I get very concerned about work which is overdue.

I don't often join in tutorial discussions: I prefer to listen.

COMPETITIVE AND EFFICIENT   (Very good degree results)

I play any game to win, not just for the fun of it.

I hate admitting defeat, even in trivial matters.

It's important for me to do really well in the courses here.

I consider the best possible way of learning is by completing the set work and doing the required reading.

At this stage it was possible to discuss our factor analyses with John Biggs of Newcastle, Australia. He had been developing a Study Behaviour Questionnaire (Biggs, 1976) which contained the ten sub-scales shown below.

Academic aspiration	Pragmatic, grade-orientated, university as means.
Academic interest	Intrinsically motivated, study as end.
Academic neuroticism	Confused, overwhelmed by demands of course work.
Internality	Sees 'truth' coming from within, not (from) external authority.
Study skills and organisation	Works consistently, reviews regularly, schedules work.
Fact-rote strategy	Centres on facts, details, rote learns.
Dependence	Rarely questions instructors, tests; needs support.
Meaning Assimilation	Reads widely, relates to known, meaning orientated.

37

Test anxiety   Very concerned about tests,
            exams, fear of failure.

Openness   (Believes) university (is) a
            place where values are question-
            ed.

          (Biggs, 1976, page 72).

The similarity between these scales and several of the dimensions described by our own inventory was striking; even the wording of many of the items was similar. Biggs indicated that his most recent work strongly suggested the existence of three main factors - utilizing, internalizing, and achieving - each of which contained both a cognitive and a motivational component as follows. (Subsequently described in Biggs, 1979):

Factor	Cognitive	Motivational
Utilizing	Fact-rote strategy	Extrinsic, fear of failure
Internalizing	Meaning assimilation	Intrinsic
Achieving	Study skills and organisation	Need for achievement

The descriptions of these three factors were similar to the ones emerging from the pilot version of our inventory. It was therefore decided to bring the inventories even closer together by introducing additional items covering scales used by Biggs, but not parelled in our inventory - intrinsic motivation, extrinsic motivation, internality and openness. The second pilot inventory contained the 82 items from the first inventory most clearly related to established factors, together with 24 items rewritten from the four scales developed by Biggs.
  Table 4.2 lists the fifteen sub-scales included in this version of the inventory, and the four factors which emerged from the analysis. Factor analysis allows us to group variables together which have elements of similarity in their inter-relationships. Thus factors are 'global' dimensions summarizing the individual scales which hang

together most closely. The meaning of a factor can be deduced from the defining items of the scales which have the highest factor loadings on that factor. A negative sign indicates that the direction has to be reversed (for example, Factor I is associated with the reverse of syllabus boundness, which is syllabus freedom).

Table 4.2   FACTOR LOADINGS OF STUDY STRATEGY SCALES

Sub-scales	I	II	III	IV
Deep approach	62		33	
Comprehension learning	73			
Intrinsic motivation	54		47	
Internality	61			
Openness	50			
Surface approach		67		
Operation learning		67		
Extrinsic motivation		61		
Fear of failure		36		-32
Syllabus bound	-41	50		
Strategic approach		41		
Organized study methods			64	
Achievement motivation		36	45	
Disillusioned attitudes			-55	
Sociability				58

The second pilot inventory was given to 767 first year (second term) students from nine departments in two universities. The disciplines covered were english, history, psychology, physics, and engineering. Principal component factor analyses, with rotation to oblique simple structure, were used to investigate the inter-relationships between the sub-scales. Four factors had eigen-values above unity and these explained 56% of the overall variance in the correlational matrix. Factor loadings are shown in Table 4.2.
The four factors can be described as follows.

Identifying Distinctive Approaches to Studying

I   DEEP APPROACH/COMPREHENSION LEARNING OR MEANING
ORIENTATION

This factor is very close to Biggs' 'internalizing'.   It carries the same emphasis on intrinsic
motivation and active search for personal meaning,
but it contains its highest loading on comprehension
learning.   This factor may thus be considered to
contain a stylistic component in addition to those
elements identified by Biggs.

II   SURFACE APPROACH/OPERATION LEARNING OR REPRO-
DUCING ORIENTATION

This shows a close similarity to the 'utilizing'
factor.   It shows high loadings on surface level
approach and also on extrinsic motivation, syllabus-
boundness and fear of failure.   But again the high
loading on operation learning could imply an
additional stylistic component.

III ORGANIZED STUDY METHODS AND ACHIEVING ORIENTATION

This is the 'achieving' factor, with high
positive loadings on organized study methods and
achievement motivation, and a high negative loading
on disillusioned attitudes.   There are also significant loadings on both deep approach and intrinsic
motivation without any hint of a stylistic component
in this case.

IV   STABLE EXTRAVERSION

The final factor appears to be a combination of
the two most basic personality traits described by
Eysenck (1970).   A similar factor was reported
earlier in work on primary school children where
scales of both motivation and personality were
included (Entwistle and Bennett, 1973).   It is
essentially stable extraversion.
This analysis appeared to support the claim by
Biggs that three second-order factors "seem to offer
a parsimonious and theoretically coherent model for
conceptualizing the more important ways in which
students may feel about, and behave towards, their
study" (Biggs, 1979, p. 383).

As the subscales of internality and openness
seemed to add little to the definition of the first
factor, they were dropped from subsequent versions of

the inventory. The isolated personality dimension
of sociability was also dropped. In their place,
it was decided to introduce sub-components of the
main explanatory concepts being investigated. In
the third pilot version of the inventory a distinction was made within approach to studying between the
intention, the process, and the outcome. Also the
styles of learning, comprehension learning and
operation learning, both of which Pask considers to
be essential in reaching understanding, were distinguished from their corresponding pathologies -
globetrotting and improvidence. Holists are likely
to exhibit both comprehension learning and globetrotting; serialists should score highly on
operation learning and improvidence. But students
adopting a deep approach, although being able to use
both comprehension and operation learning in a versatile manner, would not be expected to exhibit the
pathologies of learning.

One of the problems in developing the inventory
has been that the main theoretical constructs
identified by Marton and Pask have been evolving
during the life of the programme, partly through
new publications by the originators, partly through
seminars at which the ideas have been discussed with
other researchers, and partly through the findings
from our own inventories and interviews. Thus the
third pilot inventory had a short life. Shortly
after it had been used, an article based on the
previous version of the inventory was written
(Entwistle, Hanley, and Hounsell, 1979). In this
article a model of student learning was developed
which attempted to distinguish between deep/surface
approaches and comprehension/operation learning.
This model also distinguished two stages of both comprehension and operation learning in the way shown
in Figure 4.1.

In the final research version of the inventory
it was thus decided to restrict 'deep approach' to
the intention to understand and an active, critical
approach to learning, and to add as separate sub-
scale two of the components essential to a deep-
level outcome, but not previously covered in the
inventory. These sub-scales were labelled
'relating ideas' and 'use of evidence'.

FINAL RESEARCH VERSION OF THE INVENTORY

In deciding the items to be included in the
final research version of the inventory, all the
previous inventories were reviewed to identify items

Figure 4.1   A MODEL OF STYLES AND APPROACHES TO LEARNING

Approach or Style	Process		Outcome
	Stage I	Stage II	
Deep approach/ versatile	All four processes below used appropriately to reach understanding		Deep level of understanding
Comprehension learning	Building overal descripton of content area	Reorganizing incoming information to relate to previous knowledge or experience and establishing personal meaning	Incomplete understanding attributable to globetrotting
Operation learning	Detailed attention to evidence and steps in the argument	Relating evidence to conclusion and maintaining a critical, objective stance	Incomplete understanding attributable to improvidence
Surface approach	Memorization	Overlearning	Surface level of understanding

which had worked well at some stage within one or
other of the sub-scales now to be formed. Each
sub-scale, with the exception of surface approach
which had proved the most difficult to define, was
limited to a maximum of four items to ensure a
manageable overall length on the basis of the highest correlations between item and sub-scale total,
consistent with retaining the conceptual definition
of the sub-scales. A list of sub-scales and
defining items is shown in Table A1 (Appendix)
together with the coefficients of internal consistency (Cronbach alpha). The coefficients for the
main domains were as follows: meaning orientation
(16 items $\propto$ =0.79); reproducing orientation (16
items $\propto$=0.73); achieving orientation (16 items
=0.70); styles and pathologies (16 items $\propto$=0.59).
Although the levels of internal consistency are
rather low in some of the sub-scales, the reliability
estimates for three of the four domains are satisfactory. And there is a good reason for the lower
reliability in the fourth domain. It is unlikely
that styles and pathologies can be viewed as a single
domain. The sub-scales could well be put together
in different ways for different purposes. The total
score (with one style and pathology reversed) may
indicate an extreme 'redundant holist' say, but it
may be more meaningful to use comprehension learning
and globetrotting together to indicate a holist
style; operation learning and improvidence together
to indicate a serialist style; comprehension and
operation learning together to indicate versatility;
and globetrotting and improvidence to indicate
pathologies of learning.

MAIN STUDY

The inventory was presented to students as part
of a questionnaire in three sections. The first
section asked for background information about
school examination results and honours specialism(s),
and also contained a self-rating question in which
students were asked to assess their own academic
progress to date (How well do you think you are doing
so far on this subject/course, compared with other
students?). A similar approach to self-assessment
of mathematical aptitude proved successful in an
earlier study (Entwistle and Wilson, 1977), with a

correlation between self-rating and objective test score of +0.65. The second section contained the inventory of approaches to studying, while the final section was the Course Perceptions Questionnaire, the development of which is described in Chapter 7. A letter describing the purpose of the investigation was sent to 171 departments in 54 universities and polytechnics in England, Wales, Scotland and Northern Ireland. Ninety-five departments agreed in principle to cooperate, and an adequate proportion of completed questionnaires for anlaysis was eventually obtained from 66 of them.

The target population was second-year under-graduates (third-year in Scotland) taking honours degrees in departments of English, history, economics, psychology, physics or engineering. The six dis-ciplines were chosen to provide a range of special-isms: five of them had been used previously in the interview study (Ramsden, 1979).

Completed questionnaires were obtained from 2208 students, an estimated response rate of 73 per cent. (Returns from departments showed the class size, but it was not always possible to be sure exactly how many of the class had received the questionnaire). Students were asked to give their names (to allow degree results to be obtained sub-sequently), but they returned the questionnaires to the investigators in sealed envelopes, with a guarantee that departmental staff would not see their responses. The final sample contained 16 arts departments (491 students), 26 in the social sciences (852), and 24 in the pure and applied sciences (865).

RELATIONSHIPS BETWEEN APPROACHES TO STUDYING AND ACADEMIC PROGRESS

Although the current inventory was not designed primarily to predict academic performance, it is still of interest to examine the relationships between approaches to studying and academic progress. In this study it was only possible to investigate correlations between the inventory sub-scales and the self-rating of academic progress in the second year, but results using the second pilot inventory are available in relation to formal first-year assessment grades. It has also been possible to compare our self-rating correlations with samples of Australian first-year students who had been

given the final research version of the inventory.*
Table 4.3 presents correlations for the British and
Australian samples.

The correlations with the British students'
self-rating of academic progress by subject area,
in Table 4.3, showed consistent relationships in the
expected directions. The closest overall relationships with academic progress were found with
organized study methods and positive attitudes to
studying, followed by intrinsic motivation, deep
approach, and syllabus-freedom (changing the names to
indicate the direction of relationship). Subject
area differences show academic progress in arts to be
more closely related positively to deep approach and
comprehension learning, and negatively to all the sub-
scales within the reproducing orientation and to
operation learning and improvidence. In social
science, higher positive correlations are found with
relating ideas, intrinsic motivation, and higher
negative correlations with disorganized study methods
and negative attitudes. Social scientists appear to
be less heavily penalized for the pathologies' of
learning or adopting a surface approach. The
relationships in science follow the overall values
fairly closely with the exception of strategic
approach and disorganized study methods which show
closer relationships with progress, and operation
learning which seems to be more of a benefit in the
sciences.

The Australian samples showed lower levels of
correlation overall, which could be explained either
by the objectivity of the index of academic performance (thus avoiding the possible circularity in
comparing two sets of self-ratings), or by the
difference between first and second-year students.
The pattern of relationships was, however, very
similar, the only exceptions being that the
Australian scientists showed a negative relationship
with operation learning, and that improvidence was
more heavily penalized in sciences than in the arts.

A useful way of determining which sub-scales
predict academic progress most effectively is discriminant function analysis. In this statistical
technique, groups are formed on the basis of a
criterion (here academic performance). The
analysis then identifies a discriminant function

---

* We are grateful to David Watkins of the Australian
National University in Canberra for allowing us to
present his findings.

Table 4.3   CORRELATIONS BETWEEN APPROACHES TO STUDYING AND INDICES OF ACADEMIC PROGRESS IN BRITAIN AND AUSTRALIA

	Arts		Social Sci.		Science		British
	Brit (N=491)	Aus (295)	Brit (852)	Aus (89)	Brit (865)	Aus (156)	Total (2208)
'A' level Grades	15	–	10	–	24	–	
Meaning Orientation							
Deep Approach	30	11	23	11	21	15	24
Relating Ideas	07	07	19	12	10	-08	12
Use of Evidence	16	07	17	12	13	02	15
Intrinsic Motivation	26	21	31	16	24	13	26
Reproducing Orientation							
Surface Approach	-27	-22	-13	-27	-20	-23	-19
Syllabus-boundness	-34	-17	-24	-06	-14	-07	-22
Fear of Failure	-25	-10	-15	-14	-15	-12	-18
Extrinsic Motivation	-13	-22	-09	-07	-06	-04	-09
Achieving Orientation							
Strategic Approach	09	02	20	09	27	00	19
Disorganized Study Methods	-22	-18	-34	-27	-37	-34	-32
Negative Attitudes to Studying	-26	-25	-33	-23	-30	-30	-29
Achievement Motivation	16	04	25	18	20	28	20
Styles and Pathologies							
Comprehension Learning	15	03	08	16	05	00	08
Globetrotting	-18	-25	-11	-03	-19	-19	-16
Operation Learning	-16	-09	-03	-03	06	-12	-04
Improvidence	-23	-10	-06	-18	-17	-27	-15
Significant for r >	.12	.15	.09	.27	.09	.21	.06
Multiple Correlation	–	.41	–	.47	–	.54	–

which shows which combination of the predictive
variables (sub-scales of the inventory) most clearly
differentiates between the different criterion
groups. Using this technique on data from the
second pilot study (N= 767 first-years with a
criterion of assessment grades), the differences between the contrasting achievement groups were
associated most closely with globetrotting, disorganized studying, extrinsic and intrinsic motivation, and to a lesser extent improvidence
(Entwistle, Hanley and Hounsell, 1979).

In the main study (Ramsden and Entwistle, 1981),
two extreme groups were formed in terms of students
who said they were doing 'very well' in their courses
(N=58) and those who said they were performing
'badly' (N=43). The sub-scales which defined the
discriminant function most clearly were organized
study methods, positive attitudes to studying, a
strategic approach, and (to a lesser extent) high
scores on achievement motivation and deep approach,
combined with low scores on surface approach and
globetrotting. This function places students
correctly in their achievement category in 90% of
instances. Of course, this level of prediction is
likely to be an overestimate, due to the circularity
involved in using self-ratings of both progress and
approaches to studying. In the pilot study, with
an objective criterion but a first-year sample, the
level of correct prediction was 83% in the low group
and 75% in the high group.

RELATIONSHIPS BETWEEN APPROACHES TO STUDYING

One of the main purposes of this part of the programme was to investigate the inter-relationships
between the explanatory constructs measured by the
inventory. (The correlations between the sub-scales
can be found in Appendix Table A2). The inter-
relationships between the sub-scales of the inventory
follow the patterns anticipated. Each of the three
main domains shows fairly close inter-relationships
between the sub-scales. Even the fourth dimension,
styles and pathologies, shows a reasonable consistency - five out of the six correlations are positive
in the holist direction. The only exception was
mentioned earlier. There is a positive relationship between globetrotting and improvidence, indicating that these pathologies are more closely linked
with each other than with the stylistic component,
which would have produced a negative correlation.
Although it may be difficult at first sight to

understand how apparently opposite pathologies could be associated in this way, interview comments from some of the weaker students showed how this might occur. For example, one student said:

"I think it tends to be the case that I get bogged down in detail. I'm sure that's the case - I mean it explains why I'm so long-winded about any work that I do. I really don't find it easy to pick out the skeletal argument and just be satisfied with that ... When I'm reading to find out about a particular topic I tend to be a bit specific initially, but I do find that I get misled very easily and as soon as another area comes up which is perhaps not quite to do with the topic ... but has interesting connections, then I go off on tangents. Very regularly I end up sort of (laughs) miles away from where I originally started".

Meaning orientation was consistently related positively to the sub-scales of achieving orientation. It was also related strongly to comprehension learning (as in previous analyses), but not to globe-trotting, hence justifying the separation of style from pathology in the inventory. Reproducing orientation was positively related to serialist style and pathology and also to both disorganized study methods and negative attitudes. In this domain, however, individual sub-scales behave less coherently. For example, surface approach and fear of failure show higher relationships with the pathologies of learning, while surface approach and extrinsic motivation are positively related to both strategic approach and achievement motivation.

Factor analysis allows overall patterns of relationships to be seen more clearly. Thus, the SPSS program was used to carry out principal factor analyses, followed by rotation to oblique simple structure. Four factors had eigenvalues greater than one and they accounted for 55 per cent of the variance. The factor loadings are shown in Table 4.4.

The first two factors were almost identical to those previously described as meaning orientation and reproducing orientation. Again both factors showed a strong stylistic component. However, meaning orientation, as opposed to reproducing orientation, contained no element of pathology in its loadings. The previous third factor of achieving orientation was divided into two. Factor III had its highest loading on disorganized study methods and negative attitudes to studying, a factor similar to that which had emerged from the earlier inventory of motivation and study methods (Entwistle, 1975). This factor, which can be seen as a non-academic orientation to studying, represents disorganised and dilatory approaches to studying. Factor IV was closer to the previous achieving orientation with high loadings on strategic approach and both extrinsic and achievement motivations. There was also an apparent readiness to adopt either deep or surface approaches, which is consistent with a previous finding (Entwistle, Hanley and Hounsell, 1979) that students with an achieving orientation will seek high grades, using meaningful or rote learning, whichever seems to produce the best results.

Table 4.4   FACTOR ANALYSIS OF APPROACHES TO STUDYING SCALES (N=2208)

| Variables | Factors | | | |
	I	II	III	IV
Academic Performance				
School	(-02)	(-13)	(-15)	(-07)
Higher Education	31	-26	-39	(19)
Approaches to Studying				
(DA) Deep Approach	70			(22)
(RI) Inter-relating Ideas	65			
(UE) Use of Evidence	54			(23)
(IM) Intrinsic Motivation	72		-25	
(SA) Surface Approach		57	36	30
(SB) Syllabus-boundness	-41	58		(24)
(FF) Fear of Failure		50	34	
(EM) Extrinsic Motivation	-25	38		53
(ST) Strategic Approach	29			48
(DS) Disorganized Study Methods	-25		50	
(NA) Negative Attitudes to Studying	-39		52	
(AM) Achievement Motivation	(24)			45
(CL) Comprehension Learning	55	(-24)	30	
(GL) Globetrotting			52	
(OL) Operation Learning		62		44
(IP) Improvidence		68	(24)	26

Decimal points and most loadings less than .25 omitted.

Factor III (non-academic orientation) shows the highest (negative) loading on self-rating of academic progress. As expected, meaning orientation is positively related to achievement, while the reproducing orientation shows a negative relationship. Surprisingly, the achieving orientation itself shows only a slight association with the self-rating of academic progress. However, all these relationships will have to be re-examined subsequently, with a more satisfactory criterion of achievement (degree class).

FURTHER DEVELOPMENT WORK ON THE INVENTORY

The publication of an article describing results from the second pilot inventory (Entwistle, Hanley and Hounsell, 1979) created considerable interest among other researchers working in this field. As a result the final research version of the inventory has been used either in its original form or in a slightly amended form in studies at the Open University (Morgan, Gibbs and Taylor, 1980), at the Australian National University (Watkins, 1982) and is about to be used in Holland and Belgium (Van Rossum, personal communication).

In the Open University study, meaning orientation emerged as clearly as in our own analyses, but there was overlap between reproducing orientation, achieving orientation and styles and pathologies. The reproducing factor did not have significant loadings on extrinsic motivation, It did have loadings, not just on operation learning, but also on the two pathologies, and on disorganized studying and negative attitudes. The third factor linked together extrinsic and achievement motivation, while the fourth factor was not consistent in the two samples used.

As a result of our own factor analyses and those from the Open University, it was decided to carry out a reassessment of our sub-scales. The separation into sixteen sub-scales was designed to keep each dimension conceptually distinct; the separation could not be justified on the basis of empirical relationships. The later factor analyses made it imperative to see to what extent the current grouping of items, either within sub-scales or within four domains, could still be justified empirically. Thus alpha factor analysis was applied to data from the main study (N=2208) and 17 factors were extracted (to allow for 16 factors and the freedom to rotate created by an additional factor). Also a five-factor solution was produced to examine member-ship of domains, and repeated for each of the six disciplines separately. The 17 factor solution produced few identifiable groupings of items, so Table 4.5 summarises the factors from the 5 factor solutions.

Again the two main orientations were clear-cut and identifiable in every discipline, being meaning orientation and reproducing orientation. The clarity of the interpretation was blurred somewhat where a separate style factor was created (history and physics). Then the meaning orientation could be better described as 'deep approach out of interest', while the reproducing orientation, with operation learning removed, was more identifiable with a surface, instrumental approach. Conceptually it was this distinction which had been expected. Operation learning, with its emphasis on a cautious, logical, controlled, approach closely reliant on fact and detail, should not necessarily become a surface instrumental strategy. It was thus re-assuring to find some empirical support for this distinction.

The third main factor again differed from the achieving orientation described previously. Pre-viously it was found that disorganized study methods and negative attitudes were linked, while achievement motivation was associated with both strategic approach and extrinsic motivation. In these analyses the first two held together in most analyses, but could be separated into distinct factors. The motivational sub-scales could also be found as distinct factors, but more typically they were grouped in the ways shown in Table 4.5. An examin-ation of these, together with earlier analyses, suggests that the 'non-academic' groupings contain two components - the rejection of academic values and, in some students, an endorsement of alternative goals - social, aesthetic or sporting. It may thus be necessary to describe motivation in terms of four distinct sub-scales: achievement, extrinsic, intrinsic and social. Again in some analyses 'academic motivation', the combination of achieve-ment motivation and intrinsic motivation, was also related to strategic approach. This combination was commonly associated with elements of both deep and surface approaches - thus describing the separate 'achieving orientation' found previously.

It thus seems that there are perhaps four distinctive orientations to studying which can be

Table 4.5   SUMMARY OF ITEM FACTOR ANALYSES

Groupings of Sub-Scales	English (N=282)	History (209)	Economics (450)	Psychology (402)	Physics (357)	Engineering (508)	Total Sample (2208)
Meaning Orientation (DA + CL + RI + UE) (also IM)	X	X	X	X	X	X	X
Reproducing Orientation (SA + IP + FF + SB) (also OL)	X	X	X	X	X	X	X
Non-Academic Orientation (DS + NA + GL) (also −IM and −AM)	X	X	(two factors)	X	X	(two factors)	X
Holist Style (CL + GL)		X			X		
Serialist Style (OL + IM)					X		
Academic Motivation (AM + IM)	X			X			X
Instrumental Motovation (AM + EM)		X					
Non-Academic Motivation (EM + C* − IM)	X		X	X		X	

* C = maximum score on IM subscale (16)

identified empirically from the inventory and that these orientations are associated with characteristic forms of motivation, as Biggs has suggested:

Orientation	Motivation
Meaning Orientation (DA + CL + RI + UE)	Intrinsic (IM)
Reproducing Orientation (SA + IP + FF + SB)	Extrinsic and/or Fear of Failure (EM)
Achieving Orientation (AM + IM + ST)	Achievement
Non-Academic Orientation (DA + NA + GL)	Low levels of intrinsic combined with high extrinsic and/or social motivation

These orientations correlated with academic progress as shown in Table 4.6. Consistently the highest values are shown with the non-academic and achieving orientations. There is a subject area difference showing meaning orientation to be more effective and reproducing orientation (and serialist style) to be more heavily penalized in arts than science. The holist style is unrelated to achievement in any discipline, as is the serialist style in science and social science.

In parallel to these analyses of the final research version, work has also been progressing with a much shorter inventory of 30 items. This was devised initially for use in a book (Entwistle, 1981) to illustrate the type of scales available. For this purpose some of the items were slightly altered to make it appropriate for sixth-formers (16 - 18 year olds). The availability of this version of the inventory has allowed a pilot study* to be carried out in one school with a small sample of 51 pupils taking 'A' level (18 +) examinations. Table 4.7 shows the mean scores of pupils with the highest and lowest 'A' level performance on the shortened scales.

---

* We are grateful to Sean O'Conaill of Loretto School in Coleraine for collecting these data.

Table 4.6 CORRELATIONS BETWEEN STUDY ORIENTATION AND SELF-RATING OF ACADEMIC PROGRESS

Orientation/Style	English (N=282)	History (209)	Economics (450)	Psychology (402)	Physics (357)	Engineering (508)
Meaning	23	27	24	20	17	14
Reproducing	-39	-35	-24	-14	-26	-23
Achieving	27	24	38	38	40	28
Non-Academic	-36	-27	-39	-37	-44	-40
Holist	-02	01	-02	-00	-08	-06
Serialist	-23	-23	-06	-02	-06	-09

Decimal points omitted

Table 4.7   MEAN SCORES OF PUPILS WITH HIGH OR LOW 'A' LEVEL
GRADES ON SHORT 'APPROACHES TO STUDYING' INVENTORY

Orientation/Style	Science		Arts	
	High (N=5)	Low (7)	High (11)	Low (8)
Meaning Orientation	15.4	12.4	14.8	11.8
Reproducing Orientation	15.0	12.9	14.0	16.4
Achieving Orientation	15.2	12.4	14.4	6.6
Holist Style	13.0	11.9	14.1	13.0
Serialist Style	16.6	12.4	13.1	14.6

It was encouraging to find, even in this small
sample and using a much abbreviated inventory, a
pattern of results similar to those found with
students.   Of particular interest was a suggestion
that reproducing orientation and improvidence are
associated with success in science and with poor
performance in arts.

It is hoped that a schools version of the
published inventory will be produced and that in both
schools and higher education, the results can be
used for diagnostic purposes.   Linking this
inventory to schemes for teaching study skills in
schools and in higher education, (for example,
Tabberer and Allman, 1981;   Gibbs, 1981) it is anticipated that students could be helped to develop
appropriate skills and to become more conscious in
using those skills strategically to improve their
levels of academic performance.   Such implications
of the findings of our research will be discussed
more fully in the final chapter.

Chapter Five

PERSONALITY AND COGNITIVE STYLE IN STUDYING .

(Written in collaboration with Sarah Morison)

By now we have been able to establish clearly
from the inventory data that students adopt distinctive approaches to studying - the most insistent
contrast being between meaning and reproducing
orientations. The question posed in this chapter
is whether these approaches can be interpreted in
terms of more fundamental psychological processes.
The initial review sections introduce theories and
psychological tests which were incorporated into the
study reported in the second half of the chapter.

LEVELS OF PROCESSING IN THE MEMORY

Marton initially referred to deep level and
surface level processing, and the idea of different
levels of processing is already well established in
the psychological literature on human memory and
information processing. Models of human memory
have described generally three distinct types of
memory - a sensory register (which holds incoming
perceptions only briefly), a short-term memory (STM
- which holds a limited amount of information for up
to about 20 seconds), and a long-term memory (LTM)
which itself can be divided into episodic (storing
episodes of experience) and semantic (storing and
relating concepts).
Information can be held in store for longer
periods by internal repetition (rehearsal) and if
repeated sufficiently often (overlearning) it will
become a permanent memory trace, presumably in

The early part of this chapter contains extracts from
Entwistle (1981), Styles of Learning and Teaching.
More detailed descriptions of the psychological
literature will be found there in Chapters 7, 9 and 1(

episodic LTM. This process is what would normally be called rote memorization or surface level processing. But much incoming information is reassessed and categorized in STM before being passed to semantic LTM. This process is what is involved in deep level processing.

It comes initially as a contradiction of everyday experience to hear that we have a memory which is essentially unlimited in size and in which memories remain almost indefinitely. The apparent paradox vanishes when we realize that the ideas which go in may not necessarily come out. Retrieval from memory depends on the accuracy of a coding process which determines where the incoming information will be stored, and hence where it is expected subsequently to be found.

The long-term memory has been compared to a library, to sets of pigeon-holes and to a filing system (Broadbent, 1966). It contains what Lindsay and Norman (1972) call a data base of concepts and records of events tied together within inter-connecting systems. Each individual has a unique conceptual structure, although the linkages between concepts (which constitute definitions) have enough in common to allow effective communication of ideas. Concepts are built up by repeated comparisons of incoming perceptions or information with pre-existing concepts or linkages between images (for example, the sight of a dog and the sound of the word 'dog'). If the coding system is to be effective and recall easy, it is essential that the data base should contain a large number of clearly defined and well differentiated concepts which also carry a large number of connecting links with other concepts, ideas or events. The ability to think divergently or creatively will presumably depend on the extent to which the memory has developed a multiplicity of unusual, but valid, interconnections. It will also depend on the availability of appropriate, perhaps leisurely, search mechanisms to explore fruitful combinations of ideas.

Another model of the memory has been developed by Craik and Lockhart (1972). They broke away from the mechanistic, three-box model by proposing instead different levels of processing. Memory is seen as involving a "hierarchy of processing stages where greater 'depth' implies a greater degree of semantic or cognitive 'analysis'". Recall of complex material will also be enhanced by systematic elaboration at the same level of processing (Craik and Tulving, 1975).

Elaboration can be seen as developing linkages between the new idea and previous knowledge and personal experience.

It is therefore possible to reconsider our two main study orientations within these models of the memory. An orientation towards understanding (deep approach and comprehension learning) depends on a deep level of processing and elaboration. Reproducing (surface approach and operation learning) is more likely to involve overlearning by repetition at a shallow level of processing with little use of elaboration.

Our research strategy has involved translating constructs derived from qualitative analyses of students' reported experiences of studying into specific items of typical study processes and attitudes. We have then looked for explanations of the emerging study orientations in terms of psychological theories. It is, of course, more common to extrapolate psychological theories into educational contexts, in the expectation that basic psychological processes will be utilized wherever learning and remembering are being demanded. It is interesting, and reassuring, to discover that this research strategy converges on a description of student learning recognizably similar to our own.

From the University of Southern Illinois, Schmeck and his colleagues have reported a series of studies using an Inventory of Learning Processes (see Schmeck, in press, for an extensive summary of this work). Their approach has been to identify the processes identified most clearly in major theories of human learning and then to produce items which describe those processes in relation to the "environment and activities of the typical college student". Factor analyses of these items have produced four main dimensions describing distinct learning processes - deep processing, elaborative processing, fact retention and methodical study. Examination of the individial items shows conceptual overlap between these dimensions and our study orientations described in the previous chapter. 'Orientation to understanding' covers both deep and elaborative processing, but also contains items relating to intention and intrinsic motivation. 'Reproducing' is made up partly of the 'fact retention' dimension, but is perhaps related more strongly to shallow processing (i.e. rote memorizing processes)*. The methodical study dimension cannot be equated with our 'achieving orientation'. Schmeck describes his scale as covering the activities recommended by a 'how to study manual'. In our
* (But see Appendix, table A4).

inventory this area would be covered in part by the sub-scale of 'organised study methods', but also by 'syllabus-boundness' which is within our 'reproducing' domain. One major difference between the Schmeck inventory and our own (and Biggs') is that it does not contain either attitudinal or motivational items, which in our analyses are found to be most closely related to academic achievement.

The similarity in findings does however indicate the utility of attempting to relate our orientations to more fundamental psychological processes. Our analyses have tried to distinguish approaches (perhaps more markedly affected bv the learning context) from styles (implying links with persistent individual differences). The factor analyses did not allow this separation to be made clearly, but the conceptual distinction can be explored in relation to the existing psychological literature. A holistic style, the wide-ranging search for analogies and interconnections between ideas, could be seen as a new way of describing a more familiar term - 'divergent thinking'. Similarly serialism might be associated with convergent thinking.

STYLES OF THINKING

Hudson (1966) popularized the distinction between convergent thinking (as measured by conventional tests of reasoning) and divergent thinking, which is productive or imaginative rather than logical and analytical. Hudson used the simple 'Uses of Objects' test which asks for as many different uses as possible for such everyday objects as a barrel or a paperclip. Scores depend on both the number of responses produced and on their novelty or statistical rarity.

Hudson (1966) drew attention to the wide differences in performance on the Uses of Objects Test, even of sixth-formers who were all highly intelligent. The inability of some pupils to think of more than the most obvious uses led Hudson to designate them as 'convergers', while the superabundance of uses produced by other boys indicated that they could be called 'divergers'. The label given depends on which test score was higher - the verbal reasoning test or the open-ended test. Hudson illustrates how wide the differences can be by quoting two extreme responses. The boys had been asked to list as many uses as they could think of for a barrel. Both boys were highly intelligent, but one was a mathematician and the other was an arts specialist.

"<u>Converger</u> - Keeping wine in, playing football.

"<u>Diverger</u> - For storing old clothes, shoes,
tools, paper, etc. For pickling onions in.
For growing a yew-tree in. For inverting and
sitting on. As a table. As firewood chopped
up. As a drain or sump for rainwater. As a
sand pit. At a party for games. For making
cider or beer in. As a play-pen for a small
child. As a rabbit hutch, inverted with a
door out of the side. On top of a pole as a
dove-cote. Let into a wall as a night exit
for a dog or a cat. As the base for a large
lamp. As a vase for golden rod and michaelmas
daisies, as an ornament, especially if it is a
small one. With holes cut in the top and sides,
either for growing wall-flowers and strawberries
in, or for stacking pots, and kitchen utensils.
As a proper garbage can or wastepaper basket.
As a ladder to reach the top shelves of a high
bookcase. As a casing for a home-made bomb.
Sawn in half, as a doll's crib. As a drum.
As a large bird's nest" (Hudson, 1966, page 90-
91).

Hudson found that a majority of convergers
studied science, while divergers mainly specialized
in the arts. He also suggested that these interests,
and the cognitive abilities associated with them, have
their roots in child-rearing practices. The type of
responses made by convergers led Hudson to the conclusion that these pupils were emotionally inhibited
and he speculated that this inability to express
emotion overtly stems from cool, overdemanding
mothers. Divergent thinking is clearly a component
of problem solving, but logical thinking is also
needed. A combination of imaginative production and
analytic reasoning - the alternation of the curious
and the critical which marked Heath's 'Reasonable
Adventurer' - is often necessary.
    One of the weaknesses of the Uses of Objects
test is that it accepts both plausible and implaus-
ible uses. Raaheim (1974) has developed a 'categorizing' test which avoids this weakness by demanding realistic alternatives. In this test the names
of successive groups of three objects are presented.
In each group one name is underlined and the task is
to indicate in how many different ways the underlined
object differs from both of the other ones. Raaheim
describes the test as measuring cognitive flexibility.
It seems to be a concept similar to that used by

Bieri et al (1966) - cognitive complexity - which also demands flexible alternations of categorizations but which is described by Bieri as a cognitive style. Raaheim sees it as an ability.

The difference between divergent thinking and convergent thinking is not just one of different processes. There seem to be, as Hudson hinted, emotional and attitudinal components. de Bono (1971) has used the term 'lateral thinking' to describe the alternative to vertical, analytic thinking. He likens problem-solving to digging holes. Logical thinking often comes to the point of digging deeper and deeper holes in quite the wrong place. He suggests that 'lateral thinking' is more likely to be effective - a series of shallow, exploratory holes prior to 'deep drilling'. Lateral thinking seems to be closely allied to divergent thinking, and de Bono sees it as being necessarily leisurely, often having a dream-like quality where the emotions, as well as the intellect, are given free rein. Crutchfield (1962) suggests that

"One source of original ideas lies in the ready accessibility to the thinker of many rich and subtle (emotional) attributes of the percepts and concepts in his mental world and to the metaphorical and analogical penumbras extending out from their more explicit, literal and purely logical features. For it is partly through a sensitivity to such (emotional) and metaphorical qualities that new and 'fitting' combinational possibilities among the elements of a problem may unexpectedly emerge" (page 124).

These strategies of thinking can be readily described in the terminology of the information processing model. Divergent thinking is a search strategy which has a broad focus and allows connections between ideas to be made, even when the justifications for the associations are not obvious. The wide sweep of relevant information encompasses both semantic and episodic elements within the LTM. The search is likely to be relaxed, slow, broad, and not limited to a specific location in the information store. On the other hand convergent thinking will tend to be narrowly focused, intense, fast and limited to specific locations. This distinction between broad, leisurely, inclusive rambles through LTM, compared with narrow, fast, and limited forays, parallels Pask's distinction between holists and serialists, and seems to be at the root of the more general, but ill-defined, psychological term 'cognitive style'.

COGNITIVE STYLE

Cognitive styles, like personality traits, are considered by most psychologists to be fairly consistent, and lasting, modes of functioning:

"The stability and pervasiveness of cognitive styles across diverse spheres of behaviour suggest deeper roots in personality structure than might at first glance be implied ... Cognitive styles may entail generalized habits of information processing, to be sure, but they develop in congenial ways around underlying personality trends. Cognitive styles are thus intimately inter-woven with affective, temperamental, and motivational structures as part of the total personality ...

Cognitive styles differ from intellectual abilities in a number of ways ... Ability dimensions essentially refer to the content of cognition or the question of what - what kind of information is being processed by what operation in what form?

... Cognitive styles, in contrast, bear on the questions of how - on the manner in which behaviour occurs ... Abilities, furthermore, are generally thought of as unipolar ... (and) value directional: having more of an ability is better than having less. Cognitive styles are (bipolar and) value differentiated: each pole has adaptive value ... (depending) upon the nature of the situation and upon the cognitive requirements of the task in hand" (Messick, 1976, pages 6 - 9).

Two of the best known cognitive styles derive from perceptual tasks - Matching Familiar Figures (Kagan et al, 1964) and identifying Embedded Figures (Witkin, 1977). Figure 5.1 shows an item from one of Kogan's MFF tests which consists of a standard drawing and six or eight variants, one of which is identical to the standard, and all of which are similar. The respondent is required to answer as quickly as possible, but has to make another attempt after each incorrect response. There is thus a pressure to find the correct answer, but also to

decide quickly.   Kogan (1976) sees the situation as
building up competing anxieties towards correct, or
fast, responses.   The average time to answer
(response latency) is measured and also the number
of errors.   Two cognitive styles have been detected
with this test.   Impulsive people succumb rapidly
to the need to identify the matching figure: they
choose hurriedly and make more mistakes.   Reflective
individuals treat the task more analytically and
cautiously: they are more accurate, but slower.

The second cognitive style has perhaps attracted the greatest attention.   An item from an Embedded
Figures Test (EFT) is shown in Figure 5.2.   Witkin
(1976; 1977) has reviewed the extensive literature
on the use of this and other methods of measuring the
dimension of field dependence/field independence.
In the EFT the respondent is shown a simple geometri-
cal figure and is required to identify it in a complex figure.   The task is rather similar to the
children's puzzle in which, say, a 'hidden rabbit'
is discovered as part of the foliage of a tree.
Some people can spot the embedded figure almost
immediately: they are not distracted by the
surroundings and are categorised as field-independent.
Other people spend much longer even with the simple
items.   Witkin argues that the different scores on
this test do not simply reflect perceptual skills.
Like Pask he argues for the existence of underlying
styles of thinking.   Witkin labels these styles
articulated (field-independent) and global (field-
dependent), which seem, at first sight, to bear some
resemblance to Pask's descriptions of operation
learning and comprehension learning.

The articulated, field-independent style involves analysing and structuring incoming information; the
global, field-dependent mode of operation accepts
the totality of impressions.   The problem of Witkin's
description is that field-dependence is an inability
to impose structure.   If it is to be a style, a
rather more positive side can only be inferred from
incidental characteristics such as tendencies to be
sociable and to have an interest in other people.
Field-dependent students express this interest in
people by being drawn towards courses in the humanities and social sciences, and opting out of courses
in science and mathematics.   Field-independent
students, while found predominantly in science
faculties, are still capable of success in other areas
of study.   This facility raises the question of
whether these students might be best compared with
Pask's versatile learners, rather than with operation

Figure 5.1   Example of an Item from a Matching
Familiar Figures Test

Figure 5.2   Example of an Item from an Embedded
Figures Test.

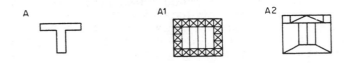

learners. But here we run up against lack of empirical evidence.

From an educational standpoint perhaps the most interesting studies reported by Witkin concern the teaching methods adopted by teachers of contrasting cognitive style. It appears that field-independent teachers or lecturers impose a tighter and more logical structure on teaching material than do 'global' teachers. They also prefer more formal approaches to teaching. Witkin argues that field-dependent students need pre-structured information, since they are less able to impose their own analytic frameworks. Hence field-dependent students ought to be more successful with teachers who have an articulated cognitive style. To date there is no evidence of differential success rates, but there is a clear indication that students prefer to be taught by teachers of the <u>same</u> cognitive style. There is thus a possible conflict here between the approach students prefer and what is considered to be most effective in helping them to learn.

PERSONALITY

Personality can be defined as "the dynamic organization within the individual of those psychophysical systems that determine his characteristic behaviour and thought" (Allport, 1963, page 28). The term 'personality' is thus the broadest of all. It can be taken to include cognitive abilities, but these are generally excluded. Styles of whatever sort are certainly contained within this definition and there are many indications in the literature that distinctive behavioural or thinking styles are a facet of personality.

The description of personality, and its measurement, has depended on the identification of what seem to be relatively consistent 'common traits'.

"Common traits are ... those aspects of personality in respect to which most people within a given culture can be profitably compared ... The scientific evidence for the existence of a trait always comes from demonstrating by some acceptable method the <u>consistency</u> in a person's behaviour" (Allport, 1963, page 343).

A useful common trait must show the consistency of representative groups of individuals both over time and between situations. A major problem is to decide <u>how much</u> consistency is required to provide

evidence for the existence of a trait. People's
behaviour, of course, is never entirely predictable
from one situation to another: it shows both consistency and inconsistency. Some psychologists have
used this fact to argue against attempts to describe
personality in terms of traits, or even against
trying to measure it at all. Labelling can be seen
as limiting human potentialities. Bronowski (1965)
has rounded on these critics and asked them a series
of awkward questions about human predictability.

> "(If) a man does not want to be law-abiding;
> very well then, it is time to ask him the rude
> but searching question "Do you want to be law-
> less?" You refuse to be predictable as an
> engine is, or an animal; do you aspire to be
> unpredictable? And if so, are you unpredict-
> able to yourself, the actor, as well as to me,
> the spectator? Do you base your claim to be a
> self on the proud assertion that your actions
> are arbitrary? (No) ... a self must have con-
> sistency; its actions tomorrow must be recog-
> nizably of a piece with the actions carried out
> yesterday" (pages 13-15).

The extent of such consistency is an empirical
question. If important traits can be measured, and
if these are also found, on the whole, to be consistently related to a variety of aspects of behaviour,
then their use in psychology is surely justifiable.
But which traits have proved most useful in describing personality?
Jung (1938), from his clinical experience,
identified what he considered to be two fundamentally
different psychological types - people who viewed the
world in opposite ways - the extravert and the introvert. The extravert, as the word implies, looks
outward. His behaviour is predominantly orientated
towards events in the outside world and his thinking
is dominated by the search for objective facts.
The introvert, on the contrary, looks inward. Outside events are, of course, perceived but they tend
to be judged by personal values and standards. The
introvert's thinking is influenced by, even obsessed
with, personal interpretations and theories. Jung
sees dangers in both extreme ways of thinking.

> "For as in the former case the purely empirical
> heaping together of facts paralyses thought and
> smothers their meaning, so in the latter case
> introverted thinking shows a dangerous tendency

to coerce facts into the shape of its image, or
by ignoring them altogether, to unfold its
phantasy image in freedom" (pages 481-482).

In Jung's theory the extraverted and introverted
tendencies are <u>both</u> present in every person.
Whichever characteristic becomes dominant in a person's behaviour and conscious thought, its opposite
continues to be represented in the unconscious as
the <u>shadow</u>, and is thought to have a continuing
effect on the development of personality.

In writing about personality theories, Jung
pointed out that the choice of a particular type of
theory, or an emphasis within that theory, was in
part a reflection of the theorists's own personality.
Thus Jung's theory, with its description of extraversion and introversion in terms of ways of
<u>thinking</u>, perhaps reflects Jung's own admitted intro-
version. He was not much concerned with outside
events. In contrast Eysenck (1965) has provided
descriptions of extraverts and introverts which
stress differences in <u>behaviour</u>.

"(The typical extravert is) sociable, likes
parties, has many friends, needs to have people
to talk to, and does not like studying by himself. He craves excitement, takes chances,
often sticks his neck out, acts on the spur of
the moment, and is generally an impulsive
individual ... The typical introvert, on the
other hand, is a quiet retiring sort of person,
introspective, fond of books rather than
people; he is reserved and distant except with
intimate friends. He tends to plan ahead,
"looks before he leaps", and distrusts the
impulse of the moment" (pages 59-60).

Eysenck and Cattell have both used personality
inventories and factor analysis in the attempt to
determine which general traits are most useful in the
description of personality. Both of them were
students of Cyril Burt who had investigated aspects
of children's personality in 1915. Burt (1965)
claimed to have originally identified a general factor of emotionality, and later described two significant bi-polar factors, one of which appears to have
been extraversion/introversion, while the other
described the contrast between optimistic and pessi-
mistic outlooks on life.

Cattell (1965) has identified sixteeen different
traits, but these overlap to some extent. A

simplified description of these traits reduces the
number to five: anxiety, extraversion, tender-
mindedness, radicalism, and conscientiousness or
moral conventionality. Eysenck's research has concentrated on the first two of these dimensions. He
has also described the second two traits, although
he originally identified these as 'social attitudes'
(Eysenck, 1970). Eysenck's most recent personality
inventories (Eysenck and Eysenck, 1969) now also contain a psychoticism scale (asocial or antisocial
morality) and a lie scale which measures the tendency
to give conventional responses. At this descriptive
level there is a good agreement between the two
theories, but Eysenck sees extraversion and what he
calls neuroticism (similar to general emotionality)
as much more basic than the other descriptions of
personality.

Eysenck assesses levels of extraversion and
neuroticism through personality inventories which are
built up from a series of questions. Each question
is an index of one particular personality trait, and
is chosen only after it has been proved to discrim-
inate between groups of people who are known to
exhibit extraverted or introverted patterns of
behaviour. Respondents are asked to reply 'yes' or
'no' to questions such as

> Can you put your thoughts into words quickly?
> Are you mostly quiet when you are with other
> people?
> Are you an irritable person?
> Are you troubled by feelings of inferiority?
> Have you ever been late for an appointment or
> work?
> Do you sometimes boast a little?

Answering 'yes' to the first question and 'no' to
the second question are indications of extraversion.
The next two questions suggest aspects of neuroticism, while the final two items are part of a 'lie'
scale designed to detect people who are trying to
present themselves in a favourable light. Considerable care and ingenuity goes into the design
of these personality inventories, and the strength
of the various traits is determined by the number
of responses given in the 'extraverted' or 'neurotic'
directions. Although a person's response to any
individual item may be affected by the wording, or by
their mood at the time, their overall score on say
25 items remains fairly consistent over time, at
least among adults.

A considerable research literature has built up which reports personality in relation both to students' academic performance and to choice of subject area (see Entwistle and Wilson, 1977). It seems as if introverts tend to be more successful students, but as indicated in Chapter 4, this is probably attributable to better study habits. There are, however, clear differences in personality between students in different subject areas and these are presented diagrammatically in Figure 5.3.

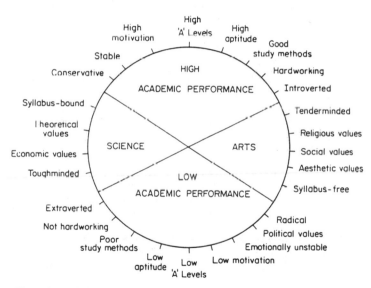

Figure 5.3 Relationship between students' characteristics, faculty membership, and level of academic performance (Adapted from Entwistle and Wilson, 1977, page 148)

The indication that cognitive styles and probably learning styles also differ by faculty reinforced the decision to include indices of personality in our investigation of the more fundamental psychological traits which may underlie approaches and styles of learning.

THE DESIGN OF THE STUDY*

The first step was to identify groups of students who had distinctively different orientations to studying. The second pilot version of the Approaches to Studying Inventory was used for this purpose. From the sample of 767 first year students, 130 were selected as having the highest or lowest scores on the sub-scales which most clearly measured meaning orientation and reproducing orientation. For this purpose the combined scores on deep approach plus comprehension learning were used. The dichotomy on each combined measure produced four groups.

The 130 selected students were sent the third version of the inventory to complete and were invited to take part in the test sessions. Seventy-two students agreed to participate and 60 finally came to the initial interviews. In spite of repeated reminders, no others came. The distribution of the 60 students between the four groups is shown below.

Surface/ Operation	Deep/Comprehension	
	High	Low
High	Strategic $N_1 = 13$	Reproducing $N_3 = 11$
Low	Meaning $N_2 = 15$	Unmotivated $N_4 = 21$

The terms used to describe the groups were chosen on the basis of the mean scores on the inventory. The smallest group (reproducing) were mainly scientists who showed a disappointing reluctance to be involved in the study. The largest group (unmotivated) were, paradoxically, very helpful and cooperative, yet their main characteristic was low scores on most of the sub-scales and subsequent tests.

The tests were given in the order shown below over a period of some 15 months. Payments were made

---

* This study was carried out by Sarah Morison (née Burkinshaw)

to every student who completed some 7 hours of testing, spread over the 6 sessions.

Session	Test	Method of Administration
1	Approaches to Studying Inventory (Third Pilot Version)	Post
2	Interviews	Individually
3	(a) Omnibus Personality Inventory (b) Matching Familiar Figures (MFF)	Individually
4	Moray House Advanced Verbal Reasoning (MHA)	Small Groups
5	(a) Test of Categorizing (TC) (b) Uses of Objects (UO) (c) Test of Generalising and Abstracting (TGA) (d) Embedded Figures (EFT)	Small Groups
6	Spy Ring History Test	Microcomputer Individually

The initial interview was designed to create interest and motivation. It was essential that every student completed the whole test battery, yet the demands on the students were very heavy. By establishing a personal relationship with each student, by providing (optionally) information about test scores and an interpretation of them, by explaining the relevance and importance of the project, by encouragement throughout, and eventually by offering a financial reward for completion of the full set of tests, all 60 students were retained in the study throughout a period of 12-15 months.

The tests used are described below in sufficient detail to ensure that the meaning of each dimension measured can be understood. The tests are introduced within five measurement areas or domains:

71

personality, reasoning ability, cognitive style,
cognitive flexibility and learning style.

PERSONALITY

The test chosen was the Omnibus Personality
Test (Heist and Yonge, 1968), as it had been
specifically designed for use with students and
contained sub-scores on 14 traits, several of
which had, in the literature, been shown to be
related to choice of subject area, and seemed also
likely to be related to differences in learning
style.   The traits measured are as follows:

Thinking Introversion	– high scorers show a preference for ideas rather than practical action; they have wide-ranging academic interests.
Theoretical Orientation	– have a logical, analytical and critical approach to problems, an interest in science and theoretical concerns and problems.
Aestheticism	– have wide interests and involvement in literature, music, painting, architecture, etc.
Complexity	– show tolerance of ambiguity, enjoy novelty; adopt flexible approaches to problems.
Autonomy	– distrust control and authority; are tolerant of other people's contrary views; prefer radical liberal thinking.
Religious Scepticism	– reject conventional religious beliefs and practices.
Social Extraversion	– enjoy being with people and attending parties or social functions; are happy to join in discussions or talk in public.
Impulse Expression	– act on the spur of the moment; are ready to express their feelings; have an active imagination

Personality and Cognitive Style in Studying

Personal Integration	– are not socially alienated or personally disturbed, having no strong feelings of paranoia, guilt, or inadequacy.
Anxiety Denial	– do not see themselves as restless, tense, anxious, over-sensitive, or highly strung.
Altruism	– show friendly concern for others; are trusting and ethical; have an interest in the community and social relationships.
Practical Outlook	– have interests in practical things; value material possessions and facts; have a tendency also to be authoritarian and conservative in outlook.
Masculinity	– have interests in science (not aesthetics); are calm, emotionally stable, and deny personal inadequacies.
Response Bias	– are attempting to make a good impression (faking good); are socially conventional, content and relaxed.

It is important to note that some of these personality scales contain items quite similar to those contained in our Approaches to Studying Inventory. There is, in terms of content, an overlap between, for example, deep approach and both thinking introversion and theoretical orientation. But the overlap is small enough to be able to accept the personality traits as distinct. Thus the measure of theoretical introversion coincides with the personality construct, particularly as described by Jung, and the validity of the other personality dimensions has also been carefully established.

REASONING ABILITY

The main test used was the Moray House Advanced Test of Verbal Reasoning (Godfrey Thomson Unit, 1971), which is a conventional 'intelligence' test. It provides a score in terms of an intelligence quotient with a mean of 100 for the population.

In addition a test of Generalizing and Abstracting (Peel, 1978) was used. A set of three words is presented; four alternatives are offered as a description of what the target words have in common.

For example: <u>Charity</u> <u>Sympathy</u> <u>Tolerance</u>
Voluntary work; Humanity; Generosity; Lacking in some people

In each item the distracting alternative responses contain a word of similar meaning but at the same level of generality, a particular instance or example, and a non-essential attribute. The items are divided into concrete and abstract terms, providing separate estimates of the ability to abstract and generalize correctly.

COGNITIVE STYLES

Field-Independence

The Group Embedded Figures Test (described in Witkin <u>et</u> <u>al</u>, 1977) produces a single score of field-independence which represents the total number of simple figures correctly identified within the complex figures (see Figure 5.2). The simple figures are shown first, followed on the next page by the complex figures. The test is in two parts with nine items in each and an overall time-limit of ten minutes.

Reflectiveness/Impulsivity

The Matching Familiar Figures Test was used in a form suitable for young adults (described in Messer, 1976). Two scores were derived from this test - the average time taken to make the first response (which indicates reflectiveness) and the total number of incorrect choices made (inaccuracy).

Cognitive Flexibility

The Uses of Objects test was used to obtain a measure of verbal fluency (total number of uses) while the Categorizing Test provided an indication of flexibility. Both tests have been described in an earlier secton.

Learning Style

Pask (1976b) has used the Spy Ring History Test to provide indices of comprehension learning, operation learning and versatility. The test is lengthy and intellectually demanding. Students are presented with detailed information about the development of an imaginary spy network operating between several countries over a period of three years. Students have to rote-learn lists and interpret diagrams to work out the communication patterns and make predictions about future developments. Besides the three indices of learning style, the test also provides a score on 'knowledge of facts'.

Because of the demanding nature of this test and the lengthy administration time, the test was mounted on a PET microcomputer *. The computer controlled the appearance of lists and diagrams and also calculated the scores.

Students' reactions to this test were, on the whole, unfavourable. They found it difficult and boring. Many students resented the demands made for continuous rote learning, and the results indicated that few students had coped adequately with these demands. Those who found the test interesting were mainly studying science or engineering. Arts students seemed to find the type of learning required alien, and were often uncomfortable with using the PET. Even the scoring procedure seemed to penalize arts students. It thus came as no surprise that the results made little sense. The scores intended to measure learning styles had weak and contradictory relationships with supposedly equivalent dimensions from the Approaches to Studying Inventory. In an exploratory factor analysis Pask's test formed its own factor with high positive loadings on all three styles and on knowledge of facts. The only significant loadings elsewhere were on verbal reasoning, field independence, and accuracy. This disappointing set of relationships, which were contrary to the patterns demanded by Pask's own descriptions of the constructs, led the test to be dropped from the main analyses. It may be that our attempts to present the test in a more attractive

---

* We are grateful to Gordon Pask for making the computer program available and to Phil Odor for adapting it for use on the PET.

way on the microcomputer interfered with the validity of the test which has been used effectively by Pask in its original form in several studies. The microcomputer presentation may have misled students into believing they had learned the material more throughly than they had, thus preventing them responding to subsequent parts of the test.

CHARACTERISTICS OF STUDENTS WITH CONTRASTING APPROACHES

The main question being asked in this part of the research was whether students adopting contrasting approaches to studying showed equivalent differences in any of the more fundamental psychological characteristics included in the study. The simplest analysis thus examined the mean scores and standard deviations of the four contrasting groups, using analyses of variance to indicate whether differences between the groups were statistically significant. With such small groups there are a large number of insignificant differences. The results were thus treated only as indicative and other analyses carried out. In terms of personality, the first indications were that students high in meaning orientation have high scores, as expected, on thinking introversion and theoretical orientation, but also on complexity (very marked) and to a lesser extent on autonomy, aestheticism, and religious scepticism. The strategic group were characterized by high anxiety, less personal integration and a higher level of impulse expression. The reproducing group had high scores on practical outlook and masculinity, combined with low scores on thinking introversion, theoretical orientation, complexity and autonomy. The unmotivated group could only be described as unresponsive and conventional. The remaining tests showed no significant differences, although there was a suggestion that high scores on meaning orientation were associated with greater facility in verbal reasoning and verbal fluency. Students with high scores on deep/comprehension learning showed a tendency towards field dependence which nearly reached statistical significance.

RELATIONSHIPS BETWEEN APPROACHES AND PSYCHOLOGICAL ATTRIBUTES

The other main analysis involved looking at the correlates of deep/surface approaches and comprehension and operation learning. The statistically significant correlations found with each of these variables are shown in Table 5.1.

These simple correlations provide an initial indication of the extent to which there may be personality correlates of learning styles or approaches to studying. The impression created by Table 5.1 is that, as predicted, styles, rather than approaches, are more closely associated with psychological attributes. Students with high scores on comprehension learning tend to have high scores on a group of personality traits which relate to interest in ideas, but they also tend to be more ready to express impulses and admit feelings of anxiety and inadequacy. Operation learners have an opposite set of personality attributes associated with interest in practical, non-theoretical areas. They also showed caution (reflectiveness) and had lower scores on the abstract items of the generalizing test.

To make sense of the total set of inter-relationships it is again necessary to carry out a factor analysis, but as there are 36 variables and only 60 students this multivariate analysis has to be treated as exploratory, rather than definitive. Given the small sample, care was taken to include only those variables which could create factors (at least two overlapping variables are necessary). After a series of exploratory analyses with different groups of variables, the clearest set of factors was produced by using principal component factor analyses with rotation to oblique simple structure to the set of variables shown in Appendix Table 3. Six factors had eigen values above unity.

The factors are mainly associated with the different measurement domains. Thus Factors I and II represent meaning orientation combined with positive attitudes to studying, while reproducing orientation is associated with strategic, achievement motivation. The personality inventory produces two factors, one of which brings together complexity, autonomy, and impulse expression (sceptical intellectual autonomy), while the other is dominated by anxiety and a lack of personal integration. Of the remaining smaller factors one seems to describe the ability to solve intellectual and perceptual

Table 5.1   SIGNIFICANT CORRELATIONS WITH APPROACHES AND STYLES (N = 60)

Deep Approach	Comprehension Learning	Surface Approach	Operation Learning
Thinking Introversion (48)	Thinking Introversion (52)	Practical Outlook (38)	Practical Outlook (39)
Theoretical Outlook (38)	Aestheticism (43)	Thinking Introversion (-31)	Complexity (-37)
Aestheticism (31)	Theoretical Outlook (39)	Theoretical Outlook (-26)	Aestheticism (-30)
Impulse Expression (28)	Complexity (33)		Abstract Generalising (-28)
Complexity (27)	Personal Integration (-31)		Reflectiveness (23)
Verbal Fluency (24)	Impulse Expression (30)		Thinking Introversion (-23)
	Practical Outlook (-23)		
	Verbal Reasoning (23)		
	Anxiety Denial (-22)		

Decimal points omitted

puzzles, while the final factor seems to describe the abilities of Hudson's 'diverger'.

It is, of course, particularly interesting to look for overlap between the final four factors and scores on the Approaches to Studying Inventory. Thus Factor III suggests that fear of failure and globetrotting, linked to disorganized surface approaches to studying, are associated with general feelings of anxiety, tenseness and inadequacy. Fransson (1977) has already shown that it is not so much a threatening learning situation which induces surface approaches to studying, as it is students' perceptions of that situation as anxiety provoking. These findings could be taken to indicate that it may be as much a student's underlying general anxiety which induces surface learning as the particular learning context experienced. But the direction of causality and the effects of previous experience cannot be determined from this type of analysis.

Factor IV is the main personality grouping of sceptical intellectual autonomy. Its fairly strong links also with degree class and deep comprehension learning are reassuring, although the element of disorganization and globetrotting is unexpected. Again it is clear that the general personality trait is reflected in approaches to studying (an indication of syllabus-freedom) and in tests of thinking (abstract generalizing and flexibility). The ability to solve puzzles links only with complexity and the use of evidence. The 'divergers' of Factor VI show readiness to express their impulses (as Hudson argued), but their deep approach, linked as it is with negative attitudes, is not associated with degree class.

Additional analyses were also carried out to identify correlates of high levels of academic performance. Overall it was clear that a deep orientation, combined with both intrinsic and achievement motivation, were the attributes most consistently related to degree class. However, anxiety was positively related to academic performance among women.

Drawing together the evidence derived from this part of the inquiry, it is possible to argue that there are underlying personality traits associated with the tendency to prefer comprehension or operation styles of learning. It also appears that a deep orientation involves, at least to some extent, the abilities to think both logically and flexibly, combined with the personality character-istics described as sceptical intellectual autonomy.

Personality and Cognitive Style in Studying

In spite of a certain circularity through similar items, the argument for personality correlates of styles of learning is still pressed, based on the validity of the traits identified in the Omnibus Personality Inventory.

STUDENTS' PREFERENCES FOR CONTRASTING STYLES OF WRITING

The next section describes an experiment, carried out after the test sessions had been completed, in which students were asked to read, and answer questions on, three short articles. As part of this experiment students were also asked to read and comment on four essays. These essays were supposed to have been written by students, although in fact they had been specially written to exhibit extremes of serialism and holism. The topic chosen was 'Alternative Sources of Energy', a title which was expected to interest both arts and science students. The essays were written to fit as closely as possible the stylistic characteristics of holists and serialists, as described by Pask and listed below.

Holist characteristics	Serialist characteristics
Comprehension Learning:	**Operation Learning:**
Creates an overall picture	Uses rules and procedures
Assimilates ideas from other subjects	Gives details in isolatic
Invents description schemes	Keeps to one topic at a time
Uses analogies	
Has broad generalizations as hypotheses	Proceeds in stepwise manner
Relates ideas to everyday experience	Gives specific hypotheses
Looks for alternative approaches to problems	
Globetrotting:	**Improvidence:**
Inappropriate links between ideas	Insufficient explanation of detail
Vacuous analogies	Failure to use common principles

The instructions given to students were as follows:

"You are to imagine that you are the tutor responsible for this course and are required to write evaluative comments on these essays indicating what you consider to be their stylistic strengths and

weaknesses and then to mark each of them on a scale
on which '9' indicates an outstanding essay and '1'
indicates one which is very poor indeed. On this
scale '5' is the mid-point which should be used to
indicate 'reasonably good'. Your comments should
make clear your reasons for allocating the mark you
decide. Please also say which essay is most
like one you might have written yourself and
which one you found easiest to read."

The sample consisted of 47 of the 60 students
described in this chapter, divided as before into the
four categories - strategic (N = 10), meaning (9),
reproducing (9), and unmotivated (19). In marking
the essays, the four groups of students showed clear,
and different, preferences for the four essays
(Serialist 1, 2 and Holist 1,2), and also different
marking standards which made comparisons difficult.
The 'unmotivated' group,with low meaning and reproducing scores, were least critical, awarding much
higher marks without any clear preference for holist
or serialist essays; they marked Serialist 2 highest
and Serialist 1 lowest. The reproducing group found
both holist essays relatively unsatisfactory, and
gave their highest average mark most clearly to
Serialist 2. The meaning group also preferred
Serialist 2, but rated Holist 1 almost as highly.
Finally the strategic group, with high meaning and
reproducing scores, were the most critical group
(particularly of Serialist 1), but marked both holist
 essays more favourably than the serialist essays.
The marking pattern of the four groups is summarized
in Table 5.2 together with their indications of which
essay they found easiest to read and which was most
like their own style of writing.
In this small-scale exploratory study it was not
expected to find clear-cut differences between the
groups. It appears that one of the essays (Serialist
1) was too extreme in its style for most of the
students, and another was generally thought to be the
best (Serialist 2). However, if the high rating for
Serialist 2 is discounted, the two groups with high
comprehension scores (groups 1 and 2) show consistent
preferences for holist essays. The unmotivated
group show in this analysis, as in earlier analyses,
no clear pattern.
Some indication of students' reasons for
choosing one or other style of writing was found
among their comments on the essays. For example, the
reproducing group indicated their preferences for
the serialist essays by saying:

Table 5.2   PREFERENCES FOR SERIALIST AND HOLIST ESSAYS

Group	Marks Given		Easiest to Read		Most Like My Own	
	Highest	Lowest	Most	Least	Most	Least
1. Strategic	H1 H2 (S2)	S1	H1 H2	S1	H1 (S2)	S1
2. Meaning	H1	H2	H1	S1	H2 (S2)	S1
3. Reproducing	(S2) S1	H1 H2	(S2)	S1	S1 (S2)	H2
4. Unmotivated	(S2)	S1	H2	S1	H2	S1

H = Holist   S = Serialist

(The Serialist 2 essay was consistently judged to be the best and so the pattern shown is best interpreted by ignoring that essay – hence the brackets around it).

"Very readable. Some of the definitions, e.g. joule, are not strictly necessary but a clear and suitably brief account of the current dilemma. Quite probing and detailed but avoids dangers of being excessively political or technological".

"Covers most aspects briefly but adequately. Easy to read. Calculations relevant and understandable. Good beginning defining what energy is and present needs. Well organized and planned".

The comments they made against the holist essays included:

"Too vague, too many cliches. Uncritical. Attempt should be made to lose flowery style and concentrate on simple sentences which are lucid and precise".

"Clear concise style. Topical. Too much on background. Readable and a lot of relevant points made but could have gone into alternative technology in more detail".

The students who had high comprehension learning seemed to have enjoyed the relaxed, conversational style of both holist essays:

"Excellent. Included political analysis. Organized. Speaks with conviction and urgency. Easy to read".

"Very interesting and lively essay taken from an unusual and worthwhile perspective. Develops logically and clearly. Last paragraph seems a bit out of joint".

The 'strategic group generally disliked the serialist style, but also recognized that the holist style was light on detail:

"Written as if to include x no. of facts. One fact after another, not enough general writing to make it readable".

"Well structured, but certainly not to be read for pleasure. Not a style I like at all".

"Narrow. Doesn't look at social/environmental/ political problems. Too much mathematics leading to arbitrary factual statements. Dry to read, no personal comment".

"Good style. Pleasant emotive reading. Would be good for getting the point across to a difficult audience. Could perhaps do with more details".

This exploratory study has provided some indication of the ways in which students may differ in their preferred styles of writing essays. Although some of the differences here may reflect little more than arts/ science divisions, other analyses have shown that important differences in style and approach remain even within the distinct disciplines.

Chapter Six

APPROACHES TO READING ACADEMIC ARTICLES

(Written in collaboration with Sarah Morison)

A QUESTIONNAIRE ON OUTCOME AND PROCESS

Marton's original experiments on how students approached the task of reading academic articles relied on interviews to establish qualitative differences in what had been learned (outcome of learning) and what strategies students had used in tackling this task (process of learning). He and his colleagues had shown clearly a link between intention, process, and outcome. Students who intended to understand were likely to interact with evidence and argument, in relation to their previous knowledge and experience, and so come to a personal understanding of the author's conclusion. Students who were more concerned to answer correctly what they anticipated to be mainly factual questions on the article concentrated instead on question-spotting and rote memorization and often finished with very little grasp of the author's argument or conclusions.

Marton's research methodology is both time consuming and limiting in sample size. It could also be argued that students are being forced to respond to questions in an unfamiliar way. Certainly in Britain, first-year students would be more used to making written, rather than oral, responses to questions. It was therefore decided to develop a questionnaire variant of Marton's procedure, recognising that what was gained in sample size might be lost in the lack of opportunity to probe the levels of understanding and approaches to learning.

The early part of this Chapter is based on work carried out by Maureen Hanley and Garth Ratcliffe and reported in a previous article (Entwistle, Hanley, and Ratcliffe, 1979).

The categories identified in the questionnaire might thus be expected to be less clear-cut, and the relationships commensurately weaker.

The main problem in developing this variant was in finding a wording for the various questions on outcome and process which enabled students to understand what was required without also indicating what type of answer was expected. It also proved extremely difficult to find a way of coding students' responses which kept sufficiently close to Marton's categories to make a convincing test of his findings on the wider sample. A further difficulty was in finding articles which were general enough to be understood by students in a particular faculty, but demanding enough and detailed enough to present a sufficient intellectual challenge.

After two pilot studies a final form of the questionnaire was produced and three articles were selected as follows:

(1) Burt (1971) - The Mental Differences between Children (4800 words).
(2) Pines (1976) - A Child's Mind is Shaped before Age 2 (3200 words).
(3) Hoyle (1950) - The Expanding Universe (3800 words).

This version of the questionnaire contained the following questions designed to cover level of understanding, previous knowledge, knowledge of details contained in the article, and approach to learning.

(1) <u>General Understanding</u> 'Write down what you have learned from the article. Imagine you were going to describe what the article was about to a friend who hadn't read it. What would you say?'

(2) <u>Attitude Statements</u> (including an index of previous knowledge). 'Rate your attitudes to this article and the ideas it contains by underlining one of EACH of the three adjectives or phrases.'

Interesting	Average	Boring
Ideas familiar to me	Average	Ideas unfamiliar to me
Enjoyable	Average	Not enjoyable

(3) <u>Knowledge of Details</u> 'Here are some specific questions on various aspects of the article. Try to answer each question as fully as you can

and where necessary explain your answer.'
Examples of typical questions in this section
are:
'How are the stars formed?
What evidence is there that the universe is ex-
panding?
Within the "new cosmology" what is the ex-
planation of the expanding universe?'

(4)   <u>Approach to Learning</u>   'Students tackle the task
of reading articles or books in many different
ways, and with different expectations of what
is required of them and of what they should be
getting out of their reading.   How did <u>you</u>
tackle this article?   Was this approach typical
of, or different from, what you would do in your
normal studying?'

<u>Procedure</u>   Groups of students were invited to take
part in the experiment.   The purpose of the study
was explained in general terms, students were then
asked to read the article as they would normally do
in preparation for, say, a tutorial.   There was a
generous time limit with no pressure to complete the
reading quickly.   Students could make notes, but
could not use them subsequently.   After reading the
article students were asked to complete a 'Uses of
Objects' test to avoid easy verbatim recall.   They
were then asked to complete the questionnaire.

<u>Coding</u>   Students wrote on average about 150 words
in response to the first question.   This was
effectively a short essay and thus created familiar
problems in coding the level of understanding reached.
The choice is essentially between impression marking
in relation to Marton's descriptions and a reliance
on specific marking criteria.   Since these studies
were carried out Biggs and Collis (1982) have published a classification system for coding the qualitative outcomes of learning (the SOLO taxonomy), and
this has been used in studies relating approach to
outcome (Biggs, 1979;   Schmeck and Phillips, in press).
In the absence of a classification scheme, simpler
approaches were adopted.   In the first study the
number of main points mentioned was used to identify
'high' and 'low' categories, but in the third study
a more effective procedure involved impression marking against the specific criteria described by Marton.
The coder made dichotomous judgements of the response
against the following questions.

(a) Has an attempt been made to integrate the
     presentation of the main points and/or facts?
     (i.e. has the student reinterpreted and re-
     organised what has been read, rather than re-
     calling points in the order read from memory?)
(b) Have a 'sufficient' number of main points been
     mentioned?   ('sufficient' being defined so as
     to produce roughly a 50/50 distribution between
     categories).
(c) Has the author's message been understood?
(d) Are details (e.g. numerical facts, specific
     names) mentioned?

   The sum of the first three codes was used as a
summary variable indicating general understanding.
The second question related to attitudes, and
students responded on the three-point scales shown
in the previous section.   Question (3) contained 12
specific questions.   These were divided into two
groups for scoring: one group had questions about
main points essential to an understanding of the
author's argument;   the other questions concerned
incidental facts.   Each question was scored on the
basis of two marks for a full answer which was
correct, one mark for an incomplete or partially
correct answer.   The two groups of marks were
summed separately to give totals for essential points
and incidental facts.
   The final question again creates great problems
in coding.   The initial approach was impression
coding into 'deep' or 'surface', but the last study
used a similar procedure to the first question, where
the coder was asked to make dichotomous judgements
against a series of questions, three of which were
indications of a deep approach and three which
suggested a surface approach.

(a) Was there a clear intention of trying to
     understand what the author was saying?
(b) Was there an intention to integrate what was
     being read with other parts of the article,
     or with facts, or with previous experience?
(c) Was there an intention to try to reach own con-
     clusion or make use of own personal experience?
(d) Was there an intention to obtain facts or
     information?
(e) Did the experimental conditions appear to have
     affected performance (for example, time limit,
     artificiality, consciousness of questions to
     be answered, anxiety etc.)?

(f) Was there an intention to memorise or try to
     learn by rote?

     The sum of the first three ratings was used as
an overall indication of a deep approach; the sum
of the second three ratings provided a similar indication of a surface approach. A different coder
was used for each article, but a sample of each set
of questionnaires was checked to ensure that the
criteria were being interpreted consistently.
     This version of the questionnaire was given to
248 first-year students from various subject areas
in two universities (N = 85), two colleges of
education (82) and first-year sixth-formers in a
further education college (81).
     The articles proved to be different both in
difficulty level and ease of coding. There could
therefore be no comparison between the levels of
understanding reached in different articles: responses had to be analysed separately by article.
Table 6.1 shows the mean scores of students in' the
different types of institution.
     There are some marked differences between the
university students and sixth-formers in the college
of further education. Note, for example, that while
on both the Burt and Hoyle articles the sixth-formers
rate themselves as almost as familiar with the ideas
as the students, they show on average only 0.77
indications of a deep approach (out of a possible
3), while the university students have 1.53 such
indications. The university students also have
higher scores on each of the three measures of the
outcome of learning.
     The intercorrelations in Table 6.2 are shown
separately for the Hoyle and Burt articles. With
the Hoyle article, the pattern of relationships is as
expected, with general understanding showing a
substantial positive correlation with the deep
approach to learning (0.45) and a negative relationship with the surface approach (-0.29). The Burt
article showed much weaker relationships, as did the
Pines article (not reported).
     To check on the justification for combining
codings within question (1) and within question (4),
and to look for further evidence of connections
between understanding and approach, principal components analyses without iteration were carried out
with oblique rotation using the SPSS program (Nie et
al, 1975). Application of the criterion of eigen-
values of unity was supported by scree plots to

Table 6.1 MEAN SCORES AND STANDARD DEVIATIONS BY TYPE OF INSTITUTION AND ARTICLES

Coding Category (N)	Burt			Hoyle		Pines	
	Univ. (16)	Coll. (25)	FE (46)	Univ. (36)	FE (35)	Univ. (33)	Coll. (57)
General understanding	1.31 (0.95)	1.36 (0.91)	1.04 (1.82)	1.75 (1.30)	1.34 (1.26)	1.94 (1.03)	1.72 (0.92)
Essential points	5.44 (2.48)	3.48 (2.16)	3.22 (2.22)	9.33 (3.96)	8.54 (3.70)	5.73 (1.84)	5.12 (1.59)
Incidental facts	5.63 (2.00)	2.52 (1.83)	2.91 (1.82)	3.03 (1.50)	2.57 (1.75)	8.33 (2.45)	7.88 (2.49)
Familiarity	2.19 (0.83)	2.32 (0.75)	1.98 (0.80)	1.94 (0.75)	1.91 (0.85)	2.06 (0.90)	2.19 (0.77)
Deep approach	1.38 (0.72)	0.72 (0.61)	0.70 (0.63)	1.67 (0.89)	0.83 (0.79)	1.45 (0.97)	1.42 (0.80)
Surface approach	1.19 (0.66)	0.92 (0.57)	1.04 (0.59)	0.83 (0.74)	1.20 (0.68)	1.21 (0.74)	1.18 (0.71)
Uses of objects	24.63 (7.54)	22.64 (9.86)	20.76 (5.59)	23.83 (7.22)	19.06 (5.52)	24.27 (7.27)	23.56 (6.90)

Table 6.2   INTERCORRELATIONS BETWEEN THE MAIN CODING CATEGORIES

	GU	EP	IF	FM	DA	SA	UO
General understanding	*	40	15	07	45	-29	15
Essential points	47	*	46	27	32	-25	29
Incidental facts	19	53	*	08	10	-06	08
Familiarity	20	07	05	*	17	-08	03
Deep approach	11	19	27	-01	*	-40	24
Surface approach	-05	07	12	04	07	*	07
Uses of objects	14	21	-08	11	13	-01	*

Notes: Correlations above the diagonal refer to the Hoyle article (N = 96);   those below the
diagonal refer to the Burt article (N = 87).

Decimal points omitted.

Correlations significant at the 5% level where r = 0.20 (Hoyle) and r = 0.21 (Burt).

suggest that five factors should be extracted.
These factors accounted for 63% of the variance, on
average.   These five factor solutions were not altogether satisfactory, as the components of general
understanding and approach to learning tended to be
associated together in rather different combinations
for the different articles.   The connection between
approach and level of understanding can, however, be
seen clearly in the three-factor solution of the
responses to the Hoyle article (see Table 6.3).
Factor I combines the three indicators of general
understanding and both detailed knowledge variables
with the first two criteria for identifying the deep
approach.   Factor III shows its high loading on
memorization, which is associated with a tendency not
to look for meaning, and a failure to mention the
main points when asked for a summary.   Factor II
shows a greater weighting on those variables relating
to facts (with the rather important exception of
'incidental facts').

Table 6.3   FACTOR LOADINGS FOR THE HOYLE ARTICLE

Coding Categories		Factor Loadings		
		I	II	III
General understanding	Integration	61		-43
	Main points	52	21	-54
	Understanding	64		-43
	Factual details		27	
Detailed knowledge	Essential points	73	48	-24
	Incidental Facts	43		
Previous knowledge	Familiarity		32	
Deep approach	Looking for meaning	26		-56
	Use of experience	37	30	-51
	Relating facts and conclusion		40	
Surface approach	Looking for information			48
	Situational anxiety	-32		20
	Memorization			68

Decimal points and loadings below 0.20 omitted.

At least with the Hoyle article it was possible

to demonstrate the predicted links between the approach to learning and both the level of understanding reached and the extent of relevant knowledge retained. The value of keeping each index of either approach or outcome separate (as opposed to Marton's method of accepting any of three indicators as sufficient to categorize as overall deep or surface) was clear in the fuller interpretation of the relationships which became possible.

STUDENTS' COMMENTS ON APPROACH TO LEARNING

Besides the quantitative analysis, it was also possible to examine qualitatively the comments made by students about their approaches to learning. In many of the answers the distinction between 'deep' and 'surface' came through clearly, and in ways which paralleled Marton's own examples of students' comments (see Marton & Säljö, 1976a, p. 9).

Consider, for example, the following extracts in relation to the coding instructions. What approach has each of these students adopted?

Student A "Whilst reading the article, I took great care in trying to understand what the author was getting at, looking out for arguments and facts which backed up the arguments ... I found myself continually relating the article to personal experience, and this facilitated my understanding of it ... The fact of being asked questions on it afterwards made my attention more intense."

Student B "In reading the article I was looking out mainly for facts and examples. I read the article more carefully than I usually would, taking notes, knowing that I was to answer questions about it. I thought the questions would be about the facts in the article ... This did influence the way I read; I tried to memorize names and figures quoted etc."

Student C "I tried hard to concentrate - too hard, therefore my attention seemed to be on 'concentration' rather than reading, thinking, interpreting, and remembering, something that I find happening all the time I'm reading text-books."

Student D "I read it in a casual interested manner, not being influenced by the fact that I was to be questioned, mainly because I did not expect the questionnaire to ask for any details from the

article. Consequently I read it with impartial
interest - extracting the underlying meaning but
letting facts and examples go unheeded."

Although these are selected extracts chosen to
demonstrate particular types of answer, many of the
replies followed Marton's examples so closely that
it seemed almost as if the students must have read
about his ideas before - but they had not.

Using Marton's approach to coding (i.e. accepting one 'symptom' of the approach as a sufficient
indication), students A and D would be classified as
having adopted a 'deep' approach, while B and C would
be coded as 'surface'. Yet students A and D have
clearly adopted very different approaches. In each
of our studies there has been a distinct group of
students who look for meaning but do not interact
with the article, relating facts to conclusion.
This group has been labelled 'deep passive' to distinguish it from the 'deep active' approach shown by
student A.

One interesting point about the two students who
adopted the surface approach is that both of them
recognised that their approach had been rather ineffective. A later question asked 'Were you satisfied with your performance (in answering the questions)?
to which student B replied: "I feel that some of my
answers are vague and need more detail ... I made the
mistake of trying to retain everything, rather than
just the important features." There is at least a
hint here of the possible advantages of helping
students to become more consciously aware of their
approaches to studying. The use of the questionnaire
proved fruitful, even though only one of the articles
seemed to be fully effective. It has provided
evidence which, in conjunction with findings from the
approaches to studying inventory, has helped to
elaborate the concept of 'approach to learning' as
originally outlined by Marton. More recent studies
at Gothenburg (Säljö, 1975; Fransson, 1977) have
independently confirmed the necessity to subdivide
approach to learning in terms of whether an active or
passive stance has been taken. Säljö described a
'technified' deep approach in which the student
looked for meaning without interacting with the detail
or the argument. This approach has since been
equated with Pask's learning pathology of 'globetrotting' or, in less extreme forms, an over-reliance
on comprehension learning to the exclusion of operation
learning.

The possible connections between the differing

categories of Pask and Marton were pointed up by the factor analysis shown in Table 6.3. Taking the two sets of categories together it seems likely that an intention to approach learning initially in what Svensson has called a holist (deep) or atomistic (surface) way will reflect,in part, the character- istic learning style of the individual. Thus the connection between a deep approach and comprehension learning becomes inevitable. Similarly operation learning, particularly where time or interest is limited, is likely to become improvidence and so re- flect at least one component of the surface approach. A holist strategy (in terms of the questionnaire res- ponses) should be shown by an emphasis on integration and on the use of personal experience, while a serialist strategy might be expected to show a greater reliance on main points and factual details. Up to a point, the distinction mentioned earlier, between factors I and II in the three-factor solution shown in Table 6.3, contains this characteristic differ- ence in emphasis. This analysis continues the pattern of results now familiar from previous analyses. The empirical findings contain hints at ways of conceptualizing learning styles, as distinct from approaches to studying. But clear empirical separation of these constructs is rarely possible.

In the study by Schmeck and Phillips (in press) relationships between levels of outcome (as measured by the SOLO taxonomy) were related to scales from the Inventory of Learning Processes. They found that deep outcome correlated 0.37 with 'deep processing', but only 0.12 with 'elaborative processing'. Schmeck comments that Marton's 'deep approach' includes "the search for personal meaning" which is a part of ela- borative processing. But the separation in Table 6.3 between two distinct types of deep approach re- inforces our view that there are contrasting styles in seeking understanding - one in which personal meaning is emphasized, and one in which the evidence is related carefully to the conclusions. In Schmeck's scheme, the first would be described as elaborative processing and the latter might, at first, be thought to be close to 'fact retention'. But there is a major problem in accepting this equivalence. Exam- ination of the items within the 'fact retention' scale (Schmeck, in press, Table 1) shows that the two items having loadings of above 0.5 are:
- "I do well on exams requiring much factual infor- mation"
- "I am very good at learning formulas, names and dates"

These items, and indeed all but two of the items in the scale, are, explicitly or implicitly, self-ratings of outcome: they do not strictly describe processes at all. Indeed the nature of the items can be used to explain the differential correlation with levels of understanding. The 'elaborative processing' scale is truly a measure of process - every item describes a process, while 'deep processing' contains an unfortunate mixture of process and outcome. Two of the items in this scale (both with loadings of over 0.40) are self-ratings of academic performance
- "I do well on essay tests"
- "I get good grades on term papers"

Thus the higher correlation between 'deep processing' and levels of outcome must, in part, be a result of having self-ratings of prior learning outcomes within the scale.

This criticism becomes even more powerful where Schmeck report that "the most successful college students were deep, elaborative, fact retainers". He comments that his inventory shows higher relationships with academic achievement than some other scales of learning processes. In Chapter 4, we used students' self-ratings of their academic progress (which would be based on essay grades and test marks) as our criterion. In relating process to outcome it is essential to keep indices of process entirely separate from criterion measures of attainment, otherwise the circularity so produced interferes with the interpretation of how the various processes and styles relate to outcome. Only by a combination of conceptual and factor analysis in scale development can such circularity be avoided.

ALTERING STUDENTS' APPROACHES TO LEARNING*

Säljö (1975) reported an experiment in which detailed factual questions about an article appeared to shift students towards a surface approach to subsequent articles. He also showed that questions about overall meaning moved some students towards a deep passive (technified) approach, without making an impact on the level of understanding reached. In our questionnaire variant of Marton's original experiment we had shown how the content and level of difficulty of an article affected the clarity with which

---

*The research reported in this section was carried out by Sarah Morison.

relationships between process and outcome could be demonstrated. Finally Fransson (1977) had shown how interest or perceived relevance affected the approach to reading an article.

These findings suggested that we should extend the use of the questionnaire variant of Marton's method of research by asking the student volunteers who had taken the psychological tests to carry out a learning experiment in which both content and question-type were varied. The materials and instructions were sent to the 48 students (out of 60) who agreed to continue their involvement with the programme beyond what had originally been negotiated.

Each student was sent three short articles, each of just under 2000 words. The first article was a shortened version of extracts from Hoyle's The Expanding Universe used successfully in the earlier study. The second was based on ideas presented by Geoffrey Ashe in his book Camelot and the Vision of Albion which described evidence linking the historical Arthur with an iron-age fort at South Cadbury. The final article was a summary of research on styles of learning and thinking, intended to have personal relevance to the students as it mentioned some of the tests they had taken during the previous year and provided the rationale for our research programme.

Students were assigned randomly to two conditions. One group was given entirely specific questions on ideas or facts presented in the article. The other group was given a general question asking them to explain 'to a friend' what the article was about. Both groups were asked after each article to suggest implications stemming from what they had read, and after the final article both types of question were given to all the students.

Both groups were also asked to comment on their approaches to reading and how the questions asked had influenced their strategies in tackling the second and third articles. They were also given a set of self-ratings about each article to indicate to what extent, on a five-point scale, they were familiar with the ideas, found the article interesting or difficult, were able to concentrate, felt tired, found illustrations useful, and could remember the main theme and the details. The instructions to the students asked them to read each article on a separate day. The instructions were as follows.

"Read this article carefully in your own time in the same way as you would if you were preparing for an examination. Take notes if you would do so normally, but you will not be allowed to use them afterwards. When you have finished reading the article put it back into the envelope together with your notes and reseal it. Take a break of 20 minutes, then open (the next) envelope and answer the questions in it, putting the questionnaire back in the envelope afterwards."

The general question was coded as before with dichotomous codes (1,0) on five indices of outcome describing whether or not the student had
(a)   reinterpreted, reorganized or integrated material
(b)   mentioned an above average number of main points
(c)   understood the author's message
(d)   used evidence appropriately
(e)   used irrelevant facts

An overall indication of a deep outcome was obtained by calculating (a) + (b) + (c) + (d) - (e) on a scale of -1 to 4 (although no one obtained a score of -1).

The answers to the specific questions were scored right or wrong in two groups - essential points and incidental facts, while the 'implications' question was coded on a four-point scale.

Approaches to reading the first article were coded as before with three indices of deep, but in this case with four criteria of a surface approach. Criteria of a deep approach were
*   a clear intention to try to understand
*   an intention to integrate separate parts
*   an intention to reach own conclusion or to use personal experience

A surface approach was indicated by
*   being influenced by the anticipated form of the questions to concentrate on either (a) the general themes, or (b) the details
*   skimming through the article with likely questions in mind relying on memorization

The questions about changes in approach when reading the second and third articles were coded in ways which distinguished various reasons for an altered strategy - in particular the types of questions experienced, the different nature of the article, greater or less interest or familiarity.

In this exploratory study only simple analyses could really be justified. Four main questions were considered. Was there evidence that the four groups of students, as originally classified by the inventory of approaches to studying, were categorized in different ways in this experiment? Did students show consistency in the outcomes reached for all three articles? To what extent did the student appear to be influenced by the experimental treatment? How did students describe their reactions to the different articles?

APPROACHES AND OUTCOMES OF CONTRASTING GROUPS OF STUDENTS

Table 6.4 summarizes the outcomes and approaches of the four groups described in Chapter 5 - strategic, meaning, reproducing, and unmotivated - in terms of the percentage of occasions on which they had been coded into each of the categories. The differences are distinct and to a large extent make good sense.

In terms of outcome, the meaning-oriented group have the highest percentage of responses classified as showing reorganization or personal reinterpretation of the material and the lowest percentage of irrelevant detail. The reproducing group contains four times as many instances of irrelevant detail but is also coded as having an 'above average' number of main points almost twice as frequently. These two groups also differ markedly in the proportions of students who provide a 'good answer' to the implications question.

In terms of approach, the individual indices differ in their discrimination between these groups. The meaning orientated group have far and away the highest percentage of students classified has having a 'clear intention to understand' and 'an intention to reach their own conclusion or to use personal experience'. While the reproducing group do have the highest percentage of each of the three indices of a surface approach, the main difference is in the tendency to try to extract specific facts by skimming. Although the strategic group also uses this tactic, these students apparently do so without relying to the same extent on memorization. The strategic group showed a very high success rate in understanding the author's message, combined with very little use of irrelevant detail. Most correct answers to specific questions were given by the meaning and the strategic groups, while the fewest came from the reproducing group. The unmotivated group did reasonably well on the general question, but were remarkably unsuccessful in recalling incidental facts.

Table 6.4   PERCENTAGE OF STUDENTS IN EACH CATEGORY OF OUTCOME AND APPROACH

Groups	(N)	Outcome — General: Interpret Points	Outcome — General: Understood Evidence	Outcome — General: Detail	Outcome — Implications: Good Answer	Outcome — Specific: Incidental/Essential	Approach — Deep: Understand	Approach — Deep: Personal Integrate	Approach — Surface: Skimming Questions	Approach — Surface: Memorize
Strategic	(12)	54 / 39	88 / 46	17	49	63 / 89	33 / 25	25	75 / 75	25
Meaning	(8)	57 / 37	60 / 47	13	53	63 / 91	88 / 25	88	13 / 75	38
Reproducing	(9)	48 / 68	58 / 53	55	39	60 / 83	44 / 33	17	78 / 78	44
Unmotivated	(19)	50 / 42	84 / 50	34	50	45 / 91	58 / 16	42	58 / 68	37

(Note: the percentages are taken across all three articles read)

EVIDENCE OF CONSISTENCY OF OUTCOME AND APPROACH

Looking at the codings of the responses to the
general question, it was possible to discover on
how many occasions students were put into the same
category for all three articles, thus providing
evidence about consistency of outcome. This
analysis could, of course, only be carried out for
the 24 students who were given the general question
each time. There were five codings made for each
student and thus there were 120 occasions when three
identical codings could be made. By chance a run
of three identical dichotomous codings would be
found on only 15 occasions. In reality three
identical codings were observed on 49 occasions and
4 other times the difference was only a single
'undecided' code. There is here considerable evidence of consistency in the outcomes of reading
articles, even under conditions deliberately arranged
to encourage change. Nevertheless, it is possible
to point to the fact that different outcomes are
found more frequently (56%) than consistent ones,
and evidence of deliberate changes in approaches can
be found in the students' open-ended responses.
Evidence of consistency was already implicit in
Table 6.4 where there was a good deal of agreement
between the assignment to groups on the basis of
inventory scores and the codings made of the approach
and outcome in the learning experiment. The agreement is all the more striking when it is recognized
that the inventory was given a full twelve months
before the experiment was carried out.

CORRELATIONAL ANALYSES TO IDENTIFY CONSISTENCY

Table 6.5 presents the correlation coefficients
between the codings made of outcome. The stability
of the values presented is low due to the small
sample (N=23 for each group; one student had incomplete data). It is clear that there are some marked
differences between articles. The historical
article showed lower and less consistent relationships with the other two articles, while the correlations between 'The Expanding Universe' and 'Study
Styles' were quite high and, with one exception
(implications), consistent. It seems that the
implications question proved unsatisfactory as
students interpreted it in different ways in
relation to the different types of article.
Table 6.6 shows the extent of consistency between the various measures of outcome derived from

Table 6.5   CORRELATIONS BETWEEN THE SAME CATEGORIES OF
OUTCOME FOR DIFFERENT ARTICLES

Categories	Expanding Universe		Arthur's Camelot
	Arthur's Camelot	Learning Styles	Learning Styles
General Question			
Personal Reinterpretation	11	20	-10
Main Points	04	65	39
Understood	-16	26	-08
Used Evidence	13	40	08
Irrelevant Detail	23	24	57
Specific Questions			
Essential Points	-09	31	-13
Incidental Facts	21	37	38
Implications	-20	-30	-26

(decimal points omitted)

the 'Learning Styles' article, for which a total set
of variables is available for all 46 students with
complete data.   Given the uncertain nature of
impression marking, correlations between different
indices of deep outcome would not be expected to
rise much above, say, 0.25 or 0.30.   In the complete
set of correlations some negative correlations might
be expected (for example between indices of a deep
outcome and both irrelevant detail and incidental
facts).   In practice rather more negative correlations emerged than anticipated.
The highest positive correlations came between
three of the deep outcome categories (main points,
understood and used evidence), as was hoped, but it
was not expected to find such high correlations between these categories and 'irrelevant detail' and
'incidental facts'.   These latter correlations imply
that a majority of the students were relying on
operation learning in seeking understanding, and this
is confirmed by the negative correlations between
'personal reinterpretation' and all of the other
categories with the exception of 'understood'.   This
pattern of correlations is in line with the two

factors within deep approach and outcome reported
in the earlier study (Table 6.3). It was thus
decided to run an exploratory factor analysis on the
'Study Styles' article with the complete set of
variables (including self-ratings and approaches),
although the sample size (N=48) hardly warrants the
use of this technique.

Table 6.6 INTERCORRELATIONS BETWEEN CATEGORIES OF OUTCOME
FOR 'LEARNING STYLES' ARTICLE

Categories	MP	U	UE	ID	EP	IF	IMP
Personal Reinter-pretation	-39	08	-14	-20	-23	-06	-21
Main Points	*	40	39	63	05	43	20
Understood		*	37	26	34	38	26
Used Evidence			*	31	05	49	19
Irrelevant Detail				*	-09	46	-06
Essential Points					*	-15	-07
Incidental Facts						*	-28
Implications							*

(decimal points omitted)

Table 6.7 shows the five-factor solution. The
first two factors show the distinction within deep
outcome already seen in the pattern of correlations.
Factor I is the clearest deep outcome factor and this
is also linked to self-ratings of 'finding the
article interesting' and 'easy to concentrate', together with an intention to reinterpret. According
to the codings of outcome, however, this intention
has not been fulfilled. Factor II shows a high
positive loading on the remaining main category of
outcome, 'personal reinterpretation', but it is
negatively related to 'main points' and to the
intention to 'concentrate on understanding'. The
'personal reinterpretation' coded here thus seems to
imply at most a 'deep passive' approach, perhaps
verging on casual globetrotting (note the use of
illustrations). Factors III and IV are the two
main 'approach' factors with what appears to be a
clear stylistic difference between them. Factor III,
with its highest loadings indicating the use of personal experience, as opposed to skimming for likely

Table 6.7   FACTOR ANALYSIS OF OUTCOMES, SELF-RATINGS AND
             APPROACHES ON 'LEARNING STYLES' ARTICLE (N=48)

Categories	Factors				
	I	II	III	IV	V
General Question					
Personal Reinterpretation		59			
Main Points	58	−55			
Understood	45				
Used Evidence	59				
Irrelevant Detail	43				
Specific Questions					
Essential Points	34			41	
Incidental Facts	70				
Implications			42		
Self-Ratings					
Interesting	59		(29)		
Familiar				−30	44
Easy to Understand					43
Easy to Concentrate	43		35		37
Not Tired		36			44
Illustrations Useful		51			
Remembered Theme					91
Remembered Details	47				57
Approach					
Concentrating on Understanding		−54			
Intending to Reinterpret	39		(26)	−35	
Using Personal Experience			62		
Looking for Theme				−59	
Looking for Details				75	
Skimming		44	−73		
Memorizing			−45	32	

Decimal points and most loadings below .30 ommitted

questions or relying on memorization, can be described as deep holism. Factor IV implies a surface
approach relying on looking for details rather than
for the theme, but the positive loading on 'essential
points' reminds us of the efficacy of operation
learning for some students.

EFFECTS OF THE EXPERIMENTAL CONDITIONS

The main differences between this experiment
and the previous one were the use of different types
of question and of contrasting articles. Table 6.8
presents a summary of the categorizations of
students under the two experimental conditions
(general question about meaning and specific questions about detail) by article.

The initial impact of the first general question
on the meaning group seems, at first sight, to have
been as intended - with a rise in the percentage
reaching a deep outcome and a drop in 'irrelevant
detail' in relation to 'Arthur's Camelot'. But
this pattern is reversed with the 'Learning Styles,'
article and the meaning group has an outcome almost
identical to the detail group. If there has been
any general effect at all of the experimental conditions, it seems to have been to push students under
the detail condition towards remembering incidental
facts, yet being better able to discuss the implications. However the large differences between
articles (with the historical article again being
most different) suggest that the effects of experiencing different types of question has been slight.

In order to explore this negative finding more
fully we need to look at the comments made by students
about their approaches. After answering the 'Expanding Universe' article, there were marked differences in some of the problems reported by students
under the different experimental conditions. By
chance, as an initial strategy, far more of the
detail group had concentrated on remembering the
theme than the meaning group (42% compared with 17%).
The general question created fewer problems than the
specific questions (46% had 'no problem' compared
with 21%). Half the detail group reported difficulty in remembering details because they had concentrated on the theme.

The meaning group, with only one exception,
maintained their initial approach after experiencing
the first general question, while 46% of the detail
group changed or attempted to change. This greater
emphasis on detail seems to have helped this group

Table 6.8 PERCENTAGE OF STUDENTS CATEGORIZED AS ANSWERING CORRECTLY OR IN DEPTH BY EXPERIMENTAL CONDITION AND ARTICLE

Category	Article/Condition					
	Expanding Universe		Arthur's Camelot		Learning Styles	
	Meaning (N=24)	Detail (N=24)	Meaning (N=24)	Detail (N=24)	Meaning (N=24)	Detail (N=24)
Deep Outcome to General Question (sum of four categories)	61		74		58	56
Irrelevant Detail	42		21		29	25
Essential Points		90		64	88	83
Incidental Facts		51		86	45	56
'Good Answer' on Implications	42	25	33	29	29	38

in answering questions on the final article.   71%
(cf. 38%) experienced no problems, while the meaning
group reported difficulties in remembering details
because they had concentrated on the theme (46% cf.
8%).
     The failure of the initial analysis to detect
evidence of change can now be attributed to the fact
that a majority of all these students seem more
ready to concentrate on the theme rather than on the
details.   But it also seems that the detail group
managed to concentrate on remembering specific facts
without sacrificing their overall grasp of the meaning.   This can be seen in several of the comments
made by students which describe how they had read
the article through as a whole first, and then gone
through concentrating on remembering details which
they thought might come up in the questions.   It
should not be surprising, perhaps, to find students
after two years in higher education adapting readily
to specific demands without sacrificing understanding.   However, the general impression left from
reading the answers was that few of the students had
gone beyond a deep passive approach to these articles ·
but again comments suggested that this in itself
might have been a tactic based on an evaluation of
the amount of effort that they were prepared to put
into the experiment, or that these particular
articles merited.
     Although no systematic qualitative analysis was
possible, given the rather brief comments made by
most students, illustrative descriptions of
approaches are worth recording.   In particular
these show something of the 'thematized' interpretation of learning developed in higher education, and
of the ways in which students recognize that their
approaches are affected by assessmentdemands, subject
content, and level of interest.

> "I began to read the article and knowing I was
> to be questioned afterwards, I was immediately
> aware of examples and figures.   I noted these
> before reading on, but found that distracting.
> So stopped taking notes and read through the
> article twice.   Then I took notes again, but
> only when I understood the concept.   Then
> wondered if questions would want facts or ex-
> planation - too many numbers to keep in my head,
> (found the simpler illustrations eg. grape-
> fruits, bees, much easier to remember than
> millions and billions) so I memorized a couple
> of important numbers and reread the theories.

"The latter were so clearly explained that I had
no difficulty understanding them and being able
to explain them to myself verbally.   I did not
attempt to memorize them or concentrate hard on
them.   They were straightforward, despite my
being completely ignorant of the subject.
Made sketchy notes on the theories but did not
re-read them having written them down.   Most
of the numbers had jumbled themselves up by
this time - glanced at the notes on the numbers
then put them in the envelope, thinking further
reading would confuse me."
*(Expanding Universe, student high on deep approach based
on inventory scores, detail condition)*

"I expected a few factual questions (eg. distance ones), therefore made notes of those.
Made a note of the content of the main theory -
expansion (bound to ask something on it).
However you wanted a recall of the article so
when I did this I also remembered things not
in the article but ones which jogged my memory
(eg. parsecs = light years) which made me
remember other related figures.   My general
plan was to note the important ideas, figures,
metaphors from each section.

I generally read articles in this way.   I try
to obtain a précis of the original.   If articles
are just a string of paragraphs without headings,
I find I try to include too much of the original.
If it is sub-headed, I just note the heading and
a few key words.   This works well if I'm
interested in the article and my concentration
is sharp.   Otherwise I stick to a lengthy
précis approach so that I have a good copy for
revision purposes.

The problem I would expect is that I'm bound by
facts.   Revision would be based on my strength
of memory.   Fortunately it works well, but I
have to work hard before exams, tests, etc.
It's a swot approach largely.   I would like to
be able to just write a page of notes (3-4 paras.)
and 'believe' I have everything there.   I
suppose this reflects a lack of understanding
in some way.   Nonetheless, my approach works
for me but from my reading and study habits it
is not particularly recommended.   I think I
need a better plan to get the most out of articles.
*(Expanding Universe, student high on surface approach,
meaning condition).*

"I concentrated more on the details since the
article did not seem to be introducing new concepts in the way the first one was.   They
were more logical and easier to grasp (for
instance I find it easier to understand how to
date a piece of pottery than to understand how
a star is formed).   In this article the details
did seem more important, dates and names were
far more vital to the theme, since the essence
of this article was the use of these details to
solve a problem.   In the first article details
tended to be simply to help you understand
something better, such as how great a distance
actually was, the details could be disregarded
and you'd still have your own representation of
how great that distance was.   But in this
article if you disregard the detail (eg. the
presence of Tintagel pottery) you lose a vital
clue to the date and consequently you lose a
part of the central theme."
(*Arthur's Camelot, student low on both deep and surface,
detail condition*).

"Generally I go through slowly, often reading
a paragraph over more than once if necessary,
take notes on details, and prompts to (indicate)
lines of thought.   I basically try to understand the passage and get the idea 'mechanism'
behind (it).   If I can get that and learn the
factual details, I can usually reconstruct the
content.

As a scientist I generally expect questions
requiring detail and so I tend to take note of
such things and just try to get the 'feel' of
the background.   It is what I want out of an
article (rather than its type) which dictates
how I read it.

(This article was) psychology, which having
done in Part I, I usually avoid like the plague!
It was necessary to force myself to concentrate
on it, and as you can see from the answers, I
haven't done so well (and know it!)   I find it
difficult to find a way to tackle this kind of
article.   If I'm not interested in a subject
it is rather doomed.

(I had a feeling that the style of questions
might change!   I don't think anything could

alter the way I read the article!)."
(Learning Styles, student high on both deep and sur-
face, meaning condition)

"I think I concentrated more on this one because the material wasn't as familiar as the
first one. If I get into it, it doesn't .
really matter as far as questions are concerned
(whether they are detailed or not). The combined effort of memory, concentration, and
thinking enable me to answer your rather simple
task."
(Arthur's Camelot, student high on surface, meaning
condition).

"I thought I'd have to explain in more detail
about the theories ... and I'm sure this influenced the way I picked up information. I
skimmed over what I thought was irrelevant and
wouldn't be asked questions on ... if I (was
reading) for an essay I would read it with the
title of the essay in mind, only picking úp
related points. Therefore what influences my
approaches depends on my reason for reading the
article."
(Expanding Universe)

"I tried to pick up the names, because there were
so many I felt sure they'd be questioned, but I
couldn't remember them very well. Couldn't
keep my interest or concentration ... as I wasn't
all that stimulated by the article. (The main
problem was) that through trying to remember, it
seemed to help me forget. I was correct about
the type of questions being asked, but felt
unsure of my answers."
(Arthur's Camelot).

"(This time) I concentrated very hard and kept
going over paragraphs trying to work it out in
relation to what I knew and to the experiments
you had given us - to try and find out which
cognitive style I had. Why? It was very
interesting and I feel I took it in better than
the others. I don't think I will forget the
main ideas, whereas I had already almost forgotten the other two. I could see its relevance to my own situation."
(Learning Styles, student low on both deep and surface,
detail condition: above three examples)

These quotations indicate some of the ways in which the context and content of learning influence students' approaches to studying. These comments came from a somewhat narrow experimental situation. The next three chapters report the attempts to look at studying in its broad natural context and to discover what aspects of departmental organization are most likely to affect students' approaches to studying.

Chapter 7

IDENTIFYING STUDENTS' PERCEPTIONS OF DEPARTMENTS

INTRODUCTION: THE STUDY OF DEPARTMENTS AS LEARNING
CONTEXTS

There are good reasons why a research programme
dealing with British students' approaches to learning should want to examine the academic departments*
in which they study.   On theoretical grounds, it
has been argued that curriculum (what is to be
taught and learnt), pedagogy (how what is to be
learnt is transmitted) and assessment (what counts
as valid realization of knowledge on the part of the
learner) are those components of the academic environment which are most intimately related to learning
(Bernstein, 1971).   British university and polytechnic departments possess a high degree of autonomy
in the organisation of courses, teaching and assessment.   Moreover, European universities - unlike
American ones - are relatively homogeneous
institutions in which most students have little contact with more than one or two academic departments.
Although many American studies have compared
institutional environments in higher education (see,
e.g., Pace, 1967;   Stern, 1970;   Peterson, 1965;
Long, 1978), the relevant focus of analysis in
Britain is probably the main discipline students
study or the one department in which they spend most
of their time, rather than the university as a whole.
On a conceptual level, a number of distinctions
between departmental contexts might be drawn.   A
department could be characterized in terms of its
relative commitment to teaching, to research and

---

* 'Department' is used here in the sense of 'smallest
basic academic unit'; it includes units called
faculties, schools, course teams, etc. in some institutions.

scholarship, or to technology (translation of theoretical ideas into practice) (Becher and Kogan, 1980). The structure of knowledge in the main discipline the department is concerned with is another possible analytic category - to what extent is the knowledge studied relativistic and contextual, or absolute, cumulative, and sequential? (see e.g., Hajnal, 1972; Schwab, 1964). Other distinctions which have been suggested include the cohesiveness of curriculum content (Becher and Kogan, 1980), the degree of control over what may and what may not be learnt and taught, and the strength of boundary maintenance between areas of knowledge in the department (Bernstein, 1971). The perceived 'quality' of a department (either in terms of its reputation as a research unit or in terms of its students' evaluations) is another possible basis for categorization. Each of these distinctions might be thought to have correlates in the teaching, assessment, and course structure of a department - the formality or informality of teaching methods, the specialization or interdisciplinarity of the courses, the openness of students' choices over content, the use of final examinations or continuous assessment, and so on.

No empirical investigation, however, has examined all or even a majority of these possible conceptual distinctions. Indeed, there are remarkably few research studies of academic departments as such. Two groups of related investigations throw some light on departmental differences. The first set of studies has looked at the cultures of academic disciplines in terms of theoretical differences between areas of knowledge and staff and student attitudes. The most pervasive difference identified in the modern literature is that between arts and social science departments, on the one hand, and science departments on the other: a version of the familiar 'two cultures' of C.P. Snow. In fields of study variously labelled paradigmatic, formal, or codified - including the sciences - lecturers are more formal in their teaching methods and less "permissive" in their attitudes to students and student learning than arts teachers: they are more likely, for example, to see assessment as a way of motivating and classifying students than as a way of providing them with feedback. (Roe, 1956; Gamson, 1966; Thompson et al, 1969; Wilson et al, 1975). Corresponding differences have been observed in the students attracted to arts and science departments, differing student orientations and personality variables being systematically related to field of study. Arts and social science departments appear to attract more nonconformist, radical, 'person-orientated', neurotic, flexible, individualistic, and divergent students; science departments are populated more heavily with stable, 'thing-orientated' convergent students; practical and applied fields not surprisingly contain more students who are vocationally-orientated.

The second group of studies has not been directly concerned with learning contexts. These investigations have, however, identified what seems likely to be another dimension of departmental contexts: students' evaluations of teaching. The studies reveal many similarities in the components students use to assess the perceived quality of teaching. Kulik and McKeachie (1975) reviewed eleven factor analytic studies of ratings of lecturers and identified considerable overlap in the factors discovered. The lecturer's skills as a teacher, his rapport with students, the amount of structure in the courses, and the amount of work students were expected to tackle, were common components. Other investigations (e.g. Payne and Hobbs, 1974: Entwistle and Percy, 1971: Brennan and Percy, 1977: Amir and Krausz, 1974) have noted the importance to students' evaluations of lecturers' concern for student learning, the amount of choice available over method and content of learning, social relationships between students, interpersonal relationships between staff and students, and clearness of grading procedures. Taken together these investigations suggest that teaching and courses are evaluated by students in different countries and disciplines in broadly similar ways, and indicate that it may be possible to characterize departments in terms of students' evaluations of the quality of the learning environment they provide.

Studies of academic departments themselves have been few and far between. An early study which suggested that the intellectual climate or ethos of individual departments in the same field might vary was carried out at Birmingham University (Beard, Levy and Maddox, 1962). Two engineering departments were found to differ in the demands they made on their ablest students. Concomitant differences in student attainment and attitudes to the subject were discovered.

Gaff et al (1976) conducted a promising study of students in four departments at a Dutch university. The authors used a questionnaire survey to examine

113

'atmosphere' in the departments, and concluded that:

> "Although there are some similarities among the
> four departments, it is apparent ... that they
> constitute markedly different learning environ-
> ments. The pressure-packed, heavily prescribed
> nature of chemistry; the relaxed somewhat un-
> certain climate in law; the memory-oriented,
> highly structured environment in medicine; and
> the free-wheeling, independent atmosphere of
> psychology - these distinctive 'atmospheres'
> of each educational environment are apparent
> from this initial analysis." (Gaff et al,1976).

A cluster analysis was then performed to identify groups of items which were answered in similar
ways. Ten scales were derived, ranging from the
amount of time students felt they must spend in
course-related activities, through the personal
attention given to students in the different departments, to the extent to which the course programmes
were prescribed by staff or defined by students.
The scales were used to identify educational 'problems'
in the departments, and the authors concluded that
steps needed to be taken to offer more attractive
learning environments if the departments were not to
suffer high rates of student attrition. Hermans (1979)
has since identified similar dimensions of departmental environments at another university in the
Netherlands.

RELATIONSHIPS BETWEEN DEPARTMENTAL OR COURSE CONTEXTS
AND STUDENT LEARNING

Gaff et al remark that the effectiveness of
learning in the departments they studied might be
related to the type of learning context provided.
How does the context of a department relate to
learning? One obvious parallel is between the
different styles of learning described by Pask (see
chapter 2, pp 22-28) and the differing demands of
arts and science departments. Simply put, comprehension learners are likely to be attracted to
departments in which knowledge is most amenable to
personal interpretation (which are mostly arts and
social science departments), while operation learners will probably gravitate towards departments in
which the knowledge is hierarchically structured and
related to accepted paradigms (i.e., science departments). Similarly, it is likely that science
departments reward and encourage operation learning,

arts and social science contexts comprehension learning. On the other hand, there may also be differences within subject areas: different departments of engineering, for example, may favour different styles of learning.

Another intriguing possible relationship is that between the characteristics of a department - its size, commitment to teaching, staff-student ratio, its assessment and teaching methods, and so on - and the quality and quantity of its students' learning. Perhaps surprisingly, research has not demonstrated any connection between objective measures of learning contexts in higher education and student learning. Dubin and Taveggia (1969) found no consistent significant differences between teaching methods in relation to student learning. Hartnett and Centra (1977) used criterion measures achievement tests to assess departmental 'effectiveness' in a study of American universities. They then attempted to find correlates of effectiveness. The analysis took into account various characteristics of the departments, including size, staff-student ratio, staff interest in teaching (self-rated) and salaries; students pre-entry levels of achievement were controlled. Although large differences in effectiveness were found between departments teaching the same disciplines, no factors consistently associated with effectiveness were discovered. The authors speculated that student perceptions may be more important in the explanation of effectiveness. Student perceptions of departmental quality do not, however, appear to be associated with other measures of departmental differences. Gaff et al (1976), for example, found that student-staff ratio and size were not connected with students' descriptions and evaluations of the departments in their study.

There is some evidence from the work on students' approaches to learning carried out in Sweden and elsewhere (see chapter 2) that levels of approach and outcome are related to the organisation of teaching, courses, and assessment. Fransson, for example, (Fransson, 1977) has shown that deep approaches are functionally related to interest in the learning material, and surface approaches to threatening assessment conditions, in one of the experiments at Gothenburg. Laurillard (1978) shows how students' approaches to learning tasks in their everyday studies are associated with their perceptions of the purposes of the task. It would seem worthwhile to explore the deduction from these findings that

academic departments, particularly as perceived by
their students, can encourage different levels of
approach. There is certainly no shortage of
historical and theoretical argument to support this
possibility. Writers as diverse as Newman (1852),
Pattison (1876), Veblen (1918), Whitehead (1932) and
Rogers (1969) have variously argued that rigid assessment systems, impersonal staff-student relationships
and lack of choice over method and content have
damaging effects on the quality of students' learning experiences, while commitment to teaching amongst
staff and freedom in learning facilitate student
understanding.

There is also empirical evidence to suggest that
assessment, teaching, and course structures in academic departments are critical variables in the
determination of student learning, and that student
perceptions are a useful way to measure these contextual characteristics. Becker et al (1968)
studied Kansas University students' perceptions of
their academic experiences. Using the sociological
device of "perspective" (consisting principally, in
this case, of the students' definition of the
situation: "the ideas describing the character of
situations in which action must be taken"), the
authors argue that students react mainly to the
environmental emphasis on grading.

Students learn the requirements of the social
situation which rewards a high grade-point-average
and turn themselves into the sort of persons the
academic context demands. Grades are described by
Becker as "the currency of the campus". High grades
in assessment tasks are seen to be the most important
goals by students, even though the members of staff
deny they are so crucial. Students come to perceive
a conflict between grades and learning and speak of
using strategies to get good grades at the expense
of understanding the material they are expected to
learn. The process of assessment comes to have the
unintended consequence of inhibiting rather than
facilitating learning.

Snyder (1971) pursued the perceived conflict
between manifest and latent functions of assessment
a stage further. He argued (as a result of a study
of students at M.I.T.) that the formal curriculum
of universities emphasises academic values: a
problem-orientated outlook, creativity, independence
of thought, originality (c.f. Entwistle and Percy,
1971). The hidden curriculum, on the other hand,
requires an answer-orientated outlook, rote learning,
and memorization. Research in this country has

116

uncovered the operation of hidden curricula.
Miller and Parlett (1974) noted the 'bureaucratic'
assessment systems in some of the university departments they studied, and found that the academic
environment defined by examinations in one department
led to the distinctive strategies of adaptation
already described (chapter 2 , pp 12-13). Even the
cue-seeking students were often uncomfortably aware
that the strategies they used - although productive
of good degrees - were detrimental to learning.
Other studies have explored relationships between
students' attitudes to learning, student achievement,
relationships with staff, and perceived quality of
teaching. Ramsden (1976) found that a perceived
lack of any direction or helpful guidance by lecturers
in an independent study course led to the development
of negative attitudes to learning. One student
commented:

> "I don't think that they have really put enough
> thought into creating learning situations. I
> think they thought 'It's a good idea, 'student-
> centred education: we"ll apply it to higher
> education'. But it's not a very stimulating
> environment. Staff seem to expect students
> to generate everything ... they seem to have
> thought that students would do things like
> coming to them and asking for series of lectures.
> As I see it, an improved version of the course
> would be if students fitted into projects
> generated by staff. They ought to take more
> initiatives themselves... On an ordinary course
> 80 per cent of the lectures may be pretty use-
> less, but at least they can be a source of
> stimulation".

When more guidance was provided in subsequent
years of the course, although no compromises were
made about the amount of choice given to students,
their attitudes to learning and to the department
improved.   Students in Miller and Parlett's study
(1974) spoke of the way in which a quite different
kind of context - impersonal, highly formalized, with
'bureaucratic' staff-student relationships - could
have similar effects in discouraging learning.
Pascarella and Terenzini (1977; 1978) studied the
association between student-teacher informal
relationships and educational outcomes.   Informal
relationships were defined as out-of-class, not
formally arranged contacts, for any purpose.   A
positive correlation between these relationships

and three dependent variables - academic performance, personal development, and intellectual development - was found. The first of these variables was a conventional assessment (students' performance in examinations and assignments as measured by the department); the others were students' self-ratings. Students who interacted more with teachers were also found to be less likely to withdraw before the end of their courses. The authors include in their discussion of these results, however, a caveat on the direction of causality in these relationships.

Recently, Fearn-Wannan (1979) has attempted to develop a path analysis model to explain Australian students' performance in chemistry. Students' perceptions of their lecturers' behaviour and satisfaction with the teaching were found to be small, but significant, mediating variables in the determination of performance. Research also exists which seems tentatively to support some of the assertions of writers like Newman and Rogers, to the effect that learning in higher education is facilitated when students are permitted greater freedom over methods and content of study, and that negative attitudes are developed when choice is perceived to be absent. Brennan and Percy (1977), reporting the analysis of data from a large-scale investigation of students in English universities and colleges, remark on the disjunction (noted also by Becker et al, 1968, and Snyder, 1971) between the avowed aims of lecturers to promote 'critical thinking' and the relatively few opportunities students said they were given to work in ways which would enable the aim to be realized. Moreover:

"It seems clear from our research that students in all fields of study believe that they would learn more, and enjoy learning more, if they had greater control over the pace of their learning, more chance to determine the subject matter of their courses and were less rigidly inhibited by traditional conceptions of disciplinary boundaries and what constitutes the proper study of a particular subject. Students very often made comments describing the 'most satisfying aspect' of their course as 'the work which I have been allowed to do myself' and were highly critical of a curriculum structure which imposed a logic and sequence of learning on them which they felt was less educational and less motivating than one suggested to them by their own developing intellectual interests". (Brennan and Percy, 1977).

Subsequently Percy and Ramsden (1980) investigated two independent study schemes in a polytechnic
and a university.   It was found that most of the
students who were interviewed in the study valued
very highly the opportunity to work independently,
that some students would have left university if they
had not been able to use the independent study programmes to pursue their own interests, and that the
standard of students' work produced in both schemes
was generally acceptable and in some cases outstanding.

IMPLICATIONS OF PREVIOUS WORK FOR THE PRESENT STUDY

Studies of academic departments as learning contexts are unusual and few of the possible discussions
suggested theoretically have been explored.   What
does seem to be clear from the work which has been
done on academic contexts in higher education is that
students' perceptions and evaluations are associated
with their approaches to studying, while systematic
differences exist in the environment provided by arts
and science departments.   Little has been done to
disentangle the effects of different subject areas
and perceived 'quality" of departments or courses on
students' approaches.   Limitations of time and resources in the programme meant that all the possible
distinctions between departments which have been
suggested could not be examined.   It was decided,
in view of the clear importance of these variables
in earlier investigations, to concentrate in particular on students' perceptions of disciplinary and
other differences in the departments in which they
studied.   However, exploratory work on defining
departmental environments was carried out in the
preliminary stages of the programme, and this is described below.

PRELIMINARY WORK

During the first year of the programme, a
number of interviews were held with staff and students
in two university departments.   One of the purposes
of these semi-structured interviews was to see whether
differences in departmental learning contexts could
be identified.   Ten social science staff, thirteen
social science students, three applied science staff,
and nine applied science students were interviewed.
The staff were asked about their aims as teachers,
the structure of their courses, how they thought
students tackled the learning tasks they were set,

their perceptions of differences between students and
the reasons for their success or failure, and the
kinds of contact they had with students.   The
students were asked, _inter alia_, about the characteristics of the courses, teaching and assessment in
their department.   Specific questions were put
about the content of lectures, seminars, and tutorials, and about the student's relationship with
members of staff.
     The staff interviews were complemented by a
study of course documents in the two departments.
These included recent examination and test papers,
syllabuses, and course handbooks outlining the second
year courses for students.   It was hoped that these
documents might provide a source from which an understanding of the context of the department might be
gained.
     The interviews revealed that students in both
departments used similar constructs to describe the
environments in which they were learning.   These
constructs were consistent with previous research
on students' perceptions of departmental environments
     (c. f. Gaff _et al_, 1976).   Particularly important
to students were the effects of their lecturers: the
extent to which they seemed to encourage learning,
lectured effectively, and offered help with study
problems.   Assessment methods and workload were also
important to students in both departments, although
they were seen rather differently;   the applied
scientists felt that a great deal of pressure was
needed in order to 'get through' the syllabus, while
the social scientists would have preferred a much
lighter workload.   Formality or informality of
teaching and learning (e.g. lectures versus discussion
methods) were also often mentioned by the students.
Although students could identify differences within
departments on all these criteria (e.g. between the
teaching abilities of different lecturers) they were
also able to speak meaningfully about the department
as a whole.   Moreover, students related their
approaches to studying to a number of characteristics
of the learning context.   On occasions the use of a
deep or a surface approach was attributed by the
students to the influence of the environment.   The
periodical tests used in the social science department, for example, seemed to encourage surface
approaches.   These relationships between perceptions
of the context and approaches are described in detail
in chapter 8.
     It was more difficult to discern any clear
patterns in the staff interviews.   There were wider

differences in the comments made by staff in the
same department than by students in the same department.   It was, however, apparent that many staff
had little knowledge of how students actually tackled
learning tasks.   The study of course documents
yielded information about the structure of the
courses which was useful briefing material to help
focus the student and staff interview questions.
But again it was not clear how the information could
be used to define differences in departmental contexts.   In view of the demonstrated effectiveness
of the student interviews, and the parallels between
the results they provided and previous work on
academic learning contexts, it was decided to concentrate attention on identifying the characteristics
of departmental environments by means of students'
perceptions.

DEVELOPMENT OF THE COURSE PERCEPTIONS QUESTIONNAIRE (CPQ) - 1

Similarities in the constructs used by students
in both departments in the preliminary interviews
suggested that a questionnaire might be an appropp-
riate instrument for identifying and comparing the
course perceptions of larger groups of students in
a number of departments.   The first task was to
collect together a number of items descriptive of
the context of learning through students' eyes.   The
items came from two principal sources: the preliminary student interviews and an earlier study of
students' perceptions of courses (Ramsden, 1976).
The 47 items thus derived were sorted into scales
reflecting hypothesized dimensions by which students
were expected to characterize their learning environments.   An attempt was made to choose scales which
would be capable of distinguishing between subject
areas or distinguishing between departments in other
ways (e.g. quality of the teaching).   The components
were as far as possible related to previous work in
associated fields.   The concept of frame strength
(Bernstein, 1971), which refers to the amount of
control over what may and may not be transmitted in
the pedagogical relationship, was incorporated into
one scale.   The recurrent notion of "rapport" in
teachers' understanding of students as a component
of effective teaching (see, e.g., Rogers, 1969,
Kulik and McKeachie, 1975; Gaff et al, 1976) was
included.   Most of the scales used in the most
closely corresponding study (Gaff et al, 1976) could
be incorporated, while two of the distinctions

121

between subject areas discovered in one of the American studies of lecturers' perceptions - existence of a paradigm and concern with application (Biglan, 1973) - also found a place. The items were provisionally grouped into the following eight scales:

Staff understanding: the degree to which students feel their teachers to provide an acceptant, understanding, and sincere environment for learning. Sample item: "Lecturers here frequently give the impression that they haven't anything to learn from students". (negatively scored)

Formal relationships: the extent of formality or informality in staff-student relationships. Sample item: "Lecturers in this department seem to go out of their way to be friendly towards students".

Relevance to work: how closely students feel the curriculum relates to vocational requirements. Sample item: "Much of the work I do here will be relevant to my future job".

Frame strength: items thought to relate most closely to the amount of discretion possessed by students in organizing their learning, selecting its content, and evaluating their progress. Sample item: "The courses in this department are highly organized".

Formal instruction: the extent to which the department emphasizes individual learning or attendance at lectures and classes. Sample item: "A great deal of my time is taken up by formal classes (lectures, practicals, tutorials, etc.)".

Workload and External pressure to work: the extent of pressure placed on students to conform to deadlines for submitted work, and the amount of material which students feel they are expected to cover in the syllabus. Sample item: "There seems to be too much work to get through in the courses here".

Homogeneity of the department: the degree to which students perceive themselves to be in a department in which the goals of their study are clear to them and shared by most other students. Sample item: "It can be hard to know how well you're doing compared to other students in this department". (negatively scored)

The first version of the CPQ was administered
to second year students in four university departments - psychology, engineering, history, and physics -
during 1977-78.   A slightly amended form was used in
two further departments (English and independent
studies) in 1978.

The results were examined by means of item
analysis: item-scale correlations and percentage
agreements to each item were calculated, and alpha
factor analysis (chosen because it is specifically
designed for use in scale development) was carried
out, using the SPSS programs.

All the significant item loadings in the first
factor were from the original 'staff understanding"
scale or the 'formal staff-student relationships'
scale.   This factor clearly represents students'
perceptions of the quality of teaching and staff-
student relationships in their department.   The
second factor appeared to identify a dimension
relating to the amount of work students are faced
with in their department: with one exception, all
the loadings were from the 'workload' or 'external
pressure to work' scales.   The third factor combined
items from the 'formal instruction', 'relevance to
work', and 'strong framing' scales, suggesting that
this dimension was one of clearly relevant curriculum
contents transmitted in a formal way.

The next factor was concerned with the social
climate or amount of interpersonal contact in a
department.   All the significant items were in the
'homogeneity' scale, but referred to aspects of
students' relationships connected with their work.
Factor V was similar to Factor IV, while the sixth
dimension identified clear goals and standards in a
department's teaching and courses (item 40, for
example, is "You usually have a clear idea of where
you're going and of what's expected of you in this
department").   Only two items reached significance
in the last two factors extracted.   The first, item
38, was "Students have a great deal of choice over
how they are going to learn in this department";
the second (in Factor VIII) was a relevance to work
item.

A second analysis was run after removing a
number of the weaker items and produced similar
results.   The CPQ scales were now revised to produce eight dimensions (Figure 7.1).   The 'staff
understanding' and 'formal staff-student relationships' scales were re-ordered to the two new scales
of commitment to teaching (dealing mainly with the
teaching climate of the department) and relationships

123

with students (referring chiefly to the quality of relationships between students and staff). It seemed useful to maintain a conceptual distinction between formal teaching methods and relevance to work; although these two aspects seemed to be empirically inseparable in the factor analyses, it might be that other samples would reveal a different picture. The former 'workload' and 'external pressure to work' scales were combined into one scale of workload. The earlier 'homogeneity' component was subdivided into two scales: social climate and clear goals and standards. The former strong framing items were mainly redistributed through the other scales, and another dimension of freedom in learning was added, corresponding to Gaff's 'room for student interests' and 'prescription in the program" scales (Gaff et al, 1976).

Figure 7.1   DIMENSIONS OF LEARNING ENVIRONMENTS DERIVED FROM FACTOR ANALYSIS OF THE FIRST VERSION OF THE CPQ

DIMENSIONS	MEANING
Relationships with students	Closeness of lecturer/student relationships; help and understanding shown to students.
Commitment to teaching	Commitment of staff to improving teaching and to teaching students at a level appropriate to their current understanding
Workload	Pressure placed on students in terms of demands of the syllabus and assessment tasks.
Formal teaching methods	Formality or informality of teaching and learning (e.g. lectures v individual study).
Vocational relevance	Perceived relevance of courses to students' careers.
Social climate	Frequency and quality of academic and social relationships between students.
Clear goals and standards	Extent to which standards expected of students are clear and unambiguous.
Freedom in learning	Amount of discretion possessed by students in choosing and organising academic work.

Identifying Students' Perceptions of Departments

Inspection of the CPQ results in terms of the eight dimensions in Figure 7.1 revealed that students saw the process of learning and teaching in quite different ways in the six departments (see Ramsden, 1979). The engineering department was thought to have very formal teaching methods, clear goals of study, high vocational relevance, and an extremely high workload, combined with close and cooperative relationships between students. Physics students also experienced a fairly formal curriculum, with little personal choice over method and content; the psychologists worked in an environment which was thought to be friendly and informal, but felt they had a heavy workload and only a very small amount of freedom over what and how they learnt. English and history students said that much individual study was required in their departments and that the courses had little relevance to their future employment; relationships with staff were rather formal in history, but informal and helpful in English. Independent studies was thought to have the best teaching, and not unexpectedly, the highest freedom in learning. Staff were said to be friendly and to make real efforts to understand difficulties students were having with their work, although the goals and stan dards expected of students were perceived to be un clear and students worked in a poor social climate.

DEVELOPMENT OF THE COURSE PERCEPTIONS QUESTIONNAIRE - 2

Further interviews of a sample of students who completed the CPQ in its original form showed that the eight main components of perceived learning environments appeared to be stable and replicable (Ramsden, 1981), although the relationships with students and commitment to teaching scales could not be clearly separated. A revised version of the questionnaire was next constructed, consisting of eight six-item scales. Items in the previous version which had not had significant loadings in the factor analysis, or which had low item-scale correlations, were deleted; other items were added to some scales (especially to the freedom in learning scale) in order to produce six-item scales in all cases.
This revised CPQ was administered to a sample of 767 students in nine departments at three universities during 1978. Item analyses largely confirmed the integrity of the revised scales, although the dis tinction between the relationships with students and commitment to teaching scales again failed to emerge

empirically. Alpha-factoring of the items, extracting eight factors, followed by oblique rotation, produced a clearly comprehensible structure: Factor I represented relationships with students plus commitment to teaching; Factor II, vocational relevance; Factor III, formal teaching; Factor IV, clear goals and standards; Factor V, workload; Factor VI, social climate; Factor VII, commitment to teaching and relationships with students; Factor VIII, freedom in learning (together with smaller loadings on several relationships with students items). In spite of large differences between individual items in terms of percentage agreements for the nine departments, item-scale correlations did not differ greatly between the departments, suggesting that the dimensions tapped by the scales were generally applicable.

Mean scale values for the departments, disciplines and subject areas were calculated. These confirmed the ability of the questionnaire to identify different departmental learning contexts. The scales of formal teaching methods, vocational relevance, and (to a lesser extent) clear goals and standards, social climate, and freedom in learning, distinguished between science and arts and social science departments. The other scales mainly seemed to differentiate between departments rather than disciplines. The scales were understandably related to each other. Freedom in learning, for example, was negatively related to formal teaching methods (freedom in learning and informal teaching are both more common in social science and arts), but was also positively associated with relationships with students (i.e. it is also an evaluative dimension).

The final research version of the CPQ was developed by re-ordering the items in the relationships with students and commitment to teaching scales into two new scales of good teaching and openness to students. The questionnaire as a whole was shortened to 40 items in eight scales by deleting the weakest item in each scale, and some of the items were re-written.

This questionnaire was administered to 2208 students in 66 departments at the same time as the approaches to studying inventory (see chapter 4; the relationships between these two sets of scales will be examined in chapter 9). It was expected - from the earlier work described above - that some of the dimensions of the CPQ would describe differences between subject areas and disciplines, while others would represent students' perceptions of differences between departments. The second group would be evaluations of the learning context in the departments.

On the whole the results confirmed these expectations. As will be seen from Table 7.1, formal teaching methods, vocational relevance, and clear goals and standards were found to be very much related to subject area; much more so, incidentally, than any of the approaches to studying subscales. The highest scores on all three of these CPQ scales were found in the engineering departments, and the lowest in the English or history departments. It was equally clear that the two evaluative scales, good teaching and openness to students, were not related to subject area. The wide ranges of departmental means within each discipline on these scales illustrate how different the departments were perceived to be by their students (see Ramsden and Entwistle, 1981, for details).

The remaining CPQ scales appear to describe differences between departments and between subject areas. For example, although the freedom in learning mean values were higher in arts and social sciences than in scientific subjects, the range of mean scores within each discipline was wide.

Factor analysis of the CPQ scale totals also revealed a familiar pattern (Table 7.2). Factor I is the evaluative dimension suggested in the interview study and the preliminary work, with its highest loadings on good teaching and openness to students. The next highest coefficient in this factor, for freedom in learning, invites the explanation that this scale is also a component of students' evaluations of departments. Social climate, clear goals and standards, and workload play lesser parts. Factor II represents differences between subject areas. The dimension is one which distinguishes between formal vocational teaching and loosely-structured informal teaching, the former being more common in science departments and the latter in arts departments. Departments with clear goals and standards, high vocational relevance, and formal teaching methods also tend to have good social climates. These results are consistent with those presented in Table 7.1.

The scales and items of the final version of the CPQ are given in Appendix A5 together with Cronbach α values which indicate a satisfactory level of internal consistency for each of the scales. An interpretation of the factor analysis of scale totals in conjunction with conceptual analysis based on the results of the

Table 7.1   STUDENTS' PERCEPTIONS OF LEARNING CONTEXTS IN
             DIFFERENT SUBJECT AREAS

Scale	Mean (1) Science (2) Social science (3) Arts	S.D.	Analysis of Variance F (df 2, 63)
Openness to students	(1) 9.04 (2) 9.31 (3) 8.36	1.47 1.82 2.14	1.42
Social climate	(1) 11.19 (2) 10.78 (3) 9.33	1.48 1.40 1.72	7.64*
Formal teaching methods	(1) 12.17 (2) 6.67 (3) 3.06	1.61 1.37 .77	232.86*
Clear goals and standards	(1) 11.83 (2) 9.62 (3) 7.35	.89 1.87 1.94	37.88**
Workload	(1) 11.19 (2) 8.86 (3) 10.58	2.26 2.71 2.33	5.95*
Vocational relevance	(1) 11.21 (2) 7.21 (3) 4.27	2.96 1.42	58.51**
Good teaching	(1) 11.63 (2) 11.74 (3) 11.63	1.02 1.48 1.65	.06
Freedom in learning	(1) 8.24 (2) 10.21 (3) 11.54	1.72 1.46 2.67	15.35**

* p < .01

** p < .001

Table 7.2   FACTOR ANALYSIS OF COURSE PERCEPTIONS SCALES
             (N = 2208)

Variables	Factors (56% variance explained)	
	I	II
Good teaching	76	
Freedom in learning	57	
Openness to students	76	
Social climate	42	32
Formal teaching methods		71
Clear goals and standards	30	57
Workload	(−24)	
Vocational relevance		72

Decimal points and most loadings less than .25 omitted

Factor I   Positive evaluation of teaching and courses

Factor II   Formal vocational teaching

interviews of 57 students in six departments (see
Chapter 8), suggested that the second-order evaluation
dimension − Factor I in Table 7.2 − might usefully be
subdivided into two components each containing two
scales.   Good teaching and freedom in learning were
combined into the scale of perceived student-centred-
ness (α = 0.75), while freedom in learning and workload (the latter scale negatively keyed) were joined
to form a scale of perceived control - centredness
(α = 0.75) in a department.   These measures of a
department's learning context were found to be
significantly associated with characteristic approaches
to learning;   the relationships will be discussed in
Chapter 9.

CONCLUSIONS

    The course perceptions questionnaire appears to
provide a useful means of describing certain important and consistent differences in the way students
perceive departments.   The relationships between
the present results and previous research into
academic environments in higher education seem to
make sense.   Dimensions of teaching quality, workload, and clarity of goals have been found to occur

consistently in factor analytic studies of student
ratings of teachers. The only other research directly
comparable to the investigations reported in this
chapter (Gaff et al, 1976) discovered similar
dimensions (and relationships between the dimensions)
to those of the CPQ, with a sample of Dutch students.
Studies of differences between the disciplinary 'ethos'
or 'culture' of different fields of study have also
produced findings compatible with those of the CPQ
(see, e.g., Smithers, 1969; Gaff and Wilson, 1971).
It is hoped that the questionnaire may prove to be a
valuable instruments for use by academic departments
as a means of obtaining information about students'
reactions to assessment and teaching methods.

The limitations of the CPQ are also apparent,
however. Firstly, the picture provided of the perceived learning context is incomplete, because the
questionnaire is unable to examine the detail of the
relationships between an individual student's
approach to a learning task and his perception of its
context. Nor can it allow for differences between
lecturers and courses in a department. Exploration
of these matters requires a different methodology,
and attention is turned towards them in the next
chapter.

Secondly, the examination of students' perceptions offers only one way (although a demonstrably
valid one) of describing departmental environments.
Within the compass of the present research programme
it was not possible to examine other potentially
important distinctions between departments except in
a very limited way. Lecturers' attitudes and
experience, curriculum structure, research and teaching orientation, and the type of institution in which
the department is situated, are among the differences
which might fruitfully be explored in future research.

Chapter Eight

STUDENTS' EXPERIENCES OF LEARNING

In the previous chapters we have dealt mainly
with research findings arising from methods
traditionally used to investigate student learning.
The approaches to studying inventory made use of
typical psychometric techniques; tests of ability
and personality were the focus of chapter 5;
chapter 6 reported experimental data on reading
academic articles.
     These approaches to understanding student learn-
ing have a common factor. They are all to some
extent removed from the immediate reality of being a
student in the natural setting of an academic
department. Even the development of the course
perceptions questionnaire inevitably tended to constrain students' experiences into a mould shaped by
the researcher. Although indications of the effects
of the context and content of learning were given in
the students' comments in chapter 6, these comments
themselves came from a rather narrow experimental
situation.
     It is important that our choice of research
methods does not undervalue the dynamic, tentative
character of student learning in favour of a static,
consistent view. Nor must we exclude potentially
critical variables in the real world of a student's
encounter with a learning task in order to achieve
experimental precision. The research methods used
by Marton and his colleagues (see chapter 2) offer
an experiential, phenomenal perspective on student
learning which can be seen as an alternative to the
experimental and correlational approaches. Typically, each student's unique experiences are examined
by qualitative analysis of interview data. A
potentially richer and more accurate picture of the
links between student learning and its context and
content is the chief return to an investment in this

approach. Of course, the qualitative approach is not without weaknesses of its own, perhaps the most important of which is the danger of bias from the subjective and impressionistic way this sort of data is sometimes handled. But careful controls can be used to minimize these difficulties.

This chapter describes the findings of a series of interviews designed to draw upon the strengths of this qualitative, experiential perspective. The interviews were used to examine students' approaches to academic tasks and their assessment strategies, and to provide a detailed picture of students' perceptions of the contexts of learning in which they worked. The results extend previous work at Lancaster, and the research of Marton (see, e.g., Marton and Säljö, 1976a, b) and Laurillard (1978; 1979) in several directions. The analyses which follow will show how categories of levels of approach, types of context, and individual differences in approach and strategic study methods were developed and subsequently used to identify differences between students and contexts. Relationships between the content and perceived context of the students' work and their approaches to academic tasks, and between approaches and degree results, will also be examined in detail.

METHODS

This is not the place to begin a discussion of the complicated issues surrounding the use of qualitative methods (see Marton and Svensson, 1979; Entwistle, 1981; Ramsden, 1981, for more extensive examinations of the relevant issues). It is, however, important to bear in mind that a qualitative perspective assumes that it is valid to consider categories of description - e.g. of different approaches to a learning task to which meaning is attributed through the learner's own perspective - as results in themselves, and not only as sources of categories to be later used in a quantitative way.

In the present study a total of 57 Lancaster University students was interviewed. Table 8.1 shows the composition of the sample, which was selected by examining students' scores on one or more subscales of the approaches to studying inventory; students with extreme scores were those chosen. The final degree results of the students, and in the case of the engineering students, the distribution of the chosen group's second year marks as well, suggested that the sample was at least broadly representative of different levels of ability.

Table 8.1   COMPOSITION OF THE INTERVIEW SAMPLE

Discipline	Year of Study	Dates Interviewed	N
Psychology	2	February—March 1977	13
Engineering	2	June 1977	9
Physics	2		10
History	2		11
English	2	January—June 1978	5
Independent Studies 2 & 3			9
TOTAL			57

The preliminary interviews used a broad range of questions, and experience with these interviews led to the development of a shorter schedule for students in the main part of the study.   This contained three groups of questions.   The focus of the first group was on reading and essay-writing (for arts and social science students) and on problem-solving and report writing (for science students).   Appropriately specific questions about relevant learning tasks (How did you go about it?   Why are you reading it? Were you looking out for anything in particular? Did you do it differently from another task of the same sort?   Why? - and so on) were asked.   The second set of questions concerned assessment strategies and the perceived outcome of the student's course.   Finally, several questions about the learning context of the student's main subject department (teaching, assessment, purpose of lectures, relationships with staff and other students) were asked.

All the interviews used a semi-structured approach;   the order and phrasing of the questions varied somewhat depending on the way in which the student answered them, and exactly the same questions were not asked of every student.   The semi-structured approach did not, however, mean that the interviews were uncontrolled.   It was always ensured that the same main points - see above - were raised.   Great care was taken not to be over-directive.   At the same time, the interviewer made a continual effort to be alert to comments made by the student which related to the hypotheses of the investigation, and which ought to be probed more fully.

The analysis of interviews of this kind presents perhaps a greater threat to the validity of the data than their conduct. At first, consideration was given to using methods such as network analysis and critical incident techniques, but the results obtained in a comparable study of students' approaches to learning (Bliss and Ogborn, 1977) seemed trite in comparison with the sophistication of the methods. More useful guidance was obtained from the methods of qualitative analysis used in the research carried out by Marton and his colleagues at Gothenburg. These techniques are designed to extract full value from the complexity of the interview data. Transcripts of the interviews are read and re-read until emergent qualities of students' experiences are consistently identified. The constructs are verified by several judges.

The present study adapted Marton's techniques to a different research situation. Practical constraints made it impossible to have all the interviews transcribed in full (a sine qua non of the Gothenburg approach). More importantly, it was felt important to avoid the dangers of a strictly inductivist approach by specifying certain guiding hypotheses derived from previous research, including the work of Marton. The categories of responses eventually used to classify the transcribed extracts were validated by means of inter-judge comparisons.

These constructs were used to direct the analysis:

1. Categories describing different levels of approach;
2. Evaluative and descriptive categories relating to the context of learning in different departments: in particular, categories relating to teaching, assessment, and course structures. The dimensions discovered in the factor analysis of the CPQ, those reported by Gaff et al (1976), and those reported in studies of lecturer evaluation (e.g. Kulik and McKeachie, 1975), were particularly considered;
3. Differences between individual students in "cue behaviour" (Miller and Parlett, 1974);
4. Differences between individual students in approaches to academic work (especially the holist-atomist dimension identified by Svensson (1977);

5. Relationships between approaches and contexts (e.g. Becker's "selective negligence" in response to assessment pressures), including associations between the conditions of the task and the type of approach used (c.f. Fransson, 1977).

Fuller details of all the techniques used in condicting and analysing the interviews can be found in Ramsden (1981).

PRELIMINARY ANALYSIS

A preliminary analysis was made by listening to each tape-recording several times and making full (or very lengthy) transcripts of a sample of interviews. With the help of Marton's judgement instructions for categorizing deep and surface level responses it eventually became clear that deep and surface categories of description could be applied to the responses of students in every department. Subcategories differing from those used by Marton were, however, needed to classify the responses satisfactorily. It was possible, in this analysis, to identify different strategic approaches related to assessment which distinguished among individual students. For example, a small number of students in all the departments took a highly strategic, assured approach to assessment tasks, while others adapted to the constraints of examinations and assignments in less positive ways. Relationships between students' perceptions of particular tasks and the approaches they used to them were also indicated in the analysis. Students who described favourable conditions for learning in relation to a subject or topic (e.g. helpful teaching) were likely to describe a deep-level approach to a task connected to it, while the reverse was true if the conditions were unfavourable (i.e. a surface level approach was described, often by the same student). An association between a student's level of interest in a task, or his background knowledge of the subject to which it referred, and level of approach, was also identified. Poor background knowledge (especially of concepts in science) or a low level of interest (particularly in arts and social science subjects) were associated with surface level approaches. These preliminary findings have been described in greater detail elsewhere (Ramsden, 1979).

CATEGORIES DESCRIBING DEEP AND SURFACE APPROACHES

The first task in the main analysis was to develop a model of deep and surface which described the approaches used by students in a wide variety of tasks in different disciplines and departments. The framework was established by means of comparing students' responses to the interview questions dealing with approaches to academic tasks with two other sets of judgement instructions: those of Marton (1975) and Laurillard (1979).

Marton used one set of judgement instructions to classify social science students' responses to interview questions about their reading of academic articles under experimental conditions, and a somewhat different set to classify responses to questions about their normal studies. Laurillard interviewed science students about their approaches to several tasks forming part of their normal studies. She did not require students to work under experimental conditions, nor did she ask them questions about their general approaches to studying. The present study was similar to Laurillard's in that students were interviewed about their approaches to tasks carried out in their normal work. But the tasks described by students were much more diverse; they included problem-solving, project work, essays, reading of books and articles, and examinations, in a number of different subject areas. It seemed advisable, moreover, to leave open the possibility of identifying consistent approaches to studying by the same student.

It was found necessary to modify the categories used by Marton and Laurillard in order to provide a model which adequately described the variability in the present data. An effort was made to develop a set of sub-categories which was both theoretically parsimonious and generally applicable to all the departments. The definitions appear in Figure 8.1. Four categories used by the previous researchers to define a deep approach are generalized to become D_2 and D_3. D_1, which has no equivalent in Laurillard's descriptions, was found to be essential to classify students' indications of a close personal relationship with the academic material with which they were dealing. It resembles one of the sub-categories used by Marton and his colleagues to classify a student's approach to his normal work. This sub-category, which describes a tendency on the part of the student to see knowledge as part of oneself, is an important component of Marton's conception of a

Figure 8.1   CATEGORIES OF DESCRIPTION FOR DEEP AND SURFACE
LEVELS OF APPROACH

D_1 Personal experience

Integrating the task with oneself.   Indicate desire
to relate the task or the subject to personal or real
life situations: to compare a task with personal
experience (outside the course);   to see a task as
part of oneself or one's personal development;   express a wish to use the knowledge forming part of the
task outside its immediate context in relation to
oneself.

D_2 Relationships

Integrating the parts into a whole.   Indicate desire
to relate parts of the task to each other or the task
DEEP   to other relevant knowledge;   indicate active attempts
to think about the relationships between different
parts of the material (e.g. relate evidence to conclusion);   try to relate material from different
sources;   try to see connections between previously
studied materials and currently studied materials.

D_3 Meaning

Integrating the whole with its purpose.   Indicate
intention to impose meaning: think about the underlying structure, or the intention of the whole task;
try to 'stand back' from the task and see it in a
wider perspective;   impose a pattern on the whole task.

S_1 Unrelatedness

Defining the task as separate or its parts as discrete.   Indicate intention or tendency to treat the
task as an isolated phenomenon: confront the
material as separate from other ideas and materials,
or from the general purpose of the task to which it
relates;   focus on the elements of the task rather
than the whole.

SURFACE S_2 Memorisation

Defining the task as a memory task.   Indicate
intention to memorize the material.

S_3 Unreflectiveness

Defining the task in an external way.   Indicate unreflective or passive approach to a task: indicate
intention not to extract meaning from the material;
see the subject-matter as external to oneself.

deep-level approach (see, e.g., Marton, 1976). The
three surface sub-categories in Figure 5.1 closely
resemble Laurillard's modifications of Marton's categories, although S_1 and S_3 are here more generally
defined.

Figure 8.1 also shows the instructions used to
classify students' responses. But the meaning of
each of the categories is properly shown through the
use of repeated instances from the student interviews.
Given below are extracts from the interviews which
exemplify the use of the sub-categories in relation
to different tasks.

D_1 Personal experience

I think I tend quite a lot to relate (this reading) to my
own experiences as well. Try and think of instances where
these experiments would be proved right. So it takes a bit
of time reading, yeah. I think if they're talking about
things like field independence I try to think about whether
people I know are field dependent or independent. (Reading
academic articles; psychology, student 6).

I got into the poem and could feel what it means. I
became part of it... I found it interesting because it had a
deep theological meaning, and I'm interested in that subject.
(Reading poetry; English, student 23).

I suppose I'm trying to imagine what the experiment is
talking about, I think, in a physical sense. Sort of get a
picture of what it's about... This one says an ultra-violet
lamp emits one watt of power; it says calculate the energy
falling on a square centimetre per second. I'm just thinking
of the light and the way it spreads out, so therefore I know
it's the inverse square law ... (Laboratory work; physics,
student 8).

To start from scratch, to basically put together information and use it... and actually build it and test it and see
that the thing, there is a fair degree of correlation between
your test results and what you actually expected the thing to
produce, I think is good... You select certain formulae to use,
and by using them... and seeing that they produce the results
you hoped they would, then, you know, you prove to yourself that
those formulae could be used. (Project work; engineering,
student 2).

D_2 Relationships

You read it, a section on precipitation hardening... and
I think well, fair enough, the material is about as strong as
mild steel or something, and I'll remember that if I can, but
I'm not going to remember that it's 297 Newtons per square mm.
if it's in such and such a state ... There are one or two

D_2 Relationships (continued)

things that do stick in your mind like the strength of mild
steel, and so on, because we've used it in the projects, so
you have a sort of relative scale whereby you can say it's
nearly as strong as mild steel ... (Reading textbooks;
engineering, student 6).

You know a method of approach, so you find usually the
thing simplifies itself greatly after you've removed a few of
the non-essentials and put it into a logical form which
relates to something you've done previously.   (Problem-
solving; physics, student 12).

I'm trying to relate it to the course as a whole.   It's
not just writing down a load of notes and thinking 'that's it
for my essay' ... You try to sort of keep a logical progression
in history, so you've some idea of the themes ... (Reading
texts; history, student 1).

You read it, you see what it's about, and usually it's
got, often it has some bearing on something else you've read
before.   It may confirm that or just add another side to it,
or be completely different.   (Reading academic articles;
psychology, student 2).

D_3 Meaning

The ideas are started by the actual question.   You realize
that it presupposes a few points that you must get into the
essay ... I list the ideas that have got to go into the essay,
because the essay, you know, entails these things.   (Essay-
writing; English, student 6).

If I feel that the article is going to be very relevant
to what I'm doing - and you can often glean that from the title
- then I'll tend to go through it fairly slowly.   Rather than
skim through it I'll read through it in a full way.   I suppose
I've got these various problem areas which I'll be looking into,
and I'll be looking, I'll be reading the article with these in
mind.   (Reading academic articles; independent studies,
student 6).

I was looking for a pattern which I could relate to the
script.   I was drawing graphs ... I knew from the script what
was supposed to be happening ... and I was looking out for it
to happen on the graph ... fortunately it did.   (Laboratory
work; physics, student 6).

You have to go through quite a few different designs to
get to the right one ... I'm sort of always thinking about
what I can put in the conclusion when I'm writing the project...

D_3 Meaning (continued)

I'll try and show what I have achieved, well, understand, from the project. (Project report writing; engineering, student 3).

It was a good chapter because it organised the readings that were to follow ... which led me off to further articles, and at the end of it, making notes on the things I was reading, I had a great wad of it, which by that time, I had an idea of how my initial conception of the problem could be used to sort out all the information I'd now got. And it all sort of fitted together quite nicely. Because I think as I was writing I was thinking about how I was going to, how the final product was going to come about, and that sort of directed my reading in fact. (Essay-preparation; psychology, student 5).

S_1 Unrelatedness

I don't exactly write down all the steps you should do. You should ... write down those sort of things – this is the result, did it work or not? If it didn't, did something else do it? That's the best way of going about it. Well, I just sort of write down what I've done. Just do the calculations and work back from there. (Projects; engineering, student 7).

This problem here, you're asked to say if it's an eigen-function, but you don't really know because he hasn't mentioned it in the lectures. He's mentioned what an eigenfunction is, but no way of telling how to work it out... You put in a formula to get the eigen energy, but to get the eigenfunction, whether it's applicable or not, there's no way of knowing (Problem-solving; physics, student 5).

I tend to give up on them. I tend to write very confused essays, because I have all these ideas going through my head, and I write them down, but I don't put them down in any particular logical sort of plan ... I tend to do better in exams, because the confusion doesn't matter so much, as long as the relevant points are there ... I don't seem to be able to link ideas together. (Essay writing; history, student 7).

I think it tends to be the case that I get bogged down in detail. I'm sure that's the case - I mean it explains why I'm so longwinded about any work that I do. I really don't find it easy to pick out the skeletal argument and just be satisfied with that. (Reading; psychology, student 10).

S_2 Memorization

Preparing for an exam, you learn your facts, then you have to memorize them, and sort of vague, sort of aspects of it... (Examination revision; history, student 2).

S_2 Memorization (continued)

I hate to say it, but what you've got to do is have a list of the "facts". You write down ten important points and memorize those - then you'll do all right in the class test. (Revision; psychology, student 5).

Formulae ... just go in (to the examination) with as many formulae as possible, so you learn those parrot-fashion. And approaches to the way you work out problems, techniques involved in maths ... I seem to remember, just sort of one day or two. (Revision; engineering, student 8).

I'm trying to remember it all - what's useful in exams. (Reading; physics, student 8).

S_3 Unreflectiveness

(This project) was just a matter of grinding the numbers out, getting some kind of solution. If it was adequate, fair enough. If it wasn't really, go back and pick different values. (Project work; engineering, student 11).

You just go straight for the section which is relevant to that particular question ... There'll be a topic in the book which the question comes under, and then you hunt through that section to see if they've got any ... Hopefully, they'll have the exact question and you can copy it straight down without doing any work at all ... Usually you have to hunt out the various related equations, then you just apply these to the problem. That's all, really. (Problem-solving; physics, student 12).

It's a bit confusing, (this subject)... I tend to rush through the books I'm reading for the essays, so I still don't really understand it when I've finished reading. And because there's such a lot of information I think you can oversimplify or go into too much detail. And I think I tend to over-simplify. (Reading; English, student 31).

You don't need to do as much background reading (for these essays). I just sort of set aside a day to do it and just write it. I don't think about it. (Essay-writing; English, student 38).

THE MEANING OF DEEP AND SURFACE IN DIFFERENT CONTEXTS

Analysis of the student interviews revealed important differences in the meanings attached to deep and surface approaches by students in different subject areas. In the previous section we looked at

the concepts in a general form in order to identify
differences which make sense in all the departments
investigated; here we examine characteristic differences in the meanings of the categories in different
learning environments. It is clear that what goes
to make up a deep or surface approach in one discipline
is not the same as in another discipline. Moreover,
while the meaning of the deep-surface dichotomy is
fundamentally the same in different subject areas,
there are important variations in emphasis. The
analysis concentrates on the clearest distinction to
emerge. This was (not unexpectedly) between arts
and social science departments (psychology, history,
English) and science and technology departments
(physics and engineering).

Deep 1

In the physics and engineering departments, this
sub-category is typically indicated by attempts to
relate the experience of the physical world to
theoretical concepts in the subject. Students frequently speak of "getting a picture of the problem"
and linking theory to practice. Student 8 in the
physics department provides the definitive example:
"I suppose I'm trying to imagine what the experiment is talking about, I think, in a physical
sense. Sort of get a picture of what it's
about ... I'm just thinking of the light and the
way it spreads out, so therefore I know it's the
inverse square law ..."(physics, student 8).

The category is also indicated by a student's
expression of the experience of personal satisfaction
while doing or in successfully completing a task:

"It's just seeing it work, you know. First of
all it looks as though it's impossible to do and
you just get, sorting through, the satisfaction
of knowing you've understood what you're doing."
(Project work; engineering, student 3).

Arts and social science students also speak of
the experience of personal satisfaction; this may be
combined with the linking of personal experience of
other people to the subject matter of the task. For
example:

"I'm very interested in social sciences generally.
I find it very enlightening, very entertaining,
very satisfying, to learn theories and then to

observe them in reality. Casually, to say,
"Christ, look, it's happening, you know, the
theory's there, that's what's going on," and I
think it adds so much, you know, to my life, to
be able to perceive what happens in everyday
society, through the eyes of a sociologist or
of a psychologist, and put a structure on what's
going on." (psychology, student 7).

The important difference to be appreciated here
is the contrast between the emphasis in arts and
social science on personal contact with the learning
task derived from the student's experience of other
people and the emphasis in science on personal
experience of the physical world. There is a
greater emphasis also on personal interpretation and
uniqueness of experience in the arts students' indications; the interpretive element is most common in
English.

Deep 2

In the science departments, indications are most
frequently of attempts to relate together the various
aspects of a problem, particularly in a logical way
(to "see how it all fits together"). See, for
example, physics student 12 above, p. 139: you "put
it into a logical form which relates to something
you've done previously".
This extract also exemplifies another typical
indication: the connection of what is known about
another problem or topic to the new task - usually,
but not always, in a very specific way. This also
happens in reading:

"You read it, a section on precipitation hardening ... and I think, well, fair enough, the
material is about as strong as mild steel or
something, and I'll remember that if I can, but
I'm not going to remember that it's 297 Newtons
per square mm. if it's in such and such a state
... There are one or two things that do stick in
your mind like the strength of mild steel, and
so on, because we've used it in the projects, so
you have a sort of relative scale whereby you
can say it's nearly as strong as mild steel ..."
(Reading textbooks; engineering, student 6).

"I'm generally trying to relate what the book
says to what you know about it already".
(Reading textbooks; physics, student 8).

143

"This book's about the relationship between the
artist and society, which is quite relevant to
the essay topic I'm doing, so I'm reading it
very thoroughly ... I'm reading and underlining
things that I think are important. And then I
find it a bit difficult because sometimes it
talks about some of the poems of the author that
I haven't read, so then I go back and read the
poems ... then afterwards I go back and make
quite detailed notes on the book, looking back at
the things I've underlined and trying to integrate it into the main topics that he's talking
about." (Reading; English, student 5).

"One of the first necessities with essays is to
have it well-planned ... I'm concentrating very
much on the organizing aspects, trying to read
through and see if it makes sense, you know,
from point to point". (Essay-writing; history,
student 8).

Indications of attempts to relate ideas from
different topics or fields to the task in hand, or to
relate ideas within the topic, are also commonly
found (see, for example, history, student 1, quoted
above, p. 139). The process of relating ideas appears
to be done much more specifically in science tasks:
concepts are related to particular problems in
science, while in arts the focus is wider and ideas
from different topics or fields are more freely
related.

Deep 3

The expression of a sense of purpose in carrying out a task is common to both main subject groups.
There is a somewhat greater emphasis in arts and
social science on underlying meanings and uniqueness
of experience, possibly because scientific fields
are characterized by single paradigms and greater
consensus about appropriate content and method (c.f.
Biglan, 1973b). For example:

"It was a good chapter because it organized the
readings that were to follow ... which led me
off to further articles, and at the end of it,
making notes on the things I was reading, I had
a great wad of it, which by that time, I had an
idea of how my initial conception of the problem
could be used to sort out all the information
I'd now got. And it all sort of fitted

together quite nicely. Because I think as I was writing I was thinking about how I was going to, how the final product was going to come out, and that sort of directed my reading in fact." (Essay-preparation; psychology, student 5).

"What I'm trying to do is find out whether Tennyson compromised his art to the age or whether he just wrote what he really wanted to write. That's what I'm thinking about all the time as I'm reading it, and reading his poems as well." (Reading; English, student 5).

"There are always underlying themes in any period of history, and if you can sort of pick out these themes and really understand what was going on and what it was all about, then you've got a good chance of discovering it on an equal sort of basis with your tutor or in an exam." (Reading; history, student 1).

"You have to go through quite a few different designs to get the right one ... I'm sort of always thinking about what I can put in the conclusion when I'm writing the project ... I'll try and show what I have achieved, well, understood, from the project." (Project report writing; engineering, student 3).

"I was looking for a pattern which I could relate to the script. I was drawing graphs ... I knew from the script what was supposed to be happening ... and I was looking out for it to happen on the graph ... fortunately it did." (Laboratory work; physics, student 6).

"If you follow the instructions to the letter, it's not so interesting. The instructions are only one way of doing the experiment, but you can develop variations that get a better answer, if you just start from scratch, really ... You know what you're heading for - say this measurement of a nucleus - so that might imply measurements of field versus frequency, say. And that keeps you on the right lines." (Laboratory work; physics, student 10).

Surface 1

This sub-category is concerned with students' descriptions of not thinking about relationships in

both science and arts.   In science, however,
students emphasize over-concentration on procedures
in performing a task: using formulae, calculations,
figures in tackling a problem without reference to
their relationship to each other or to the purpose
of the task.   Two extracts already quoted above
exemplify this sub-category (engineering, student 7,
page 140 ;   physics, student 5, page 140).   It is
sometimes difficult to separate this sub-category
from descriptions of serialist strategies demanded by
the type of task and the student's unfamiliarity with
the topic.   Particularly in science, it seems that
it may be necessary to use procedures which are
empirically inseparable from surface approaches as a
stage prior to taking a deep level approach.

Engineering and physics students also describe
a tendency to focus on factual details (in reading,
lectures, and writing reports) which are deliberately
unrelated to other parts of the course.   This is un-
mistakably a surface approach:

> "It's something completely separate from what
> we're doing in the lectures.   It's just one
> very narrow subject ... it didn't relate to
> anything else at all really ... Facts, and just
> facts.   Nothing else.   You get the facts down
> so that anybody else can read them without any
> padding or anything else."   (Project report
> writing;   engineering, student 8).

In arts, the emphasis is more likely to be on
detailed factual information which is unrelated either
to the meaning of the task or to personal meaning.
Arts and social science students are also more likely
to speak in general terms about not relating ideas.
For example:

> "A point I didn't make about the essays was that,
> I think, you're meant to express an appreciation
> of diversity, whereas in the class test, if you
> can give a bit of factual information - so-and-
> so did that, and concluded that, for two sides
> of writing, then you'll get a good mark."
> (Tests;   psychology, student 5).

> "I tend to give up on them.   I tend to write
> very confused essays, because I have all these
> ideas going through my head, and I write them
> down, but I don't put them down in any
> particular logical sort of plan ... I tend to do
> better in exams, because the confusion doesn't

matter so much, as long as the relevant points are there ... I don't seem to be able to link ideas together." (Essay-writing; history, student 7).

Surface 2

Indications of this category among the science students' transcripts typically consist of descriptions of memorizing formulae, data, factual points in reading, or transferring lecture information or reading to the memory without thinking about it. The stimulus is often an impending examination, and the approach may be either calculated or simply anxious:

"Yes, a lot of preparation to get proofs off pat ... It's no good trying to work it out when you're in the exam." (Revision; physics, student 10).

"You've just got to go over, reading the notes ... There's not really any questions you can attempt ... It's just reading the notes and hoping it sinks in". (Revision; engineering, student 3).

Similar indications are given by the social scientists and artists, although these students also mention an emphasis on memorizing vague generalities as well as specific procedures and facts:

"Preparing for an exam, you learn your facts, then you have to memorize them, and sort of vague, sort of aspects of it ..." (Exam. revision; history, student 2).

"What gets tested in the exam is short-term recall, that's all. So in revising for an exam I just cram my mind with such facts as I consider to be pertinent, to be able to trot off these names of people or places, dates or whatever ... " (Revision, history, student 4).

Surface 3

This sub-category is very often combined empirically with S_1. The conceptual distinction, however, is between purposelessness and unrelatedness. S_3 is frequently seen by students to be dissatisfying, but necessary because of contextual constraints

(such as lack of interest in a required subject).
Indications of the sub-category in engineering and
physics are descriptions of the unthinking use of
procedures (e.g. equations) in solving problems, or
the glossing-over of the meaning of the problem:

> "The first one, well I know that formula off
> from last year. It's just a simple formula.
> You shove in a number and it comes out straight
> away." (Problem-solving; physics, student 5).

> "There'll be a topic in the book which the
> question comes under, and then you hunt through
> that section to see if they've got any ... Hope-
> fully, they'll have the exact question and you
> can copy it straight down without doing any work
> at all ... Usually you have to hunt out the
> various related equations, then you just apply
> these to the problem. That's all really."
> (Problem-solving; physics, student 12).

Alternatively, science students describe a process of sorting through data without trying to
understand it, just learning techniques, or "just
getting it done without enjoying it or thinking
about it". Psychology, history and English students'
indications of this category often consist of descriptions of a passive, unthinking, vague approach to
a task; for example:

> "The topic was causes and consequences (of the
> Reform Act) so I was sort of looking through for
> causes and consequences, as opposed to anything
> else that was relevant ... I wasn't really very
> interested, so I didn't spend a lot of time on
> it basically ... I just read what it said, I
> don't know really." (history; student 2).

A slightly different indication is of being
easily distracted by similar (but irrelevant) material
when reading, and of oversimplifying, or "going off
the point" when writing:

> "I have too many ideas running through my head
> and if I let myself run away with my ideas, I
> can completely come off the subject of the
> question, and I used to be really bad about
> that, but I'm not so bad about it now." (Essay-
> writing; English, student 6).

> "I tend to be a bit specific initially, but I

do find that I get misled very easily and as
soon as another area comes up which is, perhaps,
not quite to do with the topic that I'm wanting
to look at specifically but has interesting
connections, then I go off on tangents. Very
regularly end up sort of miles away from where
I originally started." (Reading books and
articles; psychology, student 10).

STYLES AND PATHOLOGIES OF LEARNING IN DIFFERENT
SUBJECT AREAS

The differences we have described above are
clearly related to the different nature of typical
learning tasks in different subject areas. It is
difficult not to be aware of a parallel between the
differences described by Pask (1976; 1977) in
relation to learning strategies and styles and the
present findings. In arts and social science, it
appears that a deep level approach relies relatively
more - at least initially - on a holist strategy
(an emphasis on personal experiences, uniqueness of
experience, interpretation, illustration, the general
relation of ideas). In science, serialist
strategies are more common (an emphasis is apparent,
for example, on seeing relationships within the context of the task rather than in a more general way,
or in making relationships between theoretical
ideas).

It would appear that the holist-serialist and
comprehension-operation distinctions describe
differences not only between strategies and individuals within a subject area (Pask, 1976;
Laurillard, 1978), but also differences between the
demands made by learning tasks in different subject
areas. It is important to recognize the difference
in the meaning of the deep-surface dichotomy which
hinges on this distinction. Deep approaches in
science may contain elements which in arts terms
would usually be classified as surface; a serialist
strategy may involve rote learning or a very narrow
focus on procedures as a stage prior to a deep
approach. This strategy is not, of course, unique
to science tasks; but it is more common in science
tasks than in arts ones.

It is also possible to see similarities between
the surface sub-categories in the students' descriptions of their experiences and Pask's concepts of
globetrotting and improvidence. In so far as
holist strategies are more commonly used in the

first stages of arts and social science tasks or topics, and serialist strategies in science, it might be deduced that science students are more likely to display improvidence, and artists globe-trotting. The evidence from the interviews is equivocal. Arts students are more "generalized" in their indications of surface approaches, but this is not the same thing as globetrotting. S_1 describes something close to improvidence (over-cautious reliance on detail and failure to use valid analogies or to see relationships), but it occurs at least as commonly in arts and social science as in science. On the other hand, S_3 contains some suggestion of globetrotting for the arts and social science students, but not for the scientists. We shall look at further evidence concerning the presence of patholo-gies of learning in different subject areas in chapter 9.

CONTEXTS OF LEARNING

All the interviews included questions specifi-cally concerned with the students' perceptions of the learning environment. The questions dealt with teaching, assessment, and course structures; a general question about the student's perception of the good and bad features of the courses and the department was included. Except in the psychology and engineering departments, the students were also asked about the context of specific learning tasks. For example, if a student indicated a surface approach to one task and a deep approach to another - or different approaches within the same task - he was invited to give a reason for the difference.

By far the most important category to emerge from the analysis of students' descriptions of their experiences was that represented in the earlier versions of the CPQ by the commitment to teaching and relationships with students scales. This category refers to the quality of teaching in the department and to the extent to which staff seem to understand the learning requirements of the students. It was apparent in the interviews of students in all the departments:

> "The thing with the independent studies staff is that they're all so amiable ... they're so help-ful; if you go to them with a problem they can usually find some answer ... They all seem very committed to the idea of independent studies, the all feel that they're doing a worthwhile thing." (independent studies, student 2).

"Some (lectures) have been very good, partly
because they've been, well, not flippantly
delivered, but certainly humorously, and with
an entertaining streak. Others have been
putting across too many facts, and they seem to
have been badly prepared and badly put across.
There's one lecturer ... who is very clever, he
knows it all, but I wish he'd try to share it a
bit more with people, and just try and condense
the things he's saying, because he often repeats
himself and makes note-taking difficult."
(history, student 5).

"There are some lecturers who will think about
anything you say, and say, Oh, I hadn't
thought of that, let's see what it leads to.
And there are other lecturers who will just go
on talking almost to themselves ..." (physics,
student 10).

"As long as I'm doing a subject that I'm
interested in, it doesn't really matter to me
how they do it... I prefer departments to be
organized and efficient, and also, more important, that's caring about their students.
That to me is more important than the procedure
of the coursework, you know, what they decide
to do and what they decide to leave out from
their courses doesn't bother me." (English,
student 6).

"My criticisms will be very closely aligned to,
I think, the lack of empathy that some of the
staff have about the ability levels of the
students relative to their subject. Not
relative to being able to be good enough to be
at university, if you like, but relative to the
fact that the concrete knowledge that they have
is virtually nil in some of the areas that we've
talked about, at a very high level. So you can't
attach anything that you've been told to something that you already know, which of course is
a very important point in learning ... I think
it's the overall problem of the experts coming
in and having to give courses in a few weeks on
their particular interest, and they have such a
wealth of knowledge in that area that they start
at too high a level. That's what I think
happens. They've gone so far into their own
area that they've forgotten that we know nothing,
essentially, compared with them."(psychology,
student 7).

The interview data reveal an aspect of students' evaluations which the CPQ does not: staff in the same department are compared with each other, and some are seen to be more effective than others. While students do not seem to experience difficulty in describing the characteristics of the department as a whole, the interviews show that these general descriptions hide important differences.

Several other categories of description emerging from the interview analysis appear to have an evaluative element. The first of these corresponds to the freedom in learning factor discovered in the questionnaire analysis:

> "I'm not sure where the system's failing but there isn't the exchange of ideas, the sharing of information ... It's this very formal or objectified way of looking at work, at what has been produced in work, instead of ... being more informal and relaxed about it, somehow stimulating much more beneficial discussion ... there isn't enough of that - you've got to stick to the structure and plough through it." (psychology, student 10).

The assessment and workload category corresponds to the workload factor:

> "If I have started in plenty of time, then I do start thinking about the subject itself, more than perhaps if I've got to hand it in, but basically it's all a bit of a struggle, just to hand things in, as opposed to being interesting; you're working against a time deadline instead of for your own benefit." (history, student 2).

> "The exams don't exactly fill me with enthusiasm, particularly the electronics papers. We've got six papers for two units, which seems an awful lot. I know even the staff admit the workload in the second year is high, really tough on us." (engineering, student 5).

> "I look at (the topic) and I think to myself, 'Well, I can do that if I can be bothered to hunt through hundreds of textbooks and do the work' - and you sort of relate that to the value of the work in the course, which is virtually zero because it's so much exam assessment ... I just don't bother with it until the exams come round ... my revision is basically

for the exams, purely and simply aimed at passing the exams without bothering too much about studying the subject." (physics, student 12).

Social climate and clear goals and standards also seem to be evaluative, although perhaps not as strongly so as the categories already described:

"The only thing I've got against it ... is the isolation that's involved for independent studies majors. I suppose to some extent that is one's own bag, you know, and it's up to one to make more contacts, but one finds oneself rather isolated, because you're not going to routinely convened classes, very often, and that means you don't meet very many people. They tried having seminars but they were very poorly attended ..." (independent studies, student 29).

"We all do the same thing, we all talk about it more than people in most departments. You can learn a lot from this; everything's relevant to everybody else. I know 95% of the other students socially." (engineering, student 1).

"The first term, I seemed to have done a lot of work, and I hadn't got anything back at all, and I just had no idea how I was doing. I got quite worried really." (English, student 5).

Two further categories derived from the interview analysis - formal teaching methods and vocational relevance - correspond exactly to the CPQ scales of the same names. They are descriptive rather than evaluative categories.

In addition to the more general descriptions and evaluations of teaching, assessment, and courses, two categories referring to the context of specific learning tasks were apparent in the analysis of the interviews: the student's background knowledge of the topic or subject of which the task forms a part, and his level of interest in or personal commitment to a task. These categories are intimately associated in the transcripts with the approaches students describe to different tasks and will be discussed in a later secton.

The interview analysis confirms the finding of the CPQ analysis that the six departments provide very different contexts of learning. The differences between the departments correspond closely to the differences identified by the CPQ (see Chapter 7), and are not repeated here.

The categories of description themselves do not appear to differ in meaning from one subject area to another to the extent that the deep and surface approach categories do. The main evaluation variable, corresponding to the relationships with students and commitment to teaching scales (and their later refinements) of the CPQ, occurs in a similar form in all the interviews. One relatively minor difference is that social science students attach more importance to close personal relationships with staff than students in the other departments. There are more differences in emphasis in the other categories. Perceived excessive formality of the assessment system and a lack of flexibility in choosing assignments is of greater concern to arts and social scientists than to science students. In the vocationally-orientated engineering department, a heavy workload was not exactly welcomed, but was recognised as being necessary in order to fulfil the professionally-defined demands of the syllabus.

INDIVIDUAL DIFFERENCES IN STRATEGIC STUDY METHODS

We have so far focused mainly on differences between categories describing levels of approach and types of departmental context. We shall now look at some categories describing differences between individual students which emerged from the interviews.

The interviews included two questions taken from Miller and Parlett's study of students' examination strategies in a Scottish university (Miller and Parlett, 1974): "Do you think there is any technique involved in examinations, or not?" and "Do you think the staff get an impression of you during the year, or not?". To these questions were added others about techniques in essay-writing or project-report writing. The purpose of these questions was to see whether the kinds of strategies identified by Miller and Parlett would also be present in different environments - viz., in departments in which continuous assessment as well as assessment by final examinations was practised, and in science as well as in social science departments.

A preliminary analysis of the psychology students' interviews suggested that Miller and Parlett's findings were fairly closely replicated. Most students could be classified into one of the categories of cue-seeker, cue-conscious, and cue-deaf using judgement instructions similar to Miller and Parlett's modified to include continuous assessment tasks. Cue-seeking students, for example, not only tried to make favourable impressions on staff, and searched for cues to examination topics, but also took special care to select essay topics, and write essays, bearing in mind the likes and dislikes of the particular tutor who had set them.

The engineering students presented quite a different picture. Cue-seeking, as defined by Miller and Parlett, simply did not exist. Some students were more strategic than others, but instead of using cue-seeking tactics, they used other methods of maximizing assessment outcomes. These included paying special attention to the detailed requirements of a tutor when presenting written work, and the meticulous study of past examination papers. These students would probably be classified as cue-conscious in Miller and Parlett's scheme, but this would fail to distinguish a small group within this category who displayed a particularly strong determination to succeed by using these tactics. Some of them were aware that attempts to make good personal impressions and to seek out favoured examination topics might have the opposite effect in this environment to that intended, because of the formality of the teaching and staff-student relationships in the department.

These differences led to an attempt to develop a more general model of strategic methods. Miller and Parlett's study represents a special case within this model.

There are three main categories: most strategic, intermediate, and least strategic. Students who consistently indicate active attempts to use select- ive effort in relation to assessment tasks (e.g. essay preparation or examination revision) are classi- fied as most strategic. These students (n=6) often also indicate the use of impression management. They are frequently critical of the assessment system, but see it as a game to be played and won. An im- pression of a rather ruthless, calculating approach is usually given (c.f. Wankowski, 1973; Entwistle and Wilson, 1977). Within this category, cue-seek- ing students can be identified in some departments. The classic cue-seeking variant is best exemplified in the psychology department:

> "Sometimes I find myself writing for a tutor, writing for a marker ... With that essay I was just discussing, that reference group one, I wrote with the image of the marker in mind, the

personality, the person, I find that's important, to know who's going to be marking your paper ... Question-guessing is the most important (examination technique). Make a good stab at the questions that you think you are going to come up - just rationalize it and just work on the areas you think are going to be asked." (psychology, student 7).

"I like to give the impression that I'm out to get a First and hope that they'll treat me in that sort of way. I think if I stress my intention often enough, they'll sympathize with me." (psychology, student 5).

It was also apparent in some of the history and independent studies students. For example:

"Staff certainly get an impression of <u>me</u> ... All essay marking is subjective. I know <u>of</u> instances where I've handed in a good essay and got an indifferent mark for it. I had a debriefing session with the tutor ... I thought, Well, my next essay I'll get a better mark for it . And I wrote perhaps not such a good essay and got an excellent mark for it, which I didn't really deserve. But in the context of the learning process the tutor has an impression of you ... it all adds up to your essay mark and your exam marks." (history, student 4).

In the engineering department the highly strategic approach was not at all like cue-seeking. But the approach was related to an extrinsic, competitive motivation in this discipline more than in any other. Notice how the next student relates the absence of cue-seeking to the type of field in which he is studying, and at the same time illustrates his awareness of the assessment "game" in other subject areas:

"The lecturer told us his marking scheme, and 16 of the possible 20 marks went for the design, building, and performance of the bridge. It was a model bridge, and only 4 marks, 20% of the marks, were available for the report. So obviously I didn't put much effort into that at all, obviously I didn't spend three weeks writing it up ... I'm well aware that I'm here to get a degree you know, you don't write what

you think, you write what the tutor wants you
to think. And in engineering in general there's
not much room for that. I think there would be
a lot more room for it in more subjective things,
and I would do it even more then, presumably"
(engineering, student 6).

The absence of cue-seeking in the engineering
department appears to be related to the degree of
formality in the learning context. While cue-seeking may be effective in a fairly personalized and
informal environment, it is probably counterproductive
in more formally-organized departments. Even a
tactic such as selective revision of examination
topics may be less effective in departments where
knowledge is more hierarchically organised.
There were no students in the physics department
who could be unambiguously classified into the most
strategic category, but another student describes the
association between strategies and subject area:

"You sort of hear people in arts subjects saying 'He's bound to ask a question on such a
topic'. But in physics the thing's much more
continuous in a way. You can answer a question on Gladstone's foreign policy, but there's
lots of ways of setting up a question in physics.
You can never be sure exactly what questions
are going to come up." (physics, student 2).

The opposite extreme to the most strategic
students is demonstrated by the transcripts of
students in the least strategic category (n=20).
These students do not use selective effort in
relation to assessment tasks. They are often not
interested in obtaining a good degree. The assessment system is typically externalized and reified:
the students possess confidence in its reliability
and validity as a means of classification. They
think that the impression they make on staff will
probably not affect their grades; they may or may
not speak of using specific examination techniques.
A very small number of students from this category can be further classified as cue-deaf. Nearly
all students in the present investigation, however,
revealed at least a modest acquaintance with the idea
that some students might be able to influence their
grades by a judicious choice of assessment techniques.
The following extracts examplify the least strategic
category:

Just revise early, try and read through everything once
... I would have thought that (the staff's) impression of
you couldn't affect your degree to any great extent.
(physics, student 11).

You get this stuff about examination bias and all the
rest of it, but I don't really think that teachers are
that naive as to let their personal feelings about that
person influence them in any way. (psychology, student 4).

I'm not sure how they do go about marking essays and
things like that. I mean they might just go off what is
there, but they could bear in mind, perhaps, if you didn't
go to seminars ... I'm not sure. (English, student 38).

(In writing up projects) as long as you get down all the
facts you can, without padding it out too much, following
some sort of given, you know, they give you what they
think they want, and you try and follow the list, then I
think that's what they want. (engineering, student 8).

I: Do you think the impression staff get of you could
affect your degree result?
S: No, it's not, sort of, the way I could work at all.
If I do something I do it because I want to, not because
I might get a 2i instead of a 2ii, or something. That's
not particularly important to me. (history, student 2).

The largest group of students (n=28) was classified as intermediate. Some of the students were
very difficult to classify; inevitably, doubtful
cases have regressed to this category. Some students
were almost "beyond" cue-seeking, being fully aware
of the possible biases of the assessment system, but
determined to go their own way and study what they
wanted to study, despite any harmful effect on their
degree result; others were hardly conscious of the
assessment "game" at all, except for an occasional
suggestion in their interviews that they might be
aware that perfect objectivity in grading did not
exist. This category corresponds to cue-consciousness for students in some of the departments: there
was an awareness of the effects of impression-manage-
ment, and an understanding of the presence of cues
to examination topics displayed by these students,
without active and consistent attempts to seek out
cues and make favourable impressions on staff being
shown.

I think it's a favourable impression (that staff get of
me)... If people know you, know your capabilities and

how you normally work, if you're writing a question they read into it a lot of the time what they know you've meant ... I think it can have advantages. Although it shouldn't really. (independent studies, student 5).

If you really make yourself noticed it could have an effect (on degree results)... but I don't think it's significant in my case. (physics, student 13).

The main examination technique is to study past papers – as many as you can get hold of, and for as long as you've got the time ... the study of past papers is very essential. (engineering, student 2).

There's a lot of bluffing involved (in seminars). If you just know basically what you're supposed to be talking about, and throw a few intelligent comments in once in a while, you can create quite a good impression. But the impression couldn't affect my degree result much ... I'm a close friend of my tutor, but I don't play on it. (history, student 13).

You have to talk in seminars, and they hear what you say, and they can make a lot of inferences about you from what you say. And also, of course, from other things like your appearance and the way you speak, the way you put yourself over ... They know I know my stuff and that I speak when I've got something valuable to say. (English, student 6).

(Lectures are useful to get) a person's ideas, possibly, sometimes you get the lecturer's view on it, and you think – ah, that could come in handy for knowing what she thinks, playing the game or something. (psychology, student 2).

INDIVIDUAL DIFFERENCES IN DEEP AND SURFACE APPROACHES TO STUDYING

The major conclusion of Laurillard's resarch (Laurillard, 1978) was that students' strategies and approaches to learning were context-dependent: dichotomised descriptions of learning such as deep/ surface could not be applied to individual students but could be used to describe students in particular learning situations. It is nevertheless possible to maintain that while students are influenced by the demands of learning tasks and their contexts, they might also have relatively stable preferences for one approach or the other. There seems to be no logical flaw in this argument for consistency and variability in approach (Entwistle, 1979).

The interview transcripts were therefore examined again in order to see whether consistent differences between individuals could be identified, despite the fact that every student had mentioned the use of both deep and surface approaches. The following judgement instructions were developed in order to make explicit the grounds for classification:

1. What <u>general</u> approach to studying is mentioned?
    e.g.   "I <u>usually</u> find that I ..."
            "I <u>generally</u> try to ..."
            "<u>On the whole</u> I am able to ..."
            (see student 7, history, below, for a
             more extended example)

   If generally deep, classify as deep; if generally surface, classify as surface.

2. What is the relationship between intention and process?
   i.e. Does the student speak of succeeding in carrying out deep intentions (classify as deep), or does he contrast intention and process? (classify as surface)

3. Does the student concentrate in his responses on the technical aspects of studying when asked about how he goes about studying?
    e.g.   "I read this page, then I turned to the back of the book and spent ten minutes looking up the index ..." (= surface)

4. Does the student make a distinction between the merely technical and the actual process of studying?   (classify as deep)

5. Is academic knowledge seen as a part of the student?   Is an interest expressed in learning for learning's sake? (classify as deep).   Does the student talk of the excitement of learning and express a desire to learn?   Is he able to talk fluently about the process of learning (c.f. 4 above), as if it had been reflected on before the interview?   (= deep).

6. Is academic knowledge seen as external, a threat, a source of distress or anxiety, not part of oneself, something that happens to the learner? (classify as surface).

Categories 5 and 6 resemble the differences described by Saljo in his study of the development of subjective conceptions of learning (Saljo, 1979a, b,c). Learning in the "taken-for-granted" perspective is essentially a reproductive process (c.f. the earlier stages of development in Perry's model (1970)). Learning later becomes, for some experienced learners, "thematized": the learner becomes aware of the influence of the context of learning, is able to contrast learning "for life" with learning in school, and typically makes a distinction between rote learning and "real learning" (understanding).

The distinction between consistent deep and consistent surface approaches is perhaps most effectively illustrated by some rather more extensive extracts from the interview transcripts:

DEEP: I began to realize there, there was a structure in the things they were teaching us and it wasn't just a load of facts - that's only a recent, recent realization, perhaps only this term. I started to realize it when I realized that the English I'm doing for my free ninth, er, is very closely connected to psychology ... the novelist seems to be very close to the psychologist, only he writes it in a creative - no, not creative - a more artistic form. And when I realized that those were so close I suddenly realized how interrelated all the topics in psychology were. And that's when I also read some articles on creativity; that's when I suddenly realized that putting your own pattern on it would probably make a better essay, and a more enjoyable essay. And the little anecdote is that I got an A for the first essay done in the new way - so I've carried on. I can see Perry as being fairly relevant and I think, I couldn't have seen him as being relevant until I'd got into some of the stages myself. So being taught about it in the first year didn't really help because I didn't understand wha, what they were teaching, or I thought, I mean, I knew the facts sort of but I didn't know what was really meant 'cos you can't understand there are two sides to an argument - if that's what you're understanding - until you see there are two sides to an argument ... I've become more interested in the subject, I think. I've begun to understand more of the subject, and perhaps, learned, learned things that, can apply in my everyday life more successfully. I mean things like my learning. I've learned perhaps, perhaps a better way of learning ... (psychology, student 6).

SURFACE:
S: I don't really like seminars anyway.
I: Why not?
S: I don't know, er, they seem false to me, they, you've um, you all know that, that you're not enjoying them, you're just there because you have to, because they're supposed to be compulsory, your tutor's going to mark your essays anyway, so you might as well go and show willing but I don't like seminars ... I think there's a lot of bother involved in, er, I mean the two practicals count, and it's not just, I don't think it is, just the writing up the report at the end that you hand in — I mean that might be alright, but it's the way you go about organizing the practical. If you're in a state and, you go and see your tutor, and you say, er, "can't get enough subjects" or "something's gone wrong", then, it's not going to give you much. I mean you're going to feel like that aren't you — two inches tall, and you can't help but think, well when he's marking it he's going to remember that I came to him all in a state, I couldn't really organize it. I think, I think they give a lot of worry to people. (psychology, student 8).

DEEP:
I: What sorts of things were going through your head as you were reading it?
S: Pleasure at somebody being able to handle such a complex subject as what's wrong with society with great lucidity and clarity; admiration at his achievement in identifying the failures of the industrial world-view and yet also positively being able to make positive suggestions about what might be done to correct deficiencies ... I was happy too that it linked in with what I'd been reading about the development of science and scientific traditions. It just really was a book which linked together lots of different things that I already knew in one pattern ... I was continually linking together different things. (independent studies, student 29).

SURFACE:
I: Well, do you think you have to ... Do you think there's any special thing you have to do when you are preparing for them, revising for exams?
S: Um, definitely going through problem sheets and the worked solutions and that. I suppose to, find out, that way, you came across, all the likely combinations of things they're going to stick in, like rotten things ... Then you concentrate more on the, ins and outs of, the problems related to this part of the course. You know what might the prob, what might the er, what shall I say, mmm, awkward parts they are going to put in, you go through the past

problem sheets, then you can see what, um, intricate little pieces they are going to put in, you know to try and fool you and things like that. (engineering, student 7).

DEEP: I thought that was quite an interesting (essay) actually, because it was something like "What scope is there for individual initiative in a group?", and that makes me think, oh what, there's quite a few terms you've got to sort out here, er, this initiative thing, how can you take it, and I decided that, you can have initiative meaning freedom to act independently of the group and initiative being freedom to think independently of a group. And I took that sort of line on it, which I thought would be a bit different - I know how boring it must be to mark thirty essays all the same ... At first I was a bit, I thought, Oh God, how am I going to start, I don't really know where my emphasis lies at the moment before I've done a bit of work on it. I know roughly that I'm going to do this freedom to act/freedom to think bit, how does it interrelate? So I just started reading, on the first chapter I think it was on that book called "Groups", and, er it was a good chapter 'cos it organised all the readings that were to follow - it was done by the editors themselves ... Which led me off to the readings in that, ah, which led me off to further articles, and at the end of it, making notes on my, on the things I was reading, I had a great wad of it which, by that time, I had an idea of how my initial conception of the problem could be used to sort out all the information I'd now got. And it all sort of fitted together quite nicely. 'Cos I think as I was writing I was thinking about how I was going to, how the final product was going to come about and, er, that sort of directed my reading in fact. I'd read something and I'd think: well, how's this fitting in with what I've thought about so far, and once I'd got to that stage I'd think, well, where do I go from here. And so I was using what I'd just read to determine what I'd read next, and I kept going until I had to go to bed. (psychology, student 5).

SURFACE: You look for different people's ideas, the different authors' ideas, and compare, then sort of work out what you think's relevant yourself ... I find it difficult trying to work out in my own mind what I think is relevant, because obviously so many people have written pages and pages on one subject. I find it difficult to find what's relevant for myself. Making my own mind up I find very complicated. You spend such a short period of time - the other people have spent year and years ... (history, student 2).

> SURFACE: I sort of feel it's quite a challenge.   I
> like getting a lot of ideas, I like to find a particular
> angle for it, make it a bit more interesting.   But I tend
> to give up on them (essays), I tend to write very confused
> essays because I have all these ideas going through my
> head and I write them down, but I don't put them down in
> any particular logical sort of plan ... I tend to do
> better in exams, because there the confusion doesn't
> matter so much, as long as the relevant points are there
> ... I don't seem to be able to link ideas together ...
> (history, student 7).

It is possible to see a logical continuity between
the consistent deep category, Pask's concept of versatility, and strategic study methods.   Versatility
in a "thematized" learner - shown by the ability to
alternate between a grasp of the whole and its implications and the process of building up an understanding by working through details - is well demonstrated
by this student:

> What I tend to do initially on an essay or a dissertation,
> I will make up perhaps a short or a long bibliography,
> depending on what it is, of books and articles that I
> think are relevant as source material, and then at first
> I'll tend to just go through those one by one, picking out
> out points which I think are relevant, giving me some
> sort of framework to work on.   And then, after I've
> built up quite a large body of notes, possibly, from that,
> then I'll get to the stage where I've got a very good
> idea of how I'm going to organise the essay or the
> dissertation or whatever, and there'll be particular
> areas then which I'm looking for.   There may be one or
> two particular points which I want to see what other
> people have written about.   And so where previously I've
> been going through the source material perhaps one by
> one in a rather general way, then I'll get down to more
> specific details ... (independent studies, student 6).

Similarly, the concept of strategic study
methods implies an ability to choose the most effective strategy for the task in hand (sometimes this
might mean taking a surface approach) and an awareness of the purpose of the task and the way it relates
to the course as a whole.   Consistent deep approaches
were found to be positively and significantly related
to strategic study methods (Ramsden, 1981).
In the remainder of this chapter we shall examine
some functional relationships between the categories
that have been identified in the previous analyses.
We shall deal first with students' perceptions of the

relationships between different subject areas and
strategies of learning.

STRATEGIES OF LEARNING IN DIFFERENT SUBJECT AREAS

We have seen that the subjective meanings
attached to the sub-categories of deep and surface
approaches differ from one subject area to another.
The distinction between the arts and science subject
areas is related to Pask's descriptions of differing
styles and strategies of learning; it seems that
different subject areas make different demands on the
types of strategy used by students.   Although the
interviews did not measure styles and strategies of
learning, history, English, and physics
students were asked whether they felt that there were
differences between the ways in which students in
different subject areas studied.   To what extent
did the students themselves perceive differences in
the type of strategy used in arts and sciences, and
in the learning contexts provided by the different
kinds of departments?
Learning tasks in science are typically described as hierarchical, logical, heterogeneous, and
rule- and procedure-governed:

> (Science) seems to be a constant sort of building thing –
> they learn something one week and build on it ... know-
> ing the formula, and using that, and applying it to solve
> another formula, etcetera.   (history, student 9).

> A lot of our stuff is just sort of, you know, teaching us
> a logical flow of arguments, observing certain results,
> concepts and how they're related, whereas ... (physics,
> student 14).

> It's much more – exact isn't the right word – but in
> physics you're right or wrong ... here you can't think it,
> it happens.   (physics, student 5).

> But for the sciences, they have to be more calculating,
> they have to know logical concepts, they have to know
> logical things and how an answer will come out of a cal-
> culation or a few statements which have been written
> down.   (English, student 6).

Arts and social science tasks, on the other
hand, are seen to be interpretive, comparative,
generalized, more self-governed, and not as difficult
or time-consuming:

(Arts students) seem to have a much easier time of it. They read a lot more, of course, they've got to read all these books, but ... it seems much easier ... it seems to be just going on and on about what you yourself think ... In these other subjects you can just sort of go on and on: "I think this, I think that". (physics, student 5).

The work demands, in a way, a completely different intelligence. For us it's more interpretation, more analysis, more penetration into the material ... They have to look ahead to an answer: we have to look in ... For English you have to see implicit meaning. (English, student 6).

The history or politics student is trying to interpret facts; the physics student is perhaps being more and more precise whilst the history student is trying to generali e more ... the history student is going round and round, sort of thing. (history, student 8).

It's hard to explain - you're not learning something one week which will lead you on to something else, you tend to skip about ... you can see things running through the lectures, but they're very sort of tenuous ... It's not something that you can build on. (history, student 9).

A lot of (history) is just hypothesis, why did this guy do this? and so on - it's a lot less certain. (physics, student 14).

These subjectively-defined differences are surprisingly similar (the differences in workload and difficulty excepted) to Pask's definitions of operation learners and comprehension learners:

Operation learners pick up rules, methods, and details ... (the operation learner) assimilates procedures and builds concepts for isolated topics.

Comprehension learners readily pick up an overall picture of the subject matter ... (they) describe the relationships between topics. (Pask, 1976)

Moreover, although the two subject areas are seen to require different ways of learning, students in each field agree on what the differences are. And both groups relate the differences they jointly identify to characteristic differences in the environments of arts and science departments, as the following extracts show:

In physics, in the sciences, it's laid out in the lectures, everything that you do comes down, it's written on the blackboard, if you miss the lectures it's very important, really, because you miss out whole sections of the courses. Whereas with the arts you could to a certain degree, I think, be given a reading list and an essay list, and be left to tutorials and seminars ... just left to do it all yourself, with guidelines being set through the tutorials ... it's guidelines in the arts, in the sciences, it's just lines along which you have to work. There's no guiding - you have to do this, and you're not given any freedom of expression. (physics, student 12).

There is a big division between science and arts. My friend does biology, and she seems to have to learn so many more facts than us, and there's so much more pressure, especially this year. She's always being given exams, at the beginning of each term, so she has to work hard in the holidays, and you've got lots and lots of assignments to do each week, and the actual exam is a great vast area. She can't just revise particular topics, because there's a multiple choice (examination)... Sometimes she just has to memorize names, and things like that. I know some- times she feels that she'd like to be able to think a bit more about things, critically ... It's a much more specific kind of subject, it's more systematic; we're left to ourselves a lot ... we have much more work to do outside the actual set hours. (English, student 5).

We do a lot more work than they do ... more often than not, you hear people say, "Oh, I'll get an extension for my essay for another two weeks" or something; if we asked for an extension for our tutorial sheets, we'd be three weeks behind ... (physics) is far more relevant to life than the study of history is. Admittedly, if you can see what's gone on in the past, you can, it might help you, but whereas if you get a science degree you can go directly into a scientific job, with history degrees, there isn't much you can do apart from teaching, if you specifically want to use history ... They perhaps don't take it as seriously, I don't think it perhaps means as much to them as ours does. (physics, student 11).

We can hand it in and compare it with some other guy, right or wrong, with fellow-students, but there it seems to be just going on and on about what you yourself think, so you can't really compare it with other students to see what they thought of it. (physics, student 5).

My lecture timetable is pretty sparse, whereas I've got a friend who does engineering, and he's got days just full of stuff, but I've got to do a hell of a lot more reading. I go to a lecture and it just introduces me to a subject, whereas he, I suppose, gets an awful lot of it from seminars, practicals, and so on. He gets a lot more information, whereas I get an introduction to it, I suppose. (history, student 11).

(In science) I think you have to learn things you don't want to learn a lot more than in English; you can't select as much, because it all fits together. (English student 38).

These contrasting descriptions of tasks and contexts certainly support the view that Pask's concepts effectively measure differences between subject areas. Subject area and learning strategy are functionally related in the students' subjective conceptions. The match is remarkably accurate and makes good sense: science departments are seen to have clearer goals, greater vocational relevance, less freedom in learning, and more formal teaching; all these things make for an environment in which serialist strategies are encouraged (and probably rewarded), while the reverse is true for arts students and in arts departments. Although both science and arts tasks may require both types of learning strategy (we have seen that the ability to alternate between the two is a characteristic of some competent learners), the mixture is different. The students relate the differences in learning strategies to the way in which the departments are organized, as much as to inherent differences in the subject matter. A matching process, whereby students with a preference for comprehension learning gravitate towards arts departments, and operation learners towards science departments, presumably takes place. It would seem that the distinctions are continually reinforced at university.

THE EFFECT OF THE LEARNING CONTEXT ON STUDENTS' LEVELS OF APPROACH

Another important objective of the interview analysis was the exploration of possible relationships between students' perceptions of the context of learning and their levels of approach to learning tasks. How do students explain the fact that they take different approaches to different tasks?

Students' Experiences of Learning

Teaching, Assessment, Course Structure

For students in all the departments, the quality of teaching and the extent to which staff gave help and advice on approaches to studying were related to generally favourable or unfavourable attitudes towards learning and students' interest in what they were studying. The following extracts from the interviews provide examples of these relationships:

(a)   Interest in students, helpfulness of teaching

> I certainly don't like it if you get tutorials where the guy just comes along and sits down and makes you stand up and do the work on the blackboard. Usually he picks on people that can't do it, which I think is terrible because you get stuck up at the blackboard and made to look a fool, and it switches you right off... I think I'm not going to do that if this guy's going to do that to me, because I don't learn anything; nobody else learns anything because it takes you so long to do one question; and it makes you very unhappy with that particular course, so I lose interest in the course. (physics, student 12).

> I find that the courses I do most work on are the courses where I get on with the tutors best ... a tutor can put you off the subject ... some of them don't like students, so they're not interested in what students have to say unless it's relevant to their approach. (English, student 38).

> Luckily I'm doing some courses with some good tutors on them – you know, they make the books come alive because they can talk about them and they can direct you to a chapter or a passage, and that's important I think ... you could spend an hour rooting through and then just come to what you think is the essence of it all ... If you get a guideline from the tutor, and I'm quite lucky in having someone who can point the way, then it's a godsend. (history, student 5).

(b)   Commitment to the subject

> If they (tutors) have enthusiasm, then they really fire their own students with the subject, and the students really pick it up ...I'm really good at and enjoy (one subject) but that's only because a particular tutor I've had has been so enthusiastic that he's given me an enthusiasm for it and now I really love the subject. But at the beginning of (another course) the tutor was ...

169

a little bit passive for my liking ... something imaginative was lacking, there was something lacking in the seminar group ... (English, student 6).

(c)   Teaching at the students' own level

This problem here, you're asked to say if it's an eigenfunction, but you don't really know because he hasn't mentioned it in the lectures.   He's mentioned what an eigenfunction is, but no way of telling how to work it out ... You put in a formula to get the eigen energy, but to get the eigenfunction, whether it's applicable or not, there's no way of knowing.   (physics, student 5).

My criticisms will be very closely aligned to, I think, the lack of empathy that some of the staff have about the ability levels of the students relative to their subject. Not relative to being able to be good enough to be at university, if you like, but relative to the fact that the concrete knowledge that they have is virtually nil in some of the areas that we've talked at, at a very high level. So you can't attach anything that you've been told to something that you already know, which of course is a very important point in learning ... I think it's the overall problem of the experts coming in and having to give courses in a few weeks on their particular interest, and they have such a wealth of knowledge in that area that they start at too high a level.   That's what I think happens.   They've gone so far into their own area that they've forgotten that we know nothing, essentially, compared with them.   (psychology, student 7).

(d)   Lecturing ability

The concepts are really difficult anyway.   It usually takes, I think most people like, I certainly like to sit down on my own and go at my own speed.   Now the lecturers certainly assume that we know it and they just keep going. People can say, "slow down" but people of course are reluctant to say they don't understand it.   So he tends to keep going, and once you get behind it, you know, you can't really get back on terms.   (engineering, student 1).

Recently we were doing Fourier analysis, and the lecturer mentioned in passing that it was something which they used when they transmit moon pictures back to earth ... that makes a lot of difference, you can see it being used. Another example he quoted was about why when you bang a drum you get lots of different sounds rather than when you, say, play a violin when you just get one note ... he said, if you look at this you can see why - and he was right, you could see why, it did make sense.   (physics, student 3).

(e)   Feedback on performance

You give an essay in - I gave in two at the beginning of the second term and I didn't get those back till this term ... you know, it's a bit difficult, when you're writing the next essay, because you want to know where you've gone wrong and the points that have been alright ... By the time you've got it back after waiting a whole term you've forgotten what it's all about and it doesn't really mean much then.   (English, student 31).

Unfavourable attitudes to studying, lack of interest, and, significantly, surface approaches, were related by the students to deficiencies of the assess ment system (especially inappropriate assessment methods), restricted opportunities for self-direction, and excessive workload:

(a)   Inappropriate assessment methods

I look at (the topic) and I think to myself, "Well, I can do that if I can be bothered to hunt through hundreds of textbooks and do the work" - and you sort of relate that to the value of the work in the course, which is virtually zero because it's so much exam assessment ... I just don't bother with it until the exams come around ... my revision is basically for the exams, purely and simply aimed at passing the exams without bothering too much about studying the subject.   (physics, student 12).

In independent studies you've got to do the coursework and it's got to be good.   Whereas - I know some history students who've just got phenomenally good memories and have got a very good exam technique, and did very little revision, and just got good marks on the basis of, you know, parrot-fashion learning.   (independent studies, student 7).

In this department, if (the design) fails that's like a black mark.   It shouldn't be ... the French civil engineer who was the world's leading authority on the design of dams said there was more to be learned from failure than success.   He's quite right of course.   So if you have a failure, providing you can account for it, then to me that's as valid as something that passed. (engineering, student 2).

(b)   Excessive workload, lack of choice

> I'm disappointed in some respects that it isn't what I
> expected it to be ... All the time it's assessment,
> assessment, assessment.   When I got a place here I
> thought, great, this is marvellous ... I won't just be
> concentrating on ... doing it for assessment.   I'll be
> able to study ... just time to sit back and think and
> talk about a subject, and read about it.   No – it's all
> structured, you know.   When I leave here I'll go straight
> back to my room and I'll say, "Right, what've we got to
> do next?" ... It's good for individual teachers' images
> to get good marks out of their students on their courses.
> I don't think that is best achieved by following the
> academic philosophy of learning what you want to learn
> ... You've got to enforce a strong, very strong and
> carefully organized structure upon your learning, which
> is directed, aimed directly at, the assessment that exists
> ... I'm very disappointed ... that I can't just, you
> know, go through and really have a think and really work
> things out.   (psychology, student 7).

> In very few of the lectures was I picking (the principles)
> up as we did them.   It took me all my time to get the
> notes down.   So, and this in a way, the pace is so fast
> that you get the notes down and that's it.   You don't
> really follow what's going on.   You can't do two
> things at once.   You can't sit back and listen to
> what's being said.   You spend an hour taking notes
> down ... I put this down to this very keen desire to
> cover that much work.   (engineering, student 2).

> If I have started in plenty of time, then I do start
> thinking about the subject itself, more than perhaps
> that I've got to hand it in, but basically it's all a
> bit of a struggle, just to hand things in, as opposed
> to being interesting;   you're working against a time
> deadline instead of for your own benefit.   (history,
> student 2).

Departmental contexts which offer choice in
learning methods and topics to be studied seem to
be able to engender more favourable attitudes to
learning, although the freedom of choice also brings
with it greater responsibilities:

> If you're doing independent studies you're obviously
> interested in what you're doing.   Therefore you're in
> a much more relaxed mental state for approaching work: I
> am, anyway, and other people I know in the course are.
> (independent studies, student 2).

You have to take responsibility for the work yourself. You're not, you don't have the advantage of a pre-existing framework of suggested reading and suggested approaches in independent studies, so you have to be damn sure that you are interested enough and confident enough to see it through those times when you come to sort of minor crises, when you realise suddenly that it's all on your shoulders and you've got no one else to go to ... It requires commitment and personal motivation. (independent studies, student 29).

Two other context variables - clarity of goals and standards, and social climate - were also related by some students to favourable or unfavourable attitudes and to their sense of security as learners within their department.

Level of interest and background knowledge

The student's interest in an academic task (or his personal commitment to studying a particular field) and his prior possession of some understanding of the field or topic in which a task is situated were found to be associated with the probability of a deep approach to the task. For example:

(a)   Level of interest

It wasn't that interesting, there wasn't that much there. I wasn't reading it really intently, it was more skimming through, looking for certain words, science, the industrial revolution, dates as well, just to sort of pick out the points that I wanted. (history, student 14).

I: Do you try to get a grasp of the, the whole thing when you're reading an article, or ...?
S: Yeah, I try, I try to, I don't often, sometimes, depends what it's about, er, I try to.
I: But you find it difficult?
S: Mmm.   I wouldn't say I found everything, I would say I found, found it difficult according to what it was about.   I mean, the cognitive reading I was telling you about, I just couldn't be bothered to pay attention and see how one argument connected with the other. (psychology, student 8).

It's a bit confusing, (this subject).   When it comes to writing essays, because I'm not very interested in it, I tend to rush through the books I'm reading for the essays, so I still don't really understand it when I've finished reading. And because there's such a lot of information I think you can either oversimplify or go into too much detail. And I think I tend to oversimplify. (English, student 31).

(b)   Background knowledge

(The best way to study) is to go through some work, and try and get some solutions. It's difficult. It depends on how well one knows the subject as well. It's easy to write questions for something you know well. You just sort of plod through and try and understand bits here and there in something you don't know. (engineering, student 3).

I think if I already know something about the subject about which I want to write, it helps. Because then I can write something out without having to refer to the books first, sketch something out in much more detail rather than just skeletal ... this question was about popular recreations, and were attitudes to them changing. Well, having been grounded in Folklore – a consuming passion for the last eight years – I know quite a lot about that already. So I just kind of wrote out 3 or 400 words which gave a basis for it ... mentally I was much more aware of accomplishing something useful. (history, student 3).

The actual question was a particle in a box, asking you what shape it would describe ... we have come across a similar problem in chemistry ... I know, I had a picture in my mind's eye of what I was doing, most definitely. I could see it. I think that is possibly because I've already done it in chemistry, and if I hadn't I'd just have thought it a lot of figures and a lot of complicated-looking formulae, and left it at that. (physics, student 3).

It was like one of the questions from a previous course, which I could relate. It was a Schroedinger equation for a particle in a box which we'd solved generally before in chemistry, so I could relate it, I could see a picture of what I wanted. I knew basically what sort of answer I should get, and from that I could work my way through it quite simply, no problem ...

The other bit was different: I couldn't do it. Basically I gave up with it, because it was a function, which I've never really understood ... I looked at it and I thought "That looks complicated" ... it was very short, it looked like it would need a lot of rearranging.(physics, student 6)

Of course, background knowledge and level of interest are not necessarily productive of a deep approach; they provide favourable conditions for it. As might be expected, background knowledge is most often related to level of approach in the science and technology departments: when knowledge is hierarchically structured and operation learning is favoured, an understanding of new concepts is often only possible if the previous stages have been fully grasped (c.f. Biggs, 1978). Level of interest is more commonly related to deep approaches in arts and social science tasks; this result is also understandable in the light of what has already been said about the greater informality of teaching and learning, and the more opportunities for choice, in arts subjects.

The two antecedents of levels of approach are related to each other, and both are partly explained by the perceived quality of the departmental environment. Good teaching and appropriate assessment methods are ways in which interest in a subject, and background topics relating to it, can be fostered. Moreover, the way in which a department is organized may permit student choice in methods and topics of study to a greater or lesser extent. All other things being equal, freedom in learning should make for a higher level of interest.

The relationships described above seem to make sense in terms of recent theoretical work and empirical research. The investigations at Gothenburg, which provided evidence of a connection between threatening assessment conditions and surface approaches (Fransson, 1977), were carried out under experimental controls; now, there is a clear indication that the same process occurs in the natural setting of students' everyday work. The arguments of authors like Becker (1968), Snyder (1971) and Rowntree (1977) -- to the effect that assessment procedures, heavy workload, and lack of choice in methods of learning and topics to be studied can have the unintended consequences of discouraging favourable attitudes to learning and encouraging rote learning instead of understanding - are strongly supported.

The connection between level of interest and level of approach has considerable intuitive validity. Both Fransson (1977) and Biggs (1979) note the coincidence of deep level processing and expressed interest. One of the second-order factors discovered by Biggs ("internalising": see chapter 4) contains both the student's interest in the subject matter and his attempts to interrelate ideas and impose meaning.

From an entirely different standpoint, a recent study of students' attributions of reasons for success and failure in essays and examinations has produced complementary results. Interest (or the lack of it) in an essay was found to be the most commonly attributed reason for a good (or poor) level of performance in it (Hughes-Jones, 1979).

A somewhat more unusual finding is the close association revealed in the interview transcripts between good teaching, favourable attitudes, and (by implication) the conditions for deep level approaches. The accepted view has been that quality and type of teaching is unrelated to student learning (see, e.g., Dubin and Taveggia, 1969). Recent evidence (Hartnett and Centra, 1977; Centra, 1976; Fearn-Wannan, 1979) does, however, seem to suggest that student satisfaction with teaching, and perceptions of lecturers' student-orientation, may be positively related to student achievement.

STUDENTS' ACADEMIC PERFORMANCE

Levels of approach and strategic study methods are known to be positively related to the outcomes of learning, measured either qualitatively or quantitatively (see Marton and Säljö, 1976a; Miller and Parlett, 1974; Svensson, 1977; Säljö, 1981). The final section of this chapter looks at relationships between outcomes and two of the categories derived from the interview analysis: consistent deep or surface approaches and strategic study methods. We should expect deep approaches and highly strategic methods to correlate positively with the measure of outcome used (degree result).

Final degree classifications were obtained for the student sample, after each student had been categorized on the approach and strategic dimensions. It was possible to obtain the results of all but three students. (At least one of the three - classified as consistent surface - withdrew before final assessment). The results were coded by the conventional dichotomized measure of good degree (First and Upper Second Class Honours) vs. other degree (Lower Second or below).

Level of approach and degree result

Tables 8.2 and 8.3 give the degree results and interview classifications of the 42 students who could be placed into the consistent deep or surface categories and for whom degree results could be obtained. The

pattern of the relationship is clearly in the hypothesized direction. Only 5 of the 16 surface
students achieved Firsts or Upper Seconds, while 16
of the 26 deep students gained good degrees.

Strategic study method and degree result

These results appear in Tables 8.4 and 8.5.
Table 8.4 shows that strategic methods are positively
but weakly associated with good degree results.
The size of the relationship is reduced by the large
"intermediate" category, which contains several
students who were difficult to classify. Comparison
of the two extreme groups reveals that five of the
six most strategic students gained good degrees.
Table 8.5 shows that the difference between the mean
degree results of the most and least strategic
students is statistically significant.

CONCLUSIONS

The results presented in this chapter have confirmed the remarkable explanatory power of the qualitative methods first extensively used in the
Gothenburg investigations of student learning. In
particular, they have demonstrated clear functional
relationships between the context of learning - the
type of task, the quality of teaching, and the
characteristics of academic departments - and the
approaches students use.
The next chapter returns to the quantitative
data collected in the survey of students' approaches
to studying in order to examine these educationally
important connections from another standpoint.

Table 8.2   LEVEL OF APPROACH AND DEGREE RESULT

	APPROACH		
Result	Deep	Surface	Total
Good degree	16	5	21
Other degree	10	11	21
Total	26	16	42

Corrected χ^2 = 2.52 , p (one-tailed) < .06

Table 8.3   MEAN DEGREE RESULTS FOR DEEP AND SURFACE STUDENTS
(n = 42)
(where deep = 1, surface = 2, good degree = 1;
other degree = 2)

Group	Mean	S.D.	T	p (one-tailed)
Deep	1.38	.50	-1.95	.03
Surface	1.69	.48		

Table 8.4   STRATEGIC STUDY METHOD AND DEGREE RESULT

	STRATEGIC METHOD			
Result	Most strategic	Intermediate	Least Strategic	Total
Good degree	5	14	8	27
Other degree	1	14	12	27
Total	6	28	20	54

X^2 = 3.47. n.s.

Table 8.5:   MEAN DEGREE RESULTS FOR MOST STRATEGIC AND LEAST
STRATEGIC STUDENTS (n = 26)

Group	Mean	S.D.	T	p (one-tailed)
Most strategic	1.17	.41	-1.92	.03
Least strategic	1.60	.50		

Chapter Nine

APPROACHES TO LEARNING IN CONTRASTING DEPARTMENTS

The development of instruments designed to measure students' perceptions of their courses and their approaches to studying was described in chapters 4 and 7. The next stage of the research examined possible links between the scales of the two questionnaires suggested by previous research and by the results of the student interviews (chapter 8). In what ways might contrasting academic contexts affect approaches to studying? The interviews had identified functional relationships between levels of approach and students' perceptions of the teaching and assessment they experienced; it was also clear that the way students tackled academic tasks was related to the subject area in which they studied. The intention of the next part of the investigation was to test the validity of these connections, and to try to disentangle the effects of subject area and departmental organization, by using a contrasting methodology: the statistical treatment of quantitative data from a large sample of students.

METHOD AND PURPOSE

The results described in this chapter derive from the servey of 2208 students in 66 departments of engineering, physics, economics, psychology, history and English carried out in 1979-80. Students completed both the approaches to studying inventory and the course perceptions questionnaire; the methods used are presented in more detail in chapter 4. The scales of both instruments and their meaning are given in Figure 9.1.

This chapter is based on chapter 6 in Ramsden (1981).

Figure 9.1   SUBSCALES OF THE INVENTORY AND QUESTIONNAIRE

Subscale	Meaning
Deep approach	Active questioning in learning
Relating ideas	Relating to other parts of course
Use of evidence	Relating evidence to conclusions
Intrinsic motivation	Interest in learning for learning's sake
Surface approach	Preoccupation with memorization
Syllabus-boundness	Relying on staff to define learning tasks
Fear of failure	Pessimism and anxiety about academic outcomes
Extrinsic motivation	Interest in courses for the qualifications they offer
Strategic approach	Awareness of implications of academic demands made by staff
Disorganized study methods	Unable to work regularly and effectively
Negative attitudes to studying	Lack of interest and application
Achievement motivation	Competitive and confident
Comprehension learning	Readiness to map out subject area and think divergently
Globetrotting	Over-ready to jump to conclusions
Operation learning	Emphasis on facts and logical analysis
Improvidence	Over-cautious reliance on details
Formal teaching methods	Lectures and classes more important than individual study
Clear goals and standards	Assessment standards and ends of studying clearly defined
Workload	Heavy pressures to fulfil task requirements
Vocational relevance	Perceived relevance of courses to careers
Good teaching	Well-prepared, helpful, committed teachers
Freedom in learning	Discretion of students to choose and organize own work
Openness to students	Friendly staff attitudes and preparedness to adapt to students' needs
Social climate	Quality of academic and social relationships between students

The analyses were designed to investigate the following questions:

1. To what extent can differences in students' approaches to studying and perceptions of the context of learning by explained (a) by type of discipline studied (b) by type of department, after controlling for subject area?

2. What links between the two sets of scales can be identified by means of factor analysis?

3. Using departments as units of analysis rather than individual students, what associations between orientations to studying and course perceptions can be identified? In other words, do contexts of learning appear to influence approaches to studying?

4. Do some approaches to studying seem to be rewarded more highly (in terms of self-rated performance) in some contexts than in others?

DIFFERENCES IN STUDENTS' APPROACHES IN CONTRASTING SUBJECT AREAS

From previous work, including the interview study, it was expected that comprehension learning would be found to be more common in the arts and social science disciplines than the sciences, while the reverse would be true of operation learning. The two pathologies of learning would also be differentially related to subject area (although the interview results showed that both pathologies could be identified in science and arts students): improvidence should be more in evidence in science, and globetrotting in arts. The four sub-scales making up the meaning orientation scale (deep approach, relating ideas, use of evidence, and intrinsic motivation) would provide evidence of disciplinary differences if the interview results were to be replicated. Deep approach, intrinsic motivation, and relating ideas items are more characteristic of arts and social science approaches, while the use of evidence subscale is more descriptive of science approaches to learning tasks. Earlier work had also suggested that science students would be more likely to be extrinsically motivated and syllabus-bound (Entwistle and Wilson, 1977). The remaining subscales were not expected to show large differences between subject areas.

Table 9.1   MEANS OF SUBSCALES BY SUBJECT AREA

Scale	Mean (1) Science (2) Social science (3) Arts	S.D.	Analysis of Variance F (df 2, 63)
Deep approach	(1) 10.21 (2) 10.53 (3) 11.28	.90 .81 .67	8.41**
Relating ideas	(1) 9.55 (2) 10.54 (3) 10.35	.95 .77 .75	9.47**
Use of evidence	(1) 9.83 (2) 9.51 (3) 9.46	.54 .70 .46	2.51
Intrinsic motivation	(1) 8.05 (2) 8.29 (3) 9.06	1.26 1.50 .87	3.12
Surface approach	(1) 13.13 (2) 13.23 (3) 12.60	1.28 .94 1.19	1.64
Syllabus-boundness	(1) 8.96 (2) 8.18 (3) 7.22	.64 .84 .82	24.82**
Fear of Failure	(1) 5.87 (2) 5.91 (3) 5.73	.74 .74 .69	.29
Extrinsic motivation	(1) 6.93 (2) 6.01 (3) 3.08	1.69 2.01 1.09	25.45**
Strategic approach	(1) 10.37 (2) 10.27 (3) 9.80	.79 .55 .85	3.25
Disorganized study methods	(1) 9.74 (2) 9.70 (3) 8.77	.88 1.03 1.22	5.19*
Negative attitudes to studying	(1) 5.45 (2) 5.47 (3) 5.70	.75 .89 .63	.54

$*p < .01$
$**p < .001$

Table 9.1 (continued)   MEANS OF SUBSCALES BY SUBJECT AREA

Scale	Mean		S.D.	
	(1) Science			
	(2) Social science			
	(3) Arts			
Achievement	(1)	10.22	.88	
Motivation	(2)	9.45	.87	10.88**
	(3)	9.04	.64	
Comprehension	(1)	8.09	1.11	
learning	(2)	8.49	1.09	14.16**
	(3)	10.03	1.35	
Globetrotting	(1)	7.45	.57	
	(2)	8.04	.57	6.87*
	(3)	7.48	.74	
Operation	(1)	10.68	.92	
Learning	(2)	9.91	.96	12.93**
	(3)	9.12	.99	
Improvidence	(1)	7.62	.90	
	(2)	7.82	.81	5.87*
	(3)	6.88	.93	

* p < .01
** p < .001

The differences were examined in two ways.   The
mean values for each of the subscales by subject area
(science, social science, and arts) are shown in Table
9.1.   The means for each discipline and each department were also calculated.   It is clear from the
average scores for departments and subject areas that
operation learning and comprehension learning are
associated with types of discipline in the expected
way: operation learning receives higher scores in
science, comprehension learning in arts and social
science.   Globetrotting and improvidence are also
related to type of discipline, but less strongly.
Globetrotting is highest in psychology departments, and improvidence in economics departments.
Globetrotting is no more common in arts departments
than in science ones.   On this evidence, it cannot
be unequivocally stated that learning pathologies
are a function of the type of discipline studied.
Deep approach and relating ideas are most

common in arts and social science departments, confirming the predictions, but use of evidence and intrinsic motivation are only weakly associated with subject area, although in the expected directions. The other large differences between subject areas are in the subscales of syllabus-boundness, extrinsic motivation, disorganized study methods - rather surprisingly - and achievement motivation. Most of these differences conform with the theoretical predictions; for some reason, however, it would seem that arts students are less likely to have poor study methods.

Even when the effects of subject area and discipline are large and significant, it should be emphasised that there are still considerable differences between individual departments.

FACTOR ANALYSIS OF THE CPQ AND APPROACHES TO STUDYING INVENTORY

It will be remembered from chapter 7 that factor analysis of the CPQ produced two main factors: positive evaluation of teaching and courses and formal vocational teaching. Analysis of the approaches to studying inventory had revealed three principal orientations: meaning, reproducing, and achieving/disorganized and dilatory. Factor analysis of the two sets of subscales together provides one way of examining the relationships between students' approaches and the context of learning in academic departments.

Table 9.2 gives the results of this analysis. Three factors (numbers I, III and V) are recognisable as the main studying orientations; factors II and IV are the formal-vocational and evaluative dimensions respectively; factor VI describes confident students with good entry qualifications. The interviews suggested that students respond to the departmental context in which they work by adopting different levels of approach. Although there is not a lot of overlap between the two sets of scales in this analysis, what there is makes good sense when compared with the interview findings. The reproducing orientation is associated with a heavy workload (factor III), disorganized and dilatory attitudes with perceived lack of clarity in goals (factor V), the evaluative factor with intrinsic motivation and use of evidence in learning (factor IV), and the formal-vocational factor with extrinsic motivation (factor II).

184

Table 9.2   FACTOR ANALYSIS OF APPROACHES TO STUDYING AND COURSE
             PERCEPTIONS SCALES (N = 2208)

Variables	Factors (54% variance explained)					
	I	II	III	IV	V	VI
Academic performance						
School						29
Higher education	26		(-20)		-45	
Approaches to studying						
Deep approach	71			(22)	-29	
Relating ideas	67			(21)		
Use of evidence	52			28	-29	31
Intrinsic motivation	64			39	-27	-34
Surface approach			61			-30
Syllabus-boundness	-38	26	53			
Fear of failure			58		26	
Extrinsic motivation		47	37			-51
Strategic approach	27				-37	-26
Disorganized study methods					54	
Negative attitudes to studying	-28			-32	52	
Achievement motivation					-32	
Comprehension learning	60					
Globetrotting					44	
Operation learning			56		-29	-30
Improvidence			65			-33
Course perceptions						
Formal teaching methods		75				
Clear goals and standards		53		38	-25	
Workload			45	(-23)		
Vocational relevance		73				
Good teaching				77		
Freedom in learning		-28		50		
Openness to students				79		
Social climate		25		47		

Decimal points and most loadings less than .25 omitted

To what extent are the approaches to studying
factors, and the relationships between the CPQ and
approaches to studying scales shown in Table 9.2,
artefacts of area of study differences in the
relationship between learning and its context?   When
separate factor analyses by subject area are carried
out (Ramsden and Entwistle, 1981) meaning orientation
(factor 1) retains its emphasis on syllabus-freedom
and its stylistic component of comprehension learning \

across all three subject areas. This approach is
related to less formal teaching methods in science
and social science, to freedom in learning and good
teaching, and - in arts - to a good social climate
and clear goals. Reproducing orientation (factor
III) is consistently defined in all the subject
areas. It is related to a heavy workload. Factor
V, representing a disorganized and dilatory approach
to studying, is associated with the learning pathology
of globetrotting and, especially in arts, to comprehension learning. This suggests that comprehension learning carried to extremes (and unleavened
by operation learning) in arts subjects may lead to
globetrotting. A similar result was found for
certain arts and social science students in the
interviews. On the other hand, operation learning
seems to be associated with improvidence in all three
subject areas equally (factor III).

Factor IV (departmental evaluation) was linked
to positive attitudes and meaning orientation in all
three faculties. This result also conforms with
the interview data.

EFFECTS OF DEPARTMENTAL CONTEXTS ON STUDENT LEARNING

The next step was to examine in more detail the
relationships between context and approaches to
studying while controlling for the effects of subject
areas. The interviews had shown that deep approaches
and favourable attitudes to studying were functionally related to students' perceptions of good teaching. Unhelpful and uncommitted teaching was thought
by the students who were interviewed to encourage
poor attitudes to studying and surface approaches.
Surface approaches were strongly associated with perceived deficiences in the assessment system and with
a lack of freedom in learning. In spite of the
controls used in the interview analyses, however,
these findings were still to some extent impressionistic and subjective, although the relationships
appeared to be important ones. The connection
between surface approaches and assessment methods
was in accordance with deductions from earlier
findings, but the relationship betwen quality of
teaching and deep approaches had not previously been
demonstrated. Indeed, Marton's work had shown how
difficult it was to induce a deep approach experi-
mentally (Marton, 1975; Marton and Säljö, 1976b).

There are hints in the factor analyses that the
same processes identified in the interviews operate
in this larger sample of students. But the

analysis so far described are based entirely on individual <u>students</u> as cases.   Clearly, it might be argued, poor students will attribute their inability to poor teaching and too much work.   A more convincing explanation would be provided if a unit of analysis representing <u>departments</u>, rather than individual students, were employed.

In order to do this, a set of analyses of covariance was performed on the departmental mean values of several subscales, students' pre-entry levels of achievement, and composite variables formed by combining subscales identified in the factor analyses.   It was predicted that departments which were positively evaluated by their students would:

(a)   have higher meaning orientation mean scores;
(b)   have lower reproducing orientation mean scores;
(c)   have lower disorganised and dilatory mean scores

than departments which were negatively evaluated.

Composite variables measuring different orientations and evaluation dimensions were formed as follows:

Meaning orientation	Deep approach + relating ideas + use of evidence + intrinsic motivation
Reproducing orientation	Surface approach + syllabus-boundness + fear of failure + improvidence
Disorganised and dilatory attitudes	Disorganised study methods + negative attitudes to studying + globe-trotting
Evaluation variable 1	Good teaching + freedom in learning
Evaluation variable 2	Freedom in learning - workload

These variables, all of which are measurements of departments' mean scores, were constructed after examining the results of the factor analyses and also took into account the interview findings.   A third evaluation variable was used in the preliminary analysis but later rejected.   It consisted of openness to students + freedom in learning + good teaching.   A preliminary analysis showed that openness to students was unrelated to any of the criterion variables;   it seems to be a measurement of students' satisfaction with the department but does not help to explain the quality of their learning.

We can summarize the main analysis of covariance results as follows.   The effects of the evaluation

variables on orientations and attitudes were similar
in all the disciplines (there were no significant
interaction effects).* A heavy workload combined
with a lack of freedom in learning was strongly
related to an orientation towards reproducing in a
department's students (p < .001). Meaning orientation
was related to the perceived presence of freedom in
learning combined with good teaching in the department (p < .01). The way in which a department
organizes its courses, and its methods of teaching
them, seems to have a considerable effect on whether
its students develop an orientation towards meaning.
The effect is positive; one of the central results
of the interview study is confirmed.

The interviews revealed that favourable
attitudes towards studying were associated with good
teaching and with choice over method and content of
study. The inventory dimension apparently closest
to describing these attitudes is the disorganized
and dilatory component shown in the factor analyses,
with its high loadings on globetrotting, negative
attitudes, and disorganized study methods. This
orientation was found to be unrelated either to
discipline or to the evaluation variables, but
positive attitudes to studying were found to be
associated with good teaching and freedom in learning
(p < .03). This is consistent with the factor
analysis result linking departmental evaluation to
positive attitudes in all subject areas and, of
course, with the interview results reported in the
previous chapter.

Similar conclusions are reached following
multiple discriminant analyses of the departmental
mean scores. Extreme groups of departments were
formed to see whether typical orientations could be
predicted by students' perceptions. Groups were
formed by selecting the two highest and the two
lowest departmental mean scores in each of the six
disciplines, so that each group consisted of twelve
departments. This procedure automatically controlled
for the effects of different disciplines. One set
of departments was made up by choosing the highest
and lowest meaning orientation departments, another
by selecting the highest and lowest reproducing
orientation departments, and a third consisted of the
highest and lowest disorganized and dilatory attitudes

---

* It was also impossible to detect any influence on
the relationship between orientations and contexts
of the type of department defined by mean 'A' level
grade score of its students.

departments.   Separate analyses were performed on
each.
        The functions discriminating between departments
which had high and low mean scores on the disorganised and dilatory dimension were not significant.
Extreme departments in terms of meaning orientation
were predicted best by good teaching and freedom in
learning.   Using these two variables alone, 71% of
the departments could be placed in their correct
groups, the prediction being better for the low
meaning orientation departments than the high ones.
This seems consistent with the Gothenburg findings
concerning the difficulty of inducing a deep approach
and the relative ease with which its opposite can be
encouraged.   It seems that departments without good
teaching and freedom in learning effectively act to
prevent the development of meaning orientation in
their students;   departments which are positively
evaluated encourage meaning orientation by providing
the right conditions for it to grow - but it is not
a necessary consequence.
        The discriminant function for the reproducing
orientation groups was defined mainly by workload
(.84), freedom in learning (-1.20), and vocational
relevance (.77), when all the CPQ variables were
included.   The prediction results for this group
were slightly more accurate, again in accordance
with the expectation suggested by the Swedish
research.

ACADEMIC PROGRESS IN DIFFERENT DEPARTMENTAL CONTEXTS

        Relationships between approaches to studying
and academic performance (both self-rated and as
defined by first-year grades) in the different
subject areas were examined in Chapter 4.   The use
of the course perceptions questionnaire provided an
opportunity to analyse possible interactions between
approaches to studying and types of context (defined
separately from subject area) in relation to self-
rated academic progress.   Do students with contrasting orientations to studying see themselves to
be performing equally well (or equally badly) in
departments of different kinds?
        In order to examine the effect of different
orientations to studying on performance while controlling for discipline, groups of departments were
formed in terms of different extreme contexts.   Thus
the two departments in each discipline with the
highest mean scores on good teaching were compared
with the two with the lowest mean scores on good

teaching, and so on.   Correlations between self-
ratings of performance and the composite variables
representing meaning orientation, reproducing orientation, and disorganized and dilatory approaches,
were then computed.   For the purpose of these
analyses, another composite variable, accomplished
learning, was created.   This was intended to represent more accurately the consistent deep + strategic approach identified in the interviews.   It
consisted of meaning orientation + strategic approach
+ comprehension learning + syllabus-freedom + positive
attitudes to studying (compare the loadings on these
variables in the factor analyses).

The correlations presented in Table 9.3 cannot
be regarded as more than suggestive of the possible
interactions between contexts and orientations, but
they are of much interest.   Meaning orientation is
perceived to be related to academic progress most
strongly in conditions of freedom in learning with
light workload.   Reproducing orientation is least
penalized when the teaching is poor and there is
little freedom in learning, while disorganized and
dilatory approaches are least effective under the
same conditions and are always fairly strongly
related to poor performance.   Accomplished learning
is strongly favourable to progress in all conditions,
but particularly so when the teaching is poor and
there is freedom in learning.

All these associations are consistent with the
results so far presented and with the interview data.
It requires no great effort of imagination to picture
the consistent deep-level, strategic students such
as those identified in the interviews (for example,
psychology, student 5) perceiving deficiencies in the
teaching, and freedom of choice, as challenges to
perform better;   nor to see the disorganized student
hoping that the helpfulness of his lecturers will
enable him to progress more effectively.   It remains
disturbing that the reproducing students, responding
to a context of restricted choice over method and
content of study combined with ineffective teaching,
feel that their strategy will not be too heavily
penalized, while at the same time students orientated
towards meaning feel themselves least likely to do
well when the workload is heavy and there is little
freedom in learning.

CONCLUSIONS

The results we have described in this chapter,
taken in conjunction with the interview findings,

Table 9.3   CORRELATIONS BETWEEN ORIENTATIONS TO STUDYING AND PERFORMANCE UNDER DIFFERENT EXTREME CONDITIONS, CONTROLLING FOR DISCIPLINE

Conditions (types of department)	Meaning orientation	Orientations to studying Reproducing orientation	Disorganized and dilatory approach	Accomplished learning
Highest freedom in learning	28	-25	-40	35
Lowest freedom in learning	25	-23	-35	29
Highest good teaching	23	-26	-28	27
Lowest good teaching	30	-18	-42	36
Highest freedom in learning and good teaching	30	-28	-37	36
Lowest freedom in learning and good teaching	26	-16	-47	34
Highest workload	23	-24	-43	31
Lowest workload	26	-21	-27	32
Highest workload with lowest freedom in learning	22	-20	-39	28
Lowest workload with highest freedom in learning	32	-26	-33	37

Decimal points omitted

show quite clearly that students' perceptions of teaching and assessment methods in academic departments are significantly associated with, and probably causally related to, students' approaches to studying. Self-rated student performance is related both to perceptions of courses and to orientations to learning. To have identified these effects and interactions is not to imply that individual differences are unimportant variables in the explanation of approaches and academic progress. But these findings do suggest that it might be possible to make improvements in the quality of student learning in higher education by alterations to the contexts in which it occurs. These implications are examined together with conclusions drawn from the other parts of the investigation in the next chapter.

Chapter Ten

LEARNING AND TEACHING IN HIGHER EDUCATION

INTRODUCTION

This final·chapter is an attempt to highlight what we think are the distinctive contributions to understanding learning and teaching made by our research programme. Our main aims were to explore the contrasting ways in which students approach studying and in what ways academic departments may influence those approaches. What can now be said about these individual and contextual differences? What practical implications can be drawn from this research for improving teaching and learning in higher education? And finally, how successful was the attempt to make use of different methodologies in investigating how student learn?

HOW STUDENTS LEARN: APPROACHES AND OUTCOMES

The insistent contrast between students' ways of studying revealed by this research is, of course, between deep and surface (or meaning and reproducing) approaches to learning. Several different studies within our research programme show how the distinctions suggested in the work of Marton and Biggs have been developed. Repeated factor analyses of successive versions of the approaches to studying inventory confirmed the importance of the meaning and reproducing orientations in all the academic disciplines we investigated. Although it is also possible to identify other orientations to studying, the evidence here is less consistent. The final analyses suggested that the third main dimension - the achieving or strategic orientation - would have to be divided into positive and negative components (strategic orientation and non-academic orientation). The inventory has already been used with students elsewhere - the Open University and Australian National University - with similar but not identical factor structures being reported.

The questionnaire variant of Marton's research method for investigating outcomes and processes of learning with academic articles also showed the deep-surface distinction between approaches to learning. In spite of difficulties in finding appropriate articles and in coding the responses, the analysis again showed the clear links between approaches and levels of understanding reported by Marton (Marton and Saljo, 1976a). Furthermore, it indicated that there were differences within the deep approach between students who were seeking personal meaning, and those who relied more on evidence and detail in building up understanding.

Qualitative analysis of the interview data (chapter 8) confirmed the importance of the fundamental difference between deep and surface approaches. Although the distinction was seen to apply to many subject areas, it had to some extent to be re-interpreted within contrasting academic contexts. In other words, the meaning of the concepts subtly shifts in relation to different disciplines. In science departments a deep approach involves considerable emphasis on detail and procedures, and may even require a preliminary stage of rote learning difficult to distinguish from a surface approach. In humanities and social sciences, we saw how personal reinterpretation, related especially to experience of the world of people rather than things, was most important in carrying out a deep approach. A hint of a similar distinction was also found in the small-scale study of sixth-formers reported in chapter 4. Deep approaches were associated with high A-level grades in both arts and science, but successful scientists also used attention to detail and memorization.

Our research has confirmed the relationships between approaches and outcomes illustrated in the work of Marton and his colleagues. Approach and level of understanding are closely linked, not only in experimental situations but also in the realistic setting of conventional assessments. The learning experiments and the questionnaire on outcome and process (chapters 5 and 6) demonstrated the connection in a controlled context, while the inventory and interviews revealed similar relation-ships between approaches and either self-rated academic progress or degree classifications. Students in the interview study, for example, who used consistently deep approaches, and those who used highly

strategic methods to handle assessment tasks, were
more likely to obtain First or Upper Second class
honours degrees. The reproducing orientation was
related to poor self-rated performance and the
meaning orientation to higher self-ratings in the
inventory survey; similar, although rather weaker
relationships between these orientations and first
year marks have been reported in the Australian study.
The strongest relationships with poor academic performance in the Lancaster research have been with
the non-academic orientation. It is also interesting
to see indications of subject area differences in the
correlations. Reproducing orientation is associated
with poor results especially in arts, while strategic
orientation has its strongest positive relationship
with progress in science subjects. These findings
undoubtedly confirm the usefulness of the inventory
scales and the deep and surface concepts for describing realistic differences in students' ways of
approaching their work.

INTERNAL AND EXTERNAL ORIENTATIONS TO STUDYING

It may be most helpful to see the difference
between deep and surface approaches to academic tasks
in terms of the student's intention. The deep
approach is internal - to the content of the article
or problem, and to the knowledge, experience and
interests of the learner. The surface approach is
external - towards the task and its requirements, and
implies a process of learning in which alien material
is to be impressed on the memory for a limited period
and with the specific intention of satisfying external demands. There is no expectation that the content will become a continuing part of the learner's
cognitive structure.
Using this distinction between external and
internal orientations to studying, we can see how
deep and surface approaches are a special case of a
more general tendency which can be found in several
very recent studies in addition to our own. For
example, Taylor, Gibbs and Morgan (1981) have discovered marked differences between students at the
Open University and a conventional university in what
benefits they expected to derive from higher education.
The Open University students showed predominantly
personal goals, but within these the orientation could
still be external (compensating for earlier academic
failure) or internal (broadening horizons, interests,
and capabilities). At the conventional university
the students showed mainly academic or vocational

Learning and Teaching in Higher Education

goals, but again these could be subdivided into extrinsic (grades or qualifications)and intrinsic
(knowledge and skill) categories.
     The distinction between external and internal
orientation is at the heart of our own meaning and
reproducing orientations as shown in the inventory
subscales making up the two main dimensions.
Students relying on reproducing information allow
staff to define learning tasks and are interested in
courses mainly for the qualifications they offer.
In contrast students looking for meaning are interested in the work itself and interact critically with
what they are learning.   The distinction can also be
seen clearly in a recent interview analysis (Thompson,
1981) which contrasted two groups of students high or
low in scores on syllabus-boundness (Parlett, 1970).
The attitudes of these "sylbs" and "sylfs" are
dramatically different.   The sylbs accept the
lectures and examinations without question; they
focus on the course as formally defined.   In contrast
all the sylfs reject, even abhor, examinations, and
actively dislike lectures (see Entwistle, 1981).
Other interview studies (Hodgson, 1981; Manook and
King, 1981)also bring out the way in which students
see teaching in terms of its external (assessment
orientation) or internal (personal interest and
knowledge) characteristics.
     This distinction between whether a student
focuses in the intrinsic (internal) or extrinsic
(external) functions of educational experiences seems
to be the broadest way of conceptualising differences
in learning.   But by its very broadness it runs the
risk of oversimplifying the complicated differences
in how students learn.   We need to remember that
most students will be both intrinsically and extrinsically orientated at different times; that
students' approaches are strongly influenced by the
characteristics of the discipline studied and the
teaching received.   It is also important to recognize that students may have distinct preferences for
different (but equally effective) ways of tackling
academic tasks.   It is particularly important to
bear these complicating issues in mind if we seek to
apply the findings of this research to our own
learning and teaching, as will be clear in a moment.

HOW STUDENTS LEARN: STYLES, STRATEGIES AND INDIVIDUAL
DIFFERENCES

     The research reported in this book has shown
that Pask's distinctions between styles and

196

strategies of learning (see chapter 2) are an additional dimension which needs to be taken into account when we try to describe how students learn. Some of the analyses of the approaches to studying inventory made it clear that separate holist and serialist factors could be identified. The question-naire study of students' approaches to reading, described in chapter 6, revealed that the deep approach was better defined in terms of two dimensions One factor represented an emphasis on personal mean-ing, while the other showed higher loadings on previous knowledge and the use of detail. The result of the experiments in chapter 5 also seemed to indi-cate stylistic differences in studying. We saw how personal reinterpretation was again separate from concentrating on evidence, although it also seemed to be linked to a rather casual approach reminiscent of globetrotting - the overreadiness to jump to con-clusions on scanty evidence. Where globetrotting is linked with a deep approach, it is clear that we are describing no more than a deep passive approach which will shade into a surface approach. In the main approaches to studying survey a surface approach was usually associated with both learning pathologies - improvidence and globetrotting. Thus stylistic differences are apparent not only in the way differ-ent students reach understanding, but also in the ways they fail to do so.

It also seems likely that students with different styles of learning are attracted to different subject areas. We saw in chapter 8 how contrasting styles of learning are part of the common-sense understanding of students. Students' own descriptions of differences in styles and strategies of learning in arts and science departments were strongly reminiscent of Pask's characterizations of comprehension and operation learning and of Hudson's (1968) descriptions of the stereotypes of arts and science teachers held by pupils.

How should we explain these contrasting ways of seeking understanding - one relying more on personal meaning and interpretation, and the other drawing more on previous knowledge, concentration on detail, and logical argument? Analyses of the relationships between learning styles and personality traits suggested that it does make sense to regard students' patterns of studying as being relatively stable and consistent. Although there were relationships between approaches to learning and both convergent and divergent thinking, the correlations were small. Much closer associations were found between the indicators of styles of learning and personality traits. The evidence must still be treated as tentative, but it may be helpful to view styles as being more a characteristic of the individual, and approaches as being more obviously affected by the context of studying. As approaches and styles are themselves quite closely related, this separation should be seen as no more than a convenient simplification. If we stick closely to the empirical findings, we should be forced to accept that styles and approaches are both relatively stable over time and consistent over subject areas, but that both are also importantly variable between tasks or teachers. The apparent contradiction in this description may be difficult to conceptualize, but it does reflect the complexity of the inter-relationships we find among the constructs used in research on student learning.

Another attempt at simplifying the patterns of results reported in the previous chapters will be found in Figure 10.1. This framework indicates the overlapping relationships between study orientations, approaches to studying, styles of learning, personality, and probable outcomes of learning.

This framework may be helpful in summarizing some of our main empirical findings, but it is also incomplete and potentially misleading. It over-emphasizes the relatively stable individual differences identified and presents a static model of student behaviour. Yet our research contains important additional elements. As we have already argued, consistent differences in styles and approaches to studying represent only part of the whole picture of student learning. It is clear that the content and context of learning need to be taken into account: students often adopt flexible strategies to cope with different academic demands. Our theory would also need to incorporate the developmental changes which students experience through learning more effective approaches to studying.

HOW STUDENTS LEARN: THE EFFECTS OF LEARNING CONTEXT

A very important part of the studies of student learning carried out in Gothenburg was the demonstration of connections between students' approaches and the context of learning. Marton has stressed that the approach to learning should not be seen as a characteristic of the student, but as a response to a situation. The 'natural' approach is a deep

one (Marton, 1976). Although we should also want to
argue that it makes sense to speak of individual
consistency in approaches, the results presented in
the previous chapters show clearly the strong influence of the situation in which learning takes place.
There are important interactions between the context
and individual differences. For example, some
students are better able than others to 'manage'
adverse conditions.

The most crucial variable, as Fransson's
original experiment showed (Fransson, 1977) is the
student's <u>perception</u> of what he is required to do.
The effects of contrasting perceptions can be seen
at more than one level. For example, at the level
of the learning task itself, perceived interest and
relevance undoubtedly increase intrinsic motivation
and make a deep approach more likely to occur.
Tasks which are perceived as requiring only reproduction, or on which the student is mainly extrinsically motivated, increase the probability of a
surface approach. These relationships, originally
shown in Marton's work, were most apparent in the
interview study described in chapter 8. It was
also found that a student's interest in the subject
matter of the task was a crucial component of a deep
approach, especially in arts and social science
subjects, while prerequisite knowledge was most often
mentioned in relation to science tasks.

The second level at which the effects of learning context operate is that of the individual
lecturer. The attitudes and enthusiasm of a
lecturer, his concern for helping students to understand, and particularly his ability to understand the
difficulties experienced by students in dealing with
a new topic, are all likely to affect his students'
approaches and attitudes to studying. It is
perhaps important to note that our research deals
only with students' perceptions of a lecturer's
qualities, and the questionnaire covered only certain
aspects of teaching. Further research is necessary
to explore more fully the important influences of
individual lecturers on their students' approaches
to learning. It would also be necessary to explore
whether effective learning depends on a correspondence between teaching style and preferred learning style.

The final level at which perceptions affect
students' learning relates to departments. Of the
differing ways in which departments are organized,
the most crucial influences on approaches to learning concern the forms of assessment. It is

Figure 10.1 A FRAMEWORK SUMMARIZING DESCRIPTIONS OF STUDENT LEARNING

Study Orientation	Approach	Style	Stereotypic Personality	Processes	Probable Outcome
Meaning Orientation	Deep active	Versatile	Integrated and balanced personality	Uses evidence critically, argues logically and interprets imaginately	Describing, justifying and criticizing what was learned. (High grades with understanding).
	Deep passive	Comprehension learning	Impulsive introvert with a theoretical orientation	Intuitive, imaginative, thriving on personal interpretation and integrative overview but neglecting evidence	Mentioning overall argument, laced with illustration and anecdote. (Fairly high grades in arts).
Reproducing Orientation	Surface active	Operation learning (sometimes combined with improvidence	Converger with strong economic and vocational interests Neurotic introvert with obsessional characteristics	Attention to detail, cautious and limited interpretation, syllabus-bound and anxiously aware of assessment demands	Accurately describing fact and components of arguments, but not related to any clear overview. (Sometimes high grades in science)

(continued)

Figure 10.1   A FRAMEWORK SUMMARIZING DESCRIPTIONS OF STUDENT LEARNING (continued)

Study Orientation	Approach	Style	Stereotypic Personality	Processes	Probable Outcome
Non-Academic Orientation	Surface passive	Improvidence combined with globe-trotting	Social extrovert with few academic interests or vocational aspirations	Little attention to detail, overreadiness to generalize, superficial treatment and casual interpretation	Mentioning often irrelevant facts within a disordered, haphazard overview. (Low grades)
Strategic Orientation	Deep or surface as necessary	Strategic	Stability and confidence combined with competitive aggressiveness	Detail or meaning as perceived to be required by the teacher	High grades, with or without understanding

unfortunate that the most apparent effects are
negative - students are pushed towards surface
approaches by forms of assessment which seem to
invite, and reward, reproductive answers.

These relationships were shown to be functional
ones in the qualitative data from the student interviews. The correlational analyses of the course
perceptions questionnaire and approaches to studying
inventory, however, perhaps showed most convincingly
the effects of departments and lecturers on student
learning. It was clear that different departments
teaching the same disciplines provided different
learning contexts and that these contexts were
closely associated with the typical approaches to
learning adopted by the students. Perceived good
teaching, and choice over methods and content of
studying, were related to an orientation towards
meaning and to positive attitudes to studying in a
department's students. A lack of choice and a perceived heavy workload was associated with a reproducing orientation.

Besides noting the effects of departments on
their students, it is also important to remember
the characteristics which were not affected. The
differences in departments were not related to either
organized study methods or achievement motivation.
These scales in the inventory are thus probably
describing more stable individual differences or,
at least, they represent aspects of studying not
affected by differences in current departmental
practice.

Taking these findings together, combining the
impressions of causality from the interviews with
the evidence of relationships from the questionnaires,
we can begin to piece together a chain of causality
which necessarily complicates the model of student
learning presented in the previous section.

Positive attitudes to studying, a deep approach,
intrinsic motivation, and academic progress are all
related to good teaching, freedom in learning, and
an avoidance of overloading. If students perceive
the teaching they encounter to be effective, they are
more likely to be interested in the subject matter
to which it relates, and to be able to see its
relevance to their everyday lives. They are, moreover, less likely to question the worth of the
experience of higher education. Combined with
assessment methods perceived to be appropriate, these
contextual characteristics increase the probability
that students will take deep approaches. The probability is further increased, especially in science

subjects, if enough information and background
knowledge associated with the academic task is
available. But perceptions of inappropriate or
excessive assessment, together with a too rigidly
structured curriculum, encourage extrinsic motivation,
engender poor attitudes, and thereby make surface
approaches more likely. The quality of the outcome
of learning is therefore likely to be lower as well.
Of course, all these effects are mediated through
the individual differences between students: each
student will be affected in a different way. It
should also be stressed that we are not simply
arguing that freedom in learning is a guarantee of
deep approaches. Elements of choice and a clear
overall structure are both essential to this model
of the effects of course contexts on student learning.
     We must add yet another complication to the
model. It is clear from the previous chapters that
students' approaches and the effects of teaching have
to be understood in relation to the subject area in
which they take place. Disciplines differ in the
"atmospheres" of learning they provide. Generally,
science departments are seen to have more formal
teaching, clearer goals, more vocational relevance,
better social climates, and less freedom in learning
than arts and social science departments. These
differences are paralleled by typical styles of
learning: operation learning is more common in
science departments, comprehension learning in arts.
We saw earlier how deep and surface approaches have
to be redefined within contrasting subject areas.
Added to that, it seems that styles of learning are
differentially effective, depending on the subject
area. Comprehension learning is most strongly
related to self-rated academic progress in arts
subjects, while operation learning is more effective
in science. Versatility - the combination of
operation learning with comprehension learning - is
especially favourable to progress in science departments. Operation learning is apparently less
necessary in achieving high marks in the arts and
social sciences. These differences in contexts and
styles of learning suggest rather different implications for encouraging deep approaches in different
subject areas.

TOWARDS EFFECTIVE LEARNING

     It should be clear by now that our current
knowledge of student learning permits us to offer the
component parts of a theory of the process of

learning and teaching in higher education, although much work still needs to be done to reach a fully developed theory. In chapter 2 we looked at research by William Perry showing that students report a process of intellectual and ethical development during their time in higher education. The main direction of this change is away from dualistic, right/wrong views of knowledge towards contextual relativistic reasoning - the recognition of the tenative, permeable nature of academic knowledge and of the need to live with this uncertainty. The research described in the earlier chapters of this book did not involve a longitudinal study of individual students over a period of several years, and so no direct evidence of development can be presented here. However, there certainly are logical continuities between several of the concepts discussed in chapter 2, including Perry's, which our own investigations have demonstrated empirically.

The interviews of students in chapter 8 showed particularly well the links between versatility, strategic approaches, and successful learning outcomes. Certain students seem able to choose to take either deep or surface approaches to academic tasks, selecting the approach most appropriate to the demands of assessment and teaching. They adapt to, but are not dominated by, the departmental context. In chapter 9 we also saw how students who were orientated towards both meaning and achievement were apparently less affected by adverse teaching and assessment conditions. Some students in the interview study were aware of a process of development in their approaches to learning in ways reminiscent of Perry's stages or Säljö's notion of thematization in learning. Remember, for example, the psychology student who spoke of realizing that:

> "there was a structure in the things they were teaching us and it wasn't just a load of facts - that's only a recent, recent realization, perhaps only this term. I started to realize it when I realized that the English I'm doing for my free ninth, er, is very closely connected to psychology ... the novelist seems to be very close to the psychologist, only he writes it in a creative - no, not creative - a more artistic form. And when I realized that those were so close I suddenly realized how interrelated all the topics in psychology were. And that's when I also read some articles on creativity; that's when I suddenly realized that putting

your own pattern on it would probably make a
better essay, and a more enjoyable essay. I've
become more interested in the subject, I think.
I've begun to understand more of the subject,
and perhaps, learned, learned things that, can
apply in my everyday life more successfully.
I mean things like my learning. I've learned,
perhaps, perhaps a better way of learning."

Perry's idea of the relativistic reasoner, Heath's
reasonable adventurer, Pask's versatile learner -
these are all ideal types of successful student. It
would be a mistake to extend these concepts too far
and to suppose that there is one ideal personality
profile or set of values and experiences which
characterizes the effective learner in higher
education. Just as labels denoting learning disabilities in children or students (poorly motivated,
wrong family background, badly organized, and so on)
can all too easily become parts of self-fulfilling
prophecies, so models of ideal students may be unhelpful ways of encouraging effective learning. Our
research has shown, in contrast, that a bewildering
variety of approaches to learning exists in higher
education; different combinations suit different
students and can be equally successful or unsuccessful depending on the characteristics both of the
individual and of the learning context. It is
nevertheless true that the ability attributed by
Heath to the reasonable adventurer, to 'alternate
between the curious and the critical', or in our work
the alternation between a general view and the detailed examination of the evidence, is one which higher
education should aim to foster. The question which
then arises is how that ability is to be developed,
taking into account the individual, interdisciplinary,
and contextual differences, and the numerous roads
to understanding, which our research has revealed.

IMPLICATIONS FOR PRACTICE AND POLICY

The research described in this book does not
provide a blueprint for designing effective learning
in higher education. It does, however, offer a
much-needed theoretical and empirical rationale for
practical efforts to improve learning and teaching.
We have seen that the process of student learning in
relation to individual student differences and to its
context is much more complicated than lecturers and
students are often prepared to admit. The findings
of the research need to be reinterpreted by

205

lecturers in relation to the particular difficulties of their students and their subject area. Suitable teaching strategies must take account of contextual and individual differences. We hope that one of the most important messages to come from this research is that commonsense theories of "good" and "weak" students, conceptions of single "ideal" methods of studying, and teaching technologies purporting to be universally applicable in different subject areas, are all of dubious practical value to lecturers and students. But what can now be said about the steps which might be taken to improve learning in higher education?

If universities and polytechnics seek to encourage greater versatility in their students, then the evidence of this research is that a two-pronged attack is needed. On the one hand intervention focused on <u>students</u> themselves is required; on the other, efforts to change <u>teaching and assessment</u> to provide fertile conditions for the growth of approaches aimed at understanding are necessary.

IMPROVING STUDYING

We have seen that students in higher education use a variety of approaches to learning. Not only do the same students vary their approaches in response to different perceived requirements, but different students differ in their individual preferences. The finding that a deep approach can be carried out with contrasting emphases on comprehension and operation learning suggests that we should not try to change a student's learning style, except as a last resort when it is creating serious difficulties for the student. On the other hand it is valuable to help students to become more aware of their characteristic style and approach, to show how they may most effectively capitalize on their intellectual strengths and at the same time transcend the limitations of a particular style. The improvident serialist needs help to practise the skills of developing ideas and analogies; the globe-trotting holist ought to be given opportunities to practise the handling of details to support his ideas. Students could also benefit from opportunities to become more confident in exploring personal strategies which effectively cope with different academic tasks and assessment requirements. Some will probably need help with specific study skills (reading for understanding, constructing analytic essays, writing effective laboratory reports, and so on). But all students will gain from being encouraged to raise their awareness and to think about ways of developing flexible learning strategies - the higher order skill of orchestrating the component techniques.

Many students will need a good deal of help in recognizing the very different strategies required to respond appropriately to the wide variety of tasks set by lecturers. Our first recommendation is that direct teaching of study strategies, combined with individual remedial help for students experiencing special learning difficulties, ought to be provided in our universities and polytechnics. The incidence of surface approaches in students shows clearly that many have not mastered effective study processes. Students take time to develop - if they develop at all - a repertoire of strategies enabling them to deal effectively with academic demands. Although many schemes have been devised to improve study skills, few have taken seriously the wide range of strategies which can be shown to be effective. The increased use of study skills programmes concentrating solely on techniques, rather than on the development of abilities to structure material with the aim of understanding, would be worse than useless.

Inappropriate organizing techniques, for example, are more of a hindrance than a help in studying. An "ideal" approach shown to be useful for one student may suit others not at all.

Practical ways of running study skills programmes which aim at increasing awareness have already been developed, but they differ in their emphases. Main (1980) and Wankowski (Raaheim and Wankowski, 1981) advocate individual counselling, Gibbs (1981) specializes in discussion methods, while Brew (1981) concentrates on helping students to organize and structure both studying and learning. We accept the value of each of these approaches for particular purposes, but would resist any suggestion that any of these approaches was sufficient in itself. Gibbs, for example, avoids any direct teaching of study skills, partly because the psychological justifications of the 'rules' for better studying are of dubious validity, and partly because students are effective in such different ways that no general rules could be described. In our view it would be beneficial to provide students with the concepts and theories emerging from the current research on student learning. Such a study skills course would draw attention to the importance of organization and structure (in the ways described by Angela Brew, 1981), to the existence of

contrasting styles and approaches, to the need to
adopt versatile and appropriate strategies, and to
the development of a personally satisfying style of
studying which is idiosyncratic but effective.   We
recognize the value of Gibbs' (1981) technique of
helping students to discover from each other the
variety of approaches being used in a situation
which is not threatening to self-confidence.   And
finally it is clear that some difficulties in studying experienced by students have deep emotional
roots, related often to home circumstances, which
can only be helped by a student counsellor with
specialized psychiatric skills, such as Wankowski
(Raaheim and Wankowski, 1981).   This individual
counselling may also be required by other students
who have 'blocks' created by particular academic
tasks, or who cannot make the connections from a
general course or workshop to their own problems.
Alex Main (1980) describes how such students may be
helped by a counselling service.

IMPROVING TEACHING AND ASSESSMENT

      The usefulness of the sort of intervention des-
cribed above is limited.   Study skills programmes
are usually the preserve of specialists outside the
everyday context of student learning - the teaching
and assessment processes of academic departments.
What the research reported in this book has repeatedly
demonstrated is the pervasive effect of this context
of learning on students' approaches to studying and
levels of understanding.   It would probably be more
effective to change the students' environment, which
is the source of many problems, than to concentrate
on helping students to find ways of coping with those
problems (see Wankowski, 1973).   It is sadly true
that disturbing conclusions reached by researchers
and other commentators on higher education during
the last hundred years or so (see, e.g. Whitehead,
1932) are confirmed in our findings.   The evidence
is overwhelming that the quality of student learning
is adversely affected by inappropriate assessment
methods, poor teaching, and the lack of freedom
provided by some courses.   Yet the detrimental
effects may not be visible in the outcomes of conventional assessments, as 'success' is defined by
the criteria adopted by the staff.   Nevertheless
the picture is not entirely sombre.   It is equally
clear that some departments, after allowing for
subject area differences, are more effective than
others at facilitating deep approaches.   We have

seen more than once how intrinsic motivation,
interest and relevance enhance the probability of a
deep approach, while threatening assessment conditions make surface approaches more likely.
Teachers can help to encourage intrinsic motivation
and point out relevant issues; they can equally well
encourage negative attitudes by a lack of concern for
the students' learning difficulties or by a lack of
commitment to their subject. Of course, deep
approaches cannot simply be created by effective
teaching and assessment; we can, however, ensure
that the conditions for understanding are as favourable as possible.

There can be no simple advice given to lecturers,
no magic training programme, which derives from our
research. The type of learning demanded by
different disciplines is clearly different, and so
no general recipe for better teaching and assessment
can be given. In arts, students should be encouraged
to search for personal meaning, which seems to depend
on empathy and openness from staff, informal teaching
(discussion) methods, freedom for students to explore
their interests, and yet, because of that freedom,
the setting of clear goals and standards. In science
and social science, good teaching seems to depend
more on pitching information at the right level and
being alert to student difficulties. A deep
approach in science depends more on operation learning, on relating evidence and conclusion, and on the
appropriate use of a certain amount of initial rote
learning to master the terminology. But this
versatility in learning will emerge readily only
where the workload is reasonable, and where freedom
in learning is allowed. The forms of assessment, the
types of questions, will also need to be consistent
with lecturers' attempts to develop critical thinking.
If factual reproduction of memorized answers is
implicitly encouraged and actively rewarded (through
the marks given), students will shift accordingly
towards surface approaches. Remember the psychology
student in the interview study in chapter 8 who said:

> "I hate to say it, but what you've got to do is
> have a list of the "facts"; you write down ten
> important points and memorize those, then you'll
> do all right in the test ... if you can give a
> bit of factual information - so and so did that,
> and concluded that - for two sides of writing,
> then you'll get a good mark".

Staff are often unaware of the effects that their

assessment demands have on learning. Another
example comes from Gibbs (1981):

> "The scale of this problem quickly became
> apparent when, in an exercise on how students
> actually spent their time before and after the
> course started, it emerged that the students had
> actually been reading more psychology before the
> course started! But the cause was not far
> away. Three-quarters of all their time out-
> side class contact hours was spent writing up
> laboratory reports! This turned out to be
> because laboratory reports were marked severely
> and the students were worried about passing the
> first year ... Their lack of reading was a direct
> consequence of a fear of failure and the per-
> ceived demands of the assessment system ...
> Apparent poor study skill was caused by teachers."

One of the dilemmas in this area seems to be
that attempts to make assessments more reliable, by
using short-answer or multiple-choice questions, or
by introducing detailed marking schemes, are also
perceived as requiring mainly factual answers. It
is certainly clear at school level that marking
schemes are more likely to reward the accretion of
correct pieces of information than evidence of integration and personal understanding. Evidence of
personal understanding depends on the marker's judgement; it is therefore impressionistic and liable to
be unreliable. But it now seems that mechanical
marking schemes may affect not only the validity of
measurement, by concentrating too much on easily
measured aspects of the students' work, but also the
student's approach to learning. It is, however,
possible to develop systematic marking schemes which
give appropriate credit to personal understanding,
based on repeated overall impression marks on
various criteria, or the use of appropriate classification systems for evaluating qualitatively
different outcomes of learning. (Biggs, 1982).
There is, however, much work still to be done on this
problem.
The fact that lecturers in higher education
usually have a great deal of choice over how they are
going to teach and assess means that, all too often,
approaches to teaching reflect a narrow view of the
'best' pedagogical method. Frequently lecturers
will hold dogmatically to the view that one form of
teaching is necessarily superior - at one extreme,
it may be felt that computer managed instruction or

'Personalized Systems of Instruction' (Keller Plan) are the answer to learning problems; at the other, tutor-less discussion groups may be advocated as the only "true" way of learning. The argument from our research is that more, rather than less, variety of teaching methods is likely to be beneficial. Students are too rarely offered alternative ways of learning: choice over the methods of learning available (independent work, essays, lectures, tutorials, etc.) would seem to be not only highly valued by students, but a logical implication of our model of learning which stresses the wide variations among styles and approaches they prefer.

How are we to encourage staff in higher education institutions to respond to the challenge presented by these findings? In part, as we shall see in a moment, the answers must come from policy-makers, who need to offer incentives and support for improving teaching. Staff development programmes in Britain have had only very limited success in the past. We would argue that one of the reasons for their lack of impact is an excessive emphasis on a model of teaching and learning which focuses on lecturers' problems - how to address an audience effectively, how to prepare resource materials, how to run a seminar skilfully. While these things are important, they have tended to detract from the crucial links between how tutors teach and assess, and how effectively their students learn. Staff training and development programmes need to discuss students' problems, as well as those of the teachers - to discuss how the students' difficulties may be created by the staff in some instances. From the evidence of our research, many lecturers show a lack of sensitivity to students' study difficulties, while they are not sufficiently aware of students' approaches to learning or of the effects their methods of assessment have on how their students learn.

Future staff development programmes may thus have to shift away from the concern with teaching techniques towards helping lecturers to understand the effects of their teaching on students' attitudes and approaches. Good teaching, like effective learning, can be realized in many different ways; efficient techniques, either of studying or teaching, are only useful if they can be incorporated within an active and concerned approach, related to the individual's preferences but not dominated by them.

In the last few pages we have looked in turn at some of the implications of our research for helping staff and helping students in higher education. But this separation between students, on the one hand, and teaching and assessment, on the other, is slightly artificial. In the real world improvements in teaching and learning are two sides of the same coin. Perhaps a practical attempt to improve student learning in higher education ought to consider both teachers and students at the same time. This suggests that it would be worthwhile to try to develop students' learning skills by encouraging staff to involve themselves in the process of improving their students' approaches to studying. While doing this, lecturers might also be expected to improve their teaching through a clearer insight into its effects on students.

The kind of staff development and study skills programme this approach would resemble in practice is demonstrated in a continuing project at the University of Melbourne (Frederick, Hancock, James, Bowden and Macmillan, 1981). The main aim of this project has been to develop the abilities and confidence of teaching staff in the faculties of the university so that they can take on what may be an unfamiliar role - helping individual students and groups of students to improve their learning skills. Staffed by a learning skills counsellor and two members of the University's Centre for the Study of Higher Education, the project began by making contact with faculty staff and explaining what it could offer. Its potential value was emphasized by the results of a previous survey of student learning skills in the university. In spite of a highly selective admissions policy and a low withdrawal rate, both students and staff had given evidence of widespread underachievement due to inadequate learning skills.

In several faculties joint activities involving teaching staff, the project team, and students have since become part of the teaching programme. The project's work has concentrated on staff development rather than on working directly with students - an approach which is more efficient and, from the evidence of our research, likely to be more effective. Activities have included shared tutorials, segments in lectures (outlining, for example, different note-taking strategies), staff workshops on studying and learning, learning skills topics in staff development courses and course team meetings, and providing resources to help staff understand better the learning skills difficulties of their students.

What distinguishes this attempt to intervene in learning and teaching is not so much the nature of its activities as its deliberate orientation towards integrating staff development and student learning.   As this book went to press work was about to begin on a formal evaluation of the project, which will make use of several of the measures described in previous chapters to assess the effects of the interventions on the quality of students' learning.   The results of this work will be awaited with interest by all who are concerned with teaching and learning development in higher education.

IMPROVING APPROACHES TO LEARNING AT SCHOOL

It is not only in universities and polytechnics that teachers need to take account of the research presented in this book.   Teachers and examiners in secondary schools should be reminded of the importance of setting assessments which test understanding and demand independent thought, and do not seem to reward simple reproduction.   Teachers should consider ways in which they can make explicit the type of learning that is expected and should adopt teaching methods which promote active thought within a clear structure.   It is also of crucial importance that basic concepts and skills are thoroughly taught to ensure that deep approaches can be undertaken by pupils.

Orientations towards personal meaning or towards reproducing are brought to the experience of higher education by all students.   Study methods and learning pathologies in university students are fully explained neither by stable individual preferences nor by the context of learning in higher education.   It is clear that attitudes and orientations towards studying are powerfully shaped by experiences in school, in particular those associated with external examinations.   The threat of formal examinations, and the revision associated with them, may push pupils towards memorizing: worse, it may leave them with the idea that learning is nothing more than reproducing other people's facts and ideas.

Students often refer explicitly to the problems created by inappropriate approaches to learning developed at school.   For example, Mathias (1981) reports that many students felt that:

"their school experience had somehow distorted their view of learning ... Some (students) even gave fairly graphic accounts of how the 'O' and

213

'A' level system had inculcated an instrumental
view of learning. For instance ... "I used to
work for myself lots in the early days of
secondary school and it took a while to get back
into this habit because (during 'O'and'A' levels)
I was virtually being told what to do. And it
took me a while to get out of that and get back
into doing what I found interesting or if I
didn't find it interesting, to make it interesting"" (pages 6 - 7).

It is probable that a link between teaching
methods in school and approach to learning could be
demonstrated, and that again the twin attack of
modifying approaches to teaching and examining, and
developing in pupils a greater awareness of learning
strategies, could also beneficially affect the quality
of learning in schools. Indeed, it may be at school
level that the major initiative should be taken, to
prevent inappropriate learning strategies becoming
habitual before pupils move on to higher education
or employment.

POLICY ISSUES

How might the research findings presented here
be translated into policy terms, to be used in the
difficult planning issues facing post-compulsory
education in the remaining years of the century?
Educational planners and policy makers have shown a
wary attitude towards research into teaching and
learning in higher education in the past. It seems
likely that they may find themselves obliged to
change. The results of this research certainly do
not give specific procedural guidelines for policy,
but they do deserve to be taken seriously by
educational administrators and planners.
First, it is desirable that models of institutional and systems planning should build into their
analyses qualitative measures of student learning.
It is time to abandon simplistic notions of university
output couched solely in terms of quantitative criteri
- numbers of graduates produced - and to accept that
the effectiveness of a department or an educational
institution also has to take account of the quality
of understanding sought by its students. Second,
efforts need to be made to improve the learning contexts of departments and institutions. The evidence
that student learning can be improved by systematic reappraisal of teaching and courses can no longer be
ignored. Inappropriate assessment methods,

unimaginative teaching, over-rigid courses, an
excessive amount of curricular material - these
weaknesses seem to act against a high quality of
learning.   Yet all are capable of being changed.
An area deserving immediate attention is the assessment systems of our university departments.   There
is a need to develop assessment methods which
genuinely test students' abilities to think critically
and to understand the connections between activities
in the real world and the material they learn in
higher education.   The capacity to reproduce information alone is of limited value in graduate jobs,
either to employers or employees.   Improved assessment methods might decrease the chances of the process and value of university education being ignored
in the outside world (see Dore, 1977; Williams, 1978).
     Another policy issue that should be faced is
student choice of courses.   There is a growing political pressure on institutions to encourage students
to take courses of immediate benefit to the technical
and commercial future of the country.   This
 encouragement might well take the form of substantially reducing the number of places available in
the arts, humanities, and social sciences.   Such
pressure is likely to be resisted, particularly by the
universities, partly because they value a continued
balance between disciplines, but more pragmatically
because such changes imply redundancy for lecturers
in the 'irrelevant' areas of study.
     Our research, however, may suggest a reason for
looking more closely at this issue in relation to
students' academic interests.   Many employers, it
seems, are not looking to universities to supply
specific technical skills: these are taught more
effectively after graduation within the company.
Employers are expecting degree courses to develop
certain general qualities of mind, foremost of which
seems to be the ability to think critically, objective-
ly, flexibly, and quickly, and to apply that thinking
to a wide range of problem situations.   But for this
'deep' approach to occur, our research indicates that
students must have an intrinsic interest in their
content area.   That terminology is perhaps too
cautious.   Students need to engage with the subject,
to develop an intellectual passion to understand.   If
students are studying mainly to obtain a qualification
- however relevant to society's anticipated needs - our
evidence is that there is a greater likelihood that the
knowledge will be obtained passively, in a way which
would not engage those active critical 'faculties'.
It is likely then that relevance, without commitment,

will provide employers with trained personnel without
the intellectual flair which higher education is
expected to awaken.   Of course there is little known
about the extent to which intellectual skills
developed within an academic discipline are trans-
ferable to situations encountered in industry and
commerce.   The experience of, say, the Civil
Service suggests that such skills are transferred,
but the evidence is largely anecdotal.   The argument
that it would be better to develop those skills in
relevant disciplines (such as economics or law) fails
to distinguish two forms of relevance - to the anticipated needs of society and to the individual.   For
intense involvement in studying, personal relevance
is crucial, and policy makers who ignore this factor
could damage the central core of higher education.

This argument for student choice, should not,
however, be taken as a plea for the status quo.   Our
evidence has pointed clearly to the fact that the
types of assessment and teaching predominating in some
departments are unlikely to encourage the intellectual
skills most prized by lecturers.   But if systematic
reappraisal of teaching and assessment practices is
to occur, such activities must be rewarded.   At
present, in universities time spent in improving
teaching may even be indirectly penalized.   Research
output is the main criterion for promotion;   the
investment of a similar proportion of one's time in
improving teaching receives no reward, and it is not
easy to do both things properly at once.   The idea
that teaching might be evaluated is treated with outrage or dismay by many academics, although they accept
without question the judgement of others on the qualit
of their research.   Yet if quality of research may be
judged, then the quality of a teacher's teaching (and
his students' learning) should also be open to similar
evaluation.

Our research can be taken to imply that resources
diverted into changing some established course
structures, and to staff development programmes, would
represent money well invested.   The end to expansion
in higher education means that measures to maintain th
teaching vitality of staff are more than ever needed;
the spectre of an ageing academic population shot
through with cynicism about promotion prospects and
daily more uncertain of its future is depressing in
its implications for the standards of teaching in
higher education.   But at the same time declining
employment prospects mean that attempts to institu-
tionalize staff development are likely to be treated
with growing suspicion and fear.   Changes to well-

established course structures and approaches to teaching will require increased expenditure on experiments in innovation and on programmes of staff development concentrating on improving lecturers' abilities to relate more effectively to their students. It cannot be expected that a diversion of resources to these objectives will be accepted readily. It is important that changes rewarding staff and departments which try to provide high quality teaching, and which are strongly committed to helping their students to learn, should be combined with an emphasis on the individual teacher's responsibilities towards improving his own teaching. A delicate task facing managers of higher education institutions is to develop a climate of self-evaluation and simultaneously to provide rewards for units and individuals that try to enhance the quality of their students' learning.

COMPLEMENTARY APPROACHES TO RESEARCH

Our findings on the approaches to studying adopted by students emphasize the importance of flexibility and versatility; the need to adapt approach to task demands and to alternate between a holistic overall impression and the detailed examination of evidence and logical argument. These findings on students' approaches apply equally well to our own research strategies. Not only have we incorporated into the research design both qualitative methods (open interviewing of students) and quantitative methods (multivariate analyses of questionnaire responses), but there has been a deliberate alternation between the two styles of research. Each has its strengths and its limiations. The open interviews allow major explanatory constructs to emerge out of the students' own descriptions of their experiences of learning and teaching. The interviews cover, at least potentially, the whole range of influences on student learning, and allow both development and variability in strategy to emerge and experience of causality in relationships to be reported. The questionnaires are designed to measure dimensions defined in advance. The questions are closed and restrict freedom of expression. But the strength of relationships between the dimensions of studying is determined by analyzing scale scores and the multivariate analyses enable patterns of relationships to be explored in more controlled and sophisticated ways than are possible in the necessarily impressionistic analyses of interview transcripts.

The alternation of qualitative and quantitative methods can be illustrated in two main ways - first, through the development of the inventory of approaches to studying. The inventory was developed from four main sources - a previous inventory of study methods and motivation, Biggs' study processes questionnaire, Marton's and Pask's descriptions of approaches and styles, and the pilot interviews with students. The previous inventory and Biggs' questionnaire contained, in part, items designed to indicate psychological traits - four forms of motivation. These items, it could be argued, lack ecological validity - they derive from theories of motivation rather than from the experiences of students. But this is only partly true. The early stages of development of such inventories involve asking students not only to respond to the items within the controlled format provided, but also to comment on the items and suggest areas not covered. The dimensions suggested by Marton have even clearer ecological validity; they represent descriptions made by the students themselves The process of developing the inventory involved repeated reconsideration of the sub-scales, adding new items and omitting existing ones, on the basis both of factor analyses and of insights derived from the interviews with students. Thus the dimensions utlimately tapped by the inventory are firmly rooted in the experiences of the students.

The second illustration of alternation comes from the relationship between approaches to learning and methods of teaching and assessing. Repeatedly, in the interviews, students explained how their approache were affected by lecturers and by the forms of assessment they experienced. The interview transcripts provide strong evidence of the perceived causality of these relationships, and individual quotations in the previous chapters have shown in detail what specific aspects of teaching are seen to influence students' learning under particular circumstances. The interviews enable the researcher not only to describe the relationships, but through empathy with the experiences reported, to reconstruct the students' perceptions of reality imaginatively and so to understand more fully the nature of student learning. The multivariate analyses have provided both a quantitativ verification of the insights gained from the interviews, and have also provided additional insights into the complex patterns of relationships that exist, particularly between approaches and styles, and between the outcome of learning and combinations of personal characteristics (study organization and motivation) and departmental contexts (workload and freedom in learning).

We would argue that, in our experience, neither qualitative nor quantitative methods of research taken separately can provide a full and a convincing explanation of student learning. It does not seem possible to integrate the two styles of research: they pull researchers in opposite directions. It may not even be possible for a single researcher to work effectively in both ways: some people have a strong emotional attachment to a way of describing the world which precludes one or other of these styles of research. Research, like learning, is an expression of pervasive underlying cognitive preferences and value systems. Nevertheless it seems essential that an understanding of student learning should be built up from an appropriate alternation of evidence and insights derived from both qualitative and quantitative approaches to research. In our view the strength of our evidence on student learning is the direct result of this inter-play of contrasting methodologies, and has led to a realistic and useful description of approaches and contexts of learning in higher education.

REFERENCES

Allport, G.W. (1963) Pattern and Growth in Personality, New York: Holt, Rinehart and Winston

Amir, V. and Krausz, M. (1974) Factors of satisfaction and importance in an academic setting, Human Relations, 27, 211-223

Ashby, E. (1973) The structure of higher education: a world view, Higher Education, 2, 142-151.

Atkinson, J.W. and Feather, N.T. (1966) A Theory of Achievement Motivation, New York, Wiley

Bartlett, F.C. (1932) Remembering, Cambridge: Cambridge University Press

Beard, R.M., Levy, P.M. and Maddox, H. (1962) Academic performance at university. Educ. Rev., 16, 163-174

Becher, A. and Kogan, M. (1980) Process and Structure in Higher Education, London: Heinemann

Becker, H.S., Geer, B. and Hughes, E.C. (1968) Making the Grade: the Academic Side of College Life. New York: Wiley

Bernstein, B.B. (1971) On the classification and framing of educational knowledge. In Young, M.F.D.(Ed.) Knowledge and Control, London: Collier-Macmillan

REFERENCES

Bieri, J., Atkins, A.L., Briar, J.S., Leaman, R.L., Miller, H. and Tripodi, T. (1966) Clinical and Social Judgement: The Discrimination of Behavioural Information, New York: Wiley

Biggs, J.B. (1976) Dimensions of study behaviour: another look at A.T.I., Br. J. educ. Psychol., 46, 68-80

Biggs, J.B. (1978) Individual and group differences in study processes, Br. J. educ. Psychol., 48, 266-279

Biggs, J.B. (1979) Individual differences in study processes and the quality of learning outcomes, Higher Education, 8, 381-394

Biggs, J.B. and Collis, K.E. (1982) Evaluating the Quality of Learning: the SOLO Taxonomy, New York Academic Press

Biglan, A. (1973a) The characteristics of subject matter in different academic areas, Journal of Applied Psychology, 57, 195-203

Biglan, A. (1973b) Relationships between subject matter characteristics and the structure and output of university departments Applied Psychology, 57, 204-213.

Birney, R.C., Burdick, H., and Teevan, R C. (1969) Fear of Failure, New York: Van Nostrand

Brennan, J.L. and Percy, K.A. (1977) What do students want? An analysis of staff and student perceptions in British higher education. In Bonboir, A. (ed.), Instructional Design in Higher Education, European Association for Research and Development in Higher Education, 1, 125-152

Brew, A. (1981) Underlying themes in study methods teaching. Paper presented at the 5th International Conference on Higher Education, 1-4 September 1981, University of Lancaster

Broadbent, D.E. (1966) The well-ordered mind, Am. educ. Res. J., 3, 281-295

Bronowski, J. (1965) The Identity of Man, London: Heinemann

Burt, C. (1965) Factorial studies of personality and their bearing on the work of teachers, Br. J. educ. Psychol., 35, 368-378

Burt, C. (1971) The mental differences between childre In Cox C.B. and Dyson, A.E. (Eds.) The Black Papers on Education. London: Davis Poynter

Butcher, H.J. and Rudd, E. (1972) Contemporary Problems in Higher Education, London: McGraw-Hill

Cattell, R.B. (1965) The Scientific Analysis of Personality, Harmondsworth: Penguin

REFERENCES

Centra, J.A. (1976) Student ratings of instruction
    and their relationship to student learning,
    Princeton, N.J.: Educational Testing Service
Craik, F.T.M. and Lockhart, R.S. (1972) Levels of
    processing: a framework for memory research,
    J. verb. Learn. verb. Behav., 11, 671-684
Craik, F.I.M. and Tulving, E. (1975) Depth of pro-
    cessing and the retention of words in spisodic
    memory, J. exp. Psychol (Gen.), 104, 268-294
Crutchfield, R.S. (1962) Conformity and creative
    thinking In Gruber, H.E. Terrell, G., and
    Wertheimer, M. (Eds.), Contemporary Approaches
    to Creative Thinking, New York: Atherton
Dahlgren, L.O. (1978) Qualitative differences in con-
    ceptions of basic principles in Economics
    Paper read to the 4th International Conference
    on Higher Education at Lancaster, 29th August-
    1st September, 1978
Dahlgren, L.O. and Marton, F. (1978) Students' con-
    ceptions of subject matter: an aspect of
    learning and teaching in higher education,
    Studies in Higher Educ., 3, 25-35
de Bono, E. (1971) The Use of Lateral Thinking,
    Harmondsworth: Penguin
Dore, R. (1977) The Diploma Disease, London: Unwin
Dubin, R. and Taveggia, T. (1969) The Teaching-
    Learning Paradox, Eugene, Oregon: University of
    Oregon Press
Entwistle, N.J. (1975) How students learn: information
    processing, intellectual development and con-
    frontation, Higher Education Bulletin, 3, 129-148
Entwistle, N.J. (1979) Stages, levels, styles or
    strategies: dilemmas in the description of
    thinking, Educ. Rev., 31, 123-132
• Entwistle, N.J. (1981) Styles of Learning and Teaching:
    An Integrative Outline of Educational Psychology,
    Chichester: Wiley
Entwistle, N.J. and Bennett, S.N. (1973) The inter-
    relationships between Personality, Divergent
    Thinking and School Attainment, Final Report to
    the SSRC on project MR 1346
Entwistle, N.J. and Entwistle, D.M. (1970) The
    relationships between personality, study methods
    and academic performance, Br. J. educ. Psychol.,
    40, 132-41
Entwistle, N.J., Hanley, M. and Ratcliffe, G. (1979a)
    Approaches to learning and levels of understanding,
    Br. J. educ. Res., 5, 99-114
Entwistle, N.J., Hanley, M. and Hounsell, D.J. (1979b)
    Identifying distinctive approaches to studying,
    Higher Educ., 8, 365-380

REFERENCES

Entwistle, N.J. and Percy, K.A. (1971) Educational objectives and student performance within the binary system. In Research into Higher Education 1970, London: S.R.H.E.

Entwistle, N.J. and Percy, K.A. (1974) Critical thinking or conformity? An investigation of the aims and outcomes of higher education. In Research into Higher Education 1973, London: S.R.H.E.

Entwistle, N.J.,Thompson, J.B.,and Wilson, J.D. (1974) Motivation and study habits. Higher Educ., 3, 379-96

Entwistle, N.J. and Wilson, J.D. (1970) Personality, study methods and academic performance, Univ. Quart., 21, 147-66

Entwistle, N.J. and Wilson, J.D. (1977) Degrees of Excellence: The Academic Achievement Game, London: Hodder & Stoughton

Eysenck, H.J. (1965) Fact and Fiction in Psychology, Harmondsworth: Penguin

Eysenck, H.J. (1970) The Structure of Human Personality, London: Routledge and Kegan Paul

Eysenck, H.J. and Eysenck, S.B.G. (1969) 'Psychoticism in children: a new personality variable, Res. in Educ., 1, 21-37

Fearn-Wannan, H. (1979) Students' perceptions of lecturers as determinants of academic performance in first-year chemistry. Paper presented at the Annual Conference of the S.R.H.E., Brighton, December 1979

Fransson, A. (1977) On qualitative differences in learning. IV - Effects of motivation and test anxiety on process and outcome, Br. J. Educ.
* Psychol., 47, 244-257

Gaff, J.G.,Crombag, H.F.M. and Chang, T.M. (1976) Environments for learning in a Dutch university, Higher Education, 5, 285-299

Gamson, Z.F. (1966) Utilitarian and normative orientations toward education, Sociology of Education, 39, 46-73

Gibbs, G. (1981) Teaching Students to Learn, Milton Keynes: Open University Press

Glaser, B. and Strauss, A. (1967) The Discovery of Grounded Theory, New York: Aldine

Godfrey Thomson Unit (1971) Advanced Verbal Reasoning Test, Edinburgh: University of Edinburgh, Department of Education

Hajnal, J. (1972) The Student Trap, Harmondsworth: Penguin

Hartnett, R.T. and Centra, J.A. (1977) The effects of academic departments on student learning, J. Higher Educ., 48, 491-507

* (Frederick et al - see end)

REFERENCES

Heath, R. (1964) The Reasonable Adventurer,
    Pittsburgh: University of Pittsburgh Press
Heist, P. and Yonge, G. (1960), Omnibus Personality
    Inventory, New York: Psychological Corporation
Hermans, B.M.J. (1979) Student and system: academic
    success and study problems in relation with
    characteristics of the academic environment and
    of the students.   In Van Trotsenburg, E.A. (Ed.),
    Higher Education: A Field of Study, 5 vols.
    Bern: Verlag Peter Lang
Hodgson, V.E. (1981) The use of stimulated recall in
    education research. Paper presented at the 5th
    International Conference on Higher Education,1
    - 4 September, University of Lancaster
Hoyle, F. (1950) The Nature of the Universe, Oxford:
    Blackwell
Hudson, L. (1966) Contrary Imaginations, London:
*   Methuen
Jung, C.G. (1938) Psychological Types, London: Kegan
    Paul, Trench and Truber
Kagan, J., Rossman, B.l., Albert, J., and Phillips,
    W. (1964) Information processing in the child:
    significance of analytic and reflective atti-
    tudes. Psychological Monographs, General and
    Applied, 78,(1, whole no. 578)
Kogan, N. (1976) Cognitive Styles in Infancy and
    Early Childhood, Hillsdale, N.J: Lawrence
    Erlbaum
Kogan, N. and Wallach, M.A. (1964) Risk Taking, New
    York: Holt, Rinehart and Winston
Kulik, J.A. and McKeachie, W.J. (1975) The evaluation
    of teachers in higher education. In Kerlinger,
    F.N. (Ed.), Review of Research in Education 3.
    Itasca, Ill.: Peacock Publishers
Laurillard, D.M. (1978) A study of the relationship
    between some of the cognitive and contextual
    factors involved in student learning.   Un-
    published Ph.D. thesis, University of Surrey
Laurillard, D.M. (1979) The processes of student
    learning, Higher Education, 8, 395-409
Lindsay, P.H. and Norman, D.A. (1972) Human Information
    Processing, New York: Academic Press
Long, S. (1978) Student types and the evaluation
    of the university, Higher Education, 6, 417-436
Main, A. (1980) Encouraging Effective Learning,
    Edinburgh: Scottish Academic Press
Manook, S. and King. A.R. (1981) Notetaking in
    lectures. Paper presented at the 5th International
    Conference on Higher Education, 1 - 4 September,
    University of Lancaster
Marton, F. (1975) On non-verbatim learning. II - the

* (Hughes-Jones - see end)

erosion effect of a task-induced learning algo-
rithm, Reports from the Institute of Education,
University of Gothenburg, No. 40

Marton, F. (1976) What does it take to learn? Some
implications of an alternative view of learning.
In Entwistle, N.J. (Ed.), Strategies for
Research and Development in Higher Education,
Amsterdam: Swets and Zeitlinger

Marton, F. and Säljö, R. (1976a) On qualitative
differences in learning. I - Outcome and process,
Br. J. educ. Psychol., 46, 4 - 11

Marton, F. and Säljö, R. (1976b) On qualitative
differences in learning. II - Outcome as a
function of the learner's conception of the task,
Br. J. educ. Psychol., 46, 115-127

Marton, F. and Svensson, L. (1979) Conceptions of
research in student learning, Higher Education,
8, 471-486

Mathias, H. (1981) University learning and the
school experience. Paper presented at the 5th
International Conference on Higher Education,
* 1 - 4 September, University of Lancaster

Messick, S. and Associates (1976) Individuality in
Learning, San Francisco: Jossey Bass

Miller, C.M.L. and Parlett, M. (1974) Up to the Mark:
A Study of the Examination Game, London: S.R.H.E.

Morgan, A., Gibbs, G., and Taylor, E. (1980) Students
Approaches to Studying the Social Science and
Technology Foundation Courses: Preliminary
Studies, Study Methods Group Report No. 4,
Institute of Educational Technology, The Open
University

Newman, J.H. (1852) On the Scope and Nature of
University Education, London: Dent

Nie, N.J., Hull, C.H., Jenkins, J.G., Steinbrenner,
K. and Bent, D.H. (1975) Statistical Package
for the Social Sciences (2nd edition), New
York: McGraw-Hill

Pace, C.R. (1967) College and University Environment Scales, Princeton, N.J.: Educational
Testing Service

Parlett, M. (1970) The syllabus-bound student. In
Hudson, L. The Ecology of Human Intelligence,
Harmondsworth: Penguin

Pascarella, E.T. and Terenzini, P.T. (1977) Patterns
of student-faculty informal interaction beyond
the classroom and voluntary freshman attrition,
J. Higher Educ., 48, 540-552

Pascarella. E.T. and Terenzini, P.T. (1978) Student-
faculty informal relationships and freshman year
educational outcomes, J. Educ. Research, 71,
183-189

* (Messer - see end)

REFERENCES

Pask, G. (1976a) Conversational techniques in the study and practice of education, Br. J. educ. Psychol., 46, 12-25

Pask, G. (1976b) Styles and strategies of learning, Br. J. educ. Psychol., 46, 128-148

Pask, G. and Scott, B.C.E. (1972) Learning strategies and individual competence, Int. J. Man-Machine Studies, 4, 217-253

Pask, G. et al (1977) Third Progress Report on SSRC Research Programme HR 2708 (see also Fourth Progress Report, 1978, and Final Report 1979), System Research Limited, 37 Sheen Road, Richmond, Surrey

Pattison, M. (1876) Philosophy at Oxford, Mind, 1, 84-97

Payne, D.A. and Hobbs, A.M. (1979) The effect of college course evaluation feedback on instructor and student perceptions of instructional climate and effectiveness, Higher Education, 8, 525-533

Peel, E.A. (1978) Generalising through the verbal medium, Br. J. educ. Psychol., 48, 36-46

Percy, K.A. and Ramsden, P. (1980) Independent Study: Two Examples from English Higher Education, Guildford: S.R.H.E.

Perry, W.G. (1970) Forms of Intellectual and Ethical Development in the College Years: a Scheme, New York: Holt, Rinehart and Winston

Perry, W.G. (1978) Sharing the costs in growth, In Parker, C.A. (Ed.) Encouraging Development in College Students, Minneapolis: University of Minnesota Press

Peterson, R.E. (1965) On a typology of college students Research Bulletin, RB65-9. Princeton, N.J.: Educational Testing Service

Pines, M. (1976) A child's mind is shaped before age 2. In Dentler, R.A. and Shapiro, B. (Eds.), Readings in Educational Psychology: Contemporary Perspectives,New York: Harper and Row

Raaheim, K. (1976) Do we need convergent thinking? Paper presented at the 21st International Conference of Psychology, Paris, July 1976

Raaheim, K. and Wankowski, J. (1981) Helping Students to Learn at University, Bergen: Sigma Forlag

Ramsden, P. (1976) Course evaluation in higher education, Unpublished M.Phil. thesis, C.N.A.A.

Ramsden, P. (1979) Student learning and perceptions of the academic environment, Higher Education, 8, 411-428

Ramsden, P. (1981) A Study of the Relationship between Student Learning and its Academic Context Unpublished PhD thesis, University of Lancaster

REFERENCES

Ramsden, P. and Entwistle, N.J. (1981) Effects of
    academic departments on students' approaches to
    studying, Br. J. educ. Psychol., 51, 368-383
Robertson, I.T. (1977) An investigation of some
    relationships between learning and personality,
    Unpublished PhD thesis, The Open University
Roe, A. (1956) The Psychology of Occupations, New
    York: Wiley
Rogers, C.R. (1969) Freedom to Learn, Columbus, Ohio:
    Merrill
Rowntree, D. (1977) Assessing Students: How Shall
    we Know Them?, London: Harper & Row
Säljö, R. (1975) Qualitative Differences in Learning
    as a Function of the Learner's Conception of
    the Task, Gothenburg: Acta Universitatis
    Gothoburgensis
Säljö, R. (1979a) Learning in the learner's pers-
    pective: I - Some commonsense conceptions,
    Reports from the Institute of Education,
    University of Gothenburg, No. 76
Säljö, R. (1979b) Learning in the learner's pers-
    pective: II - differences in awareness, Reports
    from the Institute of Education, University of
    Gothenburg, No. 77
Säljö, R. (1979c) Learning about learning, Higher
    Education, 8, 443-451
Säljö, R. (1981) Learning approach and outcome: some
    empirical observations, Instructional Science,
    10, 47-65
Schmeck, R.R. (in press) Learning styles of college
    students. In Dillon, R. and Schmeck, R.R.
    Individual Differences in Cognition, New York:
    Academic Press
Schmeck, R.R. and Phillips, J. (in press) Levels
    of processing as a dimension of difference
    between individuals, Human Learning
Schwab, J.J. (1964) Structure of the disciplines:
    meanings and significances. In Ford, A.W.
    and Pugno, L. (eds.) The Structure of Knowledge
    and the Curriculum, Chicago: Rand McNally
Smithers, A.G. (1969) A structural study of the
    occupational value orientations of engineering
    students, Voc. Aspect, 21, 129-134
Snyder, B.R. (1971) The Hidden Curriculum, New York:
    Knopf
Stern, C.G. (1970) People in Context, New York:
    Wiley
Svensson, L. (1976) Study Skill and Learning,
    Gothenburg: Acta Universitatis Gothoburgensis
Svensson, L. (1977) On qualitative differences in
    learning. III - Study skill and learning,

REFERENCES

Br. J. educ. Psychol., 47, 233-243

Tabberer, R., and Allman, J. (1981) Study Skills at 16 plus: an interim Report, Slough: National Foundation for Educational Research

Taylor, E., Morgan, A., and Gibbs, G. (1981) Students' orientations to study. Paper presented at the 5th International Conference on Higher Education, 1 - 4 September, University of Lancaster

Thompson, J.B. (1981) An Interview Study of the Attitudes, Expectations and Motivations of 124 students in Higher Education, unpublished PhD thesis, University of Lancaster

Thompson, J.D., Hawkes, R.W., and Avery, R.W. (1969) Truth strategies and university organization, Educ. Admin. Q., 5, 4-25

Veblen, T. (1957) (First published 1918) The Higher Learning in America, New York: Hill and Wang

Wankowski, J.A. (1973) Temperament: Motivation and Academic Achievement, Birmingham: University of Birmingham Educational Survey

Watkins, D. (1982) Identifying the study process dimensions of Australian university students. Australian Journal of Education, 26, 76-85

Whitehead, A.N. (1950) (First published 1932) The Aims of Education, and other Essays, London: Ernest Benn

Williams, G.L. (1978) In defence of diplomas, Higher Education, 7, 363-371

Wilson, R.C., Gaff, J.G., Dienst, E.R., Wood, L., and Pavry, J.L. (1975) College Professors and Their Impact on Students, New York: Wiley

Witkin, H.A. (1976) Cognitive style in academic performance and in teacher-student relations. In Messick, S. (Ed.), Individuality in Learning, San Francisco: Jossey Bass

Witkin, H.A., Moore, C.A., Goodenough, D.R., and Cox, P.W. (1977) Field-dependent and field-independent cognitive styles and their educational implications, Rev. educ. Res., 47, 1 1-64

Frederick, J., Hancock, L., James, B., Bowden, J., and MacMillan, C., (1981) Learning Skills: a Review of needs and services to university students, Melbourne: Centre for the Study of Higher Educatio, University of Melbourne

Hughes-Jones, H., (1979) Attributional Analysis of Student Perceptions and the Reasons for academic success and failure. Paper presented at the Annual Conference of the S.R.H.E., Bright, December 1979

Messer, S., (1976) Reflection-Impulsivity: a review, Psychol. Bull., 83, 1026-1052.

APPENDIX

Table A1   ITEMS CONTAINED IN THE FINAL RESEARCH VERSION OF THE
APPROACHES TO STUDYING INVENTORY

MEANING ORIENTATION	Corrected* item-scale total correlation

Deep Approach (Cronbach Alpha = 0.56)

DA1	I generally put a lot of effort into trying to understand things which initially seem difficult	0.38
DA2	I often find myself questioning things that I hear in lectures or read in books	0.30
DA3	I usually set out to understand thoroughly the meaning of what I am asked to read.	0.37
DA4	When I'm tackling a new topic, I often ask myself questions about it which the new information should answer	0.33

Relating Ideas (0.47)

RI1	I try to relate ideas in one subject to those in others, whenever possible	0.31
RI2	In trying to understand new ideas, I often try to relate them to real life situations to which they might apply	0.24
RI3	I need to read around a subject pretty widely before I'm ready to put my ideas down on paper	0.20
RI4	I find it helpful to 'map out' a new topic for myself by seeing how the ideas fit together	0.30

Use of Evidence (0.38)

UE1	In reporting practical work, I like to try to work out several alternative ways of interpreting the findings	0.23
UE2	I am usually cautious in drawing conclusions unless they are well supported by evidence	0.13

* Corrected to remove contribution of that item to scale total

Use of Evidence (0.38) (continued)

UE3   Puzzles or problems fascinate me, particularly
       where you have to work through the material to
       reach a logical conclusion   0.19

UE4   When I'm reading an article or research report
       I generally examine the evidence carefully to
       decide whether the conclusion is justified   0.27

Intrinsic Motivation (0.72)

IM1   My main reason for being here is so that I
       can learn more about the subjects which really
       interest me   0.49

IM2   I find that studying academic topics can
       often be really exciting and gripping   0.55

IM3   I spend a good deal of my spare time in
       finding out more about interesting topics
       which have been discussed in classes   0.44

IM4   I find academic topics so interesting, I
       should like to continue with them after I
       finish this course   0.56

REPRODUCING ORIENTATION

Surface Approach (0.49)

SA1   Lecturers seem to delight in making the
       simple truth unnecessarily complicated   0.21

SA2   I find I have to concentrate on memorising
       a good deal of what we have to learn   0.32

SA3   When I'm reading I try to memorise important
       facts which may come in useful later   0.13

SA4   The best way for me to understand what
       technical terms mean is to remember the
       text-book definitions   0.24

SA5   I usually don't have time to think about
       the implications of what I have read   0.28

SA6   Often I find I have read things without having
       a chance to really understand them   0.32

Syllabus-Boundness (0.51)

SB1   I like to be told precisely what to do
       in essays or other assignments   0.38

Syllabus-Boundness (0.51) (continued)

SB2 I prefer courses to be clearly structured
     and highly organised   0.33

SB3 I tend to read very little beyond what's
     required for completing assignments   0.27

Fear of Failure (0.45)

FF1 The continual pressure of work-assignments,
     deadlines and competition often makes me
     tense and depressed   0.30

FF2 A poor first answer in an exam makes me panic   0.30

FF3 Having to speak in tutorials is quite an
     ordeal for me   0.22

Extrinsic Motivation (0.78)

EM1 I chose my present courses mainly to give me
     a chance of a really good job afterwards   0.63

EM2 My main reason for being here is that it will
     help me to get a better job   0.67

EM3 I generally choose courses more from the way
     they fit in with career plans than from my own
     interests   0.58

EM4 I suppose I am more interested in the qualifi-
     cations I'll get than in the courses I'm taking   0.46

ACHIEVING ORIENTATION

Strategic Approach (0.32)

ST1 Lecturers sometimes give indications of what is
     likely to come up in exams, so I look out for
     what may be hints   0.16

ST2 When I'm doing a piece of work, I try to bear
     in mind exactly what that particular lecturer
     seems to want   0.16

ST3 If conditions aren't right for me to study, I
     generally manage to do something to change them   0.18

ST4 One way or another I manage to get hold of the
     books I need for studying   0.16

*Disorganised Study Methods (0.71) (reversed
                                    scoring)*

DS1 I find it difficult to organise my study time
     effectively   0.52

Disorganised Study Methods (0.71) (reversed scoring) (continued)

DS2   My habit of putting off work leaves me with
far too much to do at the end of term   0.50

DS3   Distractions make it difficult for me to do
much effective work in the evenings   0.46

DS4   I'm rather slow at starting work in the
evenings   0.52

Negative Attitudes to Studying (0.60) (reversed scoring)

NA1   Often I find myself wondering whether the work
I am doing here is really worthwhile   0.44

NA2   Continuing my education was something which
happened to me, rather than something I really
wanted for myself   0.37

NA3   When I look back, I sometimes wonder why I
ever decided to come here   0.48

NA4   I certainly want to pass the next set of
exams, but it doesn't really matter if I
only just scrape through   0.25

Achievement Motivation (0.58)

AM1   I enjoy competition: I find it
stimulating   0.43

AM2   It's important to me to do really well in
the courses here   0.32

AM3   It is important to me to do things better
than my friends   0.48

AM4   I hate admitting defeat, even in trivial
matters   0.25

STYLES AND PATHOLOGIES OF LEARNING

Comprehension Learning (0.65)

CL1   Ideas in books often set me off on long
chains of thought of my own, only tenuously
related to what I was reading   0.45

CL2   In trying to understand a puzzling idea, I
let my imagination wander freely to begin
with, even if I don't seem to be much nearer
a solution   0.39

Comprehension Learning (0.65) (continued)

CL3   I like to play around with ideas of my own even if they don't get me very far   0.47

CL4   Often when I'm reading books, the ideas produce vivid images which sometimes take on a life of their own   0.41

Globetrotting (0.36)

GT1   Although I have a fairly good general idea of many things, my knowledge of the details is rather weak   0.13

GT2   In trying to understand new topics, I often explain them to myself in ways that other people don't seem to follow   0.16

GT3   I often get criticised for introducing irrelevant material into my essays or tutorials   0.25

GT4   I seem to be a bit too ready to jump to conclusions without waiting for all the evidence   0.24

Operation Learning (0.49)

OL1   I generally prefer to tackle each part of a topic or problem in order, working out one at a time   0.32

OL2   I prefer to follow well tried out approaches to problems rather than anything too adventurous   0.29

OL3   I find it better to start straight away with the details of a new topic and build up an overall picture in that way   0.18

OL4   I think it is important to look at problems rationally and logically without making intuitive jumps   0.34

Improvidence (0.42)

IP1   Although I generally remember facts and details, I find it difficult to fit them together into an overall picture   0.25

IP2   I find it difficult to "switch tracks" when working on a problem: I prefer to follow each line of thought as far as it will go   0.19

Improvidence (0.42) (continued)

IP3 Tutors seem to want me to be more
adventurous in making use of my own ideas 0.22

IP4 I find I tend to remember things best if I
concentrate on the order in which the
lecturer presented them 0.26

Table A2 CORRELATIONS BETWEEN SUB-SCALES OF THE APPROACHES TO STUDYING INVENTORY

	Meaning					Reproducing			Achieving				Styles and Pathologies			
	DA	RI	UE	IM	SA	SB	FF	EM	ST	DS	NA	AM	CL	GL	OL	IP
Meaning Orientation																
Deep Approach	48	43	47	-09	-28	-05	-12	24	-22	-25	19	37	-03	06	-05	
Relating Ideas		40	39	-03	-22	03	-11	22	-10	-17	13	39	08	03	02	
Use of Evidence			36	-11	-15	-06	-03	21	-14	-22	20	24	-12	15	-01	
Intrinsic Motivation				-20	-37	-08	-35	17	-22	-41	16	37	-07	-07	-12	
Reproducing Orientation																
Surface Approach					37	32	28	18	18	23	11	-09	24	29	42	
Syllabus-Boundness						27	32	06	24	22	06	-28	11	37	35	
Fear of Failure							15	03	22	21	04	-01	19	22	39	
Extrinsic Motivation								16	07	13	20	-19	04	30	27	
Achieving Orientation																
Strategic Approach									-20	-17	25	03	-09	24	12	
Disorganized Study Methods										30	-10	06	24	-05	13	
Negative Attitudes to Studying											-24	-02	25	-02	13	
Achievement Motivation												04	-02	19	08	
Styles and Pathologies																
Comprehension Learning													18	-23	-12	
Globetrotting														-07	19	
Operation Learning															41	

Decimal points omitted.
Total Sample N = 2208; correlations statistically significant with r > 0.06

Table A3   INTERCORRELATIONS BETWEEN INVENTORY SUB-SCALES AND PSYCHOLOGICAL TEST BATTERY

Test Sub-scales	Thinking Introversion	Theoretical Outlook	Aestheticism	Complexity	Autonomy	Religious Scepticism	Social Extraversion	Impulse Expression	Personal Integration	Lack of Anxiety	Altruism	Practical Outlook	Verbal Reasoning	Concrete Generalizing	Abstract Generalizing	Field Independence	Reflectiveness	Inaccuracy	Flexibility	Verbal Fluency
Deep Approach	48	38	31	27	14	21	18	28	-05	-07	12	-14	-03	-06	01	-21	20	-07	19	24
Relating ideas	36	28	33	27	26	15	10	21	-18	-19	-03	-09	03	09	13	-15	15	-03	14	17
Use of Evidence	04	15	07	-16	-09	-04	04	-04	-07	-16	-03	20	23	02	05	23	04	-13	-07	-07
Intrinsic Motivation	45	22	35	09	08	07	-11	08	-27	-22	10	-20	-16	06	01	-11	09	03	-14	-05
Surface Approach	-31	-26	-03	-18	-14	-12	01	10	-14	-17	-18	38	07	-11	-11	04	12	-10	-10	-11
Syllabus Bound	-48	-30	-26	-37	-27	0	06	0	17	03	05	47	-13	-24	-23	05	-06	02	-05	-01
Fear of Failure	-04	-03	07	-10	09	-02	-25	11	-23	-38	-21	20	14	02	-05	06	05	-13	03	-11
Extrinsic Motivation	-62	-19	-46	-47	-13	08	03	01	07	16	-06	57	-15	-10	-21	02	-17	07	-23	-14
Disorganized	-12	-13	-03	09	22	08	02	23	-08	-22	-20	-04	28	-03	16	-06	-07	-04	20	04
Strategic	02	20	13	-08	-07	20	28	15	06	10	06	37	-15	-12	-25	03	14	-15	11	11
Negative Attitude	-25	-22	-07	-07	04	-17	-15	08	-06	-26	-28	-03	28	-17	07	11	00	03	21	17
Achievement Motivation	20	18	13	-07	-17	-04	-14	03	-38	-35	30	30	-01	-05	-02	02	10	-03	-03	-04
Comprehension	52	39	43	33	17	11	04	30	-31	-22	-06	-23	23	07	13	03	-02	-04	20	16
Globetrotting	15	-04	34	23	14	-06	-01	23	-27	-27	-01	02	-03	-03	13	-06	09	09	18	-02
Operation	-23	-06	-30	-37	-16	01	02	-13	03	-02	01	39	-11	-07	-28	05	23	-11	-18	-09
Improvidence	08	06	14	-12	10	-11	-11	11	-07	-10	11	28	-26	-05	-08	-13	07	05	-09	-10

Approaches to Studying Inventory

(Continued)

Table A3   INTERCORRELATIONS BETWEEN INVENTORY SUB-SCALES AND PSYCHOLOGICAL TEST BATTERY (Continued)

Test Sub-scales	Theoretical Outlook	Aestheticism	Complexity	Autonomy	Religious Scepticism	Social Extraversion	Impulse Expression	Personal Integration	Lack of Anxiety	Altruism	Practical Outlook	Verbal Reasoning	Concrete Generalizing	Abstract Generalizing	Field Independence	Reflectiveness	Inaccuracy	Flexibility	Verbal Fluency
Thinking Introversion	52	66	51	35	13	12	16	-05	-01	26	-36	02	08	19	-12	24	-15	17	05
Theoretical Orientation		24	40	34	45	30	30	11	29	17	02	05	19	05	05	15	-12	11	05
Aestheticism			52	34	34	22	30	-12	-02	22	-09	04	-06	02	-06	19	-14	24	01
Complexity				46	33	19	53	-01	01	04	-31	19	21	30	07	11	-11	14	03
Autonomy					42	13	26	07	12	18	-27	11	17	30	-08	-05	-11	18	-05
Religious Scepticism						33	44	09	26	05	10	-09	-04	-09	08	01	-16	14	-09
Social Extraversion							19	46	46	29	17	13	-05	12	10	12	-19	14	05
Impulse Expression								-19	01	09	02	-05	-07	09	03	-04	-10	25	21
Personal Integration									61	50	12	-06	05	-02	-14	00	06	02	-06
Lack of Anxiety										49	20	-22	-16	-17	-14	-04	14	-18	15
Altruism											-04	-04	-04	-04	-26	-05	12	-02	15
Practical Outlook												-21	-13	-18	00	04	-01	-10	-25
MHA Verbal Reasoning													39	48	50	19	-38	19	-02
TGA Concrete Generalizing														56	22	22	-31	-15	-32
TGA Abstract Generalizing															07	18	-32	06	-37
EFT Field Independence																22	-42	-05	-04
MFF Reflectiveness																	-52	-01	-07
MFF Inaccuracy																		08	20
TC Flexibility																			59
VO Verbal Fluency																			

Omnibus Personality Inventory (rows: Thinking Introversion through Practical Outlook)

Decimal points omitted
Correlations of above .22 are significant at 5% level

Table A4   CORRELATIONS BETWEEN THE SCALES OF THE 'APPROACHES TO STUDYING' INVENTORY AND THE INVENTORY OF LEARNING PROCESSES (N = 269)

Learning Processes	Meaning Orientation			Reproducing Orientation					Achieving Orientation				Learning Style			
	DA	RI	UE	IM	SA	SB	FF	EM	ST	OM*	PA*	AM	CL	GL	OL	IP
Deep Processing	.14	.10	.23	.13	-.39	-.22	-41	-26	.21	28	19	04	12	-34	-13	-40
Elaborative processing	36	39	34	33	-23	-22	-22	-19	18	18	15	06	26	00	02	-14
Fact retention	05	-03	06	05	-07	-07	-18	-08	26	16	16	12	00	-27	-06	-12
Methodical study	38	30	32	43	-07	-20	00	-05	34	49	26	24	00	-06	08	12

* The directions of scoring have been reversed to indicate organized study methods and positive attitudes.

This analysis was carried out at Southern Illinois by Dr. Schmeck, and became available too late to incorporate comments on these relationships in the text. These tenative findings confirm the suggestion that our reproducing orientation is similar to 'shallow processing'. Meaning orientation turns out to overlap substantially, with elaborative processing, as expected, but also with 'methodical study'. Our achieving orientation covers deep processing, methodical study, and fact retention, while our pathology scales are negatively related to deep processing and to a less extent to fact retention. Our 'styles' dimensions show little overall correspondence, although there is some link between comprehension learning and elaborative processing. These correlations imply a good deal of overlap between the two inventories in the domain that is being measured, but little conceptual agreement on the dimensions involved.

APPENDIX

Table A5   ITEMS CONTAINED IN THE FINAL RESEARCH VERSION OF THE
            COURSE PERCEPTIONS QUESTIONNAIRE

Corrected item-scale
correlation

Formal teaching methods (alpha = 0.70)

FT1 A great deal of my time is taken up by
     timetabled classes (lectures, practicals,
     tutorials, etc)   0.49

FT2 You can learn nearly everything you need
     to know from the classes and lectures; it
     isn't necessary to do much further reading   0.56

FT3 In this department you're expected to
     spend a lot of time studying on your own *   0.38

FT4 Lectures in this department are basically
     a guide to reading *   0.44

FT5 Lectures seem to be more important than
     tutorials or discussion groups in this
     department   0.43

Clear goals and standards (0.76)

CG1 You usually have a clear idea of where
     you're going and what's expected of you
     in this department   0.54

CG2 It's always easy here to know the standard
     of work expected of you   0.60

CG3 It's hard to know how well you're doing
     in the courses here *   0.42

CG4 Lecturers here usually tell students
     exactly what they are supposed to be
     learning   0.50

CG5 Lecturers here generally make it clear right
     from the start what will be required of
     students   0.58

Workload (0.80)

WL1 The workoad here is too heavy   0.54

WL2 It sometimes seems to me that the syllabus
     tries to cover too many topics   0.19

WL3 There is so much written work to be done
     that it is very difficult to get down to
     independent reading   0.29

* reversed scoring

238

Workload (0.80) (continued)

WL4　There seems to be too much work to get
through in the courses here　　　　　　　　　0.53

WL5　There's a lot of pressure on you as a
student here　　　　　　　　　　　　　　　0.39

Vocational Relevance (0.78)

VR1　The courses in this department are geared to
students' future employment　　　　　　　　0.50

VR2　Lecturers in this department are keen to
point out that they are giving us a professional training　　　　　　　　　　　　0.34

VR3　The courses here seem to be pretty well
determined by vocational requirements　　　　0.50

VR4　The work I do here will definitely improve
my future employment prospects　　　　　　　0.19

VR5　There seems to be considerable emphasis
here on inculcating the 'right' professional attitudes　　　　　　　　　　　　0.27

Good teaching (0.67)

GT1　Lecturers here frequently give the
impression that they haven't anything to
learn from students *　　　　　　　　　　　0.32

GT2　Most of the staff here seem to prepare
their teaching very thoroughly　　　　　　　0.40

GT3　Lecturers in this department seem to be
good at pitching their teaching at the
right level for us　　　　　　　　　　　　0.42

GT4　Staff here make a real effort to understand
difficulties students may be having with
their work　　　　　　　　　　　　　　　0.49

GT5　The lecturers in this department always seem
ready to give help and advice on approaches
to studying　　　　　　　　　　　　　　0.47

Freedom in Learning (0.72)

FL1　There is a real opportunity in this department for students to choose the particular
areas they want to study　　　　　　　　　0.48

---

* reversed scoring

Freedom in Learning (0.72) (continued)

FL2	The department really seems to encourage us to develop our own academic interests as far as possible	0.38
FL3	We seem to be given a lot of choice here in the work we have to do	0.55
FL4	This department gives you a chance to use methods of study which suit your own way of learning	0.45
FL5	Students have a great deal of choice over how they are going to learn in this department	0.53

Openness to students (0.70)

OS1	Most of the staff here are receptive to suggestions from students for changes to their teaching methods	0.43
OS2	Staff generally consult students before making decisions about how the courses are organized	0.36
OS3	Most of the lecturers here really try hard to get to know students	0.53
OS4	Lecturers in this department seem to go out of their way to be friendly towards students	0.51
OS5	Lecturers in this department generally take students' ideas and interests seriously	0.47

Social climate (0.65)

SC1	A lot of the students in this department are friends of mine	0.40
SC2	Students from this department often get together socially	0.49
SC3	This department seems to foster a friendly climate which helps students to get to know each other	0.53
SC4	This department organizes meetings and talks which are usually well attended	0.25
SC5	Students in this department frequently discuss their work with each other	0.36

APPENDIX

Table A6   MEANS OF SUBSCALES AND RANGES OF DEPARTMENTAL MEAN
SCORES, BY DISCIPLINE

Subscale	ENGLISH Mean	Range	HISTORY Mean	Range
Approaches to studying				
Deep approach	11.2	10.2 - 12.7	11.3	10.4 - 12.0
Relating ideas	10.5	8.6 - 11.5	10.1	9.6 - 11.2
Use of evidence	9.4	9.1 - 9.6	9.5	8.9 - 10.6
Intrinsic motivation	9.5	8.1 - 10.3	8.5	7.3 - 9.6
Surface approach	12.9	11.0 - 14.7	12.4	11.2 - 14.0
Syllabus-boundness	7.0	5.4 - 8.1	7.6	6.4 - 8.7
Fear of failure	5.8	4.5 - 6.9	5.7	5.0 - 6.4
Extrinisic motivation	2.8	1.5 - 5.1	3.3	2.0 - 4.4
Strategic approach	9.8	8.3 - 10.6	9.8	8.9 - 11.1
Disorganized study methods	9.2	7.8 - 11.4	8.2	7.1 - 10.6
Negative attitudes	4.5	4.4 - 6.3	5.9	5.0 - 6.4
Achievement motivation	9.0	8.0 - 10.0	9.0	8.0 - 10.0
Comprehension learning	11.0	10.0 - 11.7	8.7	7.8 - 10.0
Globetrotting	7.8	6.8 - 8.9	7.2	6.3 - 8.5
Operation learning	8.6	7.5 - 9.4	9.8	8.5 - 10.7
Improvidence	6.8	4.4 - 8.4	7.1	6.3 - 8.0
Perceptions of course				
Formal teaching methods	3.3	2.5 - 5.3	2.7	2.1 - 3.6
Clear goals and standards	6.7	3.6 - 9.5	8.0	6.2 - 10.2
Workload	10.0	5.6 - 12.3	11.2	7.5 - 14.8
Vocational relevance	3.9	3.1 - 4.7	4.8	3.5 - 5.6
Good teaching	11.4	8.1 - 13.8	11.8	9.8 - 14.0
Freedom in learning	11.7	7.4 - 15.8	11.2	5.0 - 13.2
Openness to students	8.5	5.9 - 13.5	7.7	4.2 - 9.8
Social climate	9.0	6.9 - 13.6	9.2	6.9 - 10.3

(Continued)

Table A6   MEANS OF SUBSCALES AND RANGES OF DEPARTMENTAL MEAN
SCORES, BY DISCIPLINE (continued)

Subscale	PSYCHOLOGY Mean	Range	ECONOMICS Mean	Range
Approaches to Studying				
Deep approach	10.8	9.9 - 12.4	10.2	8.4 - 12.1
Relating ideas	10.9	10.1 - 12.0	10.1	8.9 - 11.8
Use of evidence	9.6	8.5 - 11.0	9.4	8.7 - 10.4
Intrinsic motivation	9.3	7.3 - 10.5	7.0	4.9 - 9.6
Surface approach	12.8	11.7 - 14.1	13.8	12.8 - 15.0
Syllabus-boundness	7.7	6.4 - 8.6	8.8	7.5 - 9.5
Fear of failure	5.9	4.8 - 7.0	6.0	4.6 - 7.5
Extrinsic motivation	4.5	2.8 - 5.6	7.9	5.1 - 9.4
Strategic approach	10.2	8.8 - 11.2	10.3	9.5 - 10.8
Disorganized study methods	9.9	8.7 - 13.0	9.4	8.1 - 11.0
Negative attitudes	5.3	4.2 - 8.6	5.6	4.3 - 6.7
Achievement motivation	8.8	7.3 - 9.9	10.0	9.2 - 11.0
Comprehension learning	9.0	7.9 - 10.1	7.7	6.2 - 9.2
Globetrotting	8.2	7.4 - 9.3	7.8	6.9 - 8.5
Operation learning	9.2	8.2 - 10.2	10.8	10.1 - 12.0
Improvidence	7.4	6.2 - 8.7	8.4	7.6 - 9.0
Perceptions of courses				
Formal teaching methods	6.7	3.8 - 9.1	6.7	5.5 - 7.8
Clear goals and standards	8.6	5.6 - 11.9	11.0	8.4 - 12.7
Workload	9.0	5.3 - 12.6	9.0	5.6 - 13.5
Vocational relevance	6.5	4.7 - 8.4	8.2	6.2 - 9.0
Good teaching	11.8	9.2 - 14.0	11.8	8.0 - 14.1
Freedom in learning	9.7	7.9 - 12.6	10.4	7.4 - 12.6
Openness to students	9.9	7.4 - 12.8	8.7	6.2 - 11.8
Social climate	11.5	10.2 - 13.5	9.9	7.8 - 12.0

(Continued)

Table A6   MEANS OF SUBSCALES AND RANGES OF DEPARTMENTAL MEAN
            SCORES, BY DISCPLINE (continued)

Subscale	PHYSICS		ENGINEERING	
	Mean	Range	Mean	Range

Approaches to Studying

Deep approach	10.1	8.5 - 11.9	10.4	8.4 - 12.0
Relating ideas	9.3	8.2 - 10.9	9.6	8.2 - 11.8
Use of evidence	9.8	8.6 - 10.3	9.9	9.0 - 11.0
Intrinsic motivation	8.8	7.9 - 9.9	7.3	5.3 - 10.1
Surface approach	13.2	10.9 - 14.7	13.2	10.8 - 16.1
Syllabus-boundness	8.6	7.6 - 9.9	9.2	8.5 - 10.1
Fear of failure	5.5	4.9 - 6.2	6.2	5.0 - 7.4
Extrinsic motivation	5.7	4.0 - 8.6	8.0	6.5 - 10.0
Strategic approach	10.6	9.2 - 11.5	10.5	8.5 - 11.5
Disorganized study methods	9.6	8.1 - 10.9	9.8	8.0 - 11.7
Negative attitudes	5.8	4.6 - 6.9	5.4	4.5 - 6.9
Achievement motivation	9.8	8.5 - 11.5	10.7	9.4 - 11.4
Comprehension learning	8.2	6.3 - 9.9	8.0	6.4 - 10.3
Globetrotting	7.4	6.3 - 8.2	7.5	6.6 - 8.6
Operation learning	10.1	9.2 - 11.8	11.1	9.7 - 12.8
Improvidence	7.4	4.9 - 8.4	7.8	6.7 - 9.3

Perceptions of courses

Formal teaching methods	12.0	9.6 - 13.5	12.1	10.0 - 16.2
Clear goals and standards	11.4	10.0 - 13.3	12.2	11.5 - 13.8
Workload	9.9	8.4 - 12.1	12.9	5.5 - 14.3
Vocational relevance	8.9	5.3 - 12.6	13.4	9.0 - 15.1
Good teaching	11.8	10.7 - 12.8	11.4	9.1 - 13.2
Freedom in learning	8.2	6.3 - 11.3	8.1	5.8 - 11.7
Openness to students	9.2	6.4 - 12.1	8.6	6.7 - 11.1
Social climate	11.2	9.0 - 12.7	11.0	8.3 - 13.9

Classroom Behaviour

Education at SAGE

SAGE is a leading international publisher of journals, books, and electronic media for academic, educational, and professional markets.

Our education publishing includes:

- accessible and comprehensive texts for aspiring education professionals and practitioners looking to further their careers through continuing professional development

- inspirational advice and guidance for the classroom

- authoritative state of the art reference from the leading authors in the field

Find out more at: **www.sagepub.co.uk/education**

CLASSROOM BEHAVIOUR

A practical guide to effective teaching, behaviour
management and colleague support

3rd Edition

Bill Rogers

Los Angeles | London | New Delhi
Singapore | Washington DC

SAGE Publications Ltd
1 Oliver's Yard
55 City Road
London EC1Y 1SP

SAGE Publications Inc.
2455 Teller Road
Thousand Oaks, California 91320

SAGE Publications India Pvt Ltd
B 1/I 1 Mohan Cooperative Industrial Area
Mathura Road
New Delhi 110 044

SAGE Publications Asia-Pacific Pte Ltd
33 Pekin Street #02–01
Far East Square
Singapore 048763

Library of Congress Control Number: 2010931528

British Library Cataloguing in Publication data
A catalogue record for this book is available from the British
Library

ISBN 978-0-85702-166-3
ISBN 978-0-85702-167-0 (pbk)

Typeset by Dorwyn, Wells, Somerset
Printed in Great Britain by TJ International, Padstow
Printed on paper from sustainable resources

Contents

What reviewers have said about *Classroom Behaviour* (first and second editions)

"Bill Rogers offers individual teachers a wide repertoire of relational management skills. He provides clear guidance for putting professional integrity and emotional literacy into practice from early, minimal intervention to responding to the most difficult student and the most challenging situation. He also suggests ways staff groups might develop a more supportive environment for each other – including mentoring. I cannot speak highly enough of *Classroom Behaviour*. All educators will identify with the situations Bill describes. He does not duck the realities in today's schools and classrooms. He manages, however, to find the balance between acknowledging the difficulties and demands on teachers, whilst also being supportive of students by responding to their needs, competencies and their right to respectful interactions. He does this with clarity, vitality and humour. Every teacher needs this book, and every student needs them to have read it."

Sue Roffey
University of Western Sydney and University of London

"Bill is unusual among authors in this field in that he works in classrooms, alongside teachers, to support and model effective practice. He is consciously reflective of day-to-day classroom experiences and this 'in touch with' dimension in his writings gives him credibility and encourages his readers to develop their own practice.

This latest publication is approaching the status of being an indispensable manual of best practice in managing pupil behaviour and effective teaching. Every teacher should have a copy as a constant companion even – and maybe especially – those teachers with long experience. The most reflective of these will recognise why, when they have good days, they are good teachers."

Mike O'Connor
The Psychology of Education Review
Vol. 27, No. 2, pp. 44–5

"Any book by Bill Rogers is eagerly grasped by classroom teachers and other professionals concerned with the behaviour and pastoral care of pupils.

Bill Rogers writes in a candid style with humour and wit. After a stressful day in the classroom this book can give you the strength to go on. It is full of practical suggestions and anecdotal stories which relate to real situations.

This book should be read by every teacher in training and NQT (newly qualified teachers) as well as the experienced teacher."

Chris Stansfield
North Lincolnshire LES, UK

"He presents with vivid authenticity – his stories are always a potent cocktail of pain and humour – tales of classroom and school challenge with which any practising teacher immediately identifies. He has that uncanny and rare knack of throwing a sharp focus on everyday classroom instances which all of us intuitively knew all along, but which we had never realised with such clarity and precision.

Having read *Classroom Behaviour* (published last year but available only at events until recently) I am seeing teachers – and my own managing and parenting skills – with such a sharp focus that it is like putting on my first set of glasses. That is the book's effect: it empowers and energises teachers, and it is a must for every department and school."

Professor Tim Brighouse
Chief Education Officer,
Birmingham
Times Educational Supplement, *19 April 2002*

"As a newly qualified teacher, I found this text extremely helpful in developing some of my key teaching skills, especially reflecting on the behaviour and practice of both teachers and students in the more 'challenging' classes."

Bill Harris
Scottish Support For Learning

"This book is a must for those entering the teaching profession and it would be really useful in a professional development programme for existing teachers"

Support For Learning

About the author

Bill Rogers taught for many years before becoming an education consultant and author; he lectures widely on behaviour management, discipline, effective teaching, stress management and teacher welfare across the UK, Australia and New Zealand. Bill also works as a mentor-teacher, team-teaching in challenging schools. He is well aware of the challenges of teacher leadership in schools today. He is a Fellow of the Australian College of Education, Honorary Life Fellow of All Saints and Trinity College, Leeds University and Honorary Fellow at Melbourne University Graduate School of

© Helen Green, 2011

Education. Dr Bill Rogers has written several books for SAGE Publications. This particular book, *Classroom Behaviour*, has been translated into several languages in its various editions.

To find out more about Bill's work, visit his website **www.billrogers.com.au** where you will find full details of how to book him for a workshop or training event.

Scope

Chapter 1 explores the dynamics of children's behaviour; how both student(s) and teacher behaviour affect each other, for good or ill. The issue of teacher "control" and management is developed as it relates to the purposes of management, teaching and discipline.

Chapter 2 addresses the critical phase of the year, the "establishment phase". Those first meetings that help define and shape our leadership, authority, discipline and our relationship with the class (as a group) and the beginnings of workable cohesion. Particular emphasis is given to the importance of a "class-room agreement" for behaviour and learning; developed with the students.

Chapter 3 develops a framework for behaviour management and explores key behaviour management and discipline skills within that framework. A number of case examples are noted to illustrate those skills.

Chapter 4 explores the fundamentals of effective teaching and outlines core understandings and skills. Case studies are, again, noted to illustrate aspects, features and skills of effective teaching.

Chapter 5 discusses behaviour management in terms of behaviour consequences and "punishment". A framework for planning and utilising consequences is developed. School-wide consequences such as detention and time-out are also discussed and suggested practices developed.

Chapter 6 addresses challenging behaviours and children who present with emotional and behavioural difficulties. A school-wide framework for supporting teachers and students is developed with an emphasis on an educational model of support for children with symptomatic or diagnosed behaviour disorders.

Chapter 7 addresses the issue of anger: our own anger as teachers and how we better communicate with and support others when they are angry. The issue of communicating with angry parents is also addressed.

Chapter 8 discusses how we can support each other, as teachers, particularly when things get difficult. Issues such as the hard to manage class, harassment (of teachers *by* students!), stress and coping are discussed in the context of colleague support. Practical strategies are explored for each of these issues with a particular emphasis on supportive mentoring.

NB   Case examples and case studies are an essential feature of this text. All the practices and skills discussed are illustrated within (and from) case studies drawn from mentor-teaching with collegues in Australian and English schools.

The case studies traverse early years to secondary school settings (with some parent–teacher examples). These case studies are listed with a brief description and page allocation in the text on pp. 249–50.

Acknowledgements

Putting a book together is time-consuming for more than the author. I want to thank my wife Lora – closest friend and fellow teacher – who gave ongoing support and tolerated an overly papered dining-room table. Thanks, too, to our daughter Sarah; we shared the dining-room table many, many times (homework and book writing). Thanks also, Sarah, for the drawing in the Epilogue.

To all my colleagues whose stories and accounts are detailed herein and to all the students who (although names are changed) would be surprised to read that their behaviour has been the subject of the many cases studies utilised in this book.

To all the team at SAGE Publications (London) who encouraged me through each edition of this book. My particular thanks to Jude Bowen, Amy Jarrold and Marianne Lagrange. Thank you, too, to Jennifer Crisp and Wendy Scott for the design motifs on each edition.

To Professor, Sir Tim Brighouse for his kind and generous review of the first edition of *Classroom Behaviour* (in the *Times Educational Supplement*).

My thanks, also, to those other reviewers who patiently waded through the book and gave feedback, encouragement and support.

To Dr John Robertson, friend and colleague, for advice, wisdom and support over the years.

My thanks, too, to Felicia Schmidt who patiently transcribed my handwriting (yes – *handwriting*) into readable text.

My thanks, lastly, to my many colleagues who put up with me as a mentor-teacher in their classrooms and whose accounts form the interactive examples about teaching, behaviour and behaviour management in this book.

All the best to my first-year colleagues embarking on their teaching journey.

We chose our profession; we chose teaching (I hope) to "make a difference" with our students – a positive difference – in the teaching and learning journey. I hope this book supports, and enables, that choice.

Bill Rogers
Third Edition
Melbourne, April, 2010

Introduction

"I never thought I'd become a teacher"

Education is simply the soul of a society as it passes from one generation to another.
G.K. Chesterton, 1924

I never thought I'd become a teacher

I never thought I'd become a teacher; I had mixed success at school. It wasn't the work; I could handle that (by and large) – it was the culture of control and authority. Few teachers encouraged or allowed students much expression of their views or ideas. I also had many "run-ins" with petty, mean-spirited and, at times, cruel teachers. Being chastised – even hit and caned – was an occupational hazard in those days (the mid-1950s to the early 1960s). On one occasion, at the age of 11, I was caned for breaking a pencil that another pupil had snatched from me. I had snatched it back; he wailed and I got "caught". I was blamed in the ensuing fracas, and later caned. I was also caned for "answering back" on a number of occasions, for drawing pictures in my workbooks instead of listening to the teacher and for sneaking off to the shops at lunchtime (a major crime in those days).

I survived – we all did – but I never thought I'd become a teacher.

In the 1950s (after the Second World War) many of the male teachers in my school would have served in the armed forces, and they didn't take kindly to students appearing as even mildly challenging to adult authority. I suppose I was heralding the view that I had basic rights. At the heart of these rights was the desire to be treated with fundamental dignity and respect; strangely I had no problems with the teachers who gave such respect.

I can recall one particular teacher walking up to me (1961), in front of the class, and grabbing my shirt. (I'd been whispering something to a friend behind me.) He then pushed me with his fingers in my chest and said, "Were you brought up or dragged up, Rogers?" He didn't like me. I stood up, heart thumping, and said, "It's none of your bloody business!" (I was a little taller than him, even at 15.) No

1

one was going to "have a go" at my parents or their parenting. I then turned and walked out of the class. The class was hushed – *waiting*; it was all very dramatic. I didn't see "the git" (as we'd nicknamed him) for a week. He didn't even put me on detention – he must have realised he'd gone too far (even then). He merely kept out of my way until the end of term.

I left school at 15; I ran away. I left because I'd been caught putting up a large picture of all the teachers I disliked on the central school noticeboard. It was 1962, just two days to go until the end of term. I'd spent a long time on this painting – in oils on a very large canvas – the faces painted in the manner of Salvador Dali; the faces of the teachers "melting", merging into the darker, swirling, background. I had come into school early, that particular day, with the unsigned painting rolled up hidden under my blazer. It was my message, my "statement"; a parting *coup de grâce*. I was observed by a prefect as I surreptitiously pinned up the painting. He reported me, although he didn't have to. At the form assembly our senior master held up the painting (thereby giving it a second public viewing), looked at me and said, "You know what is going to happen to you, don't you, Rogers?" Well, I'd been caned before. I sighed, frowned, shrugged my shoulders looking suitably mollified. He hadn't seen the joke.

He rolled up the painting and as he dismissed the class I saw him put it on the desk in his office area adjacent to the form classroom. I hid, a little way up the corridor. When he wasn't looking, I sneaked in and retrieved my property, stuck it under my school jumper and, en route to Period One, put it back on the noticeboard again (surreptitiously). Later that morning the Form 4 students were watching a film in the upstairs double classroom; a black and white nature film (*Otters in Canada* or something like that). It was probably a "filler activity", it being within the last two days of term. We were whispering in the darkness, pretending to be absorbed in the film, when a knock on the door heralded yet another prefect. The teacher turned off the projector, a beam of light from the opened door fell across the front of the darkened classroom and a voice said, "Mr Smith wants to see Billy Rogers *immediately*". The teacher said something like, "Alright, if he's here I'll send him as soon as the film has finished". He didn't seem to take the prefect's words particularly seriously – at least the 'immediacy' part. The door closed, and the darkness and the noise of the film gave me enough "cover" to sneak out. I whispered to my friend, "Don't say anything, I'm off – home". I tip-toed quietly, my back pressed along the wall, moving carefully in the darkness. I opened the door as quietly as I could and found partial freedom.

We had a letter a week later, from the headmaster (after school closure for the summer term – we didn't have a phone). "We are deeply disappointed with your son's behaviour ... " it went on, or words to that effect. My parents asked me what I wanted them to do about "all this". Wisely they let me go to another school – for six months or so. Just before my sixteenth birthday my family migrated to Australia (for ten English pounds). Excellent value. I didn't know (how could we) what future would await us as the boat left England's green and chalky cliffs …

Many years later, on one of my many trips back to England to conduct seminars on behaviour management and discipline issues in schools and universities, I met a teacher whose father had taught me at the high school where I had painted "*the* picture". I relayed the account of the painting episode and he shared it with the local press (I didn't know he had passed on the story). The article detailed, me as a self-proclaimed academic failure, who failed his 11-plus and whose strongest schoolday memories were of canings received for rebellious behaviour but who is now an education consultant on that very topic.

I was a little annoyed at the line "self-proclaimed academic failure … " (I've never said that or believed that): annoying journalistic licence, I suppose. But there is a lesson in this trip down memory lane. You can't predict where a student will go or what he or she may become. Some of my teachers had said – in effect – and sometimes in words, "You won't amount to anything …", and then had added the *because* statement of the day: "because you didn't listen" or "won't listen"; or "because you won't concentrate or apply yourself". There is also the lesson that learning is lifelong, that education doesn't finish at school, or with school. There is, obviously, a difference between *schooling* and *education*.

I recall looking out of classroom windows many, many, times (particularly when bored or when the teacher droned on and on). I could see, in the distance, the green fields and trees and gentle low hills of Hertfordshire. The window seemed to say, "Come!" I couldn't.

I eventually became a teacher – many years later. Some of my teachers at least taught me how *not* to discipline: how not to embarrass, criticise and shame children. They also taught me how *not* to teach. Of course, thankfully, I had good, kind and generous teachers too. We always remember such teachers. They affirmed, encouraged and believed in me and enabled me to continue learning and value learning to this day. They also enhanced an early, and positive, belief that "I could do it".

It was Haim Ginnot[1] who spoke of the crucial consequences of teacher's actions which have the power to affect children's lives for better or worse. Being able to open, or close, the minds and hearts of children is a responsibility for all teachers to reflect upon. In my journey as a teacher I have had to rethink many aspects of classroom behaviour, teacher behaviour, the purposes and limitations of discipline and management, and how we can establish more cooperative classrooms, where rights and responsibilities work together for the benefit of all.

This book is the outcome of many years of in-service training with teachers and countless hours in the classroom with colleagues as a mentor-teacher in Australian and British schools.

Having made over 40 visits to the UK to conduct seminars, and professional development, in schools and with education authorities and universities I hope the link between my Australian teaching and consultancy experiences and my in-service work in the UK will continue to find a receptive (and useful) audience here.

A few important prefacing notes to the text from here on ...

Tactical pausing (...)

This book has many case examples and case studies illustrating distracting and disruptive behaviours. Each case study is drawn from my work with colleagues as a mentor-teacher. All the practices and skills explored in this book are drawn primarily from those experiences (as well as supported by research in these areas).

In many of the dialogue exchanges between teachers and students throughout the book, you will find a set of brackets with an 'ellipsis' (...). This signals (in the text) a typical teacher behaviour I choose to describe as "tactical pausing". This is conscious behaviour whereby the teacher *briefly* pauses in their communication to emphasise the need for student attention, or allow some processing by the student of what the teacher has just said. It can also communicate (to older children) a sense of expectant "calming".

For example, if you beckon, or direct, a student to come across to you, in the playground, from several yards away, you need to get eye contact first. This is easier (obviously) if we know the student's name. If we don't we probably lift our voice (as we look in their direction), without shouting, and say, "EXCUSE ME (...)! EXCUSE ME (...)" Do we want to be excused? Or we may say, "Oi (...)! Oi (...)" We might use a generic, "FELLAS (...)! Fellas (...)", or "Guys (...)!" or (easier) their names (if we know them). The tactical pausing (...), in directional language, is our attempt to initiate and sustain some attention and focus.

In the classroom we frequently include tactical pausing when engaged in management and discipline. Several students are chatting away as the teacher seeks to settle the class at the beginning of a lesson. She scans the room; she tactically pauses (saying nothing). As the restlessness settles she says, "Looking this way and listening (...) ..."; she tactically pauses (again). Lowering her voice she repeats, "Looking this way and listening, thanks (...)". Sensing the class attention and focus, she then says,: "Good morning everyone ..." and begins another teaching session. Tactical pausing is a small aspect – but an important small aspect – of overall teacher behaviour.

No disclaimers

There are books whose disclaimer reads: "All characters are fictitious ... any resemblance to ...." It's the opposite in this book. Every example and case study, even the briefer "snatches" of teacher–student dialogue, are drawn directly from my teaching/mentoring role in schools.

My own teaching, these days, comes out of periodic peer-mentoring – working directly in a team-teaching role with primary and secondary teachers who are seeking to be more consciously reflective of their day-to-day teaching, behaviour leadership and discipline. Mentoring is a joint professional journey: there is no superior–inferior relationship. The aim is to build *reflective* professional practice (see later p. 17, 237f).

In this book each skill or approach suggested is supported by case examples (and case studies) taken from recent teaching situations that I have been involved in as a mentor-teacher. I have been engaged in mentorship (often in very "challenging schools") over the past 15 years.

I have changed the names of colleagues (teachers) and students wherever ethical probity demands. I have even changed grade and subject allocations and gender where I thought necessary, without changing the behavioural context and meanings of the real examples and situations noted. As I wrote each case example, each "snatch" of teacher–student(s) dialogue, the memories of particular classes, and particular students, even particular days, came back – easily; quickly. I could even "relive" some of the emotion that occasioned some of the more difficult discipline situations I have had to address.

In sharing these case examples with you, my aim is always to draw forth concepts, approaches, practices and skills of effective teaching, management and discipline. As I write, I am also acutely aware of the fact that – as a teacher – you are constantly on the go from the moment you walk in the school gates. Being acutely aware of what the day after day after day of teaching can be like, I have sought to address ineffective as well as effective teacher practice; always distinguishing between what one *characteristically* does and what one does as a result of bad-day syndrome.

There is never a stage when we stop being a reflective teacher (or learner). I hope this book enables your own professional reflection and supports and encourages you in your teaching journey.

Theories, positions and this book

There are a number of well-established theoretical positions addressing behaviour management and discipline in schools. Like any theoretical approaches, these 'theoretical positions' range across a continuum, normally categorised (in the literature) as ranging from explicit teacher control (for example, particular forms of assertive discipline) to non-directive approaches (for example, 'teacher effectiveness training').

These 'positions' – on a continuum – are in part philosophic, in part pedagogic and in part psychological – all have implications for one's values and practices as a teacher. This book is not a discussion of differing theoretical, approaches, positions or 'models'. When 'my' approach has been listed in different behaviour management texts I am portrayed as somewhere in the middle of a theoretical continuum – broadly described as 'democratic discipline' or 'positive behaviour leadership' or 'interactionist' or 'referent power'. If readers are interested to peruse theoretical models I would suggest the excellent texts of Edwards and Watts (2008); Charles (2005); Wolfgang (1999) and Tauber (1995) and McInerney and McInerney (1998).

There is, fundamentally, nothing new in these 'models'. At base they delineate the degree, and kind, of teacher leadership exercised in behaviour management and discipline. They also highlight the degree, and kind, of leadership intervention a teacher should exercise in matters of discipline. While I have found many theorists very helpful in my practice as a teacher, and in my research as university lecturer and writer, my interest has always been focused on how to bring our 'philosophy', our values, our delineation of ourselves as teacher-leader within the practicalities and *day-to-day* stresses (and joys) of teaching. And, further, how we utilise our behaviour leadership to build positive, working, relationships with our students.

In writing this text I have sought – at every point – to ask not just *why* I should lead and discipline in a given way (the value question) but *what* and *how* I should lead, guide, enable, manage, correct and support students.

Note

1. Haim Ginott was a professor of Psychology at New York Graduate School (1922–73). He did much to develop a model of discipline that advocates dignified, respectful and congruent communication with one's students. His emphasis on the positive power of teacher leadership has always been a source of great encouragement and assistance in my own journey of teaching and mentoring.

Chapter 1

The dynamics of classroom behaviour

Day-to-day school teaching normally takes place in a rather unusual setting: a small room (for what is asked of it), often inadequate furniture and space to move, a 50-minute time slot (or less) to cover set curriculum objectives, and 25–30 distinct, and unique, personalities, some of whom may not even want to be there. Some of our students come from very supportive homes, some go home to frequent shouting, arguing, poor diet, family dysfunction and worse ...

The ability and motivation to learn in this formal setting of school varies enormously. And it doesn't take long for students to work out what their teachers are like ... Why would there not be some natural, normative, stresses and strains associated with a teacher's day-to-day role?

We teach each other

Into that rather unusual setting, where students and teachers bring personal agendas, feelings and needs, and where certain obligations and rights have to be balanced, both teacher and student are "teaching" each other through their daily relational behaviours.

It is not simply enough to detail student disruption as a discrete issue only pertaining to the student. In any school the same students may behave differently, in different settings, with different teachers. The teacher's behaviour and the student's behaviour have a reciprocal effect on each other and on the ever present "audience" of peers.

The case examples that follow (as noted earlier) are taken directly from my work with colleagues as a mentor-teacher, and observing myself and my colleagues widely across the schools in which I have worked.

These shared observations are the basis of our professional self-reflection that enable and support our "choices of change" and call forth the necessary skills of our behaviour leadership.

As you read these case examples I encourage you to reflect on how teacher behaviour and student behaviour act reciprocally on each other. The nature, extent and effect of disruptive behaviour, in this sense, is not simply the result of students acting disruptively; behaviour is also learned within its context.

"Overly vigilant" management

Corey has been described by some of his teachers as "a bit of a lazy lad" and a "bit of a pain!" Any support from home for basic organisational skills and the application of day-to-day responsibility at school is "limited". In the classroom he is leaning back in his seat, a vacant look in his eyes – he's looking out of the window (to partial freedom perhaps?). His attention is hardly gripped by the task requirement in his maths class. It's his third lesson with this teacher.

The teacher walks over to him and, standing next to his table, asks, "Why haven't you started any work?"

"I haven't got a pen, have I?" Corey, at least, is honest at this point.

"Don't talk to me like that!" The teacher doesn't like Corey's tone and manner ("lazy sod").

"Well I haven't got a pen, have I? What d'you expect me to say?!" Corey folds his arms sulkily, averting his eyes.

"Well *get* a pen then!" At this, Corey gets up and walks out of the classroom. The teacher hurriedly catches up with him.

"Where do you think you're going? Get back in here!"

Corey, with feigned exasperation, says, "You *asked* me to get a pen! Gees – I'm just going to get one from my locker." He clicks his tongue and sighs loudly.

"I meant get one from another student – you just don't walk out of my class."

Corey slopes off towards the back of the classroom to a mate.

"Hey Craig, give us a pen."

Craig answers, "I'm not giving you a pen – gees I didn't get the last one back."

Corey walks back to the teacher (most of the class is now enjoying this little *contretemps*). "He won't give me a pen." He grins.

Corey's teacher says, "Look I'm sick of this. You know you're supposed to bring pen and paper ... "

Corey butts in, "Yeah well people forget sometimes y'know!"

"Look if you can't come to my class prepared to work, you can leave and go to Mr Smith (the year head)."

"Yeah – well I'm leaving. It's a shit class anyway!!" Corey storms out.

The teacher calls after him. "Right! I'll see you in detention!"
Corey (now half-way down the corridor) calls back. "I don't care!"

A small incident like a student without a pen (almost unbelievably) becomes a major fracas. I've seen this happen with some teachers. Maybe the teacher is having a bad day (maybe the student is too). Maybe the teacher is characteristically petty, churlish, pedantic, sarcastic – whatever. What can be seen, though, is that the teacher's behaviour contributes as much to this incident – and its management – as that of the student.

In another classroom a similar incident is taking place. The teacher walks across to a student who has been un-engaged in his learning task for several minutes. She has given him some take-up time – after all, he may be thinking, he may just need a few minutes to get his ideas formed and focused; he may be another lad 'with' ADSD (attention deficit spectrum disorder).

She greets him and says, "Bradley, I notice you're not working ... can I help?" She avoids asking *why* he hasn't started work yet.

He says, "I haven't got a pen."

"You can have one of mine," replies his teacher.

As it is still the first few lessons, the teacher still has not sorted out which students are genuinely forgetful, or maybe lazy, or maybe just seeking attention or indulging in some "game-playing" or even struggling with the classwork ... She has a box of blue pens and red pens, some rulers, some spare erasers and some pencils (all taped with a 1cm band of yellow electrical tape around the tip – to track them back to the box – itself yellow). On the box, in large letters, it reads: RETURN HERE – THANKS IN ADVANCE Ms Brown.

The offer of a pen is met with "Yeah – but I haven't got a red pen have I?"

"There's one in my yellow box," (she points back to the teacher's table).

"Yeah, but I haven't got any paper," (he grins).

"Bradley – there's A4 lined and plain paper next to the yellow box." She finishes with a wink and, "OK, Bradley? – I'll come and see how you're going a little later." She walks away giving Bradley some "take-up time". Her tone and manner indicate that she is aware of Bradley's avoidance "game-playing" but is confident that he will get what he needs and actually start some work. She comes back, a little later in the lesson, to chat with Bradley (in the on-task phase of the lesson), to re-establish and check on the progress of his work and to give some encouragement and support.

> NB *Some* teachers argue that in "giving" "such" students pens (and so on) we only perpetuate their irresponsibility. Would they rather simply argue? – punish? It is normally the case that only a few students come to class without pens/paper/books (and so on). My colleagues and I would rather provide such – in the critical first meetings – as we establish our leadership and relationship with the class. If the student continues to come to class without equipment (say three times in close succession) we have a one-to-one meeting to ask questions and offer support. With some students we've found it beneficial to provide a small "table pencil-case" that the student picks up at the start of the day from (say) the tutor teacher (with red and blue pen, eraser, pencil, ruler …) and then returns at the close of the day.

"Overly vigilant" behaviour

A Year 3 student (diagnosed as "special needs") has a small soft toy on her table next to her daily diary writing task. The teacher walks over and in an unnecessarily stern voice says, "You know you're not supposed to bring toys to your table don't you?" He snatches it up and walks off. The girl (naturally) protests and he adds, "Get on with your work or you'll finish it at recess … ". Who would speak to a student like that? He did. This is even more disconcerting as he knows she has special needs.

He could have walked over, looked at the toy, even smiled – (miserable sod) and given a fair and simple "directed choice". For example:

"Danielle, it's a nice toy you've got there (…), it's work time now and I want you to put it in your locker tray or on my table" (here he could use a softer directional voice), "and carry on with your writing. I'll come and see how you're getting on soon …"

This leaves her with both a behavioural choice, a "task-focus" and expectation of cooperation.

A female student walks into class a few minutes late. Melissa, a Year 9 student, likes a bit of attention, she's grinning at a few of her friends as she enters. She is wearing long, "dangly" earrings (non-regulation). She is quickly noticed by her teacher.

Teacher: "Right – come here [in a sharpish voice – visibly frustrated with Melissa's lateness and '*grand dame* entrance']. Why are you late?"
Student: "I'm just a *few* minutes late."
Teacher: "Why are you wearing those … things?"
Student: "What?"
Teacher: "*Those* things – you know what I'm talking about – those stupid earrings."

Student: "Mrs Daniels [her form teacher] didn't say anything!" [Melissa's tone is sulky, indifferent – she averts her eyes. The teacher senses – yet annoyingly "creates" – a challenge.]

Teacher: "Listen, I don't care *what* Mrs Daniels did or didn't do – get them off now. You know you're not supposed to wear them!" [He's clearly getting rattled now. He believes it's an issue on which he has to not only exercise discipline – he has to win.]

Student: "Yeah – well how come other teachers don't hassle us about it, eh?"

Teacher: "Who do you think you're talking to?! Get them off now or you're on detention!"

This happened; it still does. Some teachers believe that such teacher behaviour is "legitimate" in that it shows who is 'in control' *and* it enforces the school rules. What message do the peer-audience, and Melissa, really get from the way this teacher dealt with this "uniform misdemeanour"?

If a teacher's management style is this "vigilant" – unnecessarily and overly vigilant – there are many students who will naturally challenge and even "bait" the teacher (I was often tempted to myself, at that age!).

Non-vigilance

Walking across the playground at the end of Period Six, I noticed a couple of students riding their bikes towards the school gate doing mini-wheelies on the gravel (most students, most times, walk their bikes as per the school rule). I also noticed a colleague on end-of-day duty who couldn't have failed to see the two lads. In the brief glance (en route to the staff room) he looked wistful, oblivious to the bike riders. Perhaps he was singing (to himself) one of the favourite ditties of teachers, "How many days till the end of term ...?" I was about 20 yards away from the lads and I called them over.

"Fellas (...), Fellas (...)" – eventually getting some eye contact from distance. "See you for a few minutes over here (...) Thanks."

They stopped, akimbo their bikes, near the school gate. I thought they might just ride off (that's happened before).

"What? What d'you want?!"

They called out across the playground. They looked annoyed with a "we're-in-a-hurry-don't-hassle-us" look. I wanted them to come across to me so that I could briefly chat with them away from their immediate peer-audience. This approach is often preferable in playground settings. It avoids audience participation and the

"Greek chorus syndrome" (no offence to Greeks, you understand). I called them over again.

"Gees, what?! What d'we do?!" they called back.

"You're not in trouble – a brief chat (...) now. Thanks." I turned aside, walked a few paces and stopped facing away from them, to convey expectation (from distance) – take-up time (p. 102f).

The whole "episode" (one of countless we engage in on our teaching and management journey) hadn't taken long at all.

I saw them walking across the playground in my direction (out of the corner of my eye). I didn't want to message a visual stand-off; I've seen teachers call students over with fists curled on hips, legs astride, messaging (no doubt) a kind of "showdown".

They came over and stood nearby, with their bikes.

"Yeah? What?" (sighs, eyes averted, wry look). I tactically ignored the sighs (the sulky look, the marginal eye contact) so as to keep the focus on the main issue – bike-riding in school grounds.

I introduced myself and asked their names.

"Adam (...) Lukas" (still sulking and sighing).

"Fellas (...) I know you're on your way home. A brief chat."

"Adam and Lukas (...) what's the school rule for bike-riding in school grounds?" Avoid asking *why*.

"What?" Adam wasn't sure what I was getting at initially. I repeated the question. "What's the school rule ...?"

"Other teachers don't hassle us ..." He now knew what I was on about.

"Maybe they don't." I smiled – adding a brief "partial agreement" (p. 22) "What's the school rule?" I asked again. This time Adam looked at me, grinned.

"It depends who's here ..."

That's the point. The students tend to know which teachers are "non-vigilant".

NB   Not all students will answer a "rule-directed question". If they don't, we can answer it for them. It is a way of raising "behaviour awareness".

It does make it harder to exercise reasonable consistency in a school when some teachers ignore, or choose not to address, "small-beer" issues like "hats on in class", "chewing gum in class", "running in corridors", "testosteronic play-punching and bonding around the neck", "bike riding in school grounds", and so on.

It is easy to fall into a kind of jaded tiredness when it comes to addressing such behaviours. If such "non-vigilance" is typical across a school it makes it doubly hard for others in the team to exercise "*relaxed* vigilance".

Some students will "argue the toss" with the teacher when "called over" for a reminder about school rules (and so on). Some students will "do a runner". Rather than get into a heated argument, my colleagues and I have found it very helpful to use our small "behaviour monitoring book" (yellow cover; like the yellow card in soccer …). We record their names, incident, date, and so on. We can find the names from the photo chart (or sometimes students nearby). In 24 to 48 hours, the initiating teacher who was on playground duty will then follow up with the said student(s) *and* a senior teacher. We don't normally *chase* students (unless it is a safety issue with young children). We have learned that it is not the severity of the consequence but the fair *certainty* that is effective in communicating that teachers will follow up *and* follow through (p. 106).

Relaxed "vigilance"

As Melissa (Year 9) enters the classroom (late), to a little coterie of grins, the teacher acknowledges her with a smile, a small frown, and a welcome.

"Welcome Melissa" (her friends laugh). A little quieter: "I notice you're late; please take a seat." The teacher does not make an issue of the lateness or the fact that she is wearing dangling earrings at that point in the lesson. As Melissa walks to her seat (was that the gait of a supermodel?) the teacher is reclaiming whole-class attention and focusing on the lesson "as if nothing serious had happened at all" which is, of course, the case. The teacher's confident calmness and focus has minimised Melissa's initial audience-seeking entry.

Later in the lesson, when the students are "working", she calls Melissa aside (quietly) from her immediate peer-audience.

"Melissa – you were late last period and the one before that; we'll need to have a brief chat after class."

Melissa moans, "Why? I couldn't help it!"

"Well perhaps you can explain to me after class – I won't keep you long. Nice earrings." She quickly changes the focus.

"What?"

"Nice earrings …"

Melissa grins with ill-concealed suspicion. "Yeah!"

"What's the school rule about earrings, Melissa?"

The teacher avoids the pointless interrogative "*Why* are you …?" or "*Are* you wearing earrings?" What's the point of asking a student "why" they're doing something inappropriate if we, and they, know they're doing it?

Melissa appeals to a well worn student ploy, "But Mrs Daniels didn't say anything in form-group about them." Here Melissa sighs, folds her arms and gives a sulky, frowning, look.

"Maybe she didn't." The teacher doesn't call Melissa a liar, nor does she pass judgement on her colleague's possible ignoring of jewellery rules. "I can check that with her." The teacher's tone is pleasant, not sarcastic or in any way provocative. She repeats the question. "What's the school rule about earrings?" By using a direct question ("what?") the teacher is directing the ownership back to Melissa. Melissa, again, mentions Mrs Daniels. The teacher "partially agrees" (briefly) "Yes – you said that." but refocuses to the rule question.

"What's the rule for ...?"

Melissa sighs, "Yeah – well ... we're not supposed to." She says it, sighing, in an "I-can't-believe-why-we've-got-this-petty-rule ..." kind of voice.

The teacher then says, "Alright Melissa, it's my job to remind you; you know what to do." She smiles, "I'll come and see how your work is going later."

The teacher becomes task oriented now. She signals an end to this brief rule reminder, conveying the expectation that Melissa will take the earrings off. By giving the student some take-up time (p. 102f) she also minimises any forced "showdown" such as forcing Melissa to hand over the jewellery. If Melissa doesn't take them off then the teacher knows the underlying issue is a potential power-struggle and rather than force her to take them off will use a deferred consequence (p. 155f).

The "student tribal tom-toms" convey the message around the class that this teacher will address issues that relate to school rules (even earrings) but they also appreciate the *way* this teacher does it.

Is it worth the teacher's brief effort to address the student's lateness and earrings in *this* way? The "simple" answer is yes. *Relaxed* vigilance enables workable consistency – we'll never get perfect consistency across teacher leadership, just reasonable and workable consistency. This teacher sends the clear (fair) messages about arriving to class on time and jewellery rules but in a least intrusive way that keeps the workable and respectful relationship between teacher and student intact. She also addresses the lateness at a time of *her* choosing instead of over-reacting *at the point of attentional entrance*.

> NB If the student is late to class say three times in close succession the teacher is better served setting up a one-to-one meeting with the student (say at lunch time) to check for reasons and offer support. It is worth checking if this student is also late to other classes so that a year-level collegial response can be considered.

Inappropriate language

I was team teaching in a maths class a couple of years ago. My colleague and I had finished the whole-class teaching phase of the lesson and we were moving around the room to encourage, assist, refocus students during on-task learning time.

Out of the corner of my eye I saw a student throw an eraser, parabolically, to another student who missed the catch. Cassie called across the room – loudly – to the student who had dropped it.

"Gees, you silly bitch!" She said this in a laughing, "matey", kind of way (had she meant her friend to catch it?).

The other girl laughed – as did many in the class. My colleague was closer to the fracas than I was but hadn't taken any action regarding the student's language so I called to Cassie, across the room, to come over to me (away from her immediate coterie). She stayed seated.

"What? What do you want?!" She gave me a sulky, frowning, look across the room.

I repeated, "See you for a minute over here thanks."

I had said this in a firm (but relaxed) way while working with another group of students. She stood up, arms folded.

"What did I do then, eh?"

I wasn't going to discuss anything across the distance of several rows of students. I had directed her *away from her immediate classmates* to avoid unnecessary embarrassment (to her) and also to speak to her (briefly) about her behaviour. Cassie certainly knows how to "play to the gallery".

I added for a third (and last time), "I want to see you over here. Now (...). Thanks." I turned my eyes away from Cassie (yet again), and turned aside to the group I was working with to convey "expectation". If she had refused to come over I would have communicated a *deferred* consequence. (See later, p. 88, 146, 155f).

She came over and stood next to me, with folded arms, skewed eye contact, eyes raised to the ceiling and sighing.

"What do you want?" she said, in a careworn, "I'm-doing-you-a-favour-by-coming-across-to-you" tone of voice.

It's hard to keep the focus on the "primary" issue or behaviour. Ignoring the sulky non-verbals, I said, "I called you over so I wouldn't embarrass you in front of your classmates."

"What?" She seemed oblivious as to any reason why I'd need to speak to her.

"You threw an eraser at Melinda and she dropped it. You called across the room to her that she was a silly bitch." I'd said all this quietly. She looked at me, incredulously.

"What!? She don't care if I call her that. She's my friend anyway. Gees!!" (... the social injustice of it all!).

Should we simply accept "street" language, as some social commentators suggest we should? Should we accept "friendly banter" expressed in language that includes words like bitch, slut, a—hole, d—head, poofter, w—er, and so on? If I do let such language go I've tacitly said, "I don't care if you speak to each other like that in our class" (and I do care). (See later, p. 192f).

I *partially* agreed with Cassie. "Maybe Melinda doesn't care. I do." (I meant it.)
  She sighed and said, "So-reee!" (sorry).
  I *briefly* reminded her of our classroom agreement about respectful language.
  "Can I go back to my seat now?" Her tone and manner continued to evidence sulky indifference.

It would have been pointless at this point to add, "Look you don't really mean you're sorry! Say it properly, as if you mean it!" (I've seen teachers force students like Cassie into face-losing, or verbal slanging matches, because of the tone of voice in which an "apology" is given).

  As Cassie was leaving the class later that morning she said to me, "This class was OK till you came". That was probably true (as her version of "OK" goes.) The class had got used to being *very* noisy; with frequent calling out, cross-talking and the sort of banter I'd heard from Cassie that morning. Above all there was clearly a lack of focus during "on-task learning" time. There were several students like Cassie who hadn't had the issue of friendly banter addressed until this occasion. She was more amenable in the following lessons. We developed a basic, respectful understanding about expectations, about "focus", and why we are here together in this place. It took time, effort and continued goodwill.

Being a reflective practitioner

However many years we have been teaching we can always benefit from some reflection on our teaching and management practice. I once heard a teacher say, "You can't teach an old dog new tricks". My colleague was in a small group of teachers discussing behaviour management practices and skills. I knew my colleague had management problems in a number of classes (but unfortunately found it hard to share those concerns). The discussion group was a collegial forum to enable such general sharing of concerns. When she had said this a little too defensively, ("You can't teach an old dog new tricks"), I replied, "But you're not a dog; you're a human being". My wry smile was returned by my colleague. "If we're willing, and see a need for fine-tuning, even change, in our management practice and if we are aware of more effective management practice, we *can* always learn … with support … ". The discussion continued on about the nature of, and challenge of, change in personal behaviour as a teacher leader.

"Primary" and "secondary" behaviours

In many of the exchanges between teacher and students in this book, you will note a frequently recurring theme: that of a student's non-verbal and verbal behaviour potentially increasing the stress a teacher faces when seeking to address student behaviour. Elsewhere I have described such behaviours as "*secondary* behaviours". The student's pouting, sighing, sulking, tut-tutting, raised eyes to ceiling, and huffing behaviours and their procrastination and argumentative stance are *secondary* to the *primary* issue that the teacher addresses (Rogers 2006b). These "secondary behaviours" are also often more stressfully annoying than the "primary" issue or behaviour.

A student has not cleaned up his work area, and it is getting close to the "bell" (breaktime). The teacher reminds the student to clean up. The student says, "Alright, alright …" but sighs as he says it, rolls his eyes to the ceiling, leans back in his seat, leans forward again, but makes no initial move to start cleaning up. It is as if he's saying, "Here-we-go-again"; "blah-blah-blah".

The *primary* issue (litter on the floor) is hardly on the radar screen of teacher concern; it is merely a necessary class reminder. Even the words the student uses ("alright") are barely "amenable". It is the *tone* of the voice, the expelled sigh, the upward turn of the eyes; those body language signals appear to say, "I don't care

– don't hassle me!" It is these *secondary* behaviours that appear (quickly) as more disconcerting, or frustrating to the teacher than the issue of the litter itself.

I was teaching a Year 10 social studies class a few years back (as mentor-teacher). It was my first session with them. During the whole-class teaching phase of the lesson a student in the back row leaned back in her seat and sprayed a small can of what looked like perfume around the room. It had clearly annoyed some of the class. Others (her friends and her audience) laughed. Several boys started to join in the feigned "Ahhr!! – stinks!" It was behaviour that couldn't be ignored. I called across the room to her, by name.

"Anne (…) Anne (…)" – I'd remembered her name from roll call. She looked across the room at me with a look of (feigned?) surprise.

"Yes – what?" (oh "the sigh"). She leaned back in her chair, the can of perfume spray still on the desk. She grinned.

"You've got a can of *Impulse* (that's what I thought the brand was) and you've sprayed it around the room." It helps to be specific and briefly "describe the reality"; (a sort of "wavelength check"). "I want you to put it on my desk or put it away in your bag. Thanks." I gave her a directed choice rather than walk to the back of the room and either tell her to "hand it over" or just take it.

"It's not Impulse, it's Evoke," was her response. No doubt she said it to garner more group attention ("Notice me, everyone!") Her tone of voice seemed to suggest: "Let's play verbal ping-pong shall we?"

These kinds of "secondary behaviours" are much more annoying to teachers than the "primary behaviours" that trigger them: the sighs; the head movements; the averted eyes or the eyes to the ceiling; the supercilious grin and, of course, the annoying time-wasting things that some students say.

Rather than argue with Anne about the spray perfume ("I don't care if it's Chanel number bleedin' 9!! Put it away now or !!"), I said, "I want you to put it in your bag or on my desk," repeating the "directed choice". Her bag was under her table.

"But it stinks in here!" She still wanted to play verbal ping-pong. A bit of brief, partial, agreement can help avoid pointless argument.

"I know it stinks." She was actually right on that score. Local factories produce some awful smells that – on a hot day – waft, almost palpably, into the classrooms at this school. "And I want you to …" I repeated the directed choice.

At that point I took the minimal risk of leaving Anne with the directed "choice", as it were, and reclaimed group attention by saying something like, "Looking up here everyone (…). Thanks.", and going back to the diagram and topic I had started to address earlier. Out of the corner of my eye I noticed her slowly (ever so slowly) put the "Evoke" perfume in her bag.

If she hadn't put it away I'd have spoken to her later in the lesson, during class time, away from her direct audience. If she had refused, full stop, to put it away, a deferred consequence would have been made clear to her (see pp. 88, 155f).

The hard thing always, in such situations, is to communicate a sense of calmness and personal self-control when dealing with such "secondary behaviours". Yes, there are times when it is appropriate and necessary to communicate one's frustration and anger (Chapter 7), and to assert, but in this case, with this silly game-playing, a directed choice, avoiding argument and refocusing the class are more effective. Of course, I could have:

■ walked over and grabbed the perfume off the table, "Right! I'll have that!"
■ demanded she hand the perfume over, "Right ... give it to me ... give it to me now!" (What if she doesn't, what if she says, "No!! – can't make me!")
■ said, "Don't you ever speak to me like that! Who the hell do you think you are?" (or words to that effect)
■ been sarcastic or rude, in order to embarrass her in front of the class
■ told her to leave the room.

Some of these options (above) are no doubt transitionally tempting! What I am trying to say is that we, in effect, teach each other in these episodic transactions. Anne is learning something about *appropriate* teacher authority and leadership and (where necessary) about facing the consequences of her behaviour. So are the audience of her peers.

This is a drawing of that Year 10 class I worked with. You can see one lad throwing ("I was only passing") a ruler to a mate. Another has a iPod plugged in. Anne is into serious seat-leaning and task avoidance. It took some time to refocus this class (p. 222f).

There are always many things I *could* do or say. There are always many "ifs", "could-bes" and "what-ifs" in behaviour management with challenging students. There is also no guarantee that any approach will always work in all situations.

There needs to be, however, practices and skills that reflect our values about how we lead, guide, encourage and support young people. Later, in Chapter 3, the practices and skills of behaviour leadership are explored in some detail. This first chapter explores the natural, daily, dynamic within which we need to exercise our behaviour leadership. Behaviour is complex at times; situational and relational behaviour also has its audience-seeking effect, which can either work for the teacher's (and class's) benefit or work against the teacher.

We can ill afford to lose the goodwill of the 70–80 per cent of cooperative students by forcing the challenging student to lose face and thereby making it easy for the 70–80 per cent to "side" with the disruptive student or, conversely, allow ourselves to be "backed-into-a-psychological-corner".

In another Year 10 class I was moving around the room during on-task learning time and noticed a student with an iPod (something I come across frequently these days) – tiny earphones in his ears and clearly enjoying the music that I could hear, faintly, as I worked with students nearby. Walking over to him I made eye contact and beckoned with my fingers for him to take the earphones out. He did. I could hear the pulsating, heavy metal buzz more intensely now.

"It'll help if you turn it off," I suggested. He did.

"Nice iPod," I observed.

"Yeah," he agreed.

"Brock," I asked, "What's the school rule about iPods in class?" Students are allowed to bring iPods or hand-held electronic games or mobile phones to this particular school but they're not supposed to use them in class – for obvious reasons one would think. It's hard to communicate to a student who – in Brock's case – has serious "heavy metal" going on "upstairs".

Instead of answering the question I had asked ("What's the school rule about iPods in class?") Brock pointed to his regular teacher and said, "Ms Snaggs doesn't mind if we have them on – long as we're doing our work ..." He didn't say this rudely, even cockily (some do); he was stating it as a matter of fact.

In my team-teaching-mentoring role in this school, I had noticed that a few teachers didn't seem to care if students brought, and played, their iPods as long as they got their classwork done as well. No doubt at all – of course students can work with iPods, in their ears (even head-banging music ...); that's not the issue. The school rule is clear (and fair) and there for a reason – "no iPods in class time".

Some teachers "over-service" a student's verbal "secondary behaviour" by entering into a pointless discussion about the veracity of what the student has said, or they try to defend the reasons for the rule (generally an unwise course); "Brock ... look ... I don't make the rules do I?" Some teachers almost sound like they are "pleading". They present with a defeated, if affable, and well-meaning tone, suggesting that whatever happens the student will have their way despite what the fair rules may say. "Other teachers might let you play iPods but they're not really supposed to, *are they*?" It is pointless *asking* the student to reason (*at this point in the lesson*) about something he may see as unfair; besides it is a time-wasting exercise distracting away from the business of teaching and learning.

Some teachers become overly vigilant and defensive, and will cast ineffective aspersions on other colleagues. "Look I don't care what Ms Smith does or doesn't do! In my class you don't have personal stereos on – *full stop!* Now – give it to me." When students want to appeal to "what other teachers do (or let us do)" a *brief* partial agreement is helpful followed by a refocusing to the right or rule affected, or a refocusing to the task:

"Miss Donkin lets us have iPods in social studies."

"Maybe she does (partial agreement) (…) however in this class the rule is clear. I want you to put the iPod on my table or, if you like, in your bag (or pencil case) …". The teacher beckons to the teacher's table.

Whenever I've given this directed choice (at primary or secondary level), I've never had a student (yet) say, "OK, I'll put my expensive iPod" (or other objet d'art) "on your table".

Residual "secondary behaviour"

Jaydon is chewing a largish, viscous, fruity-smelling chewing gum. The teacher walks over and quietly says, "Jaydon (…)". Brief eye-contact is established.

"Yeah, what?" "Morning."

"Oh yeah. Morning."

The teacher asks how his work is going and adds: "The bin is over there."

"What?" he asks.

"The bin is over there." This *incidental* direction in part "describes the reality" (there is a bin) and invites some basic "behaviour awareness" (put the chewing gum in the bin) by reminding the student where the bin is. It is said respectfully, a little tongue-in-cheek, as if to say "You know that I know that you know what you should do …".

If the student engages secondary dialogue "But other teachers don't hassle us …!" (blah, time-wasting, blah), the teacher will *briefly* acknowledge with partial agreement and refocus.

"Other teachers may let you chew gum. Here, in this class, the rule is clear and the bin is near … Ta." The teacher walks off expecting cooperation by giving the student some take-up-time (p. 102f).

Ten seconds or so later the student shuffles off to the bin sighing and muttering. "I'll put it in the bin, I'll put it in the bin n'yah, n'yah (in a *sotto voce* whine) …"

The teacher *tactically* ignores this "residual secondary behaviour" and observes (out of the corner of his eye) that the student has slumped in his seat, sighed, and slowly restarted work (more residual "secondary behaviour"). A little later he goes over to the student and re-establishes the working relationship by focusing on the task. "So, how's it going then? Let's have a look. Where are you up to?"

You can imagine what could happen if the teacher over-services all those residual behaviours. "Look!! When you put chewing gum in the bin, you put it in the bin *without* a fanfare – alright?!" or, "Why can't you do a simple thing like put chewing gum in the bin without making a song-and-dance about it?!" That would unnecessarily re-escalate any residual tension as well as over-servicing this kind of attentional behaviour.

Some teachers try to ameliorate what they see as the perceived upsetness of the student; they take the huffing and puffing and muttering as an indication they've upset the student. "Troy, Troy, I don't make the rules do I ... be reasonable ...". This kind of good intent only over-services the sulkiness and pouting. It is – generally – better to *tactically* ignore such behaviours *until* the student is back on task, as it were, and then have a brief "re-establishing" that focuses on the task (the classwork) at hand (p. 100f).

If a student's "secondary behaviour" is too disturbing, or rude, in tone or manner, it will need to be addressed, briefly and firmly, and with a focus on the unacceptable behaviour and a refocus back to the task or expected behaviour: "I'm not speaking to you like that, I don't expect you to speak to me like that". This to a student whose tone of voice is rude, cocky or arrogant. At this point it is also prudent to give "take-up-time" as the student sulks off back to his seat.

If such sulking and pouting is *characteristic* of the student's behaviour, an after-class chat that involves some modelling and feedback may be a helpful way to help the student become aware of his typical behaviours and then work on a "plan of understanding" (p. 182f). If such follow-up is carried out early in the teacher–student relationship, and with supportive respect, it can go a long way to seeing a reduction in residual "secondary behaviours".

We will also come across students who, through their behaviour, say (in effect), "You can't make me!" or "I don't have to do what you say ...". I have seen some infant students really upset their teachers by turning aside and refusing to look at them after the teacher has specifically given a direction: "Bronson (...) Bronson (...) Look at me. Look-at-me!!" I've seen teachers put their hand under a child's chin and force it up to engage attentional eye contact. I've seen teachers bodily turn young children around so they are facing their teacher. I can understand such teacher behaviour, and in some *carefully thought-through* behaviour modification contexts, such teacher behaviour *may* be appropriate. But if the teacher is getting frustrated and forcing the child's head up the resistant child may well be saying (through his/her behaviour) "You can't make me!", or "I can do what I want and you can't stop me". The child's "private logic" is, at this point, "correct"; annoying, but correct. *Who is controlling whom?* The issue of challenging children is addressed more fully in Chapter 6.

- At younger primary age, children are not always aware of their 'secondary' behaviours. It will help to have a chat with them later (one to one) to explain and even briefly model such behaviours to them (see p. 108).[1]
- Sometimes "secondary behaviours" are the result of habit; the student may be unaware that their non-verbal behaviours appear as sulky; pouty; indifferent; testy – displaying a "chip on the shoulder" (with some students there is "a bucket of attitudinal chips"!). In these cases early and thoughtful follow-up to

acknowledge the teacher's concern and gain some shared understanding, and then work on changes, is crucial (p. 106f).

■ Sometimes such behaviour is the student's bad-day syndrome; sensitivity in the teacher will acknowledge this (privately) and encourage the student to be aware of their behaviour in the future.

■ Sometimes such behaviour is provoked by the teacher through their own insensitive, petty, even confrontational behaviour.

■ Sometimes the student, too, will use their secondary behaviours in a provocative way to "test" out the psychological, relational, "territory" Shakespeare speaks of: "*some kind of men … that put quarrels purposely on others … to test their valour …*" (*Twelfth Night* 3, iv). Such behaviour is often used as a territorial posturing; particularly in males.

■ For some students their secondary behaviour may be a form of "exitatory stimulation" – where the student uses his attentional behaviour as a form of "conditioned stimulation".[2]

One of the harder messages I had to learn as a younger teacher was that I cannot simply and easily "control" others' behaviour. I can control myself *in* the teaching and management situation (although that, too, is not always easy …). To the extent that I thoughtfully control myself, my language, my "manner" and my approach to the students, is the degree to which I can invite cooperation or, conversely, find my students becoming difficult, or even resistant. The skills addressed later in Chapters 2, 3 and 4, specifically address the issue of effective teaching, behaviour leadership and discipline.

I have also learned not to make demands on reality that reality won't bear.

Our "explanatory style" in behaviour management: creating or managing stress

Some teachers bring an *overly* demanding "explanatory style" to classroom management and discipline; a *characteristic* way of defining and explaining social, relational, reality. One's explanatory style can not only affect how one relates to others, but can also affect one's emotional state and well-being (Bernard 1990; Seligman 1991; Rogers 1996, 2002).

When stressful events come to us, it is not only, or *simply*, the stressful event that directly causes how we feel, and how effectively we cope and manage. Our "explanatory style", our "working beliefs" about behaviour – what students *should,* and *shouldn't* do – also contribute significantly to how effectively we manage stressful situations.

Some of the unhelpful, assumptive, beliefs that, of themselves, can increase one's stress are directly related to how we perceive and explain what is happening when a student is attentionally demanding, rude, arrogant, lazy or indifferent. "Secondary behaviour" is a typical case in point. When a student slouches, sighs, rolls his eyes to the ceiling or gives a malevolent grin, some teachers will "automatically" react to such "secondary behaviours" in a stressful way; often saying (later) that "Children *must not* question or disagree with their teachers" (their superiors), or "Children *should* do what I say the *first time*", or "Children *should not* answer back". The most common belief statement I hear is, "Children *should not* be rude, they *should* respect their teachers" (full stop).

The "should" and "must" part of the explanatory style is often the problem. There is an imperative here; a demand on reality that is often unrealistic – unrewarded in reality. There are many children who show disrespect, who do not respond, comply, or "obey" the first time; who answer back; who are *un*civil. It is unpleasant of course, and frustrating when this happens. However, when we say, "students *must* obey me ...", "*must* not answer back ..." or "*must* respect me ...", we are making absolute demands that, if not met, contribute to the level of our stress and also to how effectively we handle management situations. If we say, "He *shouldn't* answer back to me" when he did (in reality) the internal self-speech can increase the amount of stress one feels at that point; particularly if the intensity of cognitive demand (shouldn't!) is a *characteristic* way that one explains such stressful reality.

I have seen different teachers, managing the same student, in much the same situations, and seen quite different degrees of effectiveness in management, and teacher coping, that are not explained simply through personality style alone (Rogers 1996). A more *realistic* belief avoids absolutistic imperatives: "I can't stand it when ...!!" is different in kind from "It's annoying, frustrating, unpleasant when ... but I can cope if I do X, Y, Z". We might still feel stressed holding this belief, *and* explaining difficult events in this way, but we won't be *as* stressed for *as* long. Of course our beliefs need to be buttressed and supported by skills of coping in management contexts. It is the *balance* between realistic beliefs and management skill that enables less stressful, more positive, coping day after day.

A *cognitive fixation* about receiving (indeed, demanding) respect can alter how we perceive, interpret and manage the sorts of "secondary behaviours" noted earlier. Whether we like it or not, we have to "earn" respect from our students by the effectiveness of our teaching (Chapter 4), our confident management and by the effort we make to build and sustain workable relationships with our students.

Beliefs and standards

The belief "Children *must* not swear ..." is not the same as having a standard about respectful language. Having a more realistic and appropriately flexible belief about swearing – "I *don't like most swearing* however I won't let it unnecessarily stress me, while at the same time I will need to address it accordingly to situation, and circumstance" – will occasion a less stressful state of mind and (with some prior skill) enable a more effective management of swearing (see p. 192f).

It can help to learn to "tune into" and "dispute" unhelpful, self-defeating beliefs and explanatory styles that are often couched in "must" and "should" ("I *should* be able to control these kids!!"). By "reframing" the demands to preferences based in reality, we tune into workable reality without "dropping our standards". We also reduce insistence-focused statements about reality ("He *must* ...", "I *must* ...", "Others *must* ...") that can increase emotional stress levels. At the end of the day, reality has no obligation to obey our demands.

This is not mere badinage. Talking, even self-talking, is an action, and actions have effects. If I say "I'm no good", that is overgeneralising. If I have an insistent cognitive demand behind such thoughts ("I *must* get it right all the time"), I'll set an impossible personal standard. If, however, I say "Look, I'm having difficulty with (a given student or class group)" and "What skills and support do I need?", that is *accurate* self-talk. It is also realistic. Being more accurate, reasonable, and realistic about reality will help me in addressing my goals and managing inevitable, natural, stress.

Inaccurate, inflexible, demanding and negative self-talk can become an unreflective habit. If not addressed, it may become so *characteristic* that it is no longer a conscious activity. And while past performance and past experience may have interred our characteristic self-talk, it is in the present that we are using it and in the present that changes need to be made.

The bad-day syndrome

There will be days (naturally) when normative tiredness and concerns arising from one's personal life, the issues of the day and one's state of health will affect the quality of our day-to-day teaching and behaviour management. Even those days when we just feel "out-of-sorts" will have this effect. It is easy on those days for *our* frustration to spill over into our behaviour. We may become short-tempered, snappy and even angry.

It is important to telegraph to students when we're having a bad day. "You can probably tell I'm not feeling the best today. It's not your fault. ['Well it is a bit', you might be tempted to say!] I don't want to go into it all – but I'm a bit annoyed (or cheesed off). If you see me getting a bit 'snappier' today you'll know why ...".

If we are unwell it will be important to briefly explain "I've got a bad headache, or ...". If it is a more personal issue it is normally unwise to share details; it is – generally – enough to just telegraph the fact we're having a bad day. Most students cannot really cope with such personal information (nor should they have to). I am amazed at how much personal information some teachers are apparently willing (and comfortable) to share with children – even primary-aged children: information about their relationships, their divorce details, their financial hassles and even concerns they have about their fellow teachers!

Children enjoy the sort of sharing about a teacher's childhood experiences ("When I was a boy we did ...") but it is inappropriate to use the teacher–student relationship to either "offload" one's personal frustrations or to make students inappropriate confidantes.

We don't need to go into details on our bad days; it is enough to let them know so that they can have some basic awareness of how we're feeling, even occasion some sympathy with our shared humanity! Children understand that *everybody* has bad days.

There are bad days where we might say something inappropriate, or thoughtless, to a student; a throwaway line that we didn't intend to use; a sharper tone; even an insensitive, churlish or petty comment. Tiredness, stress, being rushed and hurried (and harried) by others can easily chip away at our goodwill and patience. On such days we are wise and professional – human – to remember to acknowledge and apologise. Having done so, it will then be important not to engage in self-blame and to move on.

This is to be distinguished from teachers who *characteristically* discipline and manage in petulant, petty, mean-spirited ways; destined (it seems) to create, even sustain, unnecessary anxiety and unacceptable control over their students. While such teachers may still (in some schools) get "results", they do so at a great cost to student well-being and self-esteem. I have worked with teachers who have refused to forgive students (even students who have made an attempt to apologise). I have seen teachers refuse to apologise when it was the right and proper thing to do, or who nurse a grudge against a student for a long, long time. They forget that we are all fallible. Such teaching and management behaviour needs (in my view) to be professionally confronted where it exists.

Coping with our personal, psychological, junk mail

Bad days, failure and self-criticism often seem to go together. We can at times be quite hard on ourselves, unfairly hard, when we don't perform well.

I've sat and talked with teachers who, having got angry with a student or a class, say "I *shouldn't* have got angry like that …". Why ever not? There are many situations where we will get angry with our students. Yes, there are more effective ways of managing anger than shouting or yelling, but we *did* get angry. We are not a failure for that. We can always do something about poorly handled anger (Chapter 7).

Psychological junk mail comes loaded with global, stable, self-talk: "I *shouldn't* have!" (we did); "It's *not fair*!" (really?); "I *always* get it wrong!" (always?); "I'll *never* get through to them" (never?). Maybe we shouldn't have done, or said, X, Y, Z, but we did; that's the reality. If we add to such self-talk repetitions of, and ruminations about, our failure ("I *shouldn't*!", or comments such as, "*I'm an idiot*", "*I'm* stupid, a total failure" – total?, "I *never* get a fair deal") we will naturally feel worse and cope less effectively with our failure, and our struggle.

I'm not suggesting a kind of cognitive 'shrugging it off' by saying it doesn't really matter when it does; *it can and does hurt at times*. It *does* matter when we fail, when we get things wrong; but repetitive self-talk (like that above) acts like psychological junk-mail and we feel worse than we need to feel.

Natural feelings of failure are normal, and even appropriate. Learning to fail meaningfully means we acknowledge our fallibility (in ourselves *and* others). It will help to label the failure for what it is – a mistake, a lapse in judgement (even a lack of skills) – and instead of excusing the failure we ask what can be learned from it: "Do I need to apologise to anyone?" (probably); "What do I need to do?" (specifically); "Do I need support or help to move beyond this?" We can learn as much, at times, from what goes wrong as what goes right (a message we frequently tell our students).

By *relabelling* failure – "OK, I did get it wrong. I should have done X, Y, Z" – and then asking "What can I do now and what can I do *next time* in a similar situation?", we redirect the emotional energy that can easily be eaten up by "mentally kicking oneself" (Edwards 1997). Tuning into negative self-talk is not easy; like any skill it needs to be acknowledged and practised as a kind of inner self-checking "mechanism" whenever we catch ourselves "posting psychological junk mail upstairs". Maybe we can't take control of the first thought that comes into our head but we can *learn* to take control of *subsequent* thinking and internal dialogue.

We're likely to be using negative self-talk when we're experiencing emotions such as frustration, anger or ongoing anxiety, a sense of "powerlessness", or residual jadedness towards someone or about some situation or circumstance. The reason for disputing erroneous and self-defeating thinking is that it can bring about a more effective way of coping; emotional and practical coping. We will need to ask ourselves if our current thoughts – the way we explain hurtful or bad events to ourselves – is actually helping to deal with our struggle; our failure. What are the consequences, the outcome, of *this* kind of thinking?

Failure

Professor Martin Seligman, a leading researcher on *learned* helplessness and *learned* optimism has said:

> Failure makes everyone at least *momentarily* helpless. It's like a punch in the stomach. It hurts, but the hurt goes away – for some people almost instantly … for others the hurt lasts, it seethes, it roils, it congeals into a grudge … they remain helpless for days or perhaps months, even after only small setbacks. After major defeats they may never come back. (1991: 45)

According to Seligman *learned* helplessness derives from an explanatory style that believes, and explains, difficult and bad events in several dimensions: permanence, pervasiveness and personalisation. "It's *me* …" (or, "It's *them*!") "I *never* get it right … it will last *forever* … it will affect *everything* I do …".

An *optimistic explanatory style* acknowledges the annoyance, even pain, in failure, but avoids using abiding traits to explain the failure and bad events. Using qualifiers helps reorient: "Yes, I do *sometimes* get it wrong", "*lately* I haven't been up to scratch with my lesson plans" and "it is *annoying* that I missed out on my promotion, so what do I need to do to improve or change?" The more optimistic explanatory style *acknowledges frustrating reality, but reframes* it, seeing the failure as having transient rather than permanent and pervasive causes. Further, the optimistic explanatory style avoids recumbent self-blame, or other blame: "It's *me* …", "I'll *never* change …" and "I'll *never* get it right …". Acknowledging one's *temporary* stupidity, ineptness, laziness, lack of forethought and planning is, in short, acknowledging one's humanity!

It is the *habits* of explanation that lie at the heart of explanatory styles and personal self-talk. It is not simply the explanation we make in interpreting our episodic stresses; it is the *characteristic residual* explanatory style one falls back on in seeking to cope with stressful events. Seligman's research into learned helplessness and learned optimism is a positive and very practical resource in stress management and coping.

Contrast "I *never* …", "I *always* …", "I *can't* stand it …" and "*Everybody* in this class is …" with "I *sometimes* fail; *however* …", "*Some* people are *difficult* to work, with while others are not …", "It may be *difficult* (rather than 'I *can't* stand it') … but when I …", "It *will* get better *when* …", "If I do X and Y, things will improve …" and "Even if *I've failed* I am not a failure …". Private (internal) speech has a self-guiding and self-regulatory function.

Failure doesn't mean we *are* a failure. Defining failure in global and stable terms, rather that in situational and specific terms changes our perception of both ourselves and those areas in which we failed.

Adaptive, and maladaptive, thinking behaviours are learned as well as habituated from our personal history (Rogers 1996). These thinking skills when matched with behaviour leadership and teacher skills enable effective coping and even enjoyable and effective teaching (bad days notwithstanding p. 26f).

You control us! Who controls whom and what?

Working with a new Year 9 class once, I struggled to communicate the difficult message that it was *their* job to control *their* behaviour. Apparently their previous teacher (on stress leave) had battled with this class, week in and week out, and now it was my turn.

At the classroom meeting I conducted with this class, I raised the issue of their perception of "control" (p. 223). Many students indicated that it was "the teacher's job to control the class"; "It's the teacher's job to make us behave".

I asked "how?", and in the ensuing (and lively) discussion students' comments about teacher control ranged from "shouting" behaviours through to "intimidation" and "detentions". I further asked if they *liked* that kind of behaviour; and if they believed such behaviour was fair and helpful.

As we teased this out they agreed that it wasn't helpful to anyone really – being *forced* to behave through the "controlling" behaviour of teachers. What it amounted to is that these students effectively wanted the teachers to "control us" but part of *that* arrangement meant that they would make it a challenge for the teachers to control them: "you've got to prove you can control us". When students talk like this there is also the more important underlying message of security: they expect their teachers to be able to lead, manage and direct the day-to-day complexities of 25–30 students in a small room, engaged in teaching, learning and socialisation. To this extent their "cry of control" is valid; but our role is also to lead the students beyond mere simplistic, external, control to appropriate "self" and "shared" control.

It took a while but we finally managed to shift their thinking and their game-playing towards a new understanding: "As students … we control ourselves … You (our teacher) lead, guide and support us to manage ourselves. We give you that right and that responsibility to lead us in that way."

This shift is not a simple teaching exercise. Teachers need to be able to call on student cooperation through:

- shared understandings of core rights and responsibilities. This was expressed through a collaborative classroom agreement (see Chapter 2)
- the teacher's effort to teach with some enthusiasm, skill and willingness to address a wide range of student ability and to consider a range of teaching approaches (Chapter 3)
- the teacher's effort to communicate respect and care; particularly when they discipline (Chapter 4)
- the teacher's willingness to reach individuals as well as class groups (even a brief effort to get to know, and assist, an individual has a powerful effect on teacher–student cooperation (see p. 129f)).

I have many, many, times discussed the issue of teacher management and discipline with students. They seem very able to sum up how confident, sure, "together", able, (and so on) a teacher is. They seem to gain this knowledge by *how* a teacher *initially* expresses themselves in their management and their discipline, and how effectively the teacher manages to teach (Chapters 2 and 3). Those first impressions, in those first meetings in front of the group largely determine how the class group defines the teacher's subsequent role.

> As one student wrote about taking teachers on the first impression:
> *When you can see that you can get away with things with a teacher you often be stupid [sic] and go to other people's desks and don't take any notice of them [the teacher ...].*

This student is saying, in effect, that a "good" teacher needs to control the *situation* in which students behave. They normally then discuss (as this student does) how and why students do (or don't) "take notice" of teachers. Having notice taken of one's leadership and authority is primarily related to how relaxed one appears, how confident one's leadership style appears when *encouraging* and *directing* group and individual behaviour. (See Chapter 4, p. 55f.)

One's confidence is increased by having a plan for those first meetings with our class(es). This is discussed in the section on the establishment phase (p. 38f) and in the later section on language skills of behaviour management (Chapter 3) and effective teaching (Chapter 4).

Don't smile until Christmas

This is not the clearest, most helpful, maxim in teaching! I remember being told a version of this many years ago. *Imagine* standing in front of a group (in the corridor or in the classroom) with a tense, frowning, face – heavy impatient breathing – rocking back and forth on the toes ... Such non-verbal behaviour will – more than anything – indicate a lack of confidence in one's authority and "status". It may even provoke unnecessary, contestable, behaviour in some of our students. If a teacher stands in front of a class group looking anxious, arms folded in a protective – closed – body language, or a hesitant and sheepish smile that says, in effect, "please be nice to me ...", students may well read "indecisiveness", "non-assertion" or lack of confidence.

A confident, pleasant, relaxed smile, *while* we are communicating (not a sycophantic smile) can telegraph a *potential* confidence in student cooperation.

Of course, what the maxim is meant to say is that one needs to be firm and clear at the outset of our ongoing relationship with a new class about behaviour and learning. There is truth in this. It is much harder to reclaim unfocused, off-task, distracting behaviours than to *establish* positive, clear; norms from day one – first meeting.

I have heard many teachers say that they, in effect, "lost" the class because they tried to be "too friendly" from the first meeting with the class.

The 70–80 per cent

I have seen teachers lose the goodwill and potential cooperation of most of the class by the way they treat individuals and the group. Some teachers are surprised when the bulk of the class becomes resentful if the teacher treats any *one* individual with characteristic disrespect or fosters unresolved conflict. I have seen teachers use whole-class detentions to seek to put pressure on several disruptive students only to initially frustrate and then alienate the 70–80 per cent of cooperative students when they continue to use such detentions.

While it is natural to get frustrated by some individuals in a class group, we need the cooperation of the 70–80 per cent to successfully manage and support the 20–30 per cent of more attentional, difficult or challenging students.

What we can, and can't "control"

When I write, here in this book, about managing or disciplining students, I'm not speaking about *controlling* the students; it's surprising the ease, the facility, with which we say, "I *made* the student put his hand up ...", or "I *took* the student aside and told him to ...". We can't simply *make* a student do anything, or *take* a student anywhere, unless of course he or she is either naturally cooperative, highly compliant or obedient, or unquestioningly compliant or obedient (which are not necessarily healthy personality behaviour traits at all). I have always discouraged my own children to "*simply* obey your teacher because they are a teacher". (Mind you – I've taught them skilful ways to address unfair or even unjust, teacher behaviour.)

Rather than asking myself how can I more effectively control "my" students, it is more appropriate, and much more constructive, to ask "How can I be a more effective teacher leader?" and "What can I do to bring more effective control to the teaching situation and learning context?" The way I manage myself, and my thinking and attitude, have a significant (even lasting) effect on how students behave (cooperatively or uncooperatively) when I am with them (p. 24f).

The approaches, and skills, developed in this book are a means to *that* end.

Intent and relationships

Students hear and see the teacher's intention in a teacher's discipline and management of behaviour. If the *intention* read is one where the teacher is perceived as wanting to *merely* control, embarrass, shame or "hurt" the child then the acceptance of such discipline will be (naturally) resented and often lead to an unworkable teacher–student relationship. For example, where a teacher emphasises the severity of the consequence, rather than the certainty, then that is all the child will focus on (pp. 106, 148, 157).

If it is our intention to enable a student to take responsibility for his or her behaviour and to actively consider others' rights, and if our discipline has that as its aim, the child will more likely hear and see that intention in the kind of language and manner we use. The degree of cooperation, even compliance, in student behaviour, also depends on the kind of relationship existing between teacher and student.

In the establishment phase of the year the teacher is seeking to build a workable relationship with the whole class, as a group, also with the individuals. Even deceptively mundane expressions of humanity such as learning (and using) a student's name (at all times); positive greetings to the group and individuals (even out of class); remembering aspects and details of their individuality (a student's hobbies, special interests, events and birthdays) are all indicators of a teacher's effort to build and sustain positive working relationships.

Being pleasant (not sycophantic) to "unlikeable" students; going out of one's way to say "hello" (to an unreturned or muttered response); not holding grudges and starting each day afresh are all aspects of relational teacher behaviour that children soon acknowledge, affirm and respond to in a positive way.

When students get to know that we care about them as individuals (as persons with needs, concerns, feelings), then our discipline is judged and accepted within the understanding that the teacher cares about them.

Building relationships

It is, generally speaking, the positive relationships we develop with our students that we remember long after they have forgotten the history of the Tudors or positive and negative integers. I've often asked my own children, "What was maths (or French, or history) like today?" Sometimes they'll talk about the subject matter, but more often they talk about the *kind* of teacher they have and what happens in the relational dynamics of the classroom. My children have quickly "sorted" out which teachers can manage which classes (and why); which teachers teach well (and interestingly); which are fair and considerate; and which are normally patient, have a sense of humour and, above all, care.

I went to a high school in St Albans for six months (aged 15). I was running late for science class one morning. The bus was late. I arrived at the classroom door huffing and puffing, anxious because Mr Brown was not the most empathetic teacher in the school. Entering the classroom I saw a *new* teacher; a supply teacher? (I wasn't sure). He approached me at the door, smiling, and said, "You look a bit puffed out ..." (I'd been running). "I'm Mr Ryland. What's your name?" His tone and manner immediately put me at ease. He spoke to me quietly; away from the class (and the immediate hearing of others). "Who do you normally sit next to?" Having told him I sat next to Roger (a friend), he explained we were doing an experiment on Archimedes' principle (displacement of mass in water; Eureka!). "Roger will fill you in, eh? Catch your breath Billy. I'll come over and see how you're going later." Not only did I feel better (less anxious and less embarrassed) but I was also more motivated (in a subject that wasn't a favourite). Not only did I remember Archimedes' principle, but I remembered the difference a teacher can make to how one feels and "works" as a student.

Contrast Mr Ryland's treatment of my lateness and this personal account written by our oldest daughter when she was in high school (Year 9).

Vicki and I were sitting on the wall (where we usually wait for the lift home from Vicki's grandpa) at the end of the school day. Miss Green (Vicki's maths teacher) came over to us and said, "Have you made any effort to get that maths book yet?" And before Vicki could answer she said, "No, I don't think you have. I told you to wait behind on

Friday and someone told me you only waited five minutes!"

"I couldn't wait because my grandpa didn't know I was staying behind and he would be worried."

I chipped in at this point, trying to help out. "And it's a bit hard to stay behind because we go home in a car pool."

And Miss Green said, "I don't think this has anything to do with you! I don't think you know what this is about so I think you should just keep out of this!"

Well I just shut up (being the generally angelic and compliant student I am) but the truth is I knew a damn sight more than she did and instantly made up my mind I did not like this teacher.

How might he have felt …?

A colleague of mine found this missive on the worldwide graffiti board (you know – the Internet). It describes so well the normative frustrations of a teacher; frustrations that even Jesus must have felt:

The joy of teaching

Then Jesus took his disciples up the mountain and gathering them around him, He taught them saying: "Blessed are the poor in spirit, for theirs is the kingdom of heaven. Blessed are the meek. Blessed are they that mourn. Blessed are the merciful. Blessed are they that thirst for justice. Blessed are you when persecuted. Blessed are you when you suffer. Be glad and rejoice for your reward is great in heaven." Then Simon Peter said, "Are we supposed to know this?" And Andrew said, "Do we have to write this down?" And James said, "Will we have a test on this?" And Phillip said, "I don't have any paper." And Bartholomew said, "Do we have to turn this in?" And John said, "The other disciples didn't have to learn this." And Matthew said, "May I go to the toilet?" Then one of the Pharisees who was present asked to see Jesus's lesson plan and inquired of Jesus, "Where is your anticipatory set and your objectives in the cognitive domain?" And Jesus wept.

(Anon)

Reflection

- When you reflect on your own experiences at school what qualities, attributes, do you remember with affection? (or disaffection and pain!)?
- When you look at the dynamics of your classes does the concept of "relaxed vigilance" relate to your *characteristic* behaviour leadership (p. 117)? How do

you respond to the concept of "control" noted in this chapter (p. 30f)?

■ How aware are you of "primary" and "secondary" behaviours in your students (p. 17f)? How do you conceive this 'secondary behaviour' reality? What skills, practices, enable you when you address such behaviours in your students?

■ In reflecting on your *normative* stress – how aware are you of your 'characteristic explanatory style' in coping with and managing stress (p. 24)?

Notes

1. The issue of briefly modelling or "mirroring" a student's behaviour back to them (*only* in a one-to-one relationship) should always be prefaced by a request "Do you mind if I show you what it looks (or sounds) like when you …?" Also, such mirroring should not be conducted with children with autism spectrum disorder – it will only confuse or even upset them.

2. This is an interesting theory proposed by Mills (in Robertson 1997). Some children, according to Mills, use such behaviours to 'ward off' feelings of depression or stress. In their home background they may well be in a situation of high arousal (a loud home – quarrelling and shouting; significant sibling tension; television blaring …) – the 'excitation' sought at school may well be compensatory. Robertson notes that the crucial factor in *any* effectiveness in dealing with such pupils is the calm attitude a teacher conveys (Chapter 5).

Chapter 2

New class, new year: the establishment phase of behaviour management

Habits change into characters.
Ovid (45 BC–AD 17, author of the *Metamorphoses*)

New year, new class, new start

As you stand in your classroom on the one, pupil-free day, before Day One, Term One, you scan the room and furniture (sometimes inadequate and uncomfortable). You think, "Tomorrow there will be 25–30 students in here, each with their unique personality, temperament and needs. Phew!"

For some of you it will be your first class "on your own" as it were; for others it will be another fresh new year that (at times) will soon develop into the daily, hourly, minute-by-minute juggle of demands that make up normative teaching.

Most teachers can remember their first class – and even their entire first day.

One of the important, fundamental, questions at this stage of the year is "What can I do (and what can *we* do as a collegial team) to *minimise*, and prevent (where possible), unnecessary hassles or problems in establishing positive behaviours in our classes?"

The answer to this question will focus on the necessary procedures, routines and rules to enable the smooth running of quite a complex community. It will be important to integrate routines and rules into a workable system and then *consciously teach* that "system" through discussion, modelling, encouragement and teacher-management.

There is ample and extensive research to show that effective and positive teachers are acutely conscious of the importance of the first lesson, the first few days, the first few weeks and how they establish the shared rights and responsibilities of classroom behaviour with their students (see Doyle 1986; Kyriacou 1986, 1991; McInerney and McInerney 1998; McPherson and Rogers 2008; Robertson 1997; Rogers 1998, 2006b).

Establishment phase (practices and skills)

The establishment phase of the year is a crucial time in the development of a class group (and even the school as community). In terms of basic group dynamics there is a psychological and developmental readiness in the students for their teacher to explain how things will be *this* particular year with regard to expectations about behaviour and learning in *this* class with *this* teacher. The three basic phases of the life of a classroom community are set out in Figure 2.1.

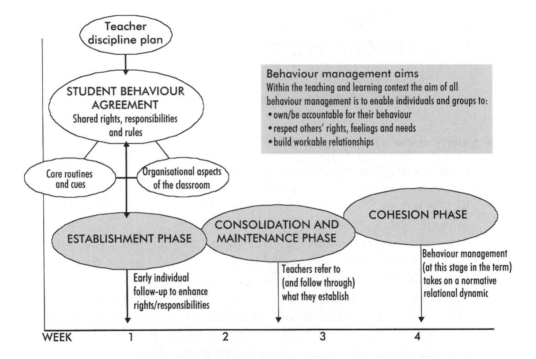

Figure 2.1 The fundamental phases of life in a classroom

Students should expect their teacher to clarify:

- lining up and room entry procedures (considerate entry, without overuse of "testosteronic-bonding" by some male students!)
- seating plans and student grouping for Week One, and possibly Term One. Such planning needs to include whether seating should occur in rows, pairs or table groups. It will often need to include, also, "who sits with whom"
- student entry to class and settling at workplaces or "carpet space" for infants. Routines and cues will need to be explained, modelled and monitored. With infants, it will also be important to explain, and model: "personal space/place"

when "on the carpet" and keeping hands and feet to oneself (although adolescents can benefit from a clear message about testosteronic bonding also!); "listening with eyes and ears"; taking your turn; hands-up without calling-out ... (see McPherson and Rogers 2008)

- organisation of locker space/place. At primary age level where locker trays are in the classroom, consideration needs to be given to how they are sited for ease of student movement
- use of cues for whole-class discussion and questions
- use of teacher cue(s) to initiate *whole-class attention* at any stage
- appropriate movement patterns between whole-class teaching time and on-task learning time (crucial transitions)
- use of appropriate cues to receive teacher assistance and support during the on-task phase of the lesson/activity
- routines for tidying work space/place
- cues and procedures for lesson closure and exit from the classroom.

These are, of course, the basic – foundational – routines/cues. Teachers also need to establish routines for lunch (dinner times); for monitor systems; for homework procedures, distribution of notices; use of school diaries; quiet reading time procedures; toilet/drink rules; dealing with students who are frequently (rather than incidentally) late to class; and so on. Most schools plan such routines and procedures on a team, or faculty, basis.

When raising student awareness about behaviour and learning (and their impact on each other) we need to emphasise the fundamentals of our learning community:

- "We share the same place, time, space, resources, every day. We have to learn to get on with each other for our own good and the good of others and to help each other in our learning here."
- "Everyone here is individual – we have our own feelings, needs, concerns."
- "As we would want others to think about us and our feelings so we, in turn ..."
- "There are rights and responsibilities we *all* share here: the right to be treated with respect, the right to learn, the right to feel safe here ..."

It can help to discuss with students the common issues and concerns about shared space, time and resources, and basic, respectful relationships. With younger children, a practical discussion on basic manners will be important initially (and revisited many times in the first few weeks): "please"; "thank-you"; "excuse me"; "asking if you want to borrow ..."; "giving/putting things back where we borrowed ..."; "sharing and cooperative behaviour ...". For some children the classroom environment (notably at infant level) presents expectations and norms of behaviour they are not used to, or that they do not easily accommodate to; it can help to conduct mini role-plays on manners and helping behaviours (McPherson and Rogers 2008).

These early discussions about behaviour and learning can be developed into a *student behaviour agreement* that can form the basis for the teacher's behaviour management and discipline on the one hand, and student–teacher cooperation on the other (see below).

Developing a student behaviour agreement with the class: rights, responsibilities and rules

Many schools now develop *classroom behaviour agreements* in the first week or two of the school year. Building on the natural readiness and expectation of students (about teachers developing rules and routines), grade teachers set aside some classroom time to develop a more collaborative model of classroom behaviour through the establishment of shared rights and responsibilities. Students participate, with their teachers, in "an agreement" addressing common rights, responsibilities and rules for behaviour and learning, core consequences for unacceptable behaviour and a framework of support to assist students when they are struggling with their behaviour and learning (Figure 2.2).

At secondary age level such an agreement is best developed by tutor (or form) teachers who set aside one full timetabled period early, in the first week, to discuss, with their form groups, the key understandings about behaviour and learning. A common framework for such discussions is conducted across all form groups (noted in Figure 2.2). Once established, such an agreement forms the basis on which subject and specialist teachers can fine-tune rules and routines pertinent to particular needs and contexts.

This agreement is published within the first fortnight of Term One and a copy is sent home to each family. At the primary level this classroom agreement (sometimes called a behaviour plan) has a cover page with a photograph of the grade teacher and the students (Figure 2.3).

Any classroom based (or year-level) behaviour agreement needs to reflect the values and aims of the whole-school policy on behaviour. The advantage of a

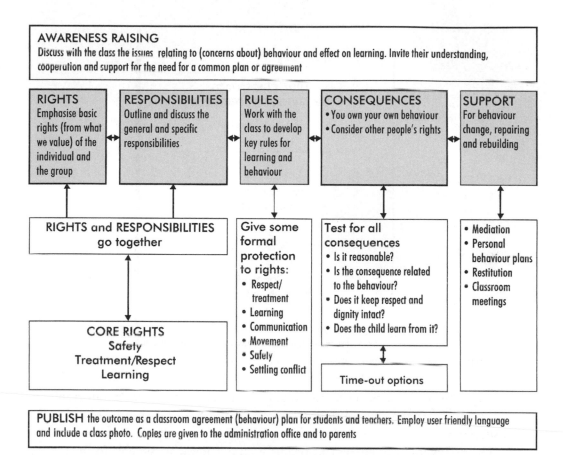

Figure 2.2 Class agreement – behaviour plan (adapted from Rogers 2006b: 51)

classroom-based policy or agreement, notably at primary and middle-school level, is that it raises a school-wide awareness and consciousness about behaviour, learning and relationships, and does so in a class-by-class, age-related and developmental way. This gives reasonable school-wide consistency on the common, and essential, aspects of behaviour policy.

A framework for such a plan or policy is set out in Figure 2.2. Each teacher, from infants to junior, junior to senior, follows the same framework; modifying the language and concepts to age and comprehension so that all students across the school share the same understandings.

The process is as important as the outcome. On the first day the class teacher sets aside time to raise whole-class awareness about behaviour and learning, inviting student participation, understanding and cooperation for a plan or agreement about fair and proper behaviour that enhances positive working relationships and learning. Some teachers will take a more discursive approach,

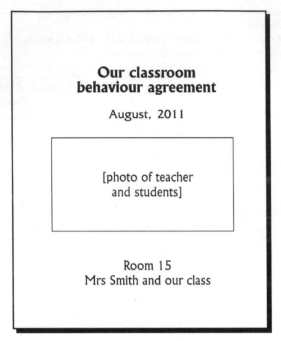

Figure 2.3 Cover of a classroom behaviour agreement

perhaps through a classroom meeting; other teachers are more comfortable with a formal approach that outlines the key areas of the plan and invites student discussion.

The policy, plan or agreement begins with a general statement, for example:

Our behaviour plan has been discussed and developed by the children and the teacher in Year [X]. It is a record of how we seek to behave towards each other. It applies to all the people who come into our class and will be used throughout the school year.

Our common rights

The key elements of a student behaviour agreement

Non-negotiable rights are the basis of a classroom agreement: the right to feel safe at school; the right to learn (without undue, unfair, distraction/disruption); and the right to be treated with respect. Rights such as the right to equality, the right to have my say, the right to be an individual and the right to teach are all subsumed within these core rights. These core rights are based on the value of mutual regard, without which no group or community could effectively cohere and work together for mutual benefit. A right – in this sense – is that which we believe is fair, *right* and proper about the way we should relate and work together.

Even very young children have an emerging concept of fundamental "rightness". Obviously they behave in contradistinction to that rightness (as do we all), but they hold to it strongly. It is the "natural law".

Simply stating that we have "a right to something" is not the same as enjoying that right. We might include in our policy, for example:

> The right to safety doesn't just mean being safe – it is about feeling safe too. Put-downs, cheap shots at others, excluding others on purpose, harassment and swearing are all ways that take away someone's right to feel safe here.
> (From a Year 6 classroom agreement)

In this sense rights imply, and necessitate, responsibilities. If we have a right to learn it implies that the teacher enables the best – most effective – learning that is *reasonably* possible. (This further implies that when we're tired, and it's cold and wet, and we're stuck in the "excuse for a classroom" that looks like a shed, then we still do our best. I actually had to teach in a bike shed over 30 years ago!)

In discussing these rights with our students we provide a common focus for the way that we look at, understand and address behaviour.

Responsibilities flow from our rights

Individual and group responsibilities overlap:

> Shared responsibilities mean that we care for ourselves and others here. Responsibilities and respect go together; when we respect others we are thinking about how our behaviour affects others.

Whole-class "brainwaving" ("surfing the collective brain space" sounds less violent than brain*storming*) will quickly elicit shared norms about the responsibility to, for example: get to class on time; have the relevant materials; share (ideas, resources and even our time); do one's best; help out; listen to others; manage our whole-class noise level. A discussion on responsibilities will also need to address respect in terms of basic manners. Basics such as saying please and thank you; asking when we borrow; returning when you've finished; saying "excuse me" when moving around others; being aware and respectful of others; allowing – and considering – others' personal space; using first names (rather than "he", "she" or "them"); taking turns; lining up without pushing; and so on, are all aspects of self-awareness as we interact with others day after day.

The *core* responsibilities can be summed up in "cooperative and respectful behaviour: the consideration of others as well as oneself".

Rules: protecting rights and encouraging responsibility

The primary purpose of a rule is to give a formal, recognised and public protection to one's rights. Fair rules also highlight and encourage one's responsibility.

In the first few weeks teachers can be heard across all classes, using rule-reminders: "remember *our* rule for asking questions". "*We've* got a rule about respectful language". In the playground teachers will be heard going up to students inviting some cognitive, behavioural awareness, by asking questions such as, "What's *our* rule about playing ball games?" and "What's *our* rule for safe play on the climbing frame?" I've italicised the plural pronouns to highlight inclusive language when we give rule reminders. Not "*my*" rule but *our* rule.

In framing rules it is important to remember some basics:

1. Develop rules that focus on the core rights: a safe place and safe behaviour; a respectful place and respectful behaviour through the way we treat others; a learning place where we give our best and cooperate to learn. Rules should be few in number but address the necessary behaviours. I have seen classrooms where teachers have posted 20 or more rules on the wall; rules often stated negatively ("You must not …", "You shall not …", "You can't …") and still not outlining the desired behaviour. Simply telling a child what he should *not* do is hardly helpful; a helpful rule should at least contain the negative *within* a positive. For example, "In whole-class learning time we put our hand up to ask questions and to contribute (the positive rule) *without calling out* (the "qualifier").

> I have usually found it helpful to have several rules covering:
> - treatment (courtesy, manners, respect)
> - communication (hands up, "partner-voices" – in on-task learning time – also positive language, active listening)
> - learning (cooperation and support, use of resources, how to fairly utilise teacher assistance)
> - movement (walking not running, considerate entry/exit to classroom, consideration of others' personal space, sensible movement)
> - problem solving (settling problems peacefully, using teacher assistance, using classroom meetings for resolving common concerns).

2. Express the rules behaviourally and positively where possible:

> To show respect in our classroom we are courteous, and we use our manners. We use positive language with each other. This means no teasing or put-downs.
>
> When we solve problems in our classroom we talk it over or ask the teacher to help. We do not fight with words or fists or feet. If we fight we will have to go to time out.

It can help highlight the key behaviour focus of the rule by having a rule heading such as: Our *Communication* Rule; Our *Respect* Rule; Our *Learning* Rule; Our *Safety* Rule.

3. Use inclusive language in framing the rules: "In *our* classroom *we* …".

4. Publish the rules in both the *classroom agreement* and on bright classroom posters (even at middle-school level). This can help with a teacher's verbal reminders about appropriate behaviour; the posters act as visual aide-memoire to the verbal reminder. Cartoon motifs can help the visual effect of the posters. At infant level teachers can further illustrate the relevant behaviour through photographs attached to the rule poster. It is often possible to attenuate the several areas (above, 1) under three poster headings such as:

- To show respect here we …
- To learn well here we …
- To feel safe here we …

Consequences

Students need to know that consequences follow inappropriate and irresponsible behaviour. Consequences are related to rules and rights. Students will need to understand that when a rule is broken, in effect a right is affected or even abused.

If a student is *repeatedly* disruptive by calling out, butting-in, talking really loudly, interfering with others' workspace or materials, or acting unsafely or aggressively, he or she is affecting others' rights to learn or even feel safe, and, of course, they are affecting the teacher's right to teach. The necessary, fair, and appropriate consequence in such a case will need to be "time out" (in-class or even out-of-class time out) (see p. 149f).

Students, therefore, can (temporarily) lose their right to be a part of the learning community through a consequence such as time out.

Students need to know that beyond rule reminders (as a verbal consequence) they may be: directed to work away from others; take cool-off time or be directed (even escorted) from the classroom for time out. They may be asked to stay back to discuss their behaviour with their teacher; or be directed into a mediation process; or be part of a parent/teacher/student meeting.

All consequences operate on a least-to-most intrusive basis. Students need to know they will always have an appropriate right of reply as part of the consequence process (see p. 106f). Behaviour consequences are discussed at length in Chapter 5.)

Support of students

It is important to balance the *corrective* and *consequential* aspects of the classroom agreement with the offer of teacher support (Figure 2.2). Here is an example of how support is expressed within a Year 5/6 classroom behaviour agreement.

Supporting each other in our classroom

There are many ways we can support each other here. Most of all we support others when we take time to think about others – to help, encourage and cooperate. Of course, there are days when things don't go right; we recognise this. It is important though, to explain to your teacher, or classmate, when you're having a "bad day". If we don't let others know they might get confused as to why we look (or sound) annoyed, upset, or angry.

Sometimes we have concerns, worries or problems outside and inside our school. It can help to talk about this. Your teacher or school counsellor are always willing to help in any way they can.

If we are making poor choices, or wrong choices about our behaviour our teacher will help us with:

- discussing our behaviour with us
- helping us with personal behaviour plans
- giving us the opportunity to put things right (restitution) – sometimes we may need to put things right by talking things through with a fellow student (mediation).

On some occasions our parents may need to be involved in helping us with our behaviour at school.

Many teachers also include an extended note (in the classroom agreement) on classroom meetings. Some parents may not be aware of this concept of whole-class discussions to share common concerns, problem-solve, work on common solutions to common concerns and problems – so a note about the positive and educational features of classroom meetings will assist in the understanding of basic classroom democracy:

We have regular classroom meetings in our class. These meetings give all students an opportunity to explore common concerns, needs and problems. These meetings allow shared understandings, active problem solving and student-assisted solutions to common issues of concern. NB Classroom meetings are also (obviously) utilised for planning time with students.

The last page of a *classroom agreement* outlines the whole-class commitment to the process.

We have discussed, drafted and edited our behaviour agreement with our teacher. We agree to use it and support it.

The classroom behaviour agreement is also a document for parents as well as students and teachers; it enables shared understandings about behaviour and learning. A copy will be sent to all parents/caregivers of all children in each grade or class group. A covering letter from the head-teacher goes home with the classroom agreement/plan.

The letter discusses the elements of rights, rules and responsibilities (and consequences) encouragement and the support and encouragement we give to our students. The letter finishes with an appeal to shared understanding and support, for example:

This behaviour agreement has been discussed, and developed, by the teacher and the children in Year 6 ... It outlines the way we address behaviour and learning in our school. We ask you to read through this agreement/plan with your son/daughter. We look forward to your understanding and support this year ...

(See particularly McPherson and Rogers 2008).

As the year plods on, all behaviour issues are, one way or another, referred back to this behaviour agreement. Whenever a parent (or school) has concerns about a child's behaviour the behaviour agreement forms an important part of the discussion and support.

Non-negotiable rules and consequences

There are rules, in a school, that are non-negotiable across all ages – all classes. These relate to issues such as health and safety, bullying, drugs, aggression and violent behaviour. These rules and consequences need to be made known in the first meetings with all students, in the school diary, in classroom agreements and school policies.

For example in Australian primary schools there is a "no hat, no outside play" (that is, no direct sunlight play) rule in the hot summer months. It is a rule directly related to health and safety.

When schools have a common framework for classroom behaviour agreements, each successive year group becomes increasingly conscious of "the way we do things here and why". This enables some sense of common understandings and expectations about appropriate and fair behaviour, and also some reasonable consistency in behaviour management by adults across the school.

As noted earlier, there are several phases in the ongoing life of a class group (Figure 2.1). If the teacher has thoughtfully established "the way we need to work here" and has developed positive routines and rules for classroom learning and social interaction, the class, as a group, becomes habituated into workably cohesive and just and fair "norms" of behaviour.

Cohesive phase (see Figure 2.1)

During the "cohesive" phase of a classroom community, the routines and rules become reasonable and *normal*: "the way we do things here". At the beginning of each term we might need to revisit the student behaviour agreement and some of the routines (such as noise monitoring) that we have established in the first few weeks. Students "forget" during term breaks, or are "resocialised" in non-school settings. A brief and positive re-establishment can help start each term with a positive, shared focus.

In this phase of the year, most of our behaviour management occurs within a *relational dynamic*. Hopefully, as teacher-leaders, we have built a positive working relationship with the individuals as well as the group. We rely less on the rules and routines, now, and the students are more self-aware and self-directed in their behaviour and learning. Students are taking appropriate "ownership" of classroom life.

During this "phase", teachers often utilise classroom meetings to discuss issues relevant to individual and group needs and concerns.

Communicating the rules to students

In communicating the necessary rules to students it is important to emphasise the *purpose of rules*: protection of rights and expectation of basic responsibilities.

In communicating the rules to a new class group (or year group) some teachers are more directive – outlining the expected rules, their reasons, and the normal consequences when rules are broken. Other teachers are more discursive in their approach, emphasising shared dialogue and engaging a *process* of agreement. Some teachers begin the year with a classroom meeting ('sharing circles' at infant level) and use the meeting to address the need for rules, responsibilities, consequences *and* support.

The approach taken will depend, in part, on the individual teacher's comfort zone about class dialogue and classroom discussion (particularly at secondary level). I have been in schools where the rules are read out almost perfunctorily by tutor teachers, or (more pedestrian) the students are directed to read the rules in the school diary – full stop.

If your preference is for a more directive approach to communicating the rules, it will be beneficial (at the very least) to give the reasons for the rules and invite student questions.

Visual reminding of routines and rules

In the establishment phase of the year the process of rule encouragement and maintenance can be assisted by basic visual posting of key rules and routines (p. 45). At infant and early years levels these could include:

- A photograph and name card for coat hooks.
- The key classroom rules can be illustrated as a visual aide-memoire posted in a prominent place at the front of the classroom. As are routines such as: "partner-voice" (working noise); what to do when the set work is completed; how to set out a piece of writing; and use of wet areas.

- At early years level teachers often take photographs of the children working cooperatively tidying the room, communicating respectfully, sharing cooperatively – and these photographs are displayed with the relevant rules the teacher has established.
- Simple signs for cupboards, quiet areas and the library corner all enable association of place, space and purpose and shared responsibilities.
- I have used simple posters to remind students at *secondary* level about tidying work space: chairs under table; straightening furniture; chairs on tables at the end of the day; cleaning up any residual litter; and leaving the room in an orderly way (p. 75f).
- Baskets can be used for "finished work here" and there can be an "early finishers" box with worksheets or activities.
- A "noise-meter" can be used to establish and monitor working voice levels (p. 69f).

Discussing rules within the wider social context

When discussing rules with students (even up to Year 10) it can help to discuss them within the students' experience of rules in many different places and contexts: the Highway Code; clubs they belong to; road rules and road signs; their families; and even board games. The purpose of and reasons for fair rules can be helpfully explored within these familiar contexts and a natural transition of understanding can be made to the classroom and playground.

Students have already learned that rules *help* guide, focus, govern behaviour, *help* protect people (at least potentially) and *encourage* shared responsibility (thinking of others), and, when broken, rules occasion consequences. They have seen the yellow card used with adult footballers and they have also seen adult footballers and other sports "heroes" throw tantrums and worse! (Shouldn't it be "champion" rather than "hero"?)

Maintenance and consolidation

It is crucial to *maintain and consolidate* the rules and routines that are established on Day One, Week One (Figure 2.1). Effective teaching and management in the establishment phase includes planning for the typical disruptions to day-to-day teaching and learning and developing a workable "system" for the smooth running of the classroom in terms of behaviour and learning. (This is discussed in Chapters 3 and 4.)

Simply stating, or even publishing, fair rules and routines is not enough. Teachers need to consciously address issues and behaviours such as lateness;

unsuitable noise levels; calling out; time off-task and task avoidance and inappropriate language on a day-to-day basis until there are "norms" of expected behaviour present in the classroom life and learning.

A teacher's "discipline plan" (pp. 83–91) forms a key feature of a workable system that thinks through typical (or likely) disruptions and plans the sorts of responses (especially one's language) that are more likely to invite student cooperation – not as a formulaic system but rather as an *enabling framework*.

None of us would ever teach a lesson or activity without some kind of lesson plan, but I'm still surprised by how many teachers continue to teach without *planning* for typical distracting and disruptive behaviours that can affect the quality of teaching and learning.

As noted earlier, students expect the teacher to clarify rules, routines and cues in terms of "how things are expected to be here and why . . ". It is important to thoughtfully plan how we will communicate, establish and monitor these rules, routines and cues; not as an end in themselves (teacher control), but as a means to an end (teacher–student cooperation in a shared learning community). In this sense this establishing *enables* effective management, teaching and learning and positive, supportive, relationships.

Seating plans and student grouping

When planning room organisation we will need to ask what the purpose of the physical seating layout serves ("U" shaped, rows, pairs, table groups) and also student placement (who sits where and with whom).

In some classes, allowing friendship groups on Day One may create unhelpful power cliques and habituated patterns of behaviour that are difficult to refocus later in the term. While it is important that teachers allow some student involvement in seating arrangements, this "freedom" is better given later in Term One (see p. 52).

On Day One it will assist in general management to have students seated in alphabetic allocation (with a name sticker on each table). This allows easy learning of students' names by the teacher and allows some early classroom socialisation outside the natural friendship groupings. "Random allocation" may also need to include gender mix and – possibly – ability mix. Also if we know that some students do not work or relate well together, that knowledge will need to be translated into student seating arrangements.

In a Year 7 class I worked with two students who had robust and motoric expressions of ADD (attention deficit disorder) had promised their teacher that they would work well if they sat together. "Really Miss! We'll be good if we sit together please Miss; please!!" It was a time-wasting mistake. After several frustrating promises we relocated their seating arrangements, and moved the whole class into rows. They eventually settled down and actually became more focused in their learning behaviour.

While socialisation is an important feature of classroom life and learning, it is also important that the students understand, from Day One, that the classroom is not merely an extension of playground socialisation; *this* place is set aside for teaching and learning. Some children are very easily distracted, for example, when sitting in table groups, so in the establishment phase of the year it may be wiser to use a more 'formal' seating plan (rows, or paired seating, facing the front of the classroom) to minimise unnecessary distraction.

Simply placing the students in table groups does not facilitate (of itself) cooperative learning behaviour. It can help to use small group seating for more focused cooperative activities and retain seating in rows for the core teaching and learning activities.

I have seen many teachers give up the positive benefits of cooperative learning by early expectations that table group seating will – of itself – engage cooperative learning; it won't. Cooperative learning needs to be structured, and taught, over time and is normally more effective when the class is more relationally cohesive.

Welfare of our students (establishment phase)

Students new to a school can often be anxious about settling in, particularly at early years and reception level, and transition to the first year at high school. It is important for teachers to be aware of, and considerate for, a student's natural concerns about how they will fit in; whether other students will accept and befriend them; whether they will be able to cope with the demands of the work; the timetable; the different teachers. In short whether – and how – they will "belong" in *this* class group, "*this* year group". The need to belong, to feel accepted and part of a group, is an important aspect of day-to-day existence at school.

Even basic considerations such as who they will be asked to sit next to and for how long (will it be every lesson?) can concern some students. It can be helpful to rotate seating pairs, or groups, over the first few weeks to enable basic group befriending. It is also important to keep an eye on students who appear to be loners or students who have difficulty befriending others, particularly at playtimes and in sports sessions. Many primary schools (and some secondary schools) now have "buddy" programmes for reception age, for pupils in Year 7 (transitional year) and for students new to a school. Older students take on a peer support role that enables the younger (or new) student to settle into the classroom group and social climate of a playground. The "peer-buddy" receives basic training beyond the natural skills and personality that equip them for such a role.

Group activities that involve games, activities and discussions, can all assist in the settling-in process and in terms of getting to know each other. Name games can sometimes lose their novelty at upper primary level but a basic seat-rotation and getting-to-know-you time can enable a *basic* sense of group cohesion and bonding.

One's welfare obligations to one's students is not confined to primary teachers. As part of a secondary year level team, the House Heads and Year Advisers (Home-room Tutors) have a particular responsibility to liaise with subject colleagues to keep the lines of communication open about how their students are coping with settling in.

When seating plans don't work

I've worked with teachers who have allowed the friendship-seating option only to find it creates little coteries or cliques; the row of students down the back whose *esprit de corps* creates contestable, time-wasting, behaviours; the little group of girls (or boys) who won't let anyone else sit with them.

I've found it helpful in such situations to change the seating plan by guided cooperation with the students. The teacher's concern about noise level, and time off-task (as it relates to learning) is briefly set out in a pro forma with an invitation to the students to assist in a seat change plan:

> As your teacher I am concerned about the level of noise, and time off-task, during class work-time. I believe a change of seating-plan will help. I would appreciate your cooperation. Please write down the names of two students you know who will make it easier for you to get on with your classwork and gain the best benefit of your time in this class/subject.
>
> While all fair suggestions will be taken on board I will be the final umpire. I will let you know next class period. Thanks for your cooperation.
>
> Mr Rogers

When handing out the pro forma I remind students to, "Choose wisely, choose thoughtfully – thanks." It is said in a spirit of goodwill.

This needs to be developed in a spirit of goodwill wherever possible. With a particularly difficult class it can help to have a supportive colleague come in and conduct the exercise with the regular class teacher (see also p. 223).

The first meeting with the students

The first meeting with a new class at secondary level can sometimes start in the corridor (outside the classroom). I've had some students in more challenging classes immediately start hassling me: "Who're you?". "What's yer name?". "You going to be our teacher today?". "Eh … where's Mr Smith …? He was our teacher last time – he's a donk!" (guffaws). Several students are talking over each other and there's some pushing, shoving or playful "testosteronic bonding".

I did this drawing of a Year 9 class arriving outside their classroom. The girl on the right, Donna, is letting the group know who the new teacher is: 'Yooooo, Mr Rogers. I seen you before in another class. Yooooo, Mr Rogers!' She had a "notice me" kind of voice, often used in wearing teachers down. I smiled at her but chose not to engage in conversation outside the class.

I've seen teachers enter into long time-wasting responses to such group banter; answering their questions; over-engaging the "attentional" students no doubt hoping they are building an early friendly relationship. The students' perception is often different; they are seeking to define how they will "work" the teacher–student relationship.

It is wiser to *tactically* ignore most of the multi-student banter and questions with a brief, polite, statement: "I'm not answering personal questions – now. We need to be ready to go into our classroom. Thanks." Our tone is pleasant, but businesslike; enabling some group "attentional focus" by a relaxed, non-verbal, "blocking hand" indicating such questioning is not on the agenda *now*. Direct group attention quickly so that the teaching and learning becomes the immediate focus, rather than whether the teacher has a boyfriend, or is married or is new here, and so on.

As Robertson (1997) reminds us, it is important to *define* the first meeting(s) in your own terms as teacher; to be confidently secure; pleasantly firm, without any overtones of "force", perception of threat or perceptible anxiety.

The *brief* "corridor-settling" by the teacher conveys the change in pace and setting: between *outside* the classroom (play, high motoric, noisy, behaviour, which is natural and OK for the playground) to *inside* (quieter, sitting – mostly focused thinking, cooperating in our learning and social interaction). It will be important to create (even here) *an expectant tone*, quickly, before going into the classroom.

Scanning the group outside the classroom the teacher will often have some expectation of "lining up" or "considerate one-at-a-time entry" to the classroom. A *reminder* to this effect can calm and focus natural student restlessness:

"Settling down everyone (...). [We'll need to repeat this whole-class cue-ing at least once!] Before we go into our classroom I notice a few hats on; if you have an iPod on remember we're going into a classroom learning environment. Thank you." The teacher smiles and nods as he gives brief, positive, feedback to the individuals as they settle. "When we go in I want you to remember ..." Here the teacher *briefly* outlines the protocol about where students will sit, where their bags go, and so on.

Teacher confidence and authority

Robertson (1997) notes that "relaxed behaviour" is consistent with high role 'status' and also implies that one is not threatened. Of course we may have natural anxiety but we need to project an approach, a manner, that in effect says, "I expect your cooperation, and compliance, in terms of reasonable behaviour". Of course such a leadership style needs to convey respect, good will and humanity.

When a teacher's manner, body language, posture and communication appear confident and authoritative, and when such confidence is further maintained in both teaching and management, students are likely to cooperate with the teacher's leadership.

There is a reciprocity at work here:

If the teacher feels confident the pupils are noticeably more responsive and this in turn reinforces his own assurance; if the teacher lacks confidence, the process can begin in reverse and he can quickly become thoroughly demoralised. (Robertson 1997: 66)

Confidence (not cockiness or arrogant self-assurance) is a crucial feature in the teacher's overall communication with a group of students.

Confidence, in part, derives from being well prepared and knowing what one intends to teach (Chapter 3) but it also derives from one's characteristic – and genuine – "presentation of self": open, relaxed body language; not appearing easily flustered (yet willing to accept fallibility without going to pieces); the ability to regain composure quickly when one has made a mistake; a confident, pleasant, engaging voice; being able to assert where necessary (pp. 84, 89, 90); effective use of eye-scanning, eye contact (p. 99f); being aware of one's body language when engaging students' personal space. These are basic but significant features of a confident teacher's behaviour (Rogers 2006b).

Establishing whole-class attention

It is important to establish, at the first group meeting, the importance of whole-class attention and focus. Developing the habit of whole-class attention is crucial to an effective beginning to any class learning, on any day.

Verbally focusing attention

Once students are sitting in their seats the teacher needs to cue for group attention and focus. This can be initiated through a combination of non-verbal cues and verbal direction(s).

- It will always help to use a positive, directional tone: "Settling down everyone (…)". Allow some, brief, tactical, pausing to give the students brief take-up time to process the teacher's cueing (p. 4, 102f). "Looking this way and listening (…). Thanks." "Thanks" at the end of an imperative form of words conveys expectation.
- Avoid questioning phrases: "*Would you* please look this way everyone?"; "*Can you* settle down please?"; "*Would you* stop talking?"; "*Why* are you talking?", "You're not supposed to be talking now *are you!*?"
- It can help to reflect on the language we use for addressing a *group*: "Class …"; "Folks …"; "Everyone …"; "Guys …"; "6D …". "Guys …" seems to be favoured as an inclusive, unisex, generic by younger teachers. It's not one of my favourites. (Must be my age!)
- Some teachers find a non-verbal cue helpful *before* they give a verbal direction. With new classes I often ting a small drinking glass with the tip of my pen; wait (some tactical pausing) then follow with the whole-class direction.
- Be aware of posture. An "open" expectant, confident posture and a positive, expectant tone in one's voice will convey our meaning ("settle", "look", "listen") as much as anything else will. We do not lounge back onto the teacher's table or lean against the whiteboard, or sit down (at upper primary or secondary level).
- Step the voice down with the *part* direction. The initial words (for example,

"Settling down everyone …") are said a little louder to gain initial attention; it may be necessary to repeat the first part of the direction.

> "*Settling* down everyone (…)"   a little louder
>   "Looking this way thanks   softer
>   and listening (…)"   softer (in concert with increasing
>   attention and focus by the students).

This verbal form ("Settling down …") is a variation of "*Stop* (what you're doing), *look* this way, and *listen*".

- Scan the eyes and faces of your class as you speak, it can communicate one's positive manner as well as giving the teacher feedback about student attention and focus. Allow time for the residual noise to settle (…), then proceed with the rest of what you want (or need) to say when the class are attending (for example, a class welcome and the whole-class teaching phase of the lesson).

Some teachers will use a raised voice to initiate group attention and, when only half the class are listening, *continue* to talk to the group while the rest of the class are still whispering or chatting. All this does (of course) is emphasise that such talking or "chatting" or calling out, or fiddling with objects on the table, is OK. It is important to scan and wait for whole-class attention. While scanning the group, it will be important to non-verbally (or verbally) affirm students who do settle, face the front and listen with readiness. We smile, give a nod, and a brief affirming comment: "Thank you, John, Damien, Tran, Bilal … you're ready"; "Nuyen, Lucien, Susan … thanks."

At early years level teachers will often give several such encouragers to emphasise the fact the students *are* listening, *are* sitting, *are* facing the front, *are* ready, and so on.

At secondary level I often add – when a class is settled and attentive … "Thanks. You're looking relaxed and ready. Good morning everyone." I will not say good morning (to the whole class) until I see (and sense) their returned settling and focus.

Always say "good morning"/"good afternoon". I have worked with some teachers who either forget, or don't bother or – even – don't see the civil necessity of whole-class greetings(!)

Teacher movement

It doesn't help student attention and focus if the teacher telegraphs too much motoric restlessness by pacing up and down at the front of the classroom; the undiagnosed "ADD students" will tend to over-focus on the teacher's movement, only half listening (if at all) to what the teacher is saying. I've watched teachers bouncing up and down on their toes while reading to the class, unaware that their overly motoric movement triggers an unconscious restlessness in the students whose eyes involuntarily track the bouncing up and down movement.

It will help to stand at the front of the room to initiate and sustain group attention: a centre-front position, facing the class group, standing relaxed and scanning the faces of the students while cueing for attention will normally (and positively) signal the teacher's readiness and expectation.

Non-verbal cues to gain group attention

One of the common non-verbal cues to initiate or signal for group attention (at primary age) is the raised hand. When the class is seated the teacher faces the class (from the centre-front of the classroom) and visually scans the room with one hand raised. At this point the teacher does not speak; the raised hand is a *cue* to which the students respond by, likewise, raising their hand in a kind of "domino effect" across the room. Students look around and, in effect, copy. It is a cue to focus and refocus attention (as is necessary during the lesson) and can be quite effective at primary age level and lower secondary level. When the class has responded (15 seconds or so) the teacher lowers his or her hand, thanks the class for their cooperation and continues with a class greeting and the session's activity.

One of my postgraduate students had been told this was a helpful signal for settling a class and proceeded to try it with a new Year 6 class. She had her hand up for a few minutes when a student finally said, "Yes, Miss … how can we help you?" When using non-verbal cues for the first time it will be important to verbally associate the expectation carried by the non-verbal cue. In the case above the teacher could have raised her hand *and* verbally directed the group, "Settling down everyone (…), looking this way (…) and listening (…)…". When they were quiet and listening she could have then explained that the next time she puts her hand up *like that* at the beginning of the lesson … So much for hindsight!

Typical non-verbal cues used by teachers include ringing a small hand-bell; a sound from an instrument (many years ago I used my guitar – strumming a chord to signal to my, then, early years class to come and sit on the mat); a hand-clap rhythm copied by all infant students, the teacher then reducing the clap to a two-finger clap and, finally, a single finger "quiet clap" and hands resting in the lap. Even standing still, relaxed, scanning the class – waiting – can, *itself*, be a non-verbal cue. *Lengthy* waiting, though, will confuse students or (with older children) trigger possible inattention and restlessness.

Re-establishing group attention

There are occasions when a teacher needs to re-establish group attention beyond the initial lesson establishment. There may be an occasion when the noise level of unnecessary off-task behaviour occurs, or the teacher may need to refocus an aspect of the lesson task. The most obvious re-establishing needs to occur before lesson closure. It is important to allow appropriate time for packing up, lesson summary (if necessary) and an orderly and calm exit (see pp. 75f).

> A primary teacher stops her class 3 or 4 minutes before the closing bell. The students are still busily colouring in or writing on their worksheet. She gives several instructions about materials and where to put finished work, adding, "Stand behind your chairs when you've finished". The problem is that the teacher is speaking over significant residual noise and activity. She is also moving around the room *while* she is giving the instruction. A third of the class is still working with pencils in hand while she is talking. She "allows" this behaviour to continue, where it would have been more effective had she gone to the front of the classroom and briefly refocused the class, and individuals, for whole-class attention.

Whenever we give *group* instructions, directions or reminders it is important to wait for whole-class attention to enable focus and processing of even routine directions. It will also help to go to the front of the classroom to consolidate the connection of whole-class teacher direction.

A further problem can occur. If the teacher frequently talks *over* students when they are talking – and talking "through" their kinaesthetic noise – the students get used to it, and this is a group habituation that is not easy to change.

- Have a positive signal or cue for group attention (verbal or non-verbal see pp. 56–8). Preferably not hands on heads (!)
- Use a brief tactical pause so students can process the direction. Repeat the group instruction if necessary: "Everyone (...) eyes and ears this way now. Thank you (...). Paul (...), Simon (...), Simone (...). Donna (...), Sean (...), Patrick (...) – pencils down." This to the several who are still not attending. "(...) Eyes and ears this way (...) Thank you." Firm, confident and pleasant, it sets the norm; the routine.
- Visual cue reminders can help at primary level (see p. 58).
- A word of acknowledegment and appreciation will encourage : "I appreciated the way in which you all packed up at your tables and put the lids on felt-tip pens – that'll help them to live longer"; "Thank you for listening, and concentrating, when I asked you all to".

Sustaining group attention

The ability to *sustain* group attention depends on the teacher's ability to engage the students in the teaching and learning focus – at that point in the flow of the lesson. The ability, and skills necessary to teach effectively and to manage disruptive behaviours is crucial to the effectiveness of any group learning. This is discussed in some detail in Chapters 3 and 4.

The seemingly non-responsive, non-attentive class (first meeting)

This phenomenon can sometimes occur with more challenging classes and is more common at secondary than primary level. The teacher enters the class with a group of restless and noisy students. It seems that they are in a world of their own (and they probably are). The teacher stands at the front of the room waiting, waiting … students are having private conversations, fiddling with objets d'art, rearranging class furniture. Does the teacher "exist"? What should he or she do?

It will be counter-productive (if tempting) to shout, though we've all done it at some stage. It might, temporarily, stop the noise and the motoric restlessness, but it will probably restart or, worse, the class will react in a hostile way. If we keep using an *overly* raised (or shouting) voice we, in effect, train our students to get used to this as the norm!

It is also unhelpful to stand there *just* waiting (p. 58).

Ideally if such a class is believed to likely behave like this (even from Day One), the establishment phase (first few lessons) should involve a team-teaching approach with one of the teachers well known to the students in that group as a teacher with credibility and respect. The new (ongoing) teacher plans the first few lessons (establishment) with this colleague; this allows a kind of "credibility by proxy" (Rogers 2006b). It has to be genuine teaming and well planned. This collegial teaming could also include some ongoing monitoring of students' behaviour in (and out of) class. What is to be avoided is any *known* "difficult class" being given to a beginning teacher or a teacher new to the school without initial and ongoing colleague support.

When faced with a seemingly unresponsive class, rather than stand at the front of the room waiting, or even cueing for group attention, I've found it helpful to leave the centre-front of the room (where students expect the teacher to try to establish some class attention and control) and move around the room initiating conversations with individuals and pairs. This is a kind of mini-establishment – in "their" space. It initially 'unsettles' *some* of the students. They don't expect *this*. No doubt some of the students are thinking, "You should be up the front where we can make life difficult for you …".

As I walk up to students and initiate conversations (beginning with a mutual name introduction) I sometimes get cocky, smart-alec responses. I find *tactical ignoring* of such behaviour (wherever appropriate, p. 100f) avoids *over*-engaging or over-servicing attentional behaviours. I seek to indicate *I'm* no threat, *nor am I threatened* by their behaviour, but at the same time I am initiating and establishing my leadership relationship with them. I ask a few questions about the sorts of things they might expect in *this* English class and assure them that our time together will be worthwhile: the process is brief, excursive and establishing. Walking back to the front of the classroom I try to hold some key student names in my short-term memory and *then* go to the centre-front of the classroom. Using the remembered names I can now cue for whole-class attention, "… settling down, thanks (…), Paul …, Dean …, Halid …, Kosta …". Most students are *now* settling, calming down and facing the front. They are affirmed (briefly), "Thanks, Crystal (…), David, Donna …". Having had some brief – relational – introductions, and chats (in the excursive roam), I can now use the names with some early, relational, confidence. After a few minutes – and several tactical pauses – the class is substantially settled. It isn't easy, but it is an approach I have found helpful to initiate group calming and focus.

If a pattern of non-attentiveness by the class is typical (and increasingly disruptive) it will be important to seek immediate, senior, colleague support:

- It may help to see if the problem is wider than your own class.
- It can help to work with the key ringleaders; those students who trigger non-attentive or provocative behaviour in their classmates. Follow-up (with such students) will need to emphasise the effect of their behaviour on the class and on the shared rights of all, and then work with them on their responsibility and commitment to change. The follow-up will also be helped by senior colleague support, but it is crucial that the class teacher engages in *any* one-to-one follow-up with these students (p. 106, see also p. 182f).
- It can help to conduct a classroom meeting outlining to the students the major concerns the teacher and the students have about behaviours such as general noise level, inattention and students talking while the teacher is talking, and then invite student responses about the need for change. Students then work with their teacher in developing a class plan to address these concerns about behaviour and learning. Such a meeting, though, will benefit from colleague support in planning, developing and follow through (see p. 223f).

Learning and using students' names

This may sound like a mundane point, but it is crucial – from Day One. I have worked with some secondary teachers who still haven't learned the names of their students by Term Three! I know it takes effort but it is significant in relational and management terms. It is basic civility. More than that it is essential in building positive relationships.

At primary level the students' names can be assigned and tagged to the desk itself for Day One; seating plans can be organised and name-games utilised (even at lower secondary level).

As a mentor/teacher in every new class I work with I ask a student to draw me a basic classroom plan of the furniture and note down the first name of the student in relation to their desk, or table group. I then use that "name plan" during the on-task phase of the lesson. I also find it helpful to double-check the *sound* of students' names so I don't cause unthinking offence (or embarrassment) to a student. I use these hand-drawn plans *at every* lesson until I've learned the names.

Some schools utilise class lists with a small photograph of each student – this assists the teacher's short-term memory in each lesson as we seek to build those workable relationships. It is also important to use the students' names in non-classroom settings (corridor and playground), even in brief, transitional, exchanges.

Small aside

It isn't easy learning students' names at high school (or if you are a "specialist" teacher at primary level). I've found that when I do forget a name I'm trying to remember it sounds a bit nicer to say to the student, "I'm trying to remember your name" (the truth), rather than, "I've forgotten your name" or even "I don't know your name".

Addressing disruptive behaviour during whole-class teaching time

When students call out, butt in or talk while the teacher is teaching or across the room to classmates ...

Like any aspect of classroom management we need to initially establish:

- discuss expected behaviours within the "class agreement" (p. 40f)

- have an age-related, established routine (at junior level it might be "hands up without calling out" whereas at senior level it might be "one at a time in class discussions")
- be able to confidently address and "manage" the calling out (or talking while the teacher is talking ...) when it occurs.

In the first few lessons the teacher will need to define, establish and maintain the fairness of one person speaking at a time and others consciously making an effort to listen. Before any group discussion we can *preface* any question time, or class discussion, by reminding students: "Remember our rule (or agreement) for ...". We might add, "I know some of you will be really keen to contribute; however if you just call out, or talk over someone, that is unfair to the other person if they are waiting. If you are waiting to make a point or contribute and others call out, you, too, would feel their behaviour is unfair." If students do forget, or call out to gain some attentional advantage, then a brief reminder of the rule will be important to the several or the individual (see below).

When giving directions or reminders it is important to be brief, giving a few seconds of take-up time, and then *re-engage* whole-group attention to and focus on the *whole-class* aspect of the lesson or discussion. If we accept calling out and easily validate such behaviour in the first few meetings we will find it difficult to re-establish those expected, fair, behaviours later in the term.

It is important not to ignore such behaviour in the hope that it will go away or that the students will "naturally" settle and listen.

I have seen teachers teach *through* such noisy, disparate, kinaesthetic behaviour *as if* they are teaching when, in fact, several or more students are actively ignoring the teacher through their private chatting, or "cross-talking". If we accept students' butting in, calling out or talking across the room to other students we – effectively – ratify that such behaviour is OK.

A "hands up" reminder is a necessary correction in most classes – even in some Year 11 and 12 classes – particularly in the establishment phase of the year. The following are some basic cues to correct and refocus calling out, or chatting while the teacher is talking.

- *A non-verbal reminder* (at infant or middle primary level). The teacher raises his or her hand (to simulate hands up) and, briefly, covers his or her mouth (to indicate hands up *without* calling out). She then acknowledges students with their hands up.
- *Incidental direction* (for older children). The teacher describes what the student is doing: "Jason (...), you're calling out and clicking your fingers". This "describes the reality" and raises some behaviour awareness. The teacher then gives some take-up time, before acknowledging other students with their hands

up, and names them – "Jason ..., Dean ..., Carla ..., I see your hands up 1, 2, 3" – and responds in turn to their questions or contributions. If a student does not "pick-up"/respond to an incidental direction we can give a brief rule reminder: "Jason (...) remember our rule for ..."

If several students are calling out it will be important to stop the class – a blocking hand – and scan the room, waiting for quiet: "Folks (...), several students are calling out (...) [a brief *descriptive* recognition]. We have a class rule. Thank you." The teacher then, in a positive, expectant manner, resumes the class flow of the discussion. "I don't mind *which* hand, as long as you have a hand up [teacher smiles]. Alright ... let's go for it ...". This, in preference to "*Don't* call out ..."; "You *shouldn't* be calling out – *Should you?*"; "*Why* are you calling out?"

Other examples of verbal cues to a group or individual:

- "Hands up without calling out, thanks ..."
- "Remember our class rule for asking questions."
- "Hands up so I can see your voice."
- "I can hear questions; I can hear calling out. I can't see hands up."
- "I get concerned when several of you call out (...) *we* end up not able to hear anyone." (This is a brief, whole-class reminder.)

If students are chatting we can also use brief descriptive cues/rule reminders, for example: "Melissa (...), Chantelle (...) you're chatting. This is whole-class teaching time (...)." Sometimes the 'descriptive cue' is enough. With some students we will need to add a brief simple direction, "... eyes and ears this way (...). Thanks." We may need to add a *brief* "... without chatting. Thanks."

The use of corrective language is discussed in some detail in Chapter 3.

If a student, has persistently called out during Day One it will be worth following up with them after class time, perhaps even making some form of verbal agreement (one-to-one) about hands up behaviour (p. 106f).

Like any discipline, we need to have the preventative focus in place, and will need to have thought-through simple, brief, *positive* forms of corrective language to remind students of their responsibility and to bring students back on task.

Transitions

When a teacher moves from the whole-class teaching phase of the lesson to the on-task phase of the lesson it is natural for the noise level of the class to rise; some students who were not listening earlier now tend to be unfocused and want teacher assistance ("Miss – what do we have to do?!", "I don't know what to do

…!"); many students will start talking to their classmate (which is obviously acceptable providing such talking is not loud or significantly non-task in focus); there will also be some students who do not have the appropriate equipment; some may go 'class walkabout' for no apparently helpful reason.

More than anything, teachers need to make the transition between whole-class teaching time and on-task time clear and definite. I've worked with teachers who have a fuzzy, inchoate transition, where the students are unclear about what they are supposed to be doing *now*. The teacher may just rattle off a series of task instructions, or even start answering individuals' questions, leaving the rest of the class uncertain as to where the focus of the lesson is *at this point*.

Basic, (but crucial) points like having the work task/activity written up as a question, or series of points/steps and having monitors for distribution of materials (particularly with group work) need to be established from Day One.

It will be important to plan for these behaviours and contingencies by explaining to the class what is meant by "working noise" and *why* a reasonable working noise level is important. It will also be important to discuss reasonable and acceptable movement *around* the classroom (this will, naturally, vary according to subject area and context). If students need teacher assistance they will need to know how they can, fairly, get teacher help in a classroom of 25–30 students (p. 74f).

It will also help to have some spare pens (blue and red), some spare rulers, pencils and erasers, and some lined (and plain) A4 paper, just in case. Initially the teacher will not know if a student without a pen is being difficult, lazy, indifferent or genuinely forgetful. A box of "necessities" is essential in the first few lessons at upper primary level onwards (p. 9). It is always worth checking if the pens work(!) before we go into class.

In developing such routines, cues and procedures with their students, teachers will find it helpful to plan ahead with colleagues who teach similar ages of students and in similar teaching/subject areas.

Cater for the visual learners in the group

Some teachers over-rely on an auditory approach to teaching. We might (sometimes) be critical of the so-called "chalk and talk" days but then, many teachers did understand the importance of visual cueing: writing key points on the board; building up concepts from main concept to subsidiary points, or using the "well-known to less-known" principle. Long before the modern emphasis on "multiple intelligences", visual, auditory and kinaesthetic learning, and left brain/right brain learning, effective teachers were using "mind-map" concepts and catering for visual and kinaesthetic learners.[1]

I was team-teaching with a senior teacher in an English class a few years ago. She was discussing (with a Year 10 class) aspects of positive communication. As she developed some quite complex ideas I noticed (ten minutes into the session) that at least a third of the class were restless and unfocused. I asked my colleague (casually) if I could "write a few of these points on the board". She replied (pleasantly), "… of course, Mr Rogers". As I wrote her key points up I noticed the students re-engage, almost straight away. It was as if the "physicality" and organisation of the words on the board had given them a visual framework for the flow of the lesson as well as their own thinking.

If, for example, I'm conducting a classroom meeting I like to have a student write up key points so the class can have a visual focus (it also validates a student's contribution). I also like to have another student record the points (as a class scribe) so I'm free (as the teacher) to manage and "chair" the class dialogue and discussion.

Noise levels

In an old *Punch*2 magazine I read an unusual word: "charivari". I couldn't figure out its meaning from the context so I looked it up. It's French in origin: "A serenade of rough music made with kettles, pans, tea-trays, etc. Used in France in derision of incongruous marriages … hence a babel of music …" (*Oxford Shorter Dictionary*). I've had quite a few Year 7–10 classes exhibit charivari! Some students are not (seemingly) aware of how loudly their voices carry (along with 25–30 others) and may be unaware of the chair scrapes; the kinaesthetic movements, of fiddling with pens, rulers, pencil cases, water bottles … (while the teacher is addressing the class). It can all contribute to a "charivari".

Teachers have differing levels of tolerance regarding noise levels. Some can tolerate very high levels of noise whereas the teacher next door may (rightly) find their next door's classroom noise inhibiting their own classroom teaching and learning. To ask a colleague if they are aware of how loud their "normal" classroom is can be a sensitive and touchy issue.

When 25–30 students are grouped several times a day in small rooms with tightly orchestrated furniture and space and are, then, expected to cohabit, think, concentrate, 'process', discuss, cooperate, work and move, there is bound to be noise. How do we manage the environment, and student behaviour, so that we have reasonable and fair levels of noise proper to the place and activities we set?

We could try Cardinal Hume's risible approach when he was a school master: "I don't mind you making noise if you don't mind me stopping you" (Mortimer 1984).

It is important that the students understand and appreciate the difference between "outside the classroom space and inside the classroom space" and the purposes of *each* "space" and "place". Some children bring all their kinaesthetic energy and louder (outside) voices into the classroom context and do not adjust and monitor their movement and voices accordingly (p. 53f).

A calm, quieter atmosphere inside a classroom will enable attention, focus and effective teacher–student communication. It also helps teacher stress levels!

- Explain why we – as a class group – need to have "inside" or "partner-voices" as distinct from louder, "outside voices". The classroom is, principally, a teaching and learning place: "we (therefore) use our voices, and the level of our voice, differently in here".
- Teach the difference between the *volume levels* of voices to emphasise whispering and appropriate "partner-voice" during on-task learning time. One of the ways I've found helpful in teaching this "difference" is to point out to the class that at any time during the on-task phase of the lesson, "I should be able to speak in a normal voice from the front of the room to the back of the room – without significantly raising my voice – and be heard". Teaching this point by modelling can help. I have frequently modelled partner-voice to a class by – say – asking a student for a pen in different levels of voice to clarify, to the whole class, the meaning and extent of partner-voice. When I ask students (even at secondary level) to describe partner-voice they invariably use qualifiers such as "soft", "close", "using eye contact", "first name", "using manners – please, thanks, and so on"; they know.
- Monitor and encourage conscious habits of appropriate and reasonable working noise. There are a number of simple, visual ways to give students feedback about 'working-noise' (see later).
- Review noise levels with the class during the first few weeks to maintain positive, and conscious, habits of monitoring, and moderation in, voice levels.

We remember to use our partner voices at our table groups

I prefer, and use, the terms "partner-voice", "working voices" our "inside voices" or "classroom voices" rather than "working *noise*": I try to avoid easy use of the "noise" motif where possible.

The teacher's voice

Sometime a teacher's normal – characteristic – voice level and volume are UNNEC-ESSARILY HIGH(!), This contributes to the raising of the residual noise level of the students' voices – creating a kind of normatively louder classroom. Often the teacher is unaware that this is a feature of their NORMAL VOICE LEVEL. The problem is that when they need to project a firmer, or slightly louder voice (for emphasis), it is not *effectively* heard. If a teacher's normal voice is particularly loud, or it sounds as if he or she is frequently (and easily) annoyed or irritated, the classroom will be an unnecessarily tense place that will inhibit effective teaching and learning, even if the teacher falsely believes he or she has "good control".

If the teacher has an overly *controlling voice*, and "peppers" their classroom communication with negative language (overusing "don't", "mustn't", "shouldn't", "why?" and "are you?"), the classroom can become an unpleasant place to be for children. I've seen older students, eventually, react against such teachers by overt or covert sabotage of classroom dynamics.

Keeping our tone and volume of voice normally pleasant, confident and adult will aid group calmness and enable student attention; it will also aid positive rela-tional tone.[3] Then when we need to raise our voice for *particular* attention, or to communicate our frustration, or even anger, (Chapter 7), it will carry an appro-priate effect and impact. When we raise our voice to *emphasise*, or to gain *attention*, it helps to – then – drop the voice (de-escalate) to a calmer or more controlled (firmer) voice. This reduces residual tension.

Caveat: I'm talking, here, about our characteristic "voice"; not bad-day syn-drome (p. 26).

Reflective teachers are well aware of the exponential axiom that 'loud teachers have loud classes'. A high level of cognitive processing is necessary – in children – to the learning experience. Noisy and distracting classroom environments (25 children in a small space for long periods) will have a detrimental effect on attention, focus and comprehension. Add to that, there are children raised in very noisy homes: televisions blaring during meal times (even breakfast) and, in some homes, overly raised voices or frequent shouting (even yelling). This necessitates – even more – that we enable calmer, more relaxing, classroom environments.

Obviously in subjects like drama, music and PE there will be a louder volume of 'social noise', at times, but not when *whole-class* focus and attention is necessary to discuss, share, explore, plan and develop the shared learning experiences.

Teaching partner-voice(s) to early years (age 5 to 7)

Like many social experiences that involve self-control we cannot assume that all the children in our classes understand what we mean by "working noise", "partner-voice", "taking turns", "lining up", "hands up without calling out" and "moving *carefully* and thoughtfully around the room"; even basic manners can't be *simply* assumed.

In the establishment phase of the year (Day One, Week, One) it will be important to explain why we need to use our "partner-voice" inside our classroom; and to teach and monitor "working voice" levels. A classroom is a physically small environment in which to creatively house and engage 20–30 young children. If poor habits of working noise volume develop it can be stressful for the teacher, who will frequently have to use a raised voice to regain group attention. It can also affect the attentional behaviour of children during on-task learning time.

The children are sitting on the carpet area at the front of the classroom – Day One. Before the first on-task session for the day the teacher talks about the large room and 25 (plus) voices, sometimes all talking at the same time. She hypothesises with them about what could happen if we talked loudly during work time at our desk. She models with her hands apart as far as she can stretch, to indicate a loud voice. She speaks, about places in the school where we would use loud(er) voices (such as the playground), and why. She asks why we need quieter (much quieter) voices *inside* our classroom. She discusses what a partner is and introduces the concept of "partner-voice" or "inside" or "working voice" (Robertson 1997; McPherson and Rogers 2008). Here she indicates a smaller, quieter voice with a non-verbal cue of hands close together.

She invites a few students to role play "partner-voice" with her in front of the class. A table has been set aside and she sits at the table with a couple of students, asks to borrow a coloured pencil, modelling "partner-voice" and asks the children what they noticed. She soon has class feedback on observed behaviours such as "softness" and "manners". She models "whisper", and "quiet-work talk" as features of partner-voice. She invites modelling from the other children in the role play. As a contrast she models "playground-voice", and the children laugh.

"Imagine if I used that kind of voice if I was asking to borrow a pencil or scissors or even if I was talking that loudly to someone about the work we were doing … What would happen …? How would we feel if we were trying to concentrate … and work …?"

The "noise meter" (Rogers 1998)

The teacher introduces some large drawings (at least A3 size) depicting children in classroom situations. The first picture illustrates the key expected student behaviours during "carpet-time", and depicts children sitting facing the teacher and listening. Some of the children in this picture have their hands up (they are not calling out). The children look relaxed and are smiling. (See over page).

"When we sit together on the carpet we face the front and listen ('listening with eyes and ears') and we sit comfortably."

It will help to explain sitting options that do not annoy others during sitting space. The teacher also discusses other behaviours such as "taking turns"; "listening when others speak" "hands up without calling out if you want to ask a question or share" and waiting for your teacher to call on you.

By having the picture, as a visual cue, the teacher can refer to it during whole-class teaching time, or class discussion time, and can simply say, "Remember our rule about hands-up ..." and physically point back to the rule reminder poster.

The second picture illustrates a table group during work time. In the background are a few faces, and in the foreground the table group are portrayed using partner-voices.

The third picture is similar to the second picture but the children at the table group are clearly using loud voices. The children in the background are frowning, indicating social disapproval.

As with all teaching concerning social behaviours we seek to emphasise the effect of individual behaviour on others and that we don't just live to/for ourselves.

The fourth picture is the same as the third picture but has a circle encompassing the loud-talkers and a diagonal line through the circle.

The teacher explains what each picture represents; what it means in terms of *how we use our voices here.*

These pictures are displayed together with a coloured meter (a circle of cardboard about 30 cm in diameter) in the centre. Each quadrant is coloured: white (carpet-time voices), green (partner-voices), orange (partner-voices getting too loud – this signals a reminder/warning) and red for stop and we all remember, we all refocus. The meter has an arrow (with split pin) that can rotate to any of the four pictures. The teacher explains what the arrow and colours represent. The teacher rotates the arrow to white during carpet-time, and green for partner-voice time.

If children become too loud during on-task learning time the teacher can put the arrow on orange as a non-verbal and visual aide-memoire. He or she will wait to see if students pick up on this visual cue. If necessary the teacher will verbally cue for class attention (wait) and point to the warning reminder picture and either non-verbally cue for partner-voice or will give a brief, positive, verbal reminder, "Remember our partner-voices. Thank you", before putting the arrow back to green.

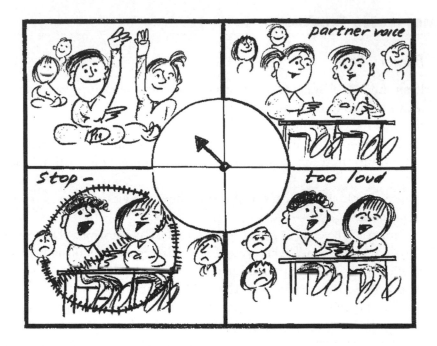

If the teacher puts it on red it signals to the class to stop and everyone has to refocus back to partner-voices. This involves a *brief*, whole-class, reminder about partner-voices. Like any routine it takes time to develop general, reasonable, habituation about noise *levels* inside a classroom.

At Year 1 to 3 level it can help to appoint noise monitors on each table group. Their role is to keep an eye on the noise meter from time to time. The teacher can assist their role by cueing the noise monitor with a brief reminder. It can also help to rotate this role in the first few weeks.

As the teacher roves the room they will also encourage students when they are using their partner-voices.

"You're using your partner voices, and I noticed you're looking at each other when you speak and you're remembering your manners … That all helps us to get our classwork done. Thank you."

In this way the teacher describes what students do that helps their table group (brief, descriptive feedback) and encourages group members.

The noise meter and picture cues are means to an end; they are props and prompts. They have their acute focus in the establishment phase of the year and can be shelved as the desired behaviour generalises.

The noise meter is both an establishment teaching device and a monitoring aide-memoire. In time it can be replaced by a simple tablecard reminder: "At our table group we use our partner-voices" (p. 67).

Partner-voice feedback

Primary level

If an individual student is still struggling with their voice *level*, and *use* of voice, it can help to develop an individual behaviour plan with them. This plan attempts to teach the child (one to one) the "why" and "how" of a quiet working voice (in effect it teaches him individually what most students have adapted to normatively as a group). In teaching a child *one to one* (in non-contact time) the teacher can:

- use simple picture cues to illustrate how individual, *noisy*, voices affect other students
- "mirror" the child's typical noisy voice (ask permission, "Do you mind if I show you how it sounds when you ...?", and keep the mirroring brief (p. 107f))
- *model* appropriate partner-voice
- practise partner-voice with the child (one to one)
- give the child a reminder plan (a small card illustrating the student using his partner-voice). The bottom picture becomes his aide memoire.

Personal reminder plan
for Travis

As with any individual plan for behaviour or learning it is developed away from other children, one to one, with an emphasis on support and encouragement (p. 129f). (See also Rogers 2003a.)

Secondary level

It can be helpful with middle-school (aged) students to give some non-verbal feedback on how the students are using their partner-voice during the lesson. A simple way to do this is through a graph on the board. The teacher uses a simple histogram. The vertical axis runs from 0 (silence), through 2 (whisper zone) and 5 (the upper limit of partner-voice) to 10. Any noise in the 5 to 10 region is too loud (10 being House of Commons on a normal day!).

The horizontal axis is divided into three to five minute sections. Every three to five minutes during the on-task phase of the lesson the teacher goes to the board and draws in the vertical line denoting the level of partner-voice at that point in the lesson (see illustration).

Students are often unaware of how loud they sound when conversing and working during on-task time. This simple graph gives the students visual feedback every five minutes (or more often if necessary). I've heard, and seen, students (many times) nudging each other as I go to the board and give the "histogrammatic" feedback.

If their noise level creeps above the 5 mark (vertical scale) it can help to see if the class picks up the visual feedback cue and brings the level down by themselves. If they do, a visual scan of the room, with a non-verbal OK sign, indicates our encouragement.

This approach is an "establishment routine": it is a means to an end, like the noise meter (p. 69f); the end being reasonable working voice levels.

- Explain and discuss 'partner-voices' with the class on the first day, or session.
- Explain visual cues (such as the graph) and the feedback cues.
- At the end of each class period give the class some descriptive feedback on how "we worked as a class group" across the on-task time period: " ... you kept your partner-voices well below 5 for most of the lesson (...) a couple of times you crept over 5, but you remembered when reminded. Thank you ... I appreciate your efforts. It helps everyone."
- As with any establishment routine it can be phased out as positive group behaviour generalises and habituates.
- With particularly loud, and kinaesthetically robust classes, I've used a points

system whereby the teacher grants points for students (as a group) when they have made the effort to keep their partner-voices below 5 (and awards more points if the level is below 4 or 3). If the class has achieved 20 points five minutes or so before the bell, the teacher, directs the class to 'pack' up early, and students chat quietly until "bell time".

Giving assistance to students during the on-task phase of the lesson

The main point behind any cue, or routine, for giving students assistance *during class time* is the reasonable fairness, and distribution, of teacher assistance and support for many students over a short period of time. Teachers, of course, should be moving around the classroom during on-task learning time to offer support, feedback, advice. This should be normative practice (unless it is a class test …).

- The teacher should explain – even discuss – how he or she can equitably support students requesting assistance during work/task time. The explanation will include the obvious point (humorously made) that a teacher is not an octopus!
- The teacher should discuss the importance of "checking set work yourself first – read through, ask yourself: 'What am I asked or required to do here and now; where should I start; how do I set the work out?'" These self-monitoring questions can be taught as part of a class discussion on positive learning habits.
- For set work procedures it can help to have a class poster with the basic reminders about drafting a piece of writing, page layout, and the writing process.
- The teacher should also remind students that they can quietly check and discuss the work with their immediate classmate (not a classmate on the other side of the classroom, or a student in a row in front, or behind them). Table groups operate differently.
- When the class group is working cohesively (several weeks into Term One) it can help to appoint classroom mentors (peer-mentors) who can assist their fellow students with conferencing about their classwork. Such students need to be held in positive regard by their class peers, and possess natural social skills such as effective listening, communication and relational empathy (high 'social intelligence').
- The teacher could also establish the basic routine: "Check (quietly) with three (directly near you) before you check with me". This can also help students to gain peer assistance before easily, and quickly, seeking out the teacher.

■ At primary age level it can help to have the key learning tasks for the day set out on a separate board, as a visual focus, so that students can rotate between tasks as they complete each appropriate phase or stage of a learning activity.

■ At upper primary onwards it will help if students go on with other work *while they wait for teacher assistance or conferencing*. One way of visually focusing the teacher assistance process is to have a *teacher help board* where the students note down their name if they need to conference with the teacher. Of course before they note down their name they will need to have:
  – checked the set work requirement/task/activity themselves
  – checked with their classmate or working partner.
If they note down their name they can go on with other set work (or other options) *while* they wait for the teacher. This avoids having children just waiting with their hands up until the teacher gets around to them. Other options can include user-friendly worksheets; ongoing project; read the class novel.

There are other 'systems' teachers use such as coloured discs (on each table) to indicate if a student needs help. The important point *in any routine* is that we have thought through why we are using *this particular* routine: how does it enable students and teachers to work more cooperatively? As always it is worth discussing the use, viability and utility of one's classroom routines with faculty (or grade team) colleagues prior to our first meetings with our classes.

Lesson closure

It is important to plan ahead for lesson closure, particularly in the first few weeks with a new class. The teacher will need to discuss with the students basic routines such as:

■ packing up and straightening the furniture; chairs under the table (or *on* the table at the end of the last class period of the day)

■ picking up any residual litter and putting it in the litter bin on the way out

■ leaving the classroom in a considerate/orderly fashion (this may need to involve dismissing the class, row by row, or table group by table group).

Remember there is a natural readiness (present in our students) on Day One, Week One, for the teacher to make these expectations and routines clear. It is also important to finish the lesson, or activity, positively (even if it has not been the best lesson in the world). Aim for a calm, positive closure with a reminder that,

"Another class is coming in after us, *let's do them a basic favour* (this is an important practice at secondary level). Chairs under ...; litter in the bin ...; we leave quietly, row by row (teacher nominates the rows). Thanks ...". At the end of the day we say something like, "Let's do the cleaner a favour, thanks ... Chairs on tables ...".

Homework cues are best written up on the board or printed reminders handed out. Auditory reminders about important topics are miscued by many students in the last few minutes of a lesson as most students are just "waiting for the bell". In fact some students will already have packed up well before the bell; it will be important to speak to such students (one to one) and encourage them to recheck their work, or read the class novel, or go on with a related activity.

It may be important to remind the class politely that the bell is a reminder to both the class, and the teacher, that *this* lesson has ended; it is the teacher's responsibility to dismiss the class.

Caveat: There are some occasions when a *brief* "stay-back" of the class may be warranted.

A quarter or more of the class make a bee-line for the door on Day One (Lesson One) as soon as the bell goes. The other 70 per cent or so (of the class) hold back.

The teacher calls the several students, who raced to the door, back inside (she does this quickly, firmly, confidently, "hopefully").

"Stop (...). Back inside, fellas (...), back inside."

If she knows their names she will use them (a small but crucial point).

"Bilal, Nazim, Craig, Dean, (...) back inside (...) *now*, thanks."

They whinge; naturally. "Gees – it's recess, come on!"

"I know it's recess," she partially agrees. She redirects: "Back inside fellas (...), won't keep you long."

Most students come back (certainly Day One, Session One, the students are generally more likely to comply, not having worked through, fully, the teacher's leadership style). They come back in (grumbling and muttering). I've been in classes where some students flop in their seats sulking and muttering ("Gees what kind of sh-t class is this!").

She stands at the front of the class, scans the group, tactically ignores the students who are sulking, and says, "When you're all settled, I'll explain (...)"

They quieten – they want to go; obviously. She is brief and clear :

"This is not a detention folks. It's not even *a minute past the bell*. In a minute you're out of here." She smiles. "This is a class reminder. In our class we leave the place tidy, straighten the tables, chairs under the tables, litter off the floor. As I said earlier (...), let's do the next class a favour. Let's try it again. Thanks to all those who did make the effort two minutes ago. So; let's all try it again. *Row by row. Thanks.*"

This time when the class leaves they are more subdued, more focused. This approach is preferable to saying, "Right!! If you're all going to waste my time, I'll waste your time!!" (and make the class suffer a lunchtime detention).

She stands at the door giving a brief goodbye as the students leave. It has only taken a couple of minutes but she has *re-established* the class routine she had discussed earlier about a "thoughtful class exit".

If something very valuable has gone missing (lost, mislaid or stolen) the teacher will (where possible) finish the lesson earlier and have a class discussion about the missing item.

"I don't know if someone has taken item X by mistake, or accidentally put it in their bag, but item X has gone missing. It is very important to _____ [the person concerned], as I'm sure you can understand. I'll stand outside this classroom for three minutes and I expect the item to be back on my desk, no questions asked. I'll *then* dismiss the class."

Prior to this mini "class meeting" the teacher might send for a senior colleague to give some immediate assistance in finding the item.

Situations like these are always tricky, especially when time is of the essence. Senior colleague support should always be involved if the item is important and is not returned.

Don Campbell (2000) notes two contrasting teachers engaging in pack-up routines in their early years classrooms. One teacher – a few minutes before lunch – sings some lines to his class, "Let's put away our pencils", the class sings back the words as they pack up. "Let's put away our work", the students musically echo back the lines ... "Let's line up at the door." It does not take long. The children enjoy the game. The teacher next door is heard – shouting – "I told you 15 minutes ago to pack up ... – Why has it taken so long?"

"One teacher," says Campbell, "is using rhythm and tone to connect with their children ..." (2000: 148). That rhythm, tone, kinaesthetic "musicality" effect motivation and emotion in a positive way and they make "routine" a more enjoyable activity.

Before you leave your working area

1. Put all materials away (lids on felt-tip pens, pencils in containers, work away).
2. Tidy your own work space; help others out too.
3. Chairs under tables. (ON tables at end of day.)
4. Litter in bin. Check.

[THANKS! Mr Rogers]

Reflection

The establishment phase of the year is crucial to the positive, working, relationship of teacher and students.

- How did you establish your class(es): individually or within a shared, team, approach?
- How clear, positive, are the rules?
- Do the rules reflect core rights? How?
- How did you communicate the rights, rules, responsibilities, routines to your class(es)? Are they published? How? Are they positively construed?
- What role does the tutor/form teacher play in communicating shared expectations across year groups? (See Figure 2.2.)
- As a primary colleague, how does the concept of a *common, published, classroom agreement* fit with your school practice? (p. 40f)
- How did you plan your first meetings with your students? (pp. 53–8)
- How aware are you of how you cue a whole class for focus, attention and engagement? Are you aware of *communicating calmness*? How?
- How have you engaged behaviour clarity (for example, *levels* of volume in

on-task time; how to get teacher assistance) with your students? Are the essential routines for behaviour and learning expressed *across a grade/year level*? How? How are such expectations fine-tuned across faculties (or grade teams)?

▪ Do you have a least-to-most intrusive framework for intervening in distracting/disruptive behaviour? How was the framework developed? Are there any – whole-school – common practices/skills to inform your "personal discipline plan"? How do the skills (in this chapter) inform/contrast with your daily practice? These skills are more fully developed in Chapter 4.

Notes

1. A "mind-map" is a visual representation of a care idea, issue, question or concept with its supporting and subsidiary ideas, concepts or questions. It can give focus and direction and help to hold several ideas or concepts together.
2. *Punch* was a popular English satirical magazine.
3. Some early years teachers affect a babyish voice when working with small children. This is unnecessary. Obviously we need to modify concepts in our language use, but we don't need to adopt the kind of tone or manner that the actress Joyce Grenfell portrayed so skilfully in some of her comic monologues.

Chapter 3

The language of behaviour management

> What do we live for, if it is not to
> make life less difficult for each other.
> George Eliot (1819–1880)

No formulas!

The language of management, and of discipline, operates in a dynamic relationship. Developing skill in this area does not simply involve our choice of words, phrases or sentences. If it is our *intention* to discipline with respect and confidence, that intention needs to come *through* the language. Only then will our language be relationally dynamic in a positive way.

Being assertive (for example), when it is called for, requires some skill in communication and control over one's non-verbal behaviour, but it is the *intention* to *assert* one's needs, or rights; or to protect someone else's needs, feelings and rights, that really signals assertive behaviour. Assertive behaviour also needs to be context appropriate. Assertion often means we communicate with a firm, resolute, unambiguous tone of voice, and manner, matched by confident (non-aggressive) body language. In this sense the *skill* of assertion is "conscious" and not simply the outcome of reactive feelings.

Two students were rearranging the furniture as I was seeking to establish class attention in a Year 9 English class. It was my first meeting with this class. They already had a "reputation". I asked them their names.

"What?" was the sulky reply.

"What is your name please," I asked again; pleasantly and indicating no threat. I was just initiating a "name check".

One of the girls leaned back, languorously – sighed – and said, "Crystal!" (a sharp, almost nasty tone in her voice) and tut-tutted loudly as if I'd asked her to do some great, onerous, task.

I said in a relaxed, but decisive, tone, "Crystal (...) I'm not speaking to you in a rude tone of voice and I don't expect you to speak rudely to me either." I then added, "You're moving the furniture and I'm ready to start the class. I want you to leave the furniture as it is and be ready for teaching time. Thank you."

She sighed (less demonstrably now) and I walked to the front of the classroom to cue for whole-class attention and focus. If she refused to cooperate with the direction about the furniture (it happens) I would have made the *deferred* consequences clear and left the "consequential choice" with the student (pp. 88, 146, 155).

Although this class had a 'reputation' there were many cooperative and supportive students. In working with them (as mentor-teacher) I believed the whole class would regain that shared sense of purpose – even enjoyment – in working together. In time even Crystal became more positive, more cooperative.

Assertion is not about winning: it's about establishing and affirming fair rights and needs.

I was discussing the issue of corrective language (discipline) with a group of teachers, we explored the issue of positive language and someone raised the question "But that language isn't *me*". We were discussing reflective rephrasing of, for example, negatives: "When ... then ..." rather than "No you can't ... because ...", or "Hands up for questions ..." rather than "Don't call out ...". I think what my colleague meant (when she said "that language isn't *me*") was, "Should we have to *think* about what we say when we discipline?" Does "being me" simply mean I say the first thing that comes into my head?

I believe we have a responsibility, as professionals, to think about the way we typically, *characteristically*, communicate in management and discipline contexts. It can even help to plan a basic repertoire of language that can enable us to discipline more effectively and (hopefully) less stressfully.

The language framework developed in this section is not formulaic; it is meant to give some conscious focus, and some utility, about management and discipline language when developing a personal discipline framework.

It is pointless (for example) to use a potentially positive sentence – "Michael (...), Dean (...), you're talking; you need to be facing this way and listening, thanks" – if we say these *words* in a mean-spirited, sharp, petty, pleading or whining tone of voice.

Language is obviously dynamic and context related; it is, though, the essential basis for positive, workable, relationships. The *skills* of corrective language that are developed in this chapter, arise from, and operate within, essential principles of behaviour leadership.

Key principles of the language of management and discipline

1. Keep the corrective interaction *"least-intrusive"* wherever possible. For example, we can manage such behaviours and issues as calling out; lateness; students overly leaning back on their chairs; uniform "misdemeanours" and students without equipment, with "low" intrusion discipline (a brief non-verbal cue, an incidental direction, a rule reminder). By keeping most correction "low" intrusive correction we keep a pleasant, positive tone to classroom life so that when we need to be *more* intrusive (as context may demand) the degree of intervention will be seen to be significant in relative terms of moral/behavioural "weight". These are times when our first response to a student's behaviour needs to be assertively intrusive, but that is the exception (reserved for unsafe, dangerous, hostile or aggressive student behaviour). (See later, p. 89.)

2. Avoid *unnecessary* confrontation (this includes embarrassment, *any* sarcasm, any sense of hostility or *threatening communication*). A core aspect of our leadership includes *the ability to communicate calmness* when addressing the group or an individual student. Such 'calmness' is not inconsistent with the need to be firm – even assertive – at times. Our 'calmness' lies in our ability to manage our own behaviour as we – in turn – seek to lead others. That calmness also includes a conscious sense of creating a calm *presence*: our body language, how we move around the classroom space, how we characteristically communicate. Humour (repartee, the bon mot, the witty Pythonesque turn of phrase ...) can, also, defuse and reframe tension and lift the spirits of teacher and student alike. Sarcasm invokes hostility and resentment – why wouldn't it?

3. Keep a respectful, positive tone of voice wherever possible.

4. Keep the corrective language itself positive where possible:
   - *"when – then"* is more invitational than "no, you can't, *because ...*"
   - avoid *overuse* of "shouldn't", "mustn't", "can't", "won't" and interrogatives such as "why?" or "are you?" (see later, p. 87)
   - avoid pointing fingers, or gesticulating, when making a corrective or assertive point – use an "open hand" when emphasizing or asserting
   - be brief where possible (avoid *long* directions or reminders about behaviour).

5. Re-establish working relationships with the student as quickly as possible. Even a brief return to a student's desk to ask how their work is going is often enough. A pleasant manner and a brief encouraging word will *always* help.

6. If we need to communicate appropriate frustration – even anger – we do so assertively rather than aggressively (see Chapter 7):

- keep the assertive statement brief
- focus on the "primary behaviour or issue" (p. 17)
- avoid over-servicing "secondary behaviours" (p. 17f)
- de-escalate any residual tension (p. 209).

I have worked with teachers who create unnecessary tension and confrontation by their overly vigilant tone, manner and language.

A teacher has just explained the rule for asking questions and a little later a student calls out. The teacher "says", "is that using the rule, *is it*?!" Does the teacher really want an answer? "Didn't I just say to you *all* to put you're hands up *without* calling out? Didn't I?!" Others add innuendo or sarcasm: "Are you deaf or what...?"; "Don't they teach you manners at home?" Such *characteristic* teacher behaviour only creates palpable tension in a room; it creates (in some students) anxious *and resentful* learners. It is unprofessional and unnecessary. In other students it creates antagonism – breeding uncooperative, even rebellious, attitudes and behaviours.

If we need to communicate annoyance, or even anger (where necessary and appropriate), we can do so in a professional manner, consistent with our feelings and focused on the behaviour (without 'attacking' the student(s) (p. 208).

7. Follow up with student(s) on issues that matter *beyond* the classroom context. This emphasises that the teacher cares enough to make clear the issue of concern with the student and to offer support to improve things (p. 106f).

A framework for management and discipline language skills

These skills are detailed in case examples used throughout this book. They are set out here – in *summary* form – to highlight the "least-to-most intrusive ..." nature of management and discipline language. These skills are illustrated, developed, explored within each case example and case study.

Tactical ignoring

The teacher selectively attends to the student when on task, *tactically* ignoring particular aspects of "secondary behaviour" (p. 17f). This is a context-dependent skill. We should *never* ignore any repeatedly disruptive behaviour, safety issues or harassment behaviours. It is combined with *selective* attention as when we acknowledge a student *when* they have got their hand up – without calling out.

Tactical pausing

The teacher briefly pauses in a spoken direction or reminder (...) to emphasise attention, and focus (p. 4).

Non-verbal cueing

The teacher communicates with a non-verbal cue that carries a clear (unspoken) message, reminder, or direction. If a student is leaning back – heavily – in their chair I will often use a non-verbal cue where I extend thumb and three fingers in a downward motion, as if to say, "… four on the floor thanks." Again – the positive tone and manner will carry the intent. (See also pp. 98–9)

Incidental language (descriptive cueing)

The teacher directs or reminds the student (or group) without directly *telling* them: for example, "There's some litter on the floor and the bell is going to go soon …" (that is, 'you know that I know that I'm encouraging you to pick it up'). In this approach the teacher describes reality and allows the student to process the "obvious" expectation: for example, "This is quiet reading time" to students who are whispering to each other. Sometimes it will be appropriate to combine the "description of reality" with a *behavioural direction*: for example, "This is quiet reading time now [the incidental descriptive comment]. Read quietly inside your heads. Thanks" (the behavioural direction: teacher taps own head). This approach is very effective from middle primary level onwards.

Take-up time

This refers to the teacher refocusing eye contact and proximity *after* having given a non-verbal cue, a direction or reminder. It most commonly involves the teacher "moving away" after having given a direction or rule-reminder. It invites and encourages (even "allows") the student to cooperate without the teacher standing "over them" as it were. (See also p. 102f)

Behavioural direction

The teacher directs a group – or individual – by referring directly to the expected or required behaviour: for example, "Jason (…), Dean (…), facing this way, thanks". Behavioural directions are appropriate for communicating the *required* behaviour, as when students are talking while the teacher is talking and the students need to be facing the front and listening.

- Focus on the expected or required behaviour.
- Use verbs/participles (rather than negative clauses): for example, "facing this way and listening …" rather than "Don't talk while I'm talking please", which

only tells the student what we *don't* want them to do.

■ Finish with "thanks", or "now" if the student/s vacillates and prompt attention is necessary.

■ Keep the direction, or instruction, brief: "Michael (…), Troy (…), sitting up and hands in laps – now" to infants. In this example, "now" is said firmly, but not sharply.

Rule reminder

The teacher briefly reminds the class group, or individual(s), of what the rule is: "We have a rule for asking questions" (a descriptive reminder); "Remember our rule for safe scissors …". The teacher does not need to *spell out* the rule each time. Rule reminders can also be expressed as a question: "What's our rule for …?" This raises the student's awareness and responsibility. If they do not answer we will remind – clearly, briefly. "Remembering to …" is more a positive verbal focus then "Don't forget …".

Prefacing

The teacher gives a positive greeting and focuses on a positive issue *before* engaging discipline (wherever possible). For example, the teacher sees students being a bit silly at their table. He has a chat about the painting they are working on. As he turns to leave he adds, quietly, yet firmly (as he scans the group), "Remember to use the paints thoughtfully". This approach is effective when one has a positive working relationship with the class. It sets the discipline within a *relational focus*.

It is obviously more effective in the on-task phase of the lesson and in non-class settings. I have also found it helpful, sometimes, to direct a student aside (from his immediate peers) to then have a *brief* disciplinary chat. The distraction, early enough, may stop a subsequent disruptive pattern of behaviour. Prefacing should also be normative in managing behaviour in non-classroom settings. The most basic 'prefacing' is to greet and ask a student's name (!)

Distraction/diversion

The example in "Prefacing" (above) is a typical "distraction".

The teacher notices that a student is folding a worksheet during the whole-class teaching phase of the lesson, and says, "Damien (…), the worksheet will be easier to read unfolded. You'll need it later". Calm, *not* sarcastic, (even a touch of humour). The teacher then gives take-up time.

One of my colleagues notes some typical distractions/diversions she uses in her infant classes. They can prevent a scenario from getting out of hand by not focusing on the negative behaviour but on the positive.

"I can see that most of you want to help in getting the plasticine. You remember I did say that we need one helper. What do you think we should do?" Then I thank the children for waiting and being patient. Or *before* saying that, I could say, "Tom has his hand up and he is also sitting quietly with his legs crossed. Tom would you like to get the plasticine?"

Ryan is playing with a pencil. "Ryan, can I see your picture please? What would you like to tell me about your picture?"

Mary is crying for her mother. "Mary, I have a picture for you to colour in and take home to show your mother. What colour are you going to use for the bow?"

Joshua is wandering around the room. "Joshua when you finish counting with the blocks would you like to paint the big picture of Humpty Dumpty?"

Joshua throws the tambourine into the box after the teacher explains to put it away carefully.

"Joshua what did you do?"

"I threw the tambourine in the box."

"What were you supposed to do? Show me the way you were meant to do it. Why do you think we need to be more careful?" If the student doesn't say what they did, then I'll remind them *how* to do the fair/right thing.

Direct questions

The teacher uses a direct form of question rather than an "open" form: for example, "what", "when", "how" or "where" rather than "why" or "are you".

"What are you doing?" rather than, "Are you being silly with the paints …?"

"What should you be doing?"

"What is our rule for …?"

"How are you supposed to …?"

These sorts of questions direct students to their responsibility rather than asking for reasons. Direct questions focus on a student responding to their *present* responsibility rather than looking for reasons *why* they are not behaving considerately or responsibly at this point.

"We need you to do your work in a way that doesn't create a problem for … How are you going to do that …?" to a Year 10 student engaged in time wasting and noisy off-task behaviour.

I asked a Year 8 student what she was doing. I had noticed her doing some maths homework instead of the set classwork.

"Jacinta (...), what are you doing ...?"

She said, "Nothing ..." and covered her work.

I gave some brief, quiet, feedback, "Actually it looks like you're doing your maths homework. What should you be doing?" (the direct question).

She answered quickly, "This shit ... I mean, sorry, this *sheet* ...". We both grinned. "Sounds like you know what to do ...". I walked off (take-up-time). I came back later to check, and encourage, her (now) now she was back on task.

Directed "choices"

A "choice" is given by the teacher within the known rules or routine: "Yes you can work on the drawing when you've finished the diary writing" ("when ... then"; "after ... then"). In this sense, the "choice" is expressed as a *conditional* direction: "We'll organise a toilet break when I've finished this part of the lesson". All "choices" given to a student are, in a sense, conditional. They refer back (one way or another) to the rights and rules and responsibilities.

"Choice"/deferred consequences

I have put the word choice in inverted commas to indicate that no choices are *free* choices as such; they are choices *within* the rights, rules, responsibility dynamic. In this case the teacher makes the consequences of *continued* disruptive behaviour clear within a consequential "choice": "If you cannot work quietly here ... I'll have to ask you to work separately ..." (to two repeatedly noisy students).

"If you choose not to put the iPod (or phone, or nail varnish, or comic) away I'll have to ask you to stay back after class [or ...] to discuss your behaviour".

This assumes that, earlier, the teacher would have reminded the student about the rule and (if necessary) given the student a directed choice to "... put the iPod in his bag or on the teacher's desk".

The language of 'choice' is not conveyed in any sense of threat or win/lose. We clarify the deferred consequence and give take-up-time. This is in preference to snatching a toy, i-Pod or phone ... Even if the school has a confiscation policy we do not *snatch* the 'object' – we extend the hand. If the student refuses to cooperate we leave the deferred consequences to their 'choice' and responsibility/accountability. It is not about 'winning', it is about *leading* and (later) carrying through the 'certainty' of the consequence away from peer audience (pp. 146, 155).

'Blocking', partial agreement, refocusing

'Blocking' is a communication approach whereby a teacher "blocks out" a student's procrastinating argument by not entering into a potential prevarication or argument.

A teacher directs two students to face the front and listen (during whole class teaching time). They whinge, "We're not the only ones talking ...". The teacher blocks their avoidance whingeing by gesturing with an open hand, palm towards the student(s) and *repeats* the direction. *In effect* she is saying, "I'm not interested in *why* you were talking, or who else was talking. Hear the direction and face the front and listen". In this, she is *redirecting* the students to the main issue (at *this* point in the lesson) and avoids over-servicing their "secondary behaviour". It is normally helpful, having "blocked" the procrastination, to give the students take-up-time and reclaim group attention (p. 102f).

There are occasions when students whine and whinge, for example when infants try to explain "who took whose toy". The teacher firmly – kindly but firmly – blocks: "Michael (...), Troy (...). Stop" (hand gesture). "I'll listen when you use reasonable voices." It can help to then tune in to how they are feeling ("I know you're feeling a bit upset ...") and then *refocus*: "What is our rule for ...?", or "How can we sort this out so that ...?".

Partial agreement

The teacher deals with the student's procrastination or avoidance by *partially* agreeing with the student (where appropriate) and refocusing back to the rule or required task. This is particularly helpful with adolescents.

A teacher reminds a student (who is chewing gum) of the rule. The student challenges by saying, "But Mr Scroggin lets us chew gum in his class" (a very common whinge ...).

Instead of arguing, the teacher *partially* agrees, "Maybe he does". The teacher *then* redirects, "In our class the rule is clear. The bin is over there; thanks" (the incidental direction). At this point it is often helpful to give the student some take-up time.

Assertive comment/direction/command

There are degrees of assertion in one's language and voice. Fundamentally, when we assert we are making our rights (or others' rights) clear, in a decisive, firm, non-aggressive way: "That language is *unacceptable* here. We have a rule for respect. I expect you to use it". *Firm* – non-aggressive – eye contact; a *clear, calm voice* and *directed, focused, language* are at the heart of assertion. Our confident "calmness" will often affect the other person's calmness, *and the peer-audience*, who naturally feel the ambient tension.

"I don't make comments about your body (or clothes or sexual orientation …). I don't want (or *expect*) you to make comments about mine."

If the student says, "I was only joking! Gees – can't you take a joke?!" the teacher will say something like, "It's not a joke to me – and it stops *now*." If the student continues, we would consider time-out provisions (see p. 149). Sexist or racist comments or put-downs should be dealt with assertively and then followed up one to one with the student (later after class time) away from peer audience. It may be helpful to ask a senior colleague to sit in during such follow-up (p. 106f).

It isn't easy. Our insides may be saying "I'd like to maim this s--!" But we're professionals. Assertion enables our professional skill to *decisively* emphasise rights and expectations, without getting into a heated argument or slanging match. If the student argues, we will need to block and refocus. In effect *reassert*.

Commands

When giving commands, it is advisable to keep them short. Establish direct eye contact: "Michael (…)!" The first word should be sharp and louder – to gain *attention*. "*Michael* (…)", bring the level of the voice *down* as eye contact is established, and cue the command in a firm, decisive, assertive voice: "get down off the table – *now*." In a fight situation (most typically in corridors or playgrounds), if the names of children aren't known, use the loud generic attentional command, "Oi (…)!, Oi (…)!" – then a firm assertive voice, "Move away *now*." Use non-verbal cues to indicate the students should separate. Direct the audience of peers away and *immediately* send for adult assistance. It is preferable to give commands in those situations where unambiguous, *immediate* stopping of disruptive behaviour is warranted. We also need to be able to back up our commands if a student refuses to obey. Our back-up should consist of a school-wide time-out plan, involving adult support, that can be invoked as quickly as possible in a crisis anywhere in the school (p. 152).

Obviously, we cannot plan for every contingency. These key principles are the underlying framework of the way we communicate and relate in our teaching and management (pp. 83–4).

The key language skills are suggestions of the sorts of things one can say in typical management, and discipline contexts. The language "forms" can serve as aides-memoire to give some prepared focus to enable the least-to-most principle (p. 83).

> NB Finding one's 'own voice' in behaviour leadership is important. Being more conscious of *how* we express ourselves, how we communicate, is essential to our leadership role. The language cues here, are based in well-established psychological theory and practice as applied to social-learning settings. By utilising these skills as a 'working template' they can enable, inform and strengthen your 'own voice' as teacher-leader.

Settling the class outside the classroom

As I approach 8D, in the corridor, I scan the students arriving. Some have US-style "baseball" caps on; some wear sunglasses; a few are still eating; a couple of students towards the back have mobile phones in their hands; a couple of students are listening to iPods; a couple of boys are "testosteronically bonding" (a mild punch, a push in the rear, a 'friendly' strangle …).

I've worked with colleagues who make no *conscious* management of this kind of corridor restlessness. Opening the classroom door they let the students in with no focused distinction made between the outside (playground) culture and the inside (teaching/learning) culture. Some teachers don't even greet the students as they form or line up outside a classroom. There are sensible reasons for corridor settling and *age-appropriate* lining up (p. 53f): the brief settling (outside the classroom) signals (by the teacher) a change of pace, place, space and purpose in terms of group behaviour.

I find it helpful to comment briefly on hats, iPods and any testosteronic bonding or pushing *before* directing the class group inside.

First a brief, group-settling direction *as we scan the group or line*.
"Settling down everyone … (…). Thank you. Morning everyone – just before we go in (…) … I notice several students with hats on …, Ben (…), Lucas (…), Marcus (…)."

This brief *description of reality* is often enough to make the issue of "hats off" clear, without directly *telling* the students. Sometimes it is enough just to give a non-verbal cue (hand to head) for caps off.

"Down the back, I can see mobile phones (…). Remember we're going into a learning environment …". Giving a non-verbal cue to the lads listening to iPods, we add, "We're going into the classroom. Remember the rule about iPods. Thanks." Rescanning the whole group, "Looks like we're ready folks. When you go in, remember to …".

This does not take long at all. It is worth it in the establishment phase (p. 38f).

It can help Day One, Session One (and the next few sessions), to emphasise our expectations about seating and settling once inside the room. With early years I find it helpful to ask them, "What do we need to do when we go *inside* our class?" and then fill the gaps in their forgetfulness as necessary (about hats, water bottles, bags … and so on).

This corridor-settling does not take long but it *prefaces* the teacher/student expectation about purposeful behaviour on the other side of the classroom door. In time, the outside settling should become a habit so that all that is necessary is a *brief* line-up, or grouping, before moving into the classroom.

It is always worth discussing with colleagues, in one's grade-team or faculty, how they normally settle a group prior to classroom entry: what sorts of things they do and say, *and why*.

The first three minutes (once inside the classroom)

The first three minutes are important in any lesson. The teacher has to *initiate*, *sustain* and *focus* group attention.

Obviously the teacher needs to allow a little time for the students to take their seats (or sit on the carpet) during which time the teacher needs to convey that he or she is purposefully waiting for the class to be seated ("eyes and ears this way …") and ready to begin.

It will help to have a brief discussion with each new class, in the establishment phase, concerning the basic expectations about classroom entry and settling at their work area or desk. Such "settling" varies with age and subject area, of course. In drama classes it may involve having shoes off, against the wall and sitting in a semicircle; in an information technology (IT) room it may mean finding a seat, turning it around to face the front and sitting, relaxed, waiting. What is important is to have a workable routine that will enable 25–30 students to settle smoothly, and consciously attend to *whole-class* teaching and learning time (even where there is no 'line-up' policy). Students also need to know that their attention (in the first three minutes) is expected ("eyes and ears at the front, thanks", "hands in lap" at infant level – explain what "lap" means).

It is worth thinking about *what* to say (as a verbal cue) to the class – particularly more restless class groups. It can even help to consider basic aspects such as making sure the class door stays open (as students enter) – asking a student to hold the door open. Avoid talking *at any length* with students *as they enter*. A brief, positive greeting is appropriate as students walk in – past the teacher to their seats. If any student wants to chat, or "raise an issue" (in the first minute or so) it is enough to assure them – briefly – you will chat later. It is then important to go to the front of the classroom to visually – then verbally – cue for whole-class settling. As noted earlier it is worth considering what we say and do in those first few minutes (p. 56f). Our ability to convey, and communicate, a sense of calmness (at that point in the lesson) is crucial to how positively students settle and focus.

■ Avoid using questioning cues to the class group. "*Would you please* be quiet and listen?", "*Can you please* stop talking and …?" (It is not a *request*.)

■ Use direct behaviour-focused language, for example, "*Settling … looking … listening … thanks …*".

■ Briefly address distractions such as overly restless seat leaning, "private chatting", loud fiddling with objects (for example, pencil cases/water bottles) *while* cueing for "settling …". Brief, descriptive, directional or reminder cueing is enough (see below).

■ Refocus the class to, "Settling … listening …".

■ Greet the class and begin. Give a whole-class greeting *when* the class has settled.

It can help (at upper primary and middle school) to establish and maintain a reasonable "target time" for group entry, settling, having relevant materials and being ready to engage in group learning. A reasonable target could be, say, 1–2 minutes. This target time is consciously set as a *class target*, and encouraged and reviewed over the first half dozen lessons or so (Pearce 1997).

Cueing for attention in some classes may mean students go straight to an activity, as in English, where students file in, take their seats, quietly get out the class novel and read for – say – five minutes. Some schools still direct students to stand behind their seats quietly at the beginning and close of each lesson. Carried through positively, even this can be a useful cue. There are a range of non-verbal cues to establish group attention in the instructional phase of the lesson (see p. 58). They should always be verbally *explained* when used for the first time.

Managing distracting and disruptive behaviour during whole-class teaching time

The typical distractions and disruptions that can occur during this phase of class time can range from rolling on the mat and hiding under tables (hopefully only at infants level – although I did have a lad hide in a low cupboard once in Year 7!), through to those annoying pockets of private chats while the teacher is seeking to engage and teach the class.

The most common disruptions in this phase of the lesson tend to be: talking while the teacher is talking; cross-talking across the classroom; calling out to the teacher; lateness; leaning chairs and motoric restlessness; fiddling with stationery (or other secreted objets d'art); and clowning (attention-seeking behaviours). Most of these behaviours tend to be exhibited in the establishment phase of the year as students test out their relationship with each other and with their teacher.

When exercising discipline in a whole-class, whole-group, context it is important to be aware of what we do and say such that we avoid alienating the cooperative students. In this part of the lesson or activity, anything we do or say, in discipline terms, has an immediate audience effect beyond the individual (or small group) that we address. For example, if we are overly confrontational we create a tone – an emotionally palpable tone – that can hinder the motivation and cooperation of all students, not only those we discipline at that point. While there are some occasions when a brief, unambiguous communication of frustration and anger is appropriate – most of the time, when we are dealing with the sort of disruptive behaviours noted earlier – it is important to be respectfully positive. Being positive, confident and *appropriately firm* are not antithetical concepts.

Several students are engaged in private conversations as the teacher is establishing initial class attention and focus. The teacher visually scans the room, standing relaxed (not slouching), and cues for group attention (p. 56f). She briefly describes the behaviour of the disruptive students.
   "A number of students across the room are talking while I'm trying to teach (…)."
   Sometimes this *description of reality* is enough; it acts as an *incidental* direction (p. 85). Sometimes we will need to add a behavioural direction.
   "Facing this way and listening, thanks." The teacher then gives take-up-time (p. 102f) and *refocuses the flow* of the lesson.

"Thanks" is to be preferred (in this context) rather than "please". "Thanks" carries an expectation of what is directed rather than a request (please).
   Sometimes this private natter – or talking while the teacher is talking – is *unfocused* student behaviour rather than *disruptive* student behaviour. Either way the approach noted above keeps the discipline least intrusive (p. 83).
   If the description and direction is focused on an individual (or several individuals) it is important to preface with the student's name(s): "Dean (…), you're fiddling with the window blinds" (the description of student behaviour). "*Facing* this way and *listening*, thanks." "Facing …" and "listening …" *behaviourally* direct the students to the expected behaviour. If the description/direction is directed to several or more students it is better to preface by saying something like, "A number of students are calling out … Remember our class rule for questions/discussions". (This acknowledges that it is not *all* the students.)

Behavioural directions

When using behaviour directions (as above) it is helpful to focus our language on the required or expected behaviour, briefly and positively wherever possible (p. 85f).

"Dean (…), you're calling out [the descriptive element]. *Hands up* and *waiting* thanks [the *behavioural* part]" is said in preference to "Don't call out …" or "Why are you calling out …". Equally unhelpful is the question "*Are you* calling out?"

Students coming late into class

A student comes into class late. The teacher has been teaching for five minutes. The teacher quickly walks over to the door and says to the student, "Are you late?" (It is surprising that the student doesn't answer, "Course I'm late!")

If the teacher asks, "*Why* are you late?" it sounds (particularly if the teacher is frustrated) as if the teacher is "interrogating" the student, when in fact the teacher may only want a reason. Does it matter (however) – at that point in the lesson – *why* a student is late? Trying to get answers, and reasons, at the classroom door only feeds (in some students) incipient attention-seeking or even power provocation.

Teacher: "Why are you late?"

Student: "People are late sometimes you know." [*If the student's tone is sulky, petulant, or hostile, the lateness issue can quickly become a scene where the student believes he must play to the 'gallery' of his peers.*]

Teacher: "Don't you speak to me like that!"

Student: "Yeah – well I'm *only late*, you don't have to hassle me. The girls are late sometimes – you don't hassle them do you?"

Teacher: [*The extended index finger appears, in the air, in the space between them. The teacher's voice is rising.*] "Who do you think you are talking to?!"

Student: "Yeah well you're hassling me about being a few minutes late – Gees!"

Teacher: "Right! Go and sit over there. Now!" [*The teacher points to the few spare seats. The student doesn't want to sit there. He wants to sit in his normal seat, which is already occupied.*]

Student: "I'm not sitting there. I sit down the back with Nathan and Travis …"

Teacher: "Look, I don't care where you sit. I said sit there!"

Student: "Nope. Why should I?" [*He sulkily folds his arms and looks away. The audience of his peers are having a "field day" on this one.*]

Teacher: "Right! Get out – go on, get out! If you're not prepared to come to my class on time you can get out. Go on, see Mr Brown!"

Student: "Yeah, I'm going anyway, this is a sh-t class …!" [*He turns and storms off.*]

Of course we need to address the issue of the student's lateness, but it is unnecessary to dwell on the lateness *in front of the class like this* and *at this point* in the lesson. Some teachers get drawn in easily by the student's "secondary behaviour" (the tone of voice and the student's reactions).

When students are late it is *always* helpful to welcome them – briefly and positively – especially in the first few lessons. We won't know, initially, if a student is late because he or she is lazy, disorganised or time-wasting, or if there are home-related issues (relevant to late arrival for Period 1 for example).

In the following example the student is five minutes late, a different class; different teacher.

Teacher: [Briefly cues the class (she had been teaching)], "excuse me for a moment class …". [*Welcomes student at the classroom door*] "Welcome (…). It's Tony, isn't it?" [*Teacher is still learning names. He puts his hand out to shake hands with Tony. Tony frowns, looks a little tentative – he was not quite expecting this approach. The teacher briefly, quietly and politely, acknowledges Tony's lateness.*] "You're late. There's a spare seat over there – next to Carlos." [*The teacher doesn't tell Tony to sit there: he "describes the obvious reality". He focuses on the important issue at this point in the lesson: direct the student to be seated and get on with the flow of the lesson.*]

Student: "I don't sit there … I sit down the back with …" [*He's less defensive with this teacher, but still procrastinates.*]

Teacher: "Those seats are taken, Tony …" [*The teacher could add, "And if you'd been here on time you would have had your seat!"… He resists the temptation.*] "We can organise a seat change later" [*This adds a (future) choice, defusing any residual tension. At this point the teacher redirects his eye-contact away from Tony, turning to re-address the class; he scans his eyes across them.*] "As I was saying folks …" [*Resuming his lesson flow, as if Tony will (naturally) sit down where the teacher has incidentally directed. He does – he walks across to the seat in a slightly exaggerated, posturing, way and flops down. The teacher tactically ignores this residual "secondary behaviour" keeping his focus – and the class's attention – on the lesson.*]

If the student blatantly refuses to sit where the teacher nominates we need to make the consequences clear – calmly, briefly. "If you choose not to sit there I'll have to ask you to leave our class and go to …". It is pointless 'pleading' or 'bargaining' with a student if there are only one or two spare seats left and they refuse to sit there; it happens. This sort of possibility needs to have been discussed within the school's time-out policy and practice (p. 149f).

He follows up with Tony later, at the end of the lesson, for a brief chat about the student's lateness. If the student is persistently late (three times over several consecutive days) he will take the lateness issue further with the year adviser to see if there is a pattern across other classes.

When students are late
- Welcome the student.
- Acknowledge (briefly) the lateness.
- Direct (incidentally where appropriate) student to a seat.
- Give take-up time (p. 102f).
- Resume the flow of the lesson or activity.

Discipline in the establishment phase of the lesson
- Scan – focus – scan (avoid maintaining eye contact for too long with any one individual or small group).
- Keep corrective language brief.
- Use positive language where possible.
- Focus on specific behaviour (when disciplining) or focus on the relevant rule.
- Avoid arguing with students – verbally block or partially agree, and refocus back to the rule or main issue, or flow of lesson.
- *Tactically* ignore non-verbal secondary behaviours wherever possible and wherever appropriate. If a student's secondary behaviour is *also* inappropriate, or disruptive, address it briefly and refocus the student(s) back to the expected rule, or behaviour.

Description of reality (directing incidentally) in a civic setting
Have you ever had someone push in on you in a supermarket queue? It surprises me how many people let others, in effect, have more "right" to the front of the queue. On these occasions I often incidentally, politely and briefly describe our little bit of shared reality: "Excuse me (...), the queue starts there." An open hand rather than a pointing finger indicates the back of the queue.

A pleasant smile – no hint of sarcasm or "I'm threatened by you" or "I'm better, more important, than you". On some occasions I've had people say, "But I'm in a hurry". I find it helpful to briefly add (before turning away and giving some take-up time), "We're in a hurry too (referring to the others in the queue) the queue starts there. Thanks." Of course if the pushing-in person is 15 stone and has emblems of the Wehrmacht tattooed on his head, let him pass (or move to another queue)!

I was in the crowded underground station at London's Victoria Station on one occasion. The many scores of commuters were going through the ticket barriers at a rapid pace. There was a New Zealand couple (I could tell by the accent from a few yards away) trying, vainly, to get their crumpled ticket into the automatic barrier. They don't have underground railways in New Zealand. I was annoyed by the several pin-stripe-suited gentlemen huffing and puffing because the couple (replete with the fruits of their London shopping) were holding them up for 30–60 seconds of their life.

I walked over and said, in a firm voice, scanning the 20 or so in the queue, "Excuse me folks (…). These people are clearly struggling with the machine (…). There're several more machines over there. Thanks." I beckoned with my hand. They moved away, frowning and huffing, a few sighing – and several looked sympathetic. I think they thought I worked for London Underground. I don't – I'm a teacher and I wanted to support my "Kiwi cousins".

I said to the older couple, "G'day – these machines aren't easy are they?" They looked relieved, more relaxed.

"You're Australian?"

"Yes …"

We had a brief chat, sorted the ticket, and they went on their way.

Kyriacou has noted, "if one behaves as if one has authority, it is surprising how far this attitude exerts a momentum of its own leading pupils to behave accordingly" (1986: 132).

I would add that even in some civic settings adults can similarly pick up the subtle cues and signals (as well as through language) and behave more considerately.

Non-verbal cueing

Many distracting behaviours can be addressed – even nipped in the bud – by a non-verbal cue.

A couple of students are leaning back in their chairs as the lesson begins. The teacher pauses in her delivery and verbally cues the students, "David and Liam (…)". They look towards her. She cues non-verbally by extending her thumb and three fingers down to indicate a chair with four feet on the floor. When she initially established this class cue she communicated both the verbal and non-verbal aspects of the cue to associate the idea of chair legs "on the floor".

Non-verbal cues minimise the need for the teacher to verbalise the required behaviour *every time*. This is particularly helpful in early years classes. Typical cues are:

- The teacher crosses his index fingers then beckons with the right hand to indicate facing the front to cue for "cross your legs and face the front".
- The teacher raises one hand, and covers his mouth with the other to indicate "hands up without calling out" (to students who call out in class discussion time). Some calling out can be *tactically* ignored if the teacher is confident with such an approach, but a non-verbal cue can act as a *brief* reminder without disturbing the flow of the lesson or activity too much.
- The teacher puts one hand over the other and pulls it into the chest to indicate "keep hands and feet to yourself". This is an important cue for restless, touchy, early years students.
- The teacher touches one eye with a forefinger, then an ear, and uses a beckoning hand to the front of the room to indicate "eyes and ears this way now".
- The teacher holds up a thumb and forefinger a little distance apart to indicate "use your partner-voice, thanks". This is an effective reminder/direction during on-task learning time as the teacher is moving around the room. He or she may be working at one table and can remind a table group nearby by cueing across the room. I have used this reminder cue countless times in secondary classrooms.
- A similar cue I have used for years is the thumb and two fingers turning down, rotating an imaginary volume control (old fashioned technology that one!).

As with any discipline strategy it is important to avoid any unnecessary tension. If any of the cues noted above were given with a jerky, thrusting, hand and a glare and a big sigh from the teacher it would hardly be seen as a *simple* reminder!

When using a non-verbal cue for the first time it will be important to associate the meaning of the cue by giving both the non-verbal cue and the spoken reminder/direction together.

Eye contact

Eye contact can engage attention, show interest and indicate intent. A stare, however, can create ambiguity if unaccompanied by verbal direction. Too long a stare may reciprocate, in some males, a perception of hostility or threat. Dodge (1981, 1985) has researched attributional bias in aggressive children, observing that aggressive boys *selectively* attend to the available cues in their environment. Overly aggressive males tend to have a *perceptual and attributional bias* towards aggressive intent in the other party.

As teachers we can avoid unnecessary hostile attributions with such pupils by considering proximity, and following eye contact with a brief direction or reminder; avoiding unnecessarily *extended* eye contact; giving take-up time; and avoiding unnecessary win–lose perception by how we frame language – that is, using appropriate choices (p. 88). It is important to be aware that in some cultures (notably South East Asian countries) extended eye contact cues do not operate in the same way we may be used to. 'Forcing' eye contact can cause significant embarrassment – even shame. Most importantly, however, we seek to communicate calmness, in tone of voice and body language (see the example on p. 96).

Tactical ignoring

Tactical ignoring is a difficult skill. It is a *conscious* decision not to attend to some student behaviours such as sulking, sighing, eyes to ceiling, the "hang-dog look". the wry mouth and frown when you direct students to do something really difficult like go back to their seats, or put their hands up without calling out, or put their pens down while you're talking to the class …

Tactical ignoring is also a form of non-verbal communication to all students (not just the student you are *tactically* ignoring). It demonstrates that the teacher is focused on the main issue – at this point – and it further avoids overly reinforcing attentional "secondary behaviours" (p. 17f): for example, "Don't you raise your eyes to the ceiling like that …!" "Why can't you do a simple thing *without sighing*? Is it *so* difficult? What's wrong with you?!"

We obviously should not ignore behaviours that the students know should not be ignored: any *repeated* and loud calling out, or butting-in that affects a teacher's right to teach; *any* verbally rude or defiant language; *any* hostile or aggressive behaviour; any unsafe behaviour. The cooperative 70 per cent of students know the difference; they know when a teacher is *tactically* ignoring.

In a class discussion, for example, it can be very effective to *tactically* ignore the few students who call out several times. It sends a message that the teacher will notice students *when* they have their hands up *without* calling out or finger clicking. Of course, the teacher needs to do this in a way that does not appear anxious, tense, uncertain or conveying superiority. Otherwise the ignoring can add confusion, or annoyance, to what is happening. A common alternative approach is to *preface* any tactical ignoring. If a student calls out (in whole-class teaching time) we give a brief rule reminder, refocus to the lesson and then – if the student calls out again – we *tactically* ignore. The 'prefacing' clarifies – and in effect cues to the class (and to the individual) – *why* we are tactically ignoring the student.

Prefacing the tactical ignoring

The teacher is moving around the Year 3 classroom assisting, encouraging and clarifying. Bilal calls out across the classroom for "Miss" to help him. He has his hand up (he thinks as long as he has his hand up, even if he is calling out or clicking his fingers, he's within the rule and will always get her attention). From a distance across the room the teacher gives a conditional direction and *then* tactically ignores Bilal's subsequent calling out: "Bilal (…), when you have your hand up without calling out then I'll come over to help". The *subsequent* ignoring now has a frame of understanding ("when … *then*").

A common example at nursery age occurs when an overly concerned, or anxious mother drops off her 4-year-old on Day One, Week One. The child cries, holds on to its mother and pleads. The mother assures the child, over and over again, "Yes I love you … my precious. I'll be back … I will. I promise … be a good boy … yes, I do love you". The child is really crying and may be anxious (although some children do learn to manufacture tears for attention). The mother naturally wants to reassure the child, but ends up reinforcing the child's attentional behaviour: "the 45-minute goodbye". Most teachers quietly reassure the mother that if she goes, leaving the child with a confident, smiling assurance (once or twice) the child *will* settle down. ("Please ring later, in half an hour, Mrs Smith …".) The teacher (after initial, warm assurance) will then *tactically* ignore the child's crying and firmly, pleasantly and kindly redirect the child without over-servicing the child's attention-seeking behaviour. She will also (obviously) distract the child by pairing them off with a more socially confident child. In this example tactical ignoring involves *selective* attention; reassuring, and refocusing as the child settles.

Take-up time

I was teaching a Year 10 class, as a mentor-teacher, and as I scanned the room during on-task learning time I noticed that a student had what looked like a novel on top of his exercise book. I walked over.

"It's Damon, isn't it?" It was my first session with the class and I was still learning names. I added, "Good morning."

He looked up (not attempting to close the book). "Yeah – it's Damon."

"I notice you've got a book there, a novel? What's it about?"

"It's about a serial killer," he said, looking up with a grin.

"Well, let's hope he's not after a teacher," I said (and meant it). This brief chat is a form of prefacing prior to some task refocusing. I thought it best to focus on the task.

"How's the work going?"

"It's boring," replied Damon.

"It may well be boring, Damon, but it's our work for today. Do you know what to do?"

My tone was pleasant; expectant of cooperation. He sighed, leaning back.

"Yeah, sort of."

"How can I help?"

I gave a brief reminder of the task, pointing back to the whiteboard and adding, "By the way, the novel. I'd like you to put it in your bag or if you like you can leave it on my desk till the bell." This was the "discipline" part of the brief engagement. He grinned back. I added, "I'll come back and check on your work a little later, Damon." The walking away, at that point, allowed some take-up time for the student and also gave a task refocus. With older children it only escalates unnecessary confrontation to take, or snatch, the distracting item. Similarly, if a directed choice is given to the student (as above) and the teacher continues to stand there, waiting, *until* the student puts the item away it also creates unnecessary tension.

Take-up time can also convey trust in the student that he or she will respond appropriately. It allows some face saving in potentially tense situations. It is important to go back to the student, later in the lesson, to check if they are back on task and also to briefly re-establish the working relationship.

A student walks into a class late. Rather than make a big fuss the teacher welcomes the student, beckons to a spare seat and continues the flow of the lesson while the student is moving towards the seat. This gives the student take-up time, increasing expectation of cooperation. The teacher quickly resumes the flow of the lesson taking the spotlight away from a potential scene (p. 96). It will be important to follow-up the lateness beyond whole-class teaching time (during the on-task time), when a brief one-to-one chat can occur (p. 106).

With younger children the teacher may need to repeat a direction or reminder a few times until the child responds, and *then* give the take-up time as the child responds.

As children get older our management and discipline language should seek to engage the emergent adult within the young person by:

- not 'talking down' to a student, or merely talking *at* them
- seeking to engage the student in thinking about their behaviour: hence incidental and 'descriptive' language (p. 85) and thoughtful use of questions; directed choices (p. 86); particularly in front of a student's peers
- not forcing students into a psychological corner (instead using deferred consequences (pp. 146, 155f).

An aside on uniform 'misdemeanours'

Some schools still retain pettifogging application to rules (and rule governance) about uniform and jewellery: only sleepers, but no pattern on the sleepers; studs, but only gold or silver, no pattern; socks must *always* be worn knee-high; no rings, or bangles, or friendship bands; hair must be a certain length; and so on (hence the word misdemeanours in inverted commas). There may well be good reasons for some of the rules but it is the application of the rules that ought to concern our *thoughtful* management.

A young girl is wearing a "non-regulation" ring in class. A present from her father. It has a sentimental, almost "Linus-like" psychological comfort for her. New to this school, she comes across a teacher who notices this major crime and asks her to hand it over. The girl is upset, confused and becoming quite frustrated.

"No. No way. I'll take it off if I have to."

"Give it to me ... now."

The teacher repeats his command and puts his hand (palm out) to indicate he expects her unquestioning compliance.

"No!" the girl clenches her fist. She (quite naturally) doesn't know if she'll ever get it back. She mentions that the teachers in the other classes hadn't said anything.

"I don't care what other teachers do. I *said* hand it over." If she doesn't (believe it ot not) he'll put her on detention!

This may sound like a manufactured example, but – sadly – it isn't. True, the teacher concerned may not have known the girl's psychological attachment to the ring. True, the teacher may be seeking to be vigilant about the uniform/dress code. The problem is he has not tuned into the girl's feelings, or considered welfare as part of the discipline process. He lacks any empathetic, perspective-taking in managing natural adolescent behaviour. He seems only concerned about the pettifogging application of the rule. He may also hold demanding, absolutist views about control and vigilant teacher discipline ("children *must* obey their teachers", "children *should not* answer back." "Good teachers must be in control of students …"). (See pp. 24–6.)

In another class at the same school a teacher comes up to a student wearing a similar ring during on-task time.

"Rachel, that's an attractive ring."

The girl has a brief chat with her teacher about the ring.

"You know the rule about large rings?" (The teacher's voice is quiet. She is keeping it low key.)

"But other teachers haven't said anything," the girl frowns.

"Maybe they haven't, Rachel, however the school rule is …" The teacher *partially* agrees (p. 89) and refocuses to the school rule. The teacher gives a non-verbal signal to the student's pocket indicating for the girl to put it away in her pocket. The girl owns her behaviour. Relaxed vigilance; even in a school with such pettifogging rules.

End of story. If the girl refuses a fair directed choice like this, the teacher will defer the matter to an out-of-class follow-up (p. 106f). If the teacher catches her with the ring on again in a school like this the issue *may* occasion a stay-back session to emphasise the rule.

If you ever happen to teach in a school that promotes a confiscation policy on "rule-breaking jewellery" (excuse my cynicism here), at least give the student the dignity of an assurance of returning it the same day. I've known "power-merchant" teachers to keep rings and non-dangerous objets d'art until the end of term! That is simply psychological harassment. It always staggers me that some students will easily hand such items over. In schools where students do not evidence such unquestioning compliance to teacher control such an order ("Hand the ring over") would be rightly laughed at.

More than personality

I have heard teachers observing some of their colleagues' behaviour management practice with the disclaimer, "Oh, it's just their personality. That's why they can get through to those students". While personality is important, if they observe more carefully, they will note that these colleagues are also aware of their own non-verbal communication and the impact of their "global set" of behaviours on others. They will note that these teachers are particularly conscious of their management and discipline language.

There are skills that can enhance 'the personality' we bring to our profession, these skills can aid positive communication: increasing positive congruence between what we communicate (content); how we communicate (non-verbal tone); timing (when we intervene) and *why we choose to communicate this way at all* (our values and our aims).

While some people are naturally effective communicators, most of us have to learn that our non-verbal behaviours and *what* we characteristically say, carry significant weight in our daily communication. These non-verbal behaviour cues can enable positive, workable, relationships with our students (and colleagues). Even when we are frustrated and angry, some non-verbal cues will make the communication process less stressful and easier to repair and rebuild when the heat has died down.

> A common belief is that group management skills are simply a natural gift. You either have it or you don't. Our evidence does not support this belief. Its most damaging feature is that teachers who have difficulty controlling classes tend to put this down to personal inadequacy rather than to a lack of particular skills that can be acquired through training or advice from colleagues.
>
> The most talented, "natural" teachers may need little training or advice because they learn so quickly from experience. At the other extreme, there are a few teachers for whom training and advice will not be properly effective because their personalities do not match the needs of the job. *It is clear, however, that the majority of teachers can become more effective classroom managers as a result of the right kinds of training, experience and support.* (Elton Report 1989: 69, emphasis added by author)

As in all reflective teaching we should, essentially, consider the *effect* of our behaviour on others and trust that they will do likewise (no new message this; just a difficult one).

Seen on a staff noticeboard

I will not yell in class and I will not throw things & I will not pinch or even hit and I will not have a temper tantrum & I must always be a good example to all the kids. ... because I am the teacher ... I am the teacher ... I am the teacher ... I am the teacher ... I am the teacher ...

Some wag had added at the bottom:

> To be read each morning in case it will be one of those days.

(When is it not?)

Following up with students beyond the classroom setting

There are a number of reasons why we will need to follow-up with students (one-to-one) beyond the classroom:

■ To clarify an issue relating to class learning (homework, or misunderstanding about class work, or a student getting behind with their work). In this case the follow-up is normally to emphasise empathetic teacher support. There should not be any emphasis on punishment for students who are currently struggling with classroom learning, or work/task assignments or homework.

■ To initiate a discussion about a concern regarding the student's behaviour.

■ To follow through with any *deferred* consequences (p. 146). A typical example is when a student has left a mess and has made no effort to clean up. At primary level, teachers sometimes use deferred consequences for students who have made no effort to complete classwork (this would assume the student was able to do the set work).

■ To initiate a process of mediation with students who have exhibited conflict behaviour in class time.

■ To initiate detention or formal stay-back procedures (p. 159f).

When following up with students in any out-of-classroom setting:

■ Consider whether a follow-up or follow-through session is merited in the first instance.

At secondary level it is often difficult to follow-up issues between classes (especially during a six-period day!). Sometimes one can manage a *brief* word of follow-up after class and sometimes that may be enough. If the issue is important enough, though, it is worth directing the student to come to a later meeting (for example, during the lunch break). In that brief moment after class we won't be able to go into the details; it will be enough to make the appointment.

Ethical probity

When conducting *any* one-to-one teacher-student stay-back session, it is crucial to be sensitive to ethical probity, particularly with a male teacher and female student. It will help in any extended one-to-one sessions to have a colleague of the opposite sex present in the room (abstractedly working on their work programme) while conducting the follow-up.

■ Whether the follow-up is a brief chat, a task based consequence (that is, cleaning up mess left), an interview with a student or even a detention (p. 159f) it is important that the teacher emphasise the fair, *certainty* rather than the severity of the consequence.

I have seen teachers confront students after class with their pointed index finger a few inches from the student's face, exhorting their "pound of psychological flesh" (emotional, psychological, pay-back). "Yes. You're inside now, eh? Missing playtime. Well it serves you right. If you had done what I said you could be outside now couldn't you?! Eh …! But no …, no …, you had to play the big man didn't you?!"

I can understand how some teachers *feel* at this point. I can understand that they may even want to make the child *feel* bad, and even "suffer", through this process. But it is counter-productive and unnecessary and unacceptable. The student, in this case, will hardly learn anything constructive about the consequential nature of his or her behaviour through such teacher behaviour.

■ Tune in briefly to how the student may be feeling at this point – they obviously want to be outside with their mates, and may be really annoyed, even angry, or possibly even anxious. By *briefly* tuning into how we think they are feeling we humanise the follow-up while retaining consequential certainty. "You're probably feeling annoyed that I've asked you to stay back after class [or to have this meeting at lunchtime, or …]". Our tone and manner here (as so often in discipline transactions) is really important. If we sound as if this follow-up session (however short in terms of time) is some kind of "win" for the teacher, the student will probably perceive and define the issue in those terms as well.

■ Focus *specifically* on the student's behaviour, or the issue of concern you have as their teacher: "I'm concerned about what happened in class when …". If it is a task-related consequence it is enough to direct the student(s) to the task-requirement: "Bradley when the work area is tidy [be brief and specific] then you'll be ready for recess …". With task-focused consequences it can help to refer to the class routine/rule: "In our class we leave our work areas tidy …".

In helping to *specifically* focus on a student's disruptive behaviour it may be appropriate to "mirror" the student's behaviour (Rogers 2003a). Mirroring involves the teacher *briefly* "acting out" the typical, characteristic, disruptive behaviour of the student (that is, calling out, frequent seat leaning, loudness or talking while the teacher is talking) and even their "secondary" behaviours (that is, *frequent* sighing, eyes raising, loud muttering, and so on (see p. 17f).

When "mirroring" a student's behaviour in this one-to-one context always:
– ask permission of the student: "I'd like to show you what I mean when I'm referring to you calling out ..."; "Do you mind if I give you a brief demo of how loud you often speak in class ...?"; "Let me show you what I see you do when you push and pinch others when you're sitting on the mat in carpet time [this to an infant student]"
– keep the actual mirroring (of the student's behaviour) brief
– avoid the impression you're getting some Machiavellian satisfaction out of showing the student how annoying, or stupid they are; we illustrate their behaviour; we don't "score" (!)
– having mirrored the student's typical classroom behaviour, we physically step back (as it were) from the kinaesthetic re-creation
– refer back to the mirrored behaviour to further clarify the issue of concern: "So; *that's* what it looks like when you ..."
– with older students it can help to invite a response to the specific behaviour: "So how many times do you think you call out like that?"

Mirroring is an attempt to *illustrate* and *clarify* a student's characteristic disruptive behaviour and to enable teacher–student dialogue. It is used in the context of teacher support, to help the student to be behaviourally "aware" and assist them in owning their behaviour.

NB   When talking one-to-one with children diagnosed with Autism Spectrum Disorder we would not – normally – use a mirroring approach. We would – instead – specifically focus the student's understanding about the necessary/appropriate behaviour/s. We do this specifically, with direct/clear language and model the behaviour to enhance clarity (see p. 170f).

We often use picture cues and brief behaviour specific cues (see p. 182f).

■ Where appropriate, invite the student's right of reply. This can be verbal or written. Ask questions that will enable the student to focus on their behaviour in the light of what happened (to occasion the staying back). We also refer back to the basic rights and responsibilities in the student behaviour agreement (p. 42f). In this, the teacher is making the important point that, in some way, the student's behaviour has affected someone else's rights.

The basic questions we can ask are: "What happened …?"; "What rule or right was affected by your behaviour …?"; "How do you see what happened, and how do you feel about it?"; "What can you do to change things … fix things up … sort things out … make things better …?". These can even be presented as a written pro forma. We call this pro forma the "4W" form, after the four questions prefaced by "What …?".

Some supplementary questions when involving a student in a longer follow-up session can include:
– "What do you want to happen – for you?"
– "What do you think will happen if you … (keep reacting in class like …)"; be specific?
– "What can you do so that others can get on with their work without [make reference, briefly, to the student's current disruptive behaviour]?" "What can you do so that others can feel safe or learn here?"
– "What can I"; "How can I, and your other teachers, help you to …" be specific about the key behaviours necessary to change for the student to get some success back into his classroom learning and social engagement?

The spirit and tone in which these questions are asked are crucial. If they are asked in a provocative, confrontational way they will (obviously) create the very resentment and resistance the teacher is seeking to refocus with the student.

The emphasis with all extended follow-up on issues of behaviour is to enable the student to become more self-aware (with regard to their behaviour).

The outcome of these questions should be some understanding, even some 'plan', that will increase the student's sense of self-monitoring and regulating behaviour (see Chapter 6).

If the student does not respond to *supportive* questioning, or even refuses to cooperate, the teacher can still make the following points clear so the student is as aware as possible of what needs to change:
– "This is what I see, and note, about your behaviour …"; be specific.
– "It isn't helping you when you …"; be specific.
– "This is what you'll need to do if you want to change your behaviour so that you can …"; be specific.
– "I'm *always* ready to help." Allow take-up time for the student to respond to *each* issue raised (above), and assure the student of your willingness to support them in making a behaviour plan.

■ Another approach when working with students who present with resistant patterns of behaviour is to explore, with them, their likely goals behind their behaviour in terms of attention and power (see Chapter 6, pp. 177–181).

Some students will frequently use the line (even whine) that "I can't …": "I can't do the work …". A firm, *supportive*, focusing can often help: "Perhaps you can't do the work:

– *because* you're not facing the front and listening during the teaching time …

– *because* you haven't got your pen, ruler and pencil ready to start …

– *because* you haven't read through the task [assuming their reading skills are proficient – if they're not we should always find creative, supportive, ways to adjust the task as well as extend their thinking] …

– *because* you're easily distracted by sitting near Dean … So let's make a plan to … [address the can'ts]."

A plan can then be developed that will incrementally build up "academic survival skills", and behaviours, to enhance the student's learning and relationships with others at school (Chapter 6).

As with all communication with students in situations where there is natural, ambient tension. We, therefore, seek to:

- calm ourselves before trying to calm the student
- avoid rushing the dialogue (allow some time for student response)
- be aware of our open, non-confrontational, body language, avoid crowding the student's personal space
- keep the focus on the "primary behaviour" or primary issue of concern (avoid pointless arguing)
- refer to the student behaviour agreement (p. 40f)
- keep a supportive, invitational, tone wherever possible.

- When we direct students to stay back for task-based consequences it is enough to direct the student to the task, give them some take-up time and check for task completion (that is, to clean up the mess, finish the piece of work …).

- Separate amicably after working through a consequence (even a brief five-minute chat after class). I've heard teachers raise the strained-relationship stakes by having the unnecessary last word: "… and if you pull that stunt again you won't just be speaking to me, or your form teacher, or the year head, or your mother! I'll ring the Minister for Education as well!"

- Track the student in terms of ongoing disruptive behaviour. If the follow-up session sees no discernible (subsequent) change in the student's behaviour or attitude it will be worth checking with other colleagues (through the team leader/year adviser) to see if this behaviour is *typical, frequent* or *characteristic* across the year level and across classes. If there is typical, frequent, disruptive behaviour in such cases it is wiser to have a year-level, whole-staff, approach to working with the student in question (p. 182f).

A colleague recently shared with me: "I followed up all my rude students, all the difficult ones, and the ones with learning problems. I even withdrew students from colleagues' classes where necessary, to follow up. I used the 4W form (p. 109) (they didn't like that; they said 'Why don't you gives us lines like the other teachers? We have to think with these questions!'). Well, by the end of first term I was buggered! But second term was a breeze."

He wasn't being smart, or clever when he said "it was a breeze". This colleague is a good, kind and patient teacher. What he was saying was that early and consistent follow-up and follow-through in the establishment phase of the year paid off.

Reflection

- How aware are you of the language you *characteristically* use in behaviour leadership? (pp. 84–91)
- How do the key practices noted earlier (p. 83) inform your own discipline practice? Do you have any school-wide expectations about *daily* behaviour leadership and discipline? Should we have some *common* school-wide discipline *practice* (beyond natural personality factors)?
- There are some quite challenging skills noted here — how aware are you of using (for example) *tactical* ignoring? (Within a framework of *selective* attention and positive feedback?)
- How do you engage students in follow up beyond the classroom? (even the five-minute chat)? How do the protocols noted (p. 83) inform your practice?

Chapter 4

Effective teaching: fundamental understandings and skills

Effective teaching: some fundamental considerations

The term "effective" needs a little reflective thought. Effective at what? For whom? At what cost? In what way?

If "effective" is pursued merely, or only, in utilitarian terms then intentional humiliation, manipulation, sarcasm, public shaming and embarrassment can all be utilised by a teacher as long as such behaviour "effectively" shuts a student up, quietens down a class, creates anxious compliance or gets the work done. Hopefully none of us would want that. Many of us grew up with teachers who made us stand when we got less than five marks out of ten in a spelling test (or whatever), or made us do a maths problem on the board (and we couldn't) or said we were "stupid" or "thick" because we didn't understand something the first time. Thankfully, there are few teachers like that in schools now. (Well – I hope.)

"Effective", in any meaningful sense, also needs to include the *values* that underlie what we aspire to in "effective teaching". Core values such as respecting all students (even basic civic respect) and equality of treatment (fairness) are universally accepted by students of any age as redolent of "effective" teaching.

There are a number of characteristics of effective teaching that are present across every age of student and teaching situation:[1]

- The teacher appears to be self-confident, patient and good-humoured (bad days notwithstanding; p. 25f). The teacher also displays a genuine interest in the topic and makes a genuine attempt to be actively involved in and concerned with each student's progress. Even a basic commitment to acknowledge and affirm a student's effort in their work, in their progress, will affect student motivation in a positive way. Of course, our acknowledgment, affirmation and encouragement need to be genuine if they are going to be accepted and valued by students (pp. 129–35).

Even a positive greeting to the whole class (as well as individuals as they enter) can assist in engaging a sense of basic *belonging* here in *this* place – our classroom.

■ The teacher's explanations and instructions are clear and pitched at a level likely to "connect" in terms of student understanding, needs and comprehension. One of the most basic aspects of effective (and competent) teaching is that the teacher explains the purpose and relevance of what they are teaching and the particular learning tasks that flow from them. They do this every lesson; every activity. When we set up learning tasks and experiences (that flow from shared dialogue in the whole-class teaching/instructional phase) we need to make the aims of the task clear to our students and outline the basic expectations (even steps) about how the learning can progress. *Task clarity* is basic, but crucial.

It is also essential that teachers make an effort to *engage* students and sustain reasonable attention to the teaching and learning process each teaching period. Such engagement also involves conveying some enthusiasm for the topic at hand.

I have heard teachers say things like, "Well … what we're doing today is pretty boring … but we have to do it … so …" (followed by a heaving sigh). If it is boring they will find out quickly enough – why tell them? If it is a routine/"boring" activity we just *do our best with it*; even a familiar, "tired" topic. We do not need to telegraph "boringness" in advance!

> Teaching is an affective process as well as a cognitive one. It is essential therefore that one conveys positive attitudes not only towards one's subject but also towards pupils … it is never advisable to devalue what one is about to teach … better to present the subject to the best of one's ability and let the pupils decide whether it has any intrinsic merit. (Robertson 1997: 70)

Mr Smith sees his class lining up haphazardly, in the corridor outside Room 15. As he walks towards them he doesn't greet them: not even a basic "Hi". He opens the door and walks in, and the students file in noisily.

He doesn't greet them, or welcome them, or consciously seek to calm the class down. He really hasn't made an effort to learn their names yet (it's Week 3). He does not introduce the topic or integrate it into any prior learning. He starts to write algorithms on the board (Year 8 mathematics), with little or no enthusiasm. There is no apparent consideration that some students who struggle with some of the more abstract aspects of mathematics may benefit from some visual connectedness, or "connectedness" to other areas of knowledge or experience.

Yes, he may be tired today. He may be bored. But if he *characteristically* teaches like this is there any wonder that there is a correlation between:
- student inattention and his approach to the topic that day?
- his lack of enthusiasm, or even basic engagement, and student indifference and lack of motivation?
- student learning outcomes and teaching style?
- behaviour distractions? (And such distractions will often arise from lack of teacher engagement.)

A lack of basic commitment to the fact that children learn in different ways will affect student learning; not all students are auditory learners.

■ The teacher is aware that his or her *characteristic* voice and actions can significantly facilitate students' attention, interest, motivation and cooperation. Although we are *not* actors we do have to project some visible presence, and pay some conscious attention to voice usage, manner, attitude and approach so as to *engage* students in our teaching presentation and communication (see Welch in Thody et al. 2000). This clearly means much more than the ability to talk, "tell", and "direct".

As Robertson notes:

> Perhaps with the exception of the first few meetings with a class, a warm and relaxed greeting before the lesson begins will often make all concerned feel better and no matter how many times a lesson has to be repeated, nor how tired one feels, one's interest with the material must be kept alive or the class will soon share the lack of interest. (1997: 69)

■ The teacher makes both a positive and *varied* use of questioning to motivate and monitor students' understanding and raise the level *and* quality of students' thinking. This issue is discussed at some length later (pp. 126–9).

■ The teacher monitors the progress of a given lesson *and* monitors general and individual behaviour as it affects teaching and learning. Such monitoring enables the teacher to make appropriate adjustments to the flow and development of a given lesson as well as addressing any inattentive or disruptive behaviour with a focus back to the central business of teaching and learning. This monitoring is conducted as unobtrusively as possible (see case study p. 135).

■ The teacher makes a conscious and willing effort to encourage students in *their* effort and progress and gives thoughtful praise and encouragement:

– keep the encouragement *descriptive* rather than global, that is, "That was a moving and thoughtful description of … in your poem about …" rather than simply noting "good work", "brilliant work" or "nine out of ten, *great* work …"

– use 'private' rather than public praise (which can create unnecessary embarrassment with older students), that is, the quiet private encouraging asides we give during on-task learning time

– focus on the students' effort and progress as well as errors and mistake; use errors and mistakes as opportunities for the student to learn and gain.

The topic of encouragement is discussed later in this chapter (p. 126f).

A colleague (Bill Kemp) outlines how he encouraged a reluctant learner in a Year 10 mathematics class.

It is Thursday afternoon, last period, in Year 10 mathematics. Students are tired and it has been a hot week. Just around the corner looms the end-of-year mathematics exam. The kids have started revision lessons with me but they are still a bit unsure about exactly which topics are in the exam and which are not.

Michelle listens as I list the topics and chapter reference and exclaims, "No, not lighthouses. I hate lighthouses!" when I mention that Chapter 7 (trigonometry) is on the list.

I continued the session with my students, building them up and encouraging them in the strange, "language other than English" subject called mathematics, and genuinely looked forward to teaching the group again first period on Friday. Michelle's comments triggered in me an automatic response to stop the standard "how high above sea-level is the lighthouse" problem being a stumbling block to her mathematical progression, and make it a springboard into a whole ocean of mathematical wonder (or at least give her the chance to pass this type of question in the exam!).

I created a hand-out sheet with three or four revision questions for the Friday morning class. The most important question on the sheet, of course, had a stick figure diagram of Michelle firing a shot from a cannon towards a lighthouse with the appropriate trigonometric detail on the diagram to help the students find out how far the shot travels to destroy the lighthouse (an old lighthouse under demolition).

The result the next day was very satisfying and fruitful. The class saw the stick figure named Michelle and the class tom-toms soon got the message around the room to check out question three on the sheet. Michelle read the question and asked me, "Did you make up this question because of what I said yesterday?" I acknowledged it and was pleased to read on her face a look of "I'm important. Mr Kemp has gone to all this trouble just for me. I better have a red hot go at these lighthouse questions". Michelle now owns that trigonometry question and, through her efforts to do her best to learn mathematics skills, has overcome the fear of the "lighthouse question".

It is my joy to be teaching in a lighthouse to shine out light to students to guide them away, around and past the dangerous rocks of doubt and "I can't do it" attitudes and "I hate maths because I don't understand it".

■ Any management of distracting and disruptive behaviour is minimised by keeping attention on the central business: teaching and learning.

"Relaxed vigilance" is a useful descriptor when addressing typical disruptions such as lateness; calling-out; butting-in; talking while the teacher is talking; inattentive motoric restlessness; and so on.

"Relaxed vigilance" describes the teacher's confident, assured, firm expectations about cooperative compliance when engaged in behaviour management. Group monitoring; through periodic scanning and eye contact (of the class as a whole as well as individuals), is a way of saying "I know that you know that I know …".

Circulating (during the on-task phase of the lesson) and proximity can even divert some potentially off-task and poor attentional behaviour. Circulating also allows teachers to monitor task engagement and to give feedback and encouragement. I've seen some teachers characteristically sit at their desk for the whole lesson and never circulate among their students.

When addressing distracting and disruptive behaviour:

– Keep the level and degree of intrusiveness low. Recall the principle of *least to most intrusive* (p. 83).

– Keep the engagement of disruptive behaviour brief and keep the language positive (where possible) (Chapter 3).

– Remember that tone of voice and manner are as important as the words themselves when communicating respectful discipline.

– Focus on the "primary" behaviour, or "primary" issue, wherever possible – avoid getting easily distracted by "secondary" issues and "secondary" behaviours (p. 17f).

– *Where possible*, conduct any 'criticism' of a student's behaviour privately, or if it has to be given publicly do so in a least-intrusive, *brief* and respectful manner.

– Give take-up time (where possible) following corrective discipline (p. 102f).

– Use directed "choices" instead of threats (p. 88).

– Refer back to the class agreement on core rights, responsibilities and rules (p. 40f).

– Have a well-planned time-out policy at the classroom and exit-from-the-class-room levels. No teacher should have to cope with a situation where a student effectively holds a class to ransom. Collegial back-up and follow-through is essential in any time-out process (p. 149f).

– Always follow-up and follow-through with a student on issues that matter. Avoid easily passing-on discipline/behaviour/management concerns to other colleagues. Utilise their skills, their relational goodwill and their expertise to *help with* the follow-up or follow-through (p. 106f).

■ There are many (and varied) *potential* disruptions to a lesson from lateness, calling out, noise levels, not having equipment and seat-rocking through to play punching, testosteronic bonding and (rarely, one hopes) hostile or aggressive behaviours. Effective teachers, and effective teaching, address potential (and likely) disruptions to learning by thinking through classroom management issues *preventatively*. Things to consider are:

– Organisational issues (from lining up and seating plans through to students who "haven't got a pen …") (p. 9f).

– Lesson materials and their distribution and use at appropriate times (so the students don't distract particularly during whole-class teaching time).

– Thinking through how we'll *engage* students' interest within a given lesson or topic and how we'll stimulate some marginal motivation through examples; current issues; use of questioning; concrete examples or illustrations; and so on.

– Thinking through how time will be managed in a lesson.

I noticed this young lad (Year 8 class) not doing his work. I also noticed that he was engaging his hormonal-bridge-building-possibility eyes on his *amour*. I asked him (quietly – an aside), "What are you doing?" He replied, wistfully, "I'm thinking love thoughts".

– Planning how we will deal with typical disruptions in the establishment phase of the lesson itself; such as lateness; noise level; settling a class; initiating and sustaining class or group attention; dealing with students who call out, butt in or seek to derail a lesson. Such planning has to include what sorts of things we'll say to address these typical, or likely, issues (Chapter 3).

– How we will deal with typical disruptions during the on-task phase of the lesson (Chapter 2 p. 64f).

The key question we need to ask is: "How can I *prevent*, or *minimise*, unnecessary hassles or problems ...?"

Most of this preventative aspect of teaching and management occurs in the establishment phase of the year. This is where we develop, then *teach* and monitor the rules, responsibilities and routines to students about lining up, hats off; phones and i-Pods away; rules about toilet provision, going for a drink even chewing gum; routines for noise level; seating and how to get reasonable teacher assistance; through to how to pack up; leaving the room tidy and how we leave and exit the classroom (Chapter 2).

In establishing these fundamental routines and rules it is essential to discuss *with* students *why* we have such routines (basically, a fair go for all), and also to try to increase some commonality of *core* routines across classes (Chapter 2).

Most of all, the preventative questions are best explored within the context of colleague support. Colleague support can give assurance that we're basically on the right track (or the best track at the moment!). Colleague support can give the moral back-up that we're all in the same boat, facing common issues, concerns and problems and have common responsibilities. Colleague support can also give us the long-term professional support we need to reflect, evaluate, assess and even appraise our day-to-day teaching. Such appraisal, of course, needs to be based in professional trust and professional goodwill. Teaching can, at times, be a lonely profession. Colleague support has the potential to meet the basic need we have to belong and work as a team of professionals.

I was sitting in a very large lecture theatre listening to an international lecturer. I was at the back – in tiered seating – and could see the few hundred fellow participants below. The lecturer was introduced. He had an hour, presenting a keynote address. Within ten minutes he had 'lost' the attention of a significant group of adults. He was hesitant and looked flustered, and his overhead sheets were complex and unreadable. His examples seemed abstruse and unrelated. His voice was often vocally monotonic and he rarely smiled or scanned the eyes of the group (scanning, of course, would have given him some feedback from sections of his audience). He frequently looked down at his notes. There were no lifting moments, or defusing moments of light humour (I'm not talking about jokes either); in effect he didn't connect with us. We never really heard *what he felt, as well as what he knew*, about the topic in question; or what impact his subject and topic had on him and his world. I'm sure his research was more than adequate. He just wasn't communicating; he wasn't making his world more common to, and with, us. I felt his struggle, his anxiety; I sensed his emotional pain.

In front of me sat two colleagues (psychologists) who had started to write notes to each other, and giggle and whisper (quite loudly – as if they were back at school!). They were completely ignoring this lecturer.

I leaned over and whispered, "He's trying to communicate to us." They replied, in a governed whisper, "But he's so bloody boring!" I thought (yet again) how fragile one's hold is on others' attention as a teacher.

I felt for this man – he was clearly nervous and anxious – yet I also understood why my colleagues behaved as they did.

Effective teaching *behaviours* are not mere technique; it is not a matter of "a bundle of skills equals an effective teacher". The skills of effective teaching can be learned, but those skills need to be engaged within a desire to teach and willingness to engage and relate to children and young people. The behaviours of effective teaching are not inconsistent with the appropriate sharing of our humanity and feelings.

Effective teaching is our normative, *professional*, responsibility.

Humour, warmth and rapport

William Glasser has said that one of our basic needs is the need for 'fun' (1992). By this he means that the classroom teacher needs to recognise the importance of feeling both emotionally and intellectually positive. It also means we seek to communicate such within the working relationship with our students.

Children of all ages value and enjoy working with teachers who have a sense of humour, which can range from the funny turn of phrase to facial expressions, Pythonesque irony, appropriate farce and self-humour (as with *faux pas*). One doesn't have to tell jokes (my memory for jokes is weak). The bon mot, repartee, and an apt turn of phrase can all defuse tension, refocus jaded students and lift their spirits (even transitionally).

I have seen classrooms where there is no laughter, warmth or basic *joi de vivre*. They are depressing places to work and learn in. Of course learning cannot always be fun. It is a bit of a grind, actually on some days. That's the point, in the "gristle" of it all, the humour gives the enabling sense that "we're all in the same boat, going in roughly the same direction". Shared humour affirms something basic about our humanity.

A note on teacher status and authority

When teachers seek to establish both appropriate moral authority, and role authority, it is important to realise that such authority is established, and earned, within the context of relationships built by the teacher. The fundamental nature of such relationships is dependent on conveying respect, knowledge and enthusiasm for what one teaches. Authority is also communicated through a relaxed confidence in one's management and teaching and a healthy acceptance of fallibility in self (and others). As Robertson notes:

> Teachers who wish to establish their authority should behave as if they are already *in* authority. This is not as simple as it sounds. A teacher by virtue of (a certain) "status" has certain rights to behave in ways denied to pupils, and in exercising those rights he reinforces his authority. This does not mean that he should be repressive or authoritarian but rather that his behaviour should be consistent with his 'status'.
>
> Pupils are less likely to question a teacher's authority if, by his behaviour, he defines the situation as one in which his authority is legitimate. It is particularly important for a teacher to do this in the first meeting with a new class. (1997: 10, 11)[2]

Some key aspects in conveying appropriate authority

- Moral authority superintends role authority. The power associated with one's authority always needs to be understood as more than power "over" others.

  We use our 'power' (as adults-in-role) *for* and *with* our students; not merely using power *over* our students. There is a conscious use of the preposition here (over). Many teachers (of my generation) grew up believing they had power *over* children. In time – of course – we learned that relational/moral power is 'earned' within our leadership and our ability to engage workable – and positive – relationships with our students.

  Do we use our leadership, experience and legitimate role authority to lead and guide young people towards increasing self-discipline and respect for others' rights? Our leadership, management, teaching and discipline are not aimed merely at controlling others but at helping them to control themselves and manage themselves, their learning and their social relationships at school.

  "Relational power", rather than the utility of "controlling power", is a crucial factor when establishing and maintaining one's moral authority with students. Relational power is in part established in the first meetings with our students and developed, and sustained, through demonstration of mutual respect and mutual regard.

■ When establishing and maintaining such authority the teacher:
  – Creates a positive tone of purposefulness about "why we are here together in school ..." and "why we are here today in *this* lesson and doing *this* activity ..." (p. 114).
  – Sustains students' attention and motivation; this is a crucial factor in effective teaching. Without the ability to initiate, engage and sustain attention and show some enthusiasm for one's subject or lesson, students are unlikely to either involve themselves in any workable (or meaningful) learning let alone behave in ways that consider classmates and teacher alike.
  – Ensures the appropriateness of the learning activity and task. This (obviously) ranges from catering for students' ability range and differentiation, through consciously considering visual (as well as auditory) learning styles, to thoughtful seating plans, and how resources can be best utilised with individual or group learning experiences.

Basically, a teacher's authority needs to be based in effective teaching rather than a status position based on coercion or displays of authoritarian management (which ultimately fail in the longer term).

Well-prepared lessons, the ability to present and communicate clearly and to communicate knowledge, information and skills with some energy and clarity, together with the ability to engage student attention and interest are fundamental to any concept of *effective* teaching. Such teaching also includes the ability to develop shared dialogue with our students, and to clarify learning tasks and activities so that students can engage meaningfully with what we seek to teach (see case study on pp. 135–9).

If, for example, a teacher typically stands in front of the class looking uninterested, or even bored with what he or she is about to teach; if he or she has not prepared some clear lesson focus and some key learning aims and tasks; if he or she does not use any visual learning cues and does not tie the learning focus into some fundamental shared experience; if his or her voice carries little engaging motivation, tone or perceptible interest (from known to less known) it will take a very patient class to sit through the lesson without some disruptive, off-task, behaviours.

■ A teacher's authority is quickly assessed by students through how they perceive his, or her, overall behaviour. The *characteristic* tone of voice; facial expressions; eye contact; scanning and posture can all signal one's emotional state, and can convey how confident, assured or anxious the teacher is. The teacher's characteristic "global set of behaviours" (verbal and non-verbal) are typically assessed by students in the early stages of their relationship with a class. (Rogers 2006a)

> Pupils are typically reported as liking teachers who can keep order (without being too strict); are fair (i.e. are consistent and have no favourites); can explain clearly and give help; give interesting lessons, and "are friendly and patient".[3] (Kyriacou 1986: 139)

■ When exercising *our rights* of leadership and authority we need to recognise that such rights depend on cognate responsibilities. There is a sense in which a teacher's authority is acknowledged and accepted by the *reciprocity* occurring in their leadership role.

For example, when a teacher walks across to a student's desk and comments about a toy on their desk and then gives a directed choice (p. 88), "David, I want you to put that toy in your bag or on my desk, thanks ...", and the student puts the toy in his bag; the student – in effect – gives the teacher *the authority that the teacher confidently exercises at that point.* This is the nature of the "reciprocity" occurring within relational authority. For one teacher the words used earlier (in the "choice" about the toy) could sound like a directed choice; in the mouth of another teacher they could well sound like a challenge or threat; yet another teacher may make such a choice appear as a plea.

When a teacher says to a class group, "Eyes and ears this way now, thanks" (or another of the many variations in the "gaining class attention" theme), the fact that most students do face the front – and actually listen – indicates a notable feature about this relational reciprocity. The authority to lead, guide, remind, direct, create (and give) 'choices', give consequences (and so on), depends on students acknowledging such authority *by their reciprocal action(s)* and responses. This is the natural – even creative – tension in teacher authority.

> Authority exists in a relationship and is to a large extent granted by the students. It is in everyone's interest that there should be a context in which teaching and learning can take place and teachers must be granted the authority required to perform this role. For their part they will have to earn this authority by the quality of their teaching but it is also helpful from the outset to behave as if they already have it, in a more formal manner consistent with their "rank".
>
> When a person behaves in a confident and efficient manner we are inclined to believe that such behaviour reflects knowledge and experience. In the school situation the reality is that teachers *are* in positions of authority in relation to students but their behaviour must be consistent with this and hence imply knowledge and experience; thus the teacher can "claim" authority. (Robertson 1997: 75)

■ Always be prepared to follow up and follow through with a student on issues that count; such as concerns about a student's learning or work; concerns about behaviour or the need to carry through with appropriate consequences (p. 147f). As with all follow-up beyond the classroom setting, a teacher needs to communicate care and concern as well as the authority to address behaviour issues or apply consequences. Alongside any such follow-up one should also be willing to repair and rebuild the relationship if there is any anxiety, tension or animosity.

In any one school, there can be significant differences in the authority granted to teachers by the students. Those differences transcend age and gender. According to Robertson (1997), Kyriacou (1986) and Rogers (2006b) it is one's personal qualities, demonstrated in effective teaching and management, rather than mere *role*, that determines one's relational authority.

While this may sound obvious in print I've seen many teachers – in practice – merely expect to have their authority accepted when they clearly are ill-prepared; do not find workable engagement, interest and entry points into student understanding; teach in a boring uninteresting way with little enthusiasm; and give infrequent encouragement and feedback to their students.

It should also be expected of teachers that they are of such a personality and character that they are able to command the respect of their pupils, not only by their knowledge of what they teach and their ability to make it interesting but by the respect which they show for their pupils, their genuine interest and curiosity about what pupils say and think and the quality of their professional concern for individuals. It is only where this two-way passage of liking and respect between good teachers and pupils exists, that the educational development of pupils can genuinely flourish. (Kyriacou 1986: 139)

Dialects and accents – an issue to be considered

There are some quite distinct dialects across the UK. I still struggle, sometimes, to understand *every* word in some UK accents. No offence – I'm sure it's the same with understanding some Aussies; although *Neighbours* has been on your television screens for a long time now! There are teachers whose dialect (or language other than English or even their *English accent*) sometimes becomes an occasion for children to tease them, or have a bit of fun. I've worked with teachers who have sometimes been demoralised by calculatingly snide comments, where several students collude by laughing loudly at the teacher's turn of phrase, use of words or accent, or fast/rapid speech pattern.

Communicating clearly, and speaking clearly, are crucial aspects of day-to-day teaching. Where teachers are aware that their accent, typical voice usage or English pronunciation may – potentially – affect their teaching and classroom management, the following will help.

- Plan ahead by discussing with colleagues what they might, or could, do – should the issue arise. This could include thinking through (ahead of time) typical responses to student comments.
- It can help to explain, briefly – and confidently – to students at the beginning of each of their first classes, that "you will, quickly, notice that my accent, in English, is a bit different. Sometimes I might mispronounce words from time to time. I work hard on my English. Thanks in advance for your understanding and support". *Prepare* a brief "explanation" beforehand. I've seen colleagues from Vietnam, Italy, Greece, India, Lebanon communicate this initial shared understanding, skilfully; with tact and even humour. It may be helpful to invite questions from the students. My own view is that the explanation should suffice. If our subsequent teaching is effective, the *accent* shouldn't matter.
- It can help, on occasion, to repeat a word (or phrase) if we think some in the class are genuinely unclear about pronunciation.
- If a student is rude or derogatory about one's accent or use of English, it will be enough to briefly, firmly – without any hostility – make the brief assertive point, "I don't make unfair (or put-down) comments about your speech; I don't expect you to make unfair comments about mine". The tone of such a statement needs to be confidently firm and calm. It is not a threat, it is an assertion – avoid any argument. In such cases it is enough to assert and then to move on with the lesson or activity. *Sometimes* even brief repartee may be appropriate. Though one should be careful not to reinforce mean-spirited, or nasty, comments with repartee.
- If some students persist in being disruptive by snide comments, "I can't understand you, Miss. You're not saying it clear. What do yer mean?" (or worse) then use the time-out provision in the short term (p. 49f). We do not want to make students' assumed misunderstanding (of one's accent) an easy affront or a "game"!
- Always follow-up *any* abusive comments made by students (p. 106f). If necessary ask a senior colleague (early in the first week) to call a meeting with the students concerned and conduct an "accountability conference" (p. 232f).

Inviting and sustaining engagement

Students need to know that their *participation* in the lesson will be expected by the teacher. At the beginning of each lesson students will need to be reminded that their contribution to their learning process will be monitored, and their involvement expected. For example, in an English lesson on Shakespeare's *Hamlet*, students know that later in the class time they will be asked to think about the main character in terms of "his relationship with his dead father" or his so-called "step-father", or "his mother", or "Ophelia" or "his moods" ("... though this be madness, yet there is method in't."). Having been given a set time students are then asked to share: "We should be ready now to hear what you think about how Hamlet coped with ...". In sharing, publicly, students will need to be given time to develop and construct their public contribution:

- "relate this topic (issue or question) to your own experiences"
- "give an example of, or analogy of ..."
- "explain 'this' (a given concept) in *your own words*"
- "give a summary of ..."
- "explain this ... as if to someone who had never seen, or heard, of ...".

Teachers will often preface their teaching time with a statement: "You will need to be listening carefully – you might be asked to contribute to someone else's answer ..."; "Listen up, here folks – you'll need to know this ..."; "I wonder if anyone will have heard of this?"; "This is going to be a little tricky so ...".

When inviting student engagement teachers can use a wide variety of approaches beyond simple public questions and answers:

- Ask all students to write their answers on a card (or mini whiteboard) and hold it up (this "old-fashioned" approach can work well for simple "scan checking" by a teacher at primary level).
- Students can answer questions in an answer notebook; they then share their answers in a paired discussion or be ready to contribute to class discussion.
- The questions asked can be answered in a daily journal.
- Students can be directed to write a brief summary in response to a teacher's questions to a whole class. This increases task focus and avoids easy distractability.

Questions and effective teaching

The purpose of questioning is to *engage* thinking; *extend* thinking; *share* thinking or *clarify* and *confirm* thinking. There are many ways questioning can be used in whole-class and small group teaching. Questions also allow the teacher to check for understanding and clarify meaning. They also provide an obvious form of feedback for the teacher. Even rhetorical questions can be used in that way.

- It is important the teacher does not do most of the talking in class dialogue. Avoid piling topic upon topic with several multiple questions that can often sidetrack and even confuse student understanding of the key issue, topic or focus. I've seen teachers talk for up to 20 minutes without any genuine student involvement. Getting students task directed (even through whole-class discussion) is a crucial feature of effective teaching and learning.

    Making the task(s) explicit (and visible) and stating the desired and positive outcomes of a lesson are basic – but crucial – in most learning tasks. It is then important (generally speaking) to stick to the aims, and the task focus, through any spoken, or written, questions.

- Some key questions are best written up on the board, or a worksheet, to *keep the focus* for the learning activity.

- Short extending and refocusing questions, can also keep the students focused. During a vigorous series of answers from students, or during a class discussion, a teacher, in responding to an individual student, can extend their thinking through short refocusing and reframing questions: "So, you're saying ... Is that right?" Even a brief, and *positive*, "So? Extend that a bit more ..." or "A bit more ...?" "And ...?" "That's clearer" can cue the student to more fully form and express their answer and ideas.

- Questions, where possible, should also link back to what students already know to extend their natural curiosity.

- After a general cue to the class, "I want you to think about the main (issue, character, point). The teacher, then, directs the class to share, or in pairs, then invites students' responses: "Alright (...), *we* should be ready to hear what you think about ... Hands up, folks, so I can see who is ready to share ...".

- Avoid discussing any *one* student's answer at length.

- If the teacher *invites* students to illustrate/develop work on the board, in front of the class, at least direct other students to work on the solution at the same time. Answers can then be compared. Any such approach requires a cohesive class environment and no student should ever be forced to display knowledge in front of the class.

- Avoid embarrassing a student by picking on them (as a discipline device): "What do you think, Mark? Eh?!" "Were you listening ...?" "So – do *you* know what we're *actually* talking about?!"

At primary age level many teachers now include a teaching unit on active listening skills to enhance student attention in shared class discussion time (see McGrath and Francey 1993).

Thoughtful questioning can also increase the active *cognitive* participation of all students. When using directed questions the teacher is also directing student effort into sharing their *thinking*; not in a merely right or wrong way, but rather supporting the process of learning.

Overuse of questions that require only one – right – answer or require a single word response can limit useful development in student thinking and expression: for example, "Who can …?"; "What is …?"; "Who is your favourite character in *Harry Potter* …?"; "Who can read *this* word?". Such questioning tends to limit extension to a student's thinking.

Contrast these questions:

■ "Share with the person next to you about who was your favourite character and *why* …". The "why" extends the sharing and allows the student to develop their thinking.

■ "Think of your own example of hope or courage in … Write the key points down … When you have several points recorded down, look up, here, to the front, so I know you're ready and we'll share as a group … *Thinking hats on everyone* …".

"Wait-time" when asking questions

Rowe (1978, in Cummings 1989) develops an interesting case for what he calls "wait-time", where teachers allow some time ("wait-time") after asking a general question to the class or an individual.

Rather than a simple "What is the …?" (expecting a right or wrong answer), the teacher frames the question more thoughtfully: "Think about the *difference* between … Raise your hand when you are ready with the answer. Take a moment to imagine …". The teacher then scans the group allowing some "wait-time" *after* asking the question and *after* the student's response.

According to Rowe, creative use of 'wait-time' can:

■ increase the length of a student's response
■ elicit a wider response rate among students
■ increase confidence in answering
■ increase the contributions of "slower" students
■ have a generally more positive effect on class behaviour.

According to Cummings (1989), teachers smile more often and nod their heads more if they perceive a student to be "bright", giving the student more encouraging non-verbal feedback and more opportunity to respond. Obversely, when teachers respond to "low-achieving" students their perception of low-achieving affects the way they interact with those students.

This is a pattern of behaviour linked to what is often termed the "expectancy effect" (see Rosenthal and Jacobsen 1968). See also Robertson (1997), McInerney and McInerney (1998) and Rogers (2009).

Using encouragement

In a Year 9 graphics class a few years ago my colleague and I were teaching calligraphy using large Gothic script with flourishes, and miniature illustrations and motifs within and around the large capital letters. Using an ink wash, fine felt-tipped pens and gold and silver pens the students were in the final stages of some demanding, well-developed and very attractive work.

I was talking with one of the lads about the shape and colours of his letters.

"So, how did you get that neat scroll effect there, with the bronze and pale blue background?" I was genuinely interested.

He shared – with some enthusiasm – the drafting and planning process that had led to this final product. I hadn't once said his work was "great", "wonderful" or "brilliant", but we did talk about his penmanship, the design, the final effect. In short, I was letting him know that I had noticed his effort, his journey (here) as a learner; an artist.

As I walked away one of the lads (who must have been listening) beckoned me over and said, "Hey, Mr Rogers, can you look at my work too?"

Students value encouragement and feedback. They benefit from the assurance that we have acknowledged their work; the effort and the direction of their work. Feedback can also clarify students' thinking and direction of their work. It can help fill in gaps, extend ideas or even just make the students aware of *their own* work.

It is important that children experience some success in their ongoing learning. Encouragement is a major way that we, as teachers, can let the students know how they are doing and where their strengths and areas of further development lie.

Positive teaching style

The most basic expression or form of encouragement is the teacher's positive body language: the encouraging and approachable manner, tone of voice and smile that says: "You can do it"; "Hang in there"; "You're trying hard"; "You handled that well"; "That's hard work, but ..."; "Give it your best shot"; "I'm sure you'll make a responsible decision".

Even basics like how we enter a student's personal space and ask to see their work; remembering to use their first name; specifically noting what they are doing and giving short-term feedback on their work and effort applied; empathising when they struggle with difficult concepts; re-explaining (several times if necessary) are all expressions of encouragement.

I have worked with teachers who will come into a student's working space (also their *personal* space), pick up a student's workbook (without asking permission) and start making comments about the work: "Is *that* what I asked you to do ... is it?" I have seen teachers walk over to a student's work and tap (with an overly motoric index finger) on their book: "... and *where's* the margin, hmm?"

I have actually heard teachers say, "Well, am I supposed to *ask permission* to see a student's work?" The answer is – of course – "Yes". It is *their* work. When we come alongside a student to chat, give feedback, or offer help (during on-task learning time) we ask: "Do you mind if I have a look at your work?" When a teacher says this (in a positive tone) she is modelling basic courtesy; it is not a matter of asking "permission".

A positive, encouraging, manner engages a more positive learning atmosphere and can help in the maintenance of long-term positive behaviour.

When students frequently hear "You *never* ...". "You *always* ...". "*Can't* you get it by now?" and the appalling "Are you thick or what ...?" one can understand that they would probably experience low motivation and feel discouraged. While it seems unbelievable that teachers would ever talk like this to students, some do. One hopes it is *never* intentional. Contrast this with teachers who will explain a difficult mathematical process many times (if necessary), assuring students that, "Yes, it can take time to come to terms with this concept. It isn't easy, but we'll get there. I struggled with positive and negative integers too ...!"

Both encouragement and discouragement contain the word *courage*. Giving a child some fundamental "courage", as a learner, is in part how we relate to the student, and in part the language we use. As an ongoing, adult learner I've noticed it was always the way I was treated, *along with* non-judgemental feedback that enabled my learning, my motivation and even my assurance that mistakes and misunderstandings did not mean that I was a failure.

When I was a full-time teacher, I started (and finished) some postgraduate study. It was long and arduous and I wondered (at times) if it was all worth it. During the course of the research I was undertaking I was required to do some statistics units. My first university teacher was somewhat offhand in his manner. He treated us (students in our late twenties or thirties, and some in their forties) as if we were a group of high school students rather than adults. He seemed unaware that we had all had busy days teaching and had trudged off, in the evening traffic, to the university to further our careers. His teaching style was high on expectation (that we all knew quadratic equations, orthogonal contrasts, and so on) and low on tolerance of struggle, confusion and "where the hell does all this fit in our postgrad studies?!". His non-verbal sighs, eyes to the ceiling and tut-tutting frustration at our "obvious" and "simplistic" questions contributed to us feeling like inadequate learners. It all came back to me; I was a student again, at high school, with a teacher I didn't like who was seemingly unconcerned about us and how we felt …

My second "teacher" (another statistics unit) was a professor (still is). The first day we entered the university classroom (as adult learners) Brian welcomed us personally and when we were sitting down as a group said, "Hello and welcome, everyone. Look, I know you're probably all feeling bushed after a long day with your Grade 5s or Year 8s … You can see I've got some tea/coffee, hot water and cups over there. I'd like you to grab a cuppa, regroup, settle down and I'll explain the course; the way in which we can work together in this unit and the sorts of projects we'll tackle together". We, all, immediately felt better (the cuppa helped). We felt we could probably do this none-too-easy subject.

Brian never failed to explain the statistics concepts carefully; in several different ways where necessary. He used visual examples and examples that would relate to our work. He encouraged us to engage in small-group work to support one other. He never failed to address and answer what we thought (at times) were simplistic or 'stupid' questions. He was always willing to chat after class, to fine-tune or qualify misunderstandings. He always gave *descriptive* feedback on our work (rather than merely "18 out of 20. Well done"). I enjoyed going to Brian's classes (although maths has never been my high-comfort-zone forte). I even passed – quite well. He wrote a personal note to me (to everyone) on the completion of the exam.

I learned a lot more than statistics from Brian. I was reminded about how to be an effective and supportive teacher.

It is easy, as teachers, to become conditioned to negative behaviour; to easily notice and over-attend to the range of distracting behaviours that occur from shuffling and whispering while the teacher is talking, to addressing lateness and calling out. While we have to manage – and correct – distracting and disruptive behaviour we also need to balance our correction with encouragement, *this should be normative in our teaching practice*. I've heard some teachers come out with the ludicrous comment (about encouraging positive behaviour and effort in work): "Well, they *are supposed* to be doing that anyway!".

It is very important to balance any correction with encouragement. This can be as basic as moving around the room and acknowledging the students' presence (smile, nod, OK sign) when they *are* working, *are* on-task; or encouragement can be as focused as specific attention to task and giving descriptive feedback and praise.

Sometimes all that is required are just a few apposite words, as when a student, answering a question in front of his or her peers, hears the teacher say, "That was a thoughtful question and an interesting way of looking at …" rather than saying, "No, that's not the right answer". If the student is wrong in his or her work or in answer to a question, a brief noting that, "… was incorrect … but you tried …" is enough. We do not need to communicate that the student is inept, stupid or can't learn.

When encouraging students

■ Be conscious of the small – as well as more involved – expressions of encouragement: the affirming smile that basically humanises; brief task-checks such as "How's it going?"; "Where are you up to?"; "How's it coming together here?"; "Have you considered?"; "Can I suggest?"; "It might help if …"

> The teacher notices a student's page without the margin and date. Instead of asking why there's no margin, the teacher asks if she can have a look at the work, gives some feedback and as she turns the book around to face the student she runs her finger non-verbally down the left-hand side of the page to indicate to the student to remember the margin, and points to the top right of the page as if to say remember the date. She winks. He smiles back. Done. Small acts – but important small acts.

■ When giving verbal or written encouragement and feedback it helps if we focus on *descriptive* comment rather than merely global praise or negation.

For example, if we say a child *is* bad because he displays frustration and anger we easily associate that *he* is bad *because* (or when) he gets angry. We all get angry on occasion, and it is our angry *behaviour* that is "good" or "bad", "right" or "wrong" helpful, constructive or destructive (p. 203f). When we focus on a child's *behaviour* we're on safer ground.

The same principle can be applied to a range of behaviours: "That desk looks tidy and well organised, Stephen … books on one side, writing materials on the other. It'll be easier to find things now, eh?" Here the teacher focuses on the child's effort (his behaviour). The teacher describes what the student has done. Rather than telling a student that she was good because she shared her play lunch we can say, "That was a kind thing to do … [or a *thoughtful* act, or was *cooperative*, or was *considerate*]". Descriptive feedback takes a little longer but it *acknowledges* – it demonstrates we know (as teacher) – and it *affirms* the student's effort and the direction of that effort. It also engages the students' self-respect as we show appreciation for their thought and effort.

This approach can be applied to the student's academic work as well. To write "Well done", "Great work", "Marvellous" or "Excellent work (9/10)" on a student's work can, of course, encourage a child but it doesn't say *what* is "great" or "marvellous" or "excellent" (or why). Compare those remarks with comments like "The words you've used to describe the loneliness and isolation of the moors ... I could feel how the main character must have felt when ...". Here the teacher is adding a few words to *describe* what was "good work"; more importantly the teacher is also affirming the student's effort. The student can also see where their strengths are demonstrated.

Errors and deficiencies can also be acknowledged: "remember to check your work for spelling and layout ...". It can help to use prearranged symbols to highlight (on their workbook) where margin, paragraphs, spelling and even grammar need to be checked. This avoids too much red marking, which can sometimes make a visible mess of a student's work. Avoid judgemental reminders: "*Don't* forget the date ... [the margin, the paras]"; or "You *should* know how to spell 'because' by now". "Remember to ..." is a more cooperative reminder to read on one's work.

■ When encouraging a student it can also help to acknowledge the effort and struggle and improvement in their progress (particularly when the student whinges that "It's too hard ..."): "Yes, it can be difficult to roll clay into a flat shape ..."; "It took me ages to understand algebra, David. It's not an easy concept to get your head around ...", "I remember how you used to struggle with this ... look how far you've come ..."

Conversely it doesn't help if we easily, and frequently, do for the student that which he can do for himself: "Here, give me the scissors ... I'll show you". It would be more helpful to say, "That's a difficult shape to cut. Can I show you how to make it easier?", "If you're not happy with it the way it is ... what do you think you could do so you'd be pleased/happier/more settled with it?"

Yes, there will be students who seemingly reject even the most supportive and well-intentioned encouragement. If a child appears to reject our feedback it is enough to meet such rejection with a brief assurance that it was well meant and leave it at that.

When using feedback to assist a student with frequent errors or unhelpful patterns of behaviour it can help to begin a one-to-one feedback session with comments like: "Have you noticed ...?"; "Are you aware that ...?"; "Do you hear yourself say ...?"; "Are you conscious of ...?"; and "How do you feel when ...?" These openers can lead to specific, supportive, feedback comments about students' work or behaviour. One of my primary teacher colleagues uses the student home–school diary to give encouragement:

> Congratulations on your spelling, David. This word list was not easy and I can see you are really trying; 7 out of 10 shows improvement and application; you're really trying. (Do you know I found spelling a bit hard when I was your age!) Mr Smith.

This brief comment shows that the teacher identifies with the student as well as giving some descriptive feedback and encouragement. What often happens is that these comments are also read by the parent who (often) gives "secondary encouragement". Here's another example:

> Karl, I noticed you shared your colouring pencils with Taylor during art time. That was a considerate thing to do. Taylor felt you cared about him (and it saved me trying to find some spare pencils) – thanks for the cooperation. Ms Joyce.

As with any comments home to parents (diary, notes, letter, certificates), their value, as encouragement, depends on the quality of the relationship between the giver (as teacher) and the receiver (the student).

■ Avoid qualifying – even discounting – the encouragement or feedback. If we notice a student putting litter in the bin thoughtfully, without a reminder, it is enough to say, "That's thoughtful, David – makes the cleaner's job easier". We don't need to add, "and if you did that more often we'd have a much tidier classroom, wouldn't we?"

If a student demonstrates neat writing (uncharacteristically? – who knows he may be on the cusp of a change), what he doesn't need to hear is, "Now – *why* can't you do that *all* the time?" Comments that begin – or include – "never" "but ..." or "always", as in "You *never* finish your work" and "You *always* call out in class" are also very discouraging.

Also, when marking a student's work be sensitive to the fact it is *their* work (and avoid scribbling comments or feedback all over the pages). Unobtrusive marking can demonstrate that you care about the student's finished product (p. 133).

■ With older students (upper primary onwards) there is a tendency to feel uncomfortable about the more public expressions of praise. A brief, positive, word to a student aside from his or her peers is often well received.

Working with a Year 8 student in a school for students with emotional and behavioural disorders (a few years ago) I was trying to encourage one young lad to use a quieter voice in class time. I made an individual behaviour plan with him to focus on "partner-voice" in class. I drew a cartoon picture of him using a quiet voice while working at his desk. I gave him a copy of this postcard-sized reminder of our plan and I had a copy for myself, and his regular teacher.

On a number of occasions during class time I noticed him making an effort to remember to use his partner-voice. I quietly beckoned him to come over to the front desk area. Here – away from his classmates – I gave him some quiet feedback. "Ahmed, I noticed you were consciously using your partner-voice. It makes it so much easier for everyone ... your teacher and me. You're remembering your plan, old chum."

I put a tick on my copy of the plan (and, later, on his copy). Sometimes I just caught his eye and gave a small OK sign. When he forgot his plan I gave a private cue to remind him of partner-voice: thumb and forefinger a little apart to show a small distance (as it were); the distance of "partner-voice".

Many teachers also use incentives such as stickers, stamps, charts, "free-time" activities, certificates and even vouchers (such as those used in primary playgrounds where naturally observed thoughtful, cooperative, behaviour is "caught" and a voucher given that can be traded for an ice-cream, and so on).

Whatever incentives teachers use it is essential that our characteristic teaching practice includes the principles of supportive and descriptive feedback and encouragement to our students regarding their effort, their goodwill, their contribution, and their thoughtful and cooperative behaviour; even if they are supposed to be doing that anyway! Like us, students benefit from – and even look for – acknowledgement and affirmation.

Case study

He had been told that it was a very difficult class; a Year 9 "low-stream" English class (predominantly boys). The teacher's personal preference was for mixed ability teaching but ability streaming was the school's current policy. He was determined to help these students go beyond their "label" and not let his personal views on mixed-ability teaching affect his desire to positively engage this new class.

It had taken him a couple of lessons to establish the beginnings of a positive working relationship.

Most of the disruptions to class learning are minor – annoying and frustrating at times, but minor. For example, as the students entered the classroom there was some general chatter and restlessness. Having greeted them in the corridor, he directed a sense of group calmness and settling (pp. 56f, 93). He now stands by the door to greet them as they come in. He doesn't, however, engage in chit-chat, or have mini discussions about homework or issues that can be addressed later (if necessary) during the on-task phase of the lesson. He smiles as he briefly greets and acknowledges the students and beckons them to their seats.

He stands at the front of the classroom – purposefully waiting – scanning the room. As they settle he cues for class attention. Sometimes he needs to raise his voice a little; he then steps the voice down as the group settles. He thanks them, greets them – as a group – and begins a fresh lesson. He never shouts at them to get quiet. They like that (I know, they told me).

Today he is developing a unit on punctuation – a revision unit. He is aware that the students may think this is "old hat" or even "kindergarten stuff", but it is part of the revision requirement. He begins by engaging a class discussion about bicycles, punctures and repair kits.

He uses the analogy of a puncture repair kit to associate "puncture" and "punctuation".

"How many of you still ride bikes?" Hands go up. "What sort of bikes do you ride?" Some students excitedly call out; some attentionally call out; he reminds them of the rule, "Remember our rule for sharing ... Thanks."

As the sharing proceeds, one of the students comments that, "Gavin's bike is a shit bike."

It's just audible. The snigger goes around the room. The teacher looks in the direction of the comment (he's not sure who said it) and says, "That's not a helpful comment (even if it's true)." His tone is pleasant, matter of fact and he moves on.

"How many of you have ever got a puncture?" Several hands go up. They're interested, they still like their bikes. A few students call out. The teacher reminds them (briefly) of the rule. Scanning the faces he says, "Remember our class rule for questions ..., thanks."

"Jacinta (...)," he nods and smiles toward her, "tell us about the worst puncture you remember." Several students laugh. She recounts her story. As others contribute he is aware of not over-engaging on any one answer or contribution, and he continues to periodically scan the class group (making brief eye contact) even as he listens to each individual contribution. A student walks in late, posturing a little. The teacher welcomes him quietly, acknowledges that he's late and directs him to a seat (p. 96f). He continues with the lesson, not making a big deal of the lateness.

He develops the analogy from a puncture (a hole, or several holes, like Jacinta's punctured tyre) to *punctuation* in a mass of words (commas, full stops, question marks, "talking marks" to show where direct speech is being used, exclamation marks and even capital letters). He puts up a large poster with a dozen sentences. The written vignette is an account about "my first bike", written in the first person without punctuation, so it is quite confusing to read; a mass of words. He invites a few students to read it. They find it, naturally, difficult. There's good humoured laughter as one idea runs into another giving confusing messages from the text. He is clearly enjoying himself, although he must have taught punctuation many, many times. He is aware that each lesson is a fresh lesson. He does his best (bad day notwithstanding). He doesn't overdramatise; he is not overly ebullient, but he has a relaxed, positive, good humoured rapport that is able to engage interest and sustain motivation – he can even enthuse his students on most days.

He notices Jason leaning back a bit heavily and noisily on his seat. He's aware that this is probably just unconscious restlessness.

"Jason (...) four on the floor, thanks."

He adds a non-verbal cue with his hand (p. 98). He moves on with the flow of the lesson. He notices a few students chewing gum. He tactically ignores this now;

the chewing isn't affecting the flow of teaching and learning. He'll address it later; in the on-task phase of the lesson.

Krista has her hand up. He acknowledges her question, and she asks to go to the toilet. He suspects she might be wanting just to get out for a few minutes. He says, "When I've finished this part of the lesson, Krista, we'll organise a toilet break." She frowns and leans back, satisfied. (If she had appeared desperate he would have given her the benefit of the doubt and addressed the issue later if repeated requests were made in subsequent lessons.) He moves on.

"So, folks," he scans the group, "what can we do to this mass of print to make it *meaningful* and *sensible*?" He discusses the role of punctuation; these marks (punctuation) help us to clarify meaning in written expression. "How? We 'puncture' the text – all these words. We need to make *sense* of it all." He taps the text on the board (with his finger), "We use *capital* letters to begin *every* sentence; we use commas for ... we use speech marks for ... What difference does it make *now* when we read the text?"

As the answers come he sometimes extends or develops them. "So, what you're saying, Matt, is ... is that right?" If a student is on a helpful track with their answer or contribution he extends by simply adding "So ...?", or "and ...?", or "keep going ...?" with a smile and eye contact that says: "Keep going, you're on the right track".

"So, what does punctuation *do* then ...?"

"What *purpose* does it serve?", "How will this knowledge – today – help you in your writing?"

"Think about the tyre on the bike that's punctured. Remember when Jacinta and Rob shared how they learned to fix punctures themselves using a puncture kit?"

"I have a *punctuation* kit here, which is a kind of reverse of what a bike repair kit does." He holds up a poster of an open tin. "Right, what do we need in this kit? This little kit will help us repair our writing; put it in some ordered form so it makes reasonable sense, eh?" He puts up a poster that illustrates the tin and its contents: capitals, full stops, commas, speech marks, question marks. He then takes suggestions from the class on how to repair the text on the board using the "punctuation kit".

The rest of the lesson (and the next lesson) is involved with focused activities to apply the punctuation repair kit to differing texts (on worksheets). They are now developing the *skills* of punctuation.

Before they move on to the on-task phase of the lesson he reminds them of the task requirement; the need for "partner-voice, thanks" (p. 67); "and you know what to do if you need my assistance – check the set task, read through, check with your immediate classmate first, ask for my help, go on with the class novel while you're waiting for me to assist ...". (He has a poster at the front of the classroom with those positive reminders noted ...)

If students talk at any time when he is engaged in group teaching or discussion he will not talk over them. He knows how easy it is to reinforce the tacit acceptance (in students) that it is OK to chat and natter quietly while the teacher is talking. Sometimes he just tactically pauses, sometimes he just gives an incidental reminder to the group (or individuals): "A number of students are talking …"; or "You're talking and I'm trying to teach". His primary focus is not the disruptive behaviour itself; it is always the teaching and learning process for that class session. Any discipline is a means to enable the protection of fundamental rights and the engagement of focused learning. Many times in a lesson he will periodically scan the group, and call on students at random to check for understanding – most of all to engage and extend their thinking.

As he moves around the room later, in the on-task phase of the lesson, chatting, encouraging, refocusing and clarifying, he asks questions that assist, probe and encourage: "Anything still unclear?"; "What questions do you have about …?"; "Is it easy or difficult – why?"; "What do you need to know to help it connect?"

At the close of the lesson (a double period) he has a "round-Robin" of class questions, calling on students at random to invite responses about the lesson topic and asking questions such as: "What do you think the purpose of today's activity was?"; "Is there anything that still isn't clear …?"; "Does anyone have any questions …?"; "Would you be able to use what you've learned today in any other classes? How?"; "How can you recall, remember, the key ideas from today?"; "Would anybody like to share how they could punctuate more easily, clearly, now?"; "What's made the difference?" (He has a "summary session" – like this – every 3–4 lessons.)

He finishes the lesson early enough to briefly summarise, collect work, cue homework and remind the students to leave the room tidy and leave the room in a "non-Darwinian-survival-of-the-fittest-way" (p. 75). Most of all, he tries to end each lesson in a positive way (even if it has not been the best lesson).

Those students who do not really apply themselves, or are "calculatedly lazy", he speaks to away from their peers (one to one; p. 106f). He doesn't berate them, or make them feel guilty or punish them for poorly developed and poorly applied work. He does point out (privately) that he knows they can do better, that the choices we make about learning now affect what we do later and that he'll always be available to help.

He knows that building a cohesive class group takes time, but he plans thoughtfully towards that end, not leaving such cohesion to mere chance.

The lessons do not always go this well. There are some difficult days (from time to time) but he has built up the general confidence, and cohesion, of the students in this class to believe they can communicate more thoughtfully, more effectively and more interestingly (even) in their written expression.

When he's had a particularly good session – a lesson that has gone well – he spends some time (personally) reflecting on what happened to contribute to the relative success. Was it the lesson content? Was it the engagement and the way he taught that day? Could it have been the timetable slot at that point in the week? Was he feeling particularly well?

When he's had a particularly difficult session with the class he similarly reflects. How did he deal with the students who were late? Was the learning task clear? Was he trying to cover too much? Did he give enough feedback? He discusses these issues with his colleagues from time to time as well.

He is a reflective practitioner. I know; I've worked with him.

Skill development takes time

Working as a mentor-teacher I have noticed colleagues struggle with new skills; notably new ways of communicating when managing, disciplining or even encouraging students. As with any new skill it is important to remember that it takes time to develop any skills within the "comfort zone" wherein the language comes easily and naturally, without too much conscious thought.

I've played golf only several times (by invitation – it's not my game). As I watch others play, as I watch their fluidity of stroke and eye, and follow through, it *looks* easy. When I try to play I *feel* wooden. My legs don't seem to connect with my arms and head. I hit the ground several times with the club, then I hit the ball too hard. I can't even see where it is going. It skews off a long way from the green I aimed at. I *over*-concentrate.

But I can still swim quite well; and dive; ride a bike (although infrequently); draw reasonable pictures (there are some in this book); and juggle three balls in the air quite well. Why? Because I *practised* these skills many times; I had felt a need; I was motivated and I kept at it until there was a kind of "second nature" about the skills I chose, and wanted to learn and develop.

To get to that habituation level one has to go through the discomfort zone, as it were. That is normal. Knowing about skills (through reading or in-service education and training) and being able to use them in an integrated way – as a teacher – are two different things. Initially the new skill *feels* uncomfortable; the words, the tone, the manner, may not seem "to be me". As P.G. Wodehouse once put it, "My tongue seems to get entangled with my brain". However, if we see a need and value in the skills, and if we see how those skills can be integrated into our *overall* teaching and management, we will succeed (with effort, time, normative failure and some colleague encouragement).

In time we won't need to think, "Am I avoiding unnecessary focus on the secondary behaviour by *tactically* ignoring the residual secondary behaviour; and refocusing the procrastinating and reframing to the core issue?" We'll just do it.

Home truths

My daughter once said to me, "Dad, why do some teachers bother to get into teaching when they hate kids?" By "hate" she meant dislike expressed (at its worst) in mean-spirited, churlish, petty, unthinking (well – we hope it is unthinking) behaviour; a lack of fundamental humanity expressed in a sense of caring, positive support and mutual regard. Having worked with some teachers who seem to present a *characteristically* "miserable-soddish attitude" to teaching and to their students, I know what she meant.

Whenever I've discussed the issue of "good teachers" with students they always emphasise several key aspects of teacher behaviour. The comments below in brackets are directly drawn from high school students I have taught. (Some of the positive behaviours are expressed in negative terms.)

Effective teachers:

- teach clearly and with interest in the subject and the students' needs: – "the work is interesting"; "they try to help you connect to what they're talking about"; "they help us with the work"; "they don't moan if you ask them to re-explain things"; "they give us a chance to talk and explain too"
- build a sense of class cohesion as it relates to learning together and being together here in "this place" – the classroom "They let you all know why we're doing this subject or lesson"; "they give choices"; "they have manners"; "they trust you"; "they have a sense of humour" [this is a very frequent descriptor]; "they're not chauvinistic or sexist"; as one student said with a wry smile, "If we're stuck here together … and we're all human beings … we have to do it with less pain!" I knew what he meant
- discipline fairly: – "they discuss/explain the rules"; "they don't take sides"; "they don't shame you in front of the class"; "you get a fair chance"; "they give you fair warning even non-verbal [*sic*]"; "you make mistakes but they don't hold it against you"; "because they have a good relationship with the class the correction is accepted better"; "they're fair"; "there's give and take"; "They hear your side of the story …".

The kind of relationship a teacher builds, and sustains, is central to effective teaching and learning. It also increases the likelihood that the students will cooperate with us when we exercise necessary discipline.

My own children have said – about their teachers – that they often enjoyed a *particular* subject because of the *particular* teacher who taught it that semester or that year.

One of the most powerful and influential aspects of a teacher's relationship with individuals and groups of students is the teacher's willingness to empathise. Perspective-taking means the ability to see a student's struggle with work or behaviour or their relationships in a school; to tune-in to a student's frustration or anxiety; to give feedback on learning and behaviour, and always to give a right of reply. As Branwhite (1988) reported, a teacher's capacity to empathise was the most valued teacher quality cited by pupils (cited in Kyriacou 1991: 57).

I wonder how our students would describe our *characteristic* teacher leadership behaviour? (*Not* what we're like on our bad days.)

Teaching is not for everyone

Teaching in schools is clearly not for everyone. It is a profession that is naturally, inherently, even normatively, stressful. Its daily demands are multiple and various and simultaneously require one to not only have planned well on the one hand, but also to be flexible and able to think on one's feet.

The ability to relate well to others and to communicate clearly and effectively, the ability, and skill, to enthuse and motivate, and the ability to cope with multi-task, group-oriented activities, as well as individual activities, are not merely desirable; they are essential attributes and skills.

There are teachers who present with poor – or ineffective – teaching and management practice. Supporting teachers who struggle because they, themselves, are a key factor in a hard-to-manage-class setting is not easy, in part because we need to see, and support, the colleague's failure and struggle without seeing them *as* a failure (Chapter 8).

If such teacher behaviour can be addressed within a school-wide perspective of shared values, aims and practices about managing classroom behaviour the task is made somewhat clearer, although not necessarily easier.

If a struggling teacher does not request or invite colleague support it will be important to approach that colleague to informally share – at the very least – concerns about their welfare. If we have walked past a really loud class on enough occasions to know that the behaviour in that class (even briefly observed) is more than bad-day syndrome, it is professionally irresponsible not to meet with the colleague in question and offer support. In providing such support we will need to consider the following:

- Wherever possible any offered support should be "early-intervention"; before a spiral of discouragement, or defeat, sets in.
- Senior teacher involvement can often set up further colleague networking (even mentoring) and address more serious concerns such as harassment by students (p. 230f).
- The offer of support should be made discreetly and confidentially.
- The emphasis in the first meeting allows the colleague to share their concerns, needs and problems with honesty and balance. Emphasise the positive areas of their teaching and management as well as the areas of concern.
- Set up a plan of support, developed with other colleagues (perhaps even a

mentor; p. 237f) to enable ongoing support. Early features of any support options may need to include thoughtful, careful, time-out plans (see p. 149f).

Where there is *characteristic* laziness; indifference; lack of commitment; poor teaching; inappropriate management and discipline; insensitivity and even active dissent in some teachers' behaviour this will need to be supportively confronted within the school's shared values and practices as they relate to a teacher's professional rights and responsibilities.

Teachers who *characteristically* present as ineffective in their teaching practice (global descriptors such as "ineffective" and "poor" need careful and thoughtful delineation) are best advised and counselled to reconsider if the profession of teaching is really for them.

A cooperative and supportive school based appraisal system working with a more consciously supportive Office for Standards in Education (Ofsted) could help such teachers to reassess their professional choices, obligations and responsibilities earlier in their teaching journey. (We do not have an equivalent of Ofsted in Australia.)

The drawing shows an infant class (5-year-olds). The teacher on the right, Joy, is comforting a young boy who is upset. I am supervising play-lunch. (In Australian schools, children eat packed lunches in the classroom with their class teacher.) Infants have morning play at 11.00 a.m., but play-lunch needs to start aeons before then. They take a long, long time!

I'm also singing to the group. "I can see some sandwiches, some sandwiches … I can see yummy sandwiches in your play-lunch today." As I sing a student comes to my chair with a pencil and starts to comb my hair. I hadn't asked her. I am thinking of a cup of tea (meagre pleasure!). I ask myself, "Why does it seem so really long 'til morning tea time?" – Teaching infants is different. On top of the whiteboard is Boris the mouse. I'd made him out of Blu-Tack.

Reflection

The issue of what we mean by *"effective* teacher" needs values and utility to enable any purposeful, and appropriate, sense of *effective*?

- What *indicators* does your school note/suggest for "effective" teaching? (beyond Ofsted!)
- How do the noted understandings of effective teaching in this chapter reflect your normative practice? The research on effective teaching has a clear – anchor – variable: that of personal and collegial reflection. Do you take time to personally/collegially reflect on your teaching practice? How?
- If you sought to consciously address change in your teaching practice, what would motivate or occasion such consciousness? Where would you start?
- How do you respond to the distinctions made between encouragement and praise? How aware are you of your characteristic use of encouragement and supportive feedback to your students? (verbally and in writing?)
- Research distinguishes between authority (earned/developed in relationships) and – more crucially – our ability to engage a positive teaching and learning culture; how do sense and perceive your "authority" in relationship to your students? How do you think they perceive your authority? (bad days notwithstanding of course!)
- Have you reflected on your use of questions – and questioning – within your teaching practice (p. 126f)? How do the suggestions of use of questioning inform your practice?

Notes

1. These are drawn principally from Kyriacou (1986), Robertson (1997) and Rogers (1998 and 2002).
2. The best text I have read in this tricky area is John Robertson's *Effective Classroom Control* (3rd edition, 1997).
3. While this sounds like a tall order, it is not inconsistent at all with the

bad-day syndrome. Children fully understand and respect bad-day syndrome in adults, and if the teacher communicates, briefly and respectfully, why they are having a bad day, children are normally quite forgiving. Of course, if our frustration or anger have been disrespectful, we should always apologise.

Chapter 5

Management beyond the classroom: behaviour consequences

When I do good no one remembers,
when I do bad no one forgets.
Anon

Behaviour consequences (punishment?)

During most of my teaching career teachers used the word "punishment" to describe what happened when a student had to face the consequences of inappropriate or wrong behaviour. The verb "to punish" was often used – uncritically – to mean anything we did *to* a child such as detention; "giving lines"; withdrawing a privilege (such as missing out on a valued activity); wearing the dreaded dunce's cap (a conical hat with "D" for dunce[1] written on it and worn by the student while standing in the corner of the classroom) or, of course, the cane (whoosh! ouch!). I had that a number of times. We even had "public caning" (on school stage) for the worst offenders (1960s).

I put the word *punishment* in parenthesis in the heading (adding a question mark) because I wanted to question the easy facility with which we use the word. Whether we use the word "punishment" or "consequences" may mean little to the child. It is what *happens* to the child through the process of consequential outcome that matters.

The degree to which a child will see the teacher's action as fair "punishment" depends on several factors:

■ Do we set out to punish? Engage accountability? Teach (that is, teach the child to *own* their behaviour *and* its consequences)?
■ The intent we convey through the "consequential process".
■ Whether we use the "consequential process" as an end in itself (mere punishment) or as a means to an end – the end being some understanding, some learning (in the student), about their behaviour.

For example, a fair consequence can easily be applied punitively by a teacher whose intent is to make the child *feel* punished by the way he or she speaks to, and treats, the child through the consequential process (p. 106).

Behaviour consequences, as a feature of thoughtful discipline, are an attempt by the teacher to link the disruptive or wrong behaviour of the student to an outcome that, hopefully, will emphasise fairness and justice, and may even teach the child something about accountability and responsibility.

When we apply a consequence, even a simple consequence of directing students to stay back after class and "clean up their mess", we are organising outcomes so the students experience the consequences of their own behaviour. Through *behaviour consequences* teachers seek to emphasise that as students "choose" to be disruptive they also "choose" to face the consequences of their behaviour; they are not *simply* pawns or victims when they do the wrong thing. We treat the students as if they are responsible for what they do and how they treat others.

One of my colleagues has introduced her Year 5 class to the term "reparation":

Sometimes we let classmates and teachers down by choosing not to be responsible towards people or property. Sometimes we're irresponsible because we do not care enough.

Sometimes we do the wrong thing by mistake; we don't mean to.

When that happens we work to fix things, or sort things out through an apology or paying back that person in a helpful, positive way. We call this "making reparation".

When we do the unfair and wrong thing our reparations help earn our class's and our school community's trust back again.

All our behaviour has consequences and we are responsible for the consequences of our behaviour.

In this sense the teacher is emphasising a consequence as something the child is involved in as well as something organised by the teacher.

In working through consequences with children we need to make clear that all behaviour, (one way or another) has consequences. Some consequences are naturally occurring: when we stay out too long in the sun without a hat, sunglasses and sun-cream, we risk sunburn; unbrushed teeth, in time, will need dental work, and may lead to halitosis (phew!); if you don't plan the progress of a long assignment the due date comes quickly (help!). Children can see the reality of situational consequences like these and – hopefully – learn from them. *Behavioural* consequences are also an attempt to teach responsibility and accountability. The teacher links a consequential outcome to a behaviour: "If you choose to leave the mess like that you'll need to stay back at play-time and ..."; "If the work is not completed now ... then"; "If the assignment is in on a due date ... then ..."; "If you continue to make it difficult for others to work you'll have to work away from others ..." .

Managing consequences

- *All* consequences are referred back to the student behaviour agreement, which outlines the rights, responsibilities, rules and consequences (p. 40f). It is within the emphases of the classroom agreement that the student needs to see his or her inappropriate behaviour, while also being encouraged to accept the support offered to face the consequences of thoughtless, irresponsible and wrong behaviour.

- Consequences are both "non-negotiable" and "negotiable":
  - *Non-negotiable consequences* should be known in advance, clearly stated in the school policy and applied decisively. Non-negotiable consequences are applied for such behaviours as: repeated, and *very frequent*, *disruptive* behaviour in the classroom (this would occasion time-out, see p. 149); swearing at a teacher; any possession (or use) of drugs or weapons; violent behaviours; harassment and bullying. Non-negotiable consequences normally occasion some form of time out, detention, or formal suspension procedures. They may also include withdrawal of privileges, as when a repeatedly aggressive student is denied (excluded) from a school camp after due process.
  - *Negotiable consequences* normally refer to consequences worked through with the teacher who is witness to the inappropriate or disruptive behaviour. Teachers often use a stay-back session (or even a detention) to discuss with the student questions such as: "What happened?"; "What rule (or right) was affected by your behaviour?"; "What's your side of the story?"; "How do you see what happened …?"; "What can you do to fix things up [sort things out, make things right] …?" Teachers will also – often – ask "How can I help …?"

    Most students actually come up with a tougher consequential outcome, through such negotiation, than their teacher. We often have to help them trim their consequential suggestions back to workable reality.

- A consequence is more than mere punishment; we seek to address the reality of the inappropriate or disruptive behaviour by applying a consequence that seeks to gain some *relationship* between the behaviour and its consequential outcome.

    For example, when a student is caught smoking at school, the rule, and consequence, is clear: a detention. In this case though, the "smoker's detention" occasions a "Quit" video (a positive educational video addressing the habit of smoking and how to seek support to break the habit).

    If a student has damaged school property, or another individual's property, he is required to make "reparation". This normally occurs after some "cool-off time" and subsequent discussion or mediation with a teacher who has some skill in this area.

An infant child uses the class waste-paper bin as a urinal (he knows the difference). It was attention-seeking behaviour. In his own time, later, he washes the bin out with detergent. Another infant washes out a boy's jumper that he has thrown mud on. Many reparative, and "task-related", consequences can be applied in this way.

The emphasis is one where the students experience the consequences of their own behaviour and (hopefully) see some relevance in the applied consequence; they are encouraged to be more responsible next time in similar situations.

■ Concentrate on the *present* and the future change flowing from the consequence. Avoid over-focusing on the child's past misdemeanours.

■ *Keep the respect intact* when working through a consequence with a student. I have seen (too many times) a teacher keep a student back after class for a talk, or a detention, only to berate the student and harp on at the student about why he or she is a rotten, unthinking, uncaring, nasty "piece of work" (or words to that effect!).

Keeping the respect intact means that even when we have to apply significantly serious consequences we do so without the easy temptation to engage in some kind of psychological payback. The *certainty* of the consequence has a more powerful teaching effect than *intentionally applied severity*: "You could be outside playing now couldn't you?! But you're not, you're in here with me! What did I say to you before in class? Didn't I say that if you kept wasting my time, and your time, you would have to stay back at recess? Didn't I – um?! Well? You've lost your playtime now – serves you right doesn't it?"

■ Consequences should also be applied within a school-wide framework that has "degrees of seriousness". We wouldn't, for example, give detention for not completing homework, whereas we might give detention for *continued* refusal to cooperate with reasonable teacher requests in class time. We would, then, probably use the detention process to sort out the problem behaviour with the student (p. 159f).

> The key questions to ask when framing and applying any behaviour consequence include:
>
> ■ Is the consequence *related*, in some way, to the disruptive behaviour?
> ■ Is the consequence *reasonable* in terms of "degrees of seriousness"?
> ■ Do we keep the *respect* intact?
> ■ What does the student *learn* from the consequence?

The messages of *consequential* discipline – whether an after-class chat or a detention – emphasise:

- our school has fair rights and rules expressed in the behaviour agreement (p. 40f)
- "your behaviour is effectively your choice" (even if others were involved)
- when teachers apply consequences to irresponsible and wrong behaviour they do so because people's rights are affected and individuals ought to be fairly held accountable for their behaviour and to face their responsibilities.

We also need to balance consequential aspects of discipline with appropriate *support* such as mediation, restitution, counselling and (when appropriate) individual behaviour plans (p. 182f).

Time out

I can recall my primary school years at Harlesden in London in the 1950s. It was a drab, brick school with a few scraggly trees, asphalt playgrounds and narrow stairs to the headteacher's office (a place of fear!). The pointed iron railings gave a prison-like appearance to the enclosed asphalt, concrete and brick. I recall standing in the corner of the classroom with a dunce's cap on: it was that school's version of time out!

Time out, thoughtfully utilised, is a consequential step or process that seeks to link separation from the classroom group with serious infringement, or abuse, of others' rights.

Reading a story to a Year 1 class, I saw a boy at the back of the group (sitting on the carpet) pinch the lad in front of him a few times. I gave Patrick the rule reminder: "Patrick (...), hands and feet to yourself." He stopped. A little later he started again – pushing the boy this time in the small of his back – and the other lad fell forward. This time I directed him to take time out (cool-off time). "Patrick (...), Patrick (...), cool-off time. Over there – *now.*" I started to walk over to the cool-off-time area (to convey take-up time).

I pointed to an area at the back of the room, with a chair, a small table, an egg-timer (5 minutes) and a sign on the wall simply saying "cool-off time" (the term in this infant classroom for time-out consequence).

He whined back at me, "No, I'll be alright, Mr Rogers, I will!" I repeated, "Patrick (...), Cool-off time. Over there – *now.*"

On such occasions our voice needs to be calm but firm – decisive. There should be no plea-bargaining ("Are you sure you'll be good now, Patrick, will you promise me?"); forget that. Once we have decided on a consequence like time out it is the certainty of the consequence that will carry the message that "If you keep annoying others, or hurt them or make it *repeatedly* difficult for them to learn you will have to have cool-off time (time out)". In-class time out like this is quite effective at infant and even middle primary level.

There are some important considerations when using this approach to time-out.

- Time out is a short-term consequence; it is never an end in itself. As a means to an end, it can help and support disruptive students by giving them a chance to calm themselves (away from their immediate audience) and give them a chance to think about their behaviour. It is also fair for the other students in that they, too, have a chance to refocus (to class learning and activities) beyond the disruption to their basic rights.
- Time out, as a school-wide consequence, needs to be utilised as a least- to most-intrusive option in managing disruptive and unsafe behaviour. At the least intrusive level, *in-class* time out may be an option; at the most intrusive level of application students may need to be escorted from the classroom to a time-out place where they can calm down and, if necessary, parents (or caregivers) may need to be notified.

When applying time out as a consequence it is important that the teacher exhibits calmness *and* firmness. If the teacher starts shouting and grabbing the student, not only will many students become uncooperative and resistant (or even violent), but the students watching will become unnecessarily anxious or give unhelpful attention to the disruptive student. There are some (rare) occasions when a teacher will need to physically restrain a student. The school should have a policy on this sensitive aspect of behaviour management (p. 153).

There may be occasions when a student's behaviour is too disruptive for in-class time out. On these occasions the teacher will:

- Direct the student to leave the classroom and go to a nominated teacher or place in the school. The nominated place will often be a classroom next door, or nearby. Some schools have "time-out rooms" set aside where students can be directed for time out. Here they are supervised for the class period during which the disruptive behaviour occurs. Infant-age children will need to be escorted from their classroom, by an adult, to a time-out place.
- In directing students to take time-out it is important that the initiating teacher makes clear to the student what is happening. The teacher needs to communicate that it is the student's behaviour that is being addressed; we are not rejecting the student: "Troy, I've asked you several times to work in your seat and not wander and annoy the other students. If you're not willing to settle down here you'll have to leave our classroom and take time out. You know the class rules. I will get together with you later to help you sort things out."
- If a student refuses to leave the classroom to take time out, or we suspect that

in directing the student to leave he will become even more disruptive, the initiating teacher should have the back-up of colleague-assisted time out. All teachers have a cue card in their classroom – a poster-sized card with a symbolic colour (for example, red) and the classroom number on it. This cue card can be sent – with a trusted student – to a colleague teaching nearby (maybe even next door). In a more disturbing (or dangerous) discipline situation the card will be sent to a senior colleague (team leader, year head, deputy) who will come speedily to escort the student from the classroom (and their audience) to a "time-out place". Some schools use internal phone cues to call a senior colleague to the classroom for time-out support.

There are occasions when even senior teachers (yes, even senior teachers) cannot 'make', or get, a disruptive student to leave a classroom or playground setting where they are engaged in *repeatedly* disruptive, or dangerous, behaviour. In these rare situations it is wiser for the senior support colleague to stay *in* the classroom with the disrupting student while the host teacher calmly escorts the rest of the class away from the classroom (in effect escorts the "audience" away). The supervising teacher then stays with the student until they have calmed down and are ready to leave the classroom.

- With infant and middle-primary aged children any directed exit from the room for time-out should be accompanied by an adult. In many schools, teachers utilise the support of a teaching colleague next door. The cue-card (mentioned earlier) is sent to the support colleague, who briefly leaves her class (door open for line of sight) and escorts the disruptive student to the next door classroom to calm down.

- Teachers should *always* follow up with any student later that day (or later that week at secondary level) to work through the concerns or issues that occasioned time out. This is especially important at secondary level where a teacher may not see a student for a day or two. If there is no follow-up the old animosities may still be there and brought back in the classroom (unresolved) later that week.

- During the time-out period it is important that the student is not unhelpfully reinforced, or over-attended to, by counselling, or special activities or "jobs for the teacher". Time out is not primarily a punishment; it is a decisive consequence where we send the clear message that "if you *continue* to make it difficult for others in our class to work, feel safe or be treated with respect *then* you will have to take time out away from your classmates until you have calmed down and are prepared to work by the fair rights and rules here". Counselling, and reparation, can occur later. If students associate time out with counselling, or special jobs (or activities), some students may use disruptive patterns of behaviour to gain what they perceive to be special privileges, or time away from class work, during time out.

No student should be allowed to hold a classroom to ransom by *repeatedly* disruptive behaviour in the course of a lesson or activity. Nor should we ever convey the message to students that we will ever tolerate *repeatedly* disruptive, unsafe, threatening, dangerous or aggressive behaviours.

Students should be made aware of what time out is, and what it means. This awareness-raising can be occasioned when teachers are developing their student behaviour agreements in the first week of Term One (p. 40f).

If a student has been in time out on several occasions, in close succession, they will probably benefit from an individual behaviour plan to help them with the behaviours or learning issues that have necessitated time out (p. 182f).

Extreme situations – "restraint"

There are – sometimes – very extreme situations in schools where forms of restraint procedure may be necessary; where there is likelihood of serious injury to a student (or teacher).

This issue is not addressed in this text. The overriding message of this book is that teachers should seek to use *their* leadership and support behaviour in a calm and positive way (wherever possible) to defuse, direct, de-escalate potential conflict and hostility. Such "calmness" is not inconsistent with appropriate assertion.

The successive Children's Acts (in the past 20 years) have rightly stressed the nature and purposes of professional, supportive, care for the child. The actual, specific, guidance regarding appropriate and strategic use of restraint (in situations of danger) is less clear. Teachers and care workers in special schools; care settings; pupil-referral centres and young offenders institutions do receive particular, and focused, training – teachers in regular schools do not.

Whenever an adult uses physical force – in a controlled, restraining, way – as a necessary option, they are in a vulnerable position; physically and legally. Terms like "positive handling"; "minimal restraint"; "proportionate restraint"; "safe restraint ..."; "restrictive intervention" are widely used in the literature addressing this issue. All schools are required to have a Behaviour and Management and Discipline policy. Such policies, however, rarely mention *restraint* (for obvious reasons); they will speak about *staged intervention* (including time out) or *levels of intervention*. On the rare situations where a teacher might restrain a child (in some way – even minimally) risk assessment is always a challenge in the immediate emotional moment. Many teachers have taken the risk and intervened in very serious fights (where a child is at risk of serious hurt and they've been physically hurt) – I have done it myself a number of times over the years. We, hopefully, do so with protective goodwill, and using calm verbal cueing to de-escalate emotional arousal in the child. It is never easy or simple. We often have to act in "the heat of the emotional moment" – risk assessment often has to be swift.

Using common sense – professional common sense – informed by our experience and shared practice is our starting point. "How dangerous is *this* behaviour, *this* situation, in terms of what I know about these 'types' of experience?"

Knowing those students who are most at risk at school will help us fine-tune our policy and practice so we are as clear as we can be in this difficult area. Any practice, and "form" of restraint: even holding a student's arm, or placing an arm, or one's body, between students engaged in a potential fight (or engaged in a "full-on" fight) should always be conducted within the least-to-most principle.

This is not the book to address 'techniques' and practices. There are a number of training providers who address this topic in the UK.

Any teacher who decides to use any form of restraint should always, *carefully* report what they *actually* did; the predisposing factors, the participant children, any adult witnesses (hopefully there were!) how the incident progressed and its outcome (McPherson and Rogers 2008).

The teacher, too, should debrief with senior colleagues and be given support after any restraint episode. Obviously parents, too, should be notified of *any* restraint procedures involved in a critical incident – no second guessing.

Key education department Acts and Directives regarding this topic are noted in the Bibliography under "Extreme situations".

Deferred consequences

While consequences for serious disruptive behaviour need to be applied immediately, or close to the occurrence of disruptive behaviour, there are occasions when behavioural consequences need to be deferred to a later stage.

It is pointless to force a behaviour consequence in the immediate emotional moment if a student is too upset or angry. The student (and sometimes the teacher) needs time to calm and settle before the consequences of their disruptive behaviour can be worked through.

Nathan (Year 2) had left his work area messy (pencils on the floor, bits of screwed up paper). I had reminded him, prior to lunch play, that he needed to clean up. He didn't; he groaned and moaned and complained that other students hadn't cleaned up yet, although they were actually doing it.

He prevaricated. I gave him a choice, with a deferred consequence: "If the workspace is not tidied before big play (I beckoned him non-verbally to the mess) you will need to stay back to clean up."

He moaned. "I don't care!"

I replied, "I care, Nathan. We always clean up our work area." (It can help with reminders about classroom routines to use inclusive language: our, us "we", p. 44)

When I directed him to stay back, at the close of the lesson, he did so, but sulkily. I reminded him of our class agreement and directed him to clean up (the deferred consequence). The message that I was trying to convey – through the consequence – was that if the mess is left it will need to be cleaned up later and that an individual's responsibility will be called in, eventually.

I had been teaching a social studies class and I was moving towards lesson closure. I noticed Anne get up out of her seat in the last few minutes, walk from the back of the room and stand with her bag in the doorway. I saw the class watch her as she moved towards the denouement of this potential little *contretemps*. It was my first lesson with this Year 10 class and I had been warned that it was a difficult class. I looked across to Anne standing there (as did the class).

"Anne." She looked back at me from the door. "You're out of your seat – we haven't finished yet and the bell hasn't gone yet."

The class was watching. I could feel that ambient tension – the students wondering what was going to happen and what I was going to do.

With hand on hip she said, "If the bell's about to go I might as well stay here then, mightn't I?" The voice carried (it was meant to) a clear tone of "What are you going to do then?" Anne's little power play with the new teacher. It's wearisome at times, isn't it? A few minutes to go and I'm thinking of a well-earned cuppa and also saying to myself (at nano-second speed), "Well, what do you do next, old chum?"

In the language of *deferred* consequence I said, "Anne, if you stay there and choose not to leave with the rest of us I'll have to ask you to stay back after class."

"I don't care!" How many times have I heard this? The hands on the hips said it all. I can understand teachers who, at this point, want to rush over, wag a finger, and say, "You will care!! I'll make you care!! I've got the power to …!" The power to what? To yell? To threaten? To play the game of "I have more power than you have?" Who is the adult here? I cannot (in reality) make this young girl do anything. I cannot control her, or force her to go back to her seat.

When Anne said, "I don't care!" I replied that I did care.

"Do you?" was the sarcastic reply.

At that point, with the bell about to go, I turned my attention back to the class group, some of whom had possibly been disappointed that I hadn't given Anne a chance to over-react and storm away.

"Alright, folks, time to pack up. I'll see you again on Thursday. Remember there's another class coming in next period. Let's do them a favour …" (the cue for straightening the furniture, picking up any litter and leaving quietly in an orderly fashion). Anne was still standing there, arms crossed now. I imagined she was waiting for her friends. The bell went. As her friends met up with her at the door, she walked away. I called her back.

"Anne (…), Anne (…), I need to talk with you now thanks." "Naa! – gees, it's recess." I could sense she was "winding herself up"."I know it's recess. I still need to speak to you … for a minute or so.""Nope, I'm going …," she whined."If you leave now it will get messy. I'll have to involve the coordinator." Another *deferred* consequence – not a threat. I walked back into the classroom leaving the choice (in effect) with her. Less than a minute later she came into the classroom. "Well – what do you want?!" Her face had a practised scowl; her tone and manner sulky. I said that I knew she was annoyed and I knew she wanted to be with her friends. I would not keep her long. We had a calmer chat, her audience having gone. I briefly recounted her behaviour and how I felt it affected the class, and also me as a teacher. I then asked her how she saw the whole thing. She complained that she didn't like social studies. This is not untypical of the "secondary behaviour" noted earlier (p. 17f).

I explained that she didn't have to like social studies; the issue I was wanting to focus on was "getting out of your seat, throwing your bag in the doorway and refusing to go back to your seat before the class was dismissed". We also briefly discussed her tone and manner. She grinned through this; a "knowing" grin. And I gave a wry smile back.

The chat was brief, by the open door (for ethical probity). We parted amicably and I noticed that Anne was far less abrasive during the next lesson. We were on that road – that sometimes slow road – to a "workable relationship".

■ Deferred consequences can often be linked to a choice statement or reminder: "If the work is not completed now, you will need to …". This assumes, of course, that the student is able to do the work but has been task-avoiding. No student should ever be forced to do a set amount of work that he or she is unable to realistically manage.

■ Deferred consequences can carry the message of certainty: "If ... then"; "When ... then". If (however) the language is framed as a threat, or carries a *tone* of threat, the deferred consequence loses the message of fair certainty. It is not about winning; the process of deferring consequences is to create a management context of fairness, and justice, through reasonable certainty.

■ Deferred consequences allow there to be a calmness between the initial disruptive event and the consequence applied, enabling the parties to more effectively address the behaviour and appropriate recovery or restitution. For example, it is unhelpful to force a student to apologise in the heat of the moment (to an adult or a child). I have seen some teachers make an already difficult situation significantly more difficult by forcing the student to "apologise *now* or else ...". Even adults would find that difficult.

■ Deferred consequences need to be established fairly, with appropriate certainty, rather than any *intentional* severity.

Students who don't/won't stay back after class

It was Period 6 and my colleague, Frank, and I had been team teaching a Year 7 English class. Matt and Craig had thrown pencil cases at each other. From a brief glance, as it happened, it looked as though Matt had started it. I quickly redirected them to work separately. Matt picked up his pencil case and walked over to another desk muttering "oaths and incantations". He sulked and did no work during the last 15 minutes of class.

Just before lesson closure (and the bell for freedom) I reminded the class about "doing the cleaner a favour" (chairs up, litter in the bin, and so on). Taking my notebook from my top pocket I directed my gaze at Matt and Craig and said, briefly, "I'll need to see you both *briefly* after class."

I always carry a notebook with me in (and out) of class to record names of students I need to follow up with for a chat about either work-related issues or behaviour concerns. It acts as an aide-memoire for me and acts as a "quasi-legal" reminder to the student that I'll need to follow through on issues of concern with them from time to time.

When I gave Craig and Matt the direction about the brief stay-back (to make a further appointment for some follow-up about pencil case throwing) Matt got really agitated.

"I'm not staying back for you!! I gotta get a bus!!" He nearly shouted the words.

I said, "It'll only be for a few minutes, Matt."

Craig's body language indicated he was ready (maybe not willing but ready) to stay back. But Matt was adamant.

"Nahh!! I gotta get a bus!!"

He dropped a few, muttered, f—ings en route. I noticed my colleague, Frank, tense up as Matt started to badmouth me. I knew that Frank (a beginning teacher) had had a number of earlier run-ins with Matt. I tactically ignored the outburst and finalised the class dismissal (as positively as I could).

The bell went; as the class filed out Craig stood to the side of the room and leaned against the wall. In a flash the other student, Matt, raced for the door like a jack rabbit! I managed a quick command.

"Matt, back inside – c'mon."

"I'm f—ing going – I gotta get a bus!!" were the last words as he raced away.

My colleague started to chase after him into the now-busy corridor; students from all directions were all leaving classes near us. I called him back.

"Frank! Frank (...) Leave it." He came back into the room, very tense, fists clenched and forgetting Craig was there, and said, "Just once Bill, just once I'd like to get him!" I could see he was really tensed up so I said I'd go through the chat with Craig and suggested he get a coffee and I'd catch up with him a bit later.

Ten minutes later we were having a coffee in the English staffroom. He was noticeably calmer.

I asked him, "Frank, if you had *actually caught* Matt, as he ran down the corridor; what would you have done and said? Presumably you would have had to restrain him. Just calling 'Halt' or 'Running is *verboten!*' would probably have had little effect."

He gave a weary, frustrated, laugh and said: "*I don't know* what I'd have done!"

And that's the real issue – he *didn't know what he'd do.*

"Neither of us are fit enough to chase a student like Matt – no offence, Frank. If you had caught him in the *mêlée* of the Years 7 and 8 scrum, and restrained him, can you imagine his mum within 24 hours, at the newspaper or on the television: 'Teacher maims boy on way to get bus!' Frank, it's not worth it mate. The Pyrrhic victory is not worth it ... Your career ..."

In the larger scheme of things whether we "win" in the immediate moment at 3.40 p.m. today is not important. Even the concept of "I must win", in this context, is inappropriate.

We discussed the certainty of the consequence as distinct from the severity of the consequence.

"We can catch up with him tomorrow ..." and we did – after the heat had died down. Matt was a lot more reasonable (next day); we used the lunch detention time to work through some of the issues about his disruptive classroom behaviour.

I remember viewing a short BBC television series, a drama. It was a very challenging school that set out to show how a newly qualified teacher had coped in his first school. It was pretty black (and bleak) at times, illustrating the pressures of one's first year, and first school. The struggle for class management as it interfaced with the struggle for teaching and learning was the dominant theme.

At one point in this bleak picture of modern schooling, an older teacher (early fifties) is seen chasing a Year 8 lad down a busy corridor. The boy has refused to stay back after class and has bad-mouthed the teacher. The teacher finally grabs the boy, pulls him into a vacant room and knocks him over and is seen raining frustrated blows on him. The newly qualified teacher is half a minute behind his colleague. He pulls his older colleague off with some difficulty. Standing between the puffing, angry older colleague, and the student on the lino he tries to calm him. The older man says words to the effect that, "There [puff, puff!] wouldn't be a teacher here [puff!] who hasn't wanted [puff] to do that to him!"

I can understand how such a teacher in real life (convincingly played by this actor) would have felt. But it's just not worth it.

Detention

Most schools utilise detentions of some kind, even if they do not use the term as such (other terms I've seen used are "stay-backs" and "time-in"). Essentially, the consequence of detention emphasises detaining a student (during the day or at the end of the day or even weekend detentions in fee-paying, private schools (!)) because of certain kinds of disruptive behaviour. Theoretically the purpose of detention is to link the withdrawal of time privilege (or right) with some attempt at helping the student to reflect on his or her behaviour.

Detention is a significant behaviour consequence. Its effective currency can be devalued, or even abused, when teachers:

- merely use detention as a *stand-alone* punishment.
- use detentions for minor behaviour management issues such as homework not completed or "uniform misdemeanours". These issues can be addressed more thoughtfully by the teacher following up the issue with the student in a supportive discussion. In such cases it is important to assure the student that this "is not a detention but an opportunity to work through the issue or concern".
- keep whole classes back for (say) a lunchtime detention. This strategy is sometimes used by teachers in the mistaken belief that they can set in motion peer-pressure from the more responsible students. That does not work (of course); it does lead to resentment from the more responsible, and cooperative, students.

     I've worked with teachers who have used whole-class detentions as threats and pay-backs ("I'll make you suffer"). When I've explained to such teachers that they are – effectively – losing their class, I've had some say, "I don't care – they've *got* to *learn*", as if this indefatigable exercise will eventually turn the tide on the disruptive element; it doesn't. *We have to care*; if there are several students who are disruptive we use the detention system for these students, and not for the whole class. If the disruptive behaviour is low level, but disparate *across* the class (talking/chatting while the teacher is talking, calling out, general noisiness), it will be more effective to have a classroom meeting to assess and refocus group behaviour (see p. 223f).

■ use detention merely to punish the student by making them sit and do nothing for half an hour or more.

It is important to clarify what we are seeking to achieve through detention. Is it *just* a punishment or is it a means to assess *what* happened, seek some student reflection and further reparation? Many schools use the following general approach for detentions.

When a student enters a detention room (sounds a bit like a prison doesn't it?) they are welcomed by the supervisory teacher. They are given a pro forma that has four or five questions on it:

■ "What happened ...?" (that is, "that caused you to be in detention")
■ "What is your side of the story ...?" (a right of reply question)
■ "What rule or right was affected by your behaviour?"
■ "What can you do to fix things up/make things better?" (p. 109)

A supplementary question can be added:

■ "What can your teacher do to help you fix things up ... ?"

A copy of this completed pro forma goes back to the tutor/form teacher, a copy stays with the initiating teacher (who supervises the detention) and a copy may be sent to the administration (with date, name, form group, etc.). In some schools, students keep a copy.

It is pointless getting the student merely to "write lines" during detention ("I must not ...", "I must ...") or copy out the school rules (I have actually seen some schools who still use the practice of "writing lines"!) If we are going to use writing as a consequence, at least we should direct, and focus, the student to write *about their behaviour.* In some schools each detention session begins with a brief referral by the supervising teacher to the rights/responsibilities code (p. 40f) as a context for why the student's behaviour has occasioned detention.

As with any consequence we need to try to link the disruptive behaviour to the detaining (time) experience. Getting students to use detention time to clean up will be less effective if the reason for their detention was repeated calling out in class, or being rude to a teacher. In this last instance the student should use the detention time to work through an appropriate apology and reparation. The supervising teacher's role is to enable that process. In this sense detention is *part* of a more involved consequential chain.

Hopefully your school will have a thoughtful detention policy that addresses questions and issues such as:

- What sorts of behaviours or issues do we detain students for?
- What are we primarily seeking to teach the student through detention (time)?
- How should we conduct a detention session? What sorts of things do we typically seek to do (and say) in managing the detention session? What should the student, normally, be directed to do? What are the preferred options? (That is, the protocols for after-school or lunchtime detention.)
- What is the role of supervising teacher?
- How do we utilise incident report sheets and the 4W pro forma noted earlier (p. 160)?
- What is the link between detention as a "primary" consequence and the "secondary" consequences that may need to be developed from detentions such as apologies, some restitutional process or some behaviour agreement for the future? (After – say – several detentions).

One of my colleagues was supervising the school buses at the end of the day (bus duty – a large primary school). One of the boys on the bus was teasing a student walking by. His response to the teasing was to kick the bus in a fit of frustration and pique. The bus duty teacher called the boy over but he ran away, shouting. Rather than chasing him (unwise) the teacher followed it up the next day with a lunchtime detention. During detention she discussed what happened, how the student had felt about being teased and the fact that he had run away, ignoring the teacher. She communicated her care and understanding but spoke about the "kicking-the-bus" incident. She asked how the bus driver might have felt. She further asked, "What can you do to help fix things up, or sort things out?"

Through the teacher's mediation the student agreed that even if he was angry he shouldn't have kicked the bus and he should explain to the driver what had happened.

He wrote a letter to the bus driver apologising that he had kicked the bus but he was angry because of the teasing from the boy in the bus. He assured the driver he wouldn't kick the bus again.

The teacher took the young lad to the bus driver – early (before the Period 6 bell) and the lad nervously gave his written apology to the bus driver and said, "I'm sorry for …". The bus driver read it and said, "It's not easy to apologise, is it?" tuning into the lad's probable feelings, "Especially to an adult, but you did. I can see a little scuff mark on the bus. Next time you get angry with another student let your teacher know rather than the bus, eh?" and he shook the lad's hand.

The bus driver's goodwill and the teacher's mediation skill enabled a useful outcome from the detention. In this sense the detention was used as a primary consequence with the apology/restitution acting as a "secondary consequence".

In some schools detentions are conducted by senior staff on referral from their colleagues. In other schools, each teacher conducts his or her own (subject or class based) detentions. Some schools use a combination of both systems. If a teacher initiates a detention carried through by another colleague it will be important for the initiating teacher to effect some repairing and rebuilding with the student concerned rather than seeing the incident as handled, and somehow finished, by the colleague conducting the detention. If the initiating colleague does not make an effort to be involved in some checking and re-establishing with the student, the detention process may adversely affect the ongoing teacher–student relationship.

Detentions can also to be used to track which students, classes and teachers are experiencing difficulties. They are an "early warning", from which senior colleagues can (and should) offer moral and practical support.

Bullying

Bullying has always been a disturbing feature of school life; any large social mix will experience bullying behaviour as insecure individuals seek to exercise their distorted sense of social power. I saw bullying as a student at school. I saw disgusting – unchecked – bullying as a young army conscript (during the Vietnam conflict). I saw bullying when I worked on building sites. I always fought back verbally and, at times, physically – it always stopped but I saw many go under; hurt, damaged even destroyed by this gutless feature of human behaviour.

Anti-bullying policies have been a feature of schools for several decades now – they do have an effect if the emphasis is more than *anti* (it is easy to frame policy language in the negative). In effect any feature of a whole-school policy needs to focus on *pro*-rights – essentially the right to feel psychologically as well as physically safe. Our emphasis needs to be the building – and enabling – of a school culture where it is not "normal" or "OK" to hurtfully tease, harass and bully.

In supportive school cultures, key features are consistently noted – in the literature – that enable rights affirming and rights protection and confront bullying *at every level* (Lee 2004; Rogers 2003a, 2006a).

■ The issue, and clarification, of *what constitutes bullying is made clear generally* to students in the establishment phase of the year. A clear understanding that bullying is more than *physical* is essential. *Most bullying is psychological/social*: teasing and name-calling; racist/sexist/homophobic language; threats, friendship/play exclusion; "posting" message texts, photo/captions or "video links" on phones or Facebook – "Facebook mobbing"(!)

■ Many schools conduct educational programmes using discussion groups, drama and literature-based examples to raise a shared consciousness about:
  – Why does anyone bully others (?)
  – What is the role/responsibility of onlookers (?) – when we see someone bullying others, what should we do? What can we do?
  – What to do when others seek to harass/bully you (?)
  – Why you need to report it when it *continues* (as bullying often does); *to whom and how?*

■ Students know that all staff are committed to confronting bullying (in all its expressions).

■ Some schools conduct "bully-proofing" coaching: how to "ignore" or speak assertively to a student when they seek to tease, harass or threaten.

■ Many schools have also found success in helping students understand the role of "spectator"; what happens when students "watch" bullying episodes and some collude and join in by "laughing along with" or goading the bully. Bullies rarely exercise their bullying behaviour "in secret" (apart from secrecy from adults of course). They need their sense of 'social power and prestige'. As Peter Fonagy suggests, bullying is often "performance art" of which only 10–20 per cent of the school population are involved, though it is supported by the bystander audience (Labi 2001: 45).

■ Many schools use surveys (among students and teachers and, even, parent groups) to ascertain attitude; kinds of bullying; and the extent of bullying in the school (and even nomination of bullies) "in-house surveying" (Rogers 2003a).

■ Any school approach to bullying must make clear that it is not "wrong" or "tale-telling" to let an adult know when you're being bullied. *We need to let an adult know so they can help make this stop* … It is crucial that the students be reassured on this matter. I have seen far too many examples where it is the victim who ends up having to leave the school rather than the bully.

■ A key feature of any approach to victim support is to encourage the victim to confront the bully in a planned, supported one-to-one meeting. "Confront" sounds like a tough verb to use here; I mean the opportunity for the victim to sit and speak to the bully clearly, specifically, about what they have done, said, implied, written about them and the effect such behaviour has had, and to have a clear assurance – from the bully – that such behaviours will stop. Any such meeting must have the consent of the victim and discussion *and planning* needs to occur prior to any one-to-one meeting with the bully.

Most victims want (and rightfully deserve) clear assurance that the bullying behaviour will stop.

Review meetings are conducted within a week/fortnight to see what has occurred regarding the bullying behaviour. It is helpful to also meet with the collusive bullies (one at a time).

■ There also needs to be a consequential framework for bullying behaviour in schools including exclusion for repeated bullying. Where a student refuses to cooperate within a safe-school policy and is persistently refusing any and all support, exclusion is a just – and necessary – consequential necessity.

One of the best texts I've read for developing a whole-school approach is Chris Lee's book *Preventing Bullying in Schools* (2004).

The issue of bullying of teachers *by students* is addressed in Chapter 8.

Reflection

■ How do you distinguish between behaviour consequences and punishment?

■ Is there a *framework* for behaviour consequences in your school? (That is, beyond non-negotiable consequences for serious behaviour?)

■ Are there suggestions, or guidelines, for *typical behaviour consequences* as utilised by class teachers? How do they fit with the 3Rs framework (*Related? Reasonable? Conveying Respect?*)?

■ Do you have a "staged model" for consequences; *degrees* of time-out options and usage? How does your school utilise time out on a least-to-most intrusive continuum? Is this published? At what point(s) are senior teachers engaged?

■ What are the protocols/practices for time-out usage in your school?
 – Are they published?
 – What is the moral responsibility – and professional role – of the teacher who initiates *any* time-out consequence *regarding follow up with that student later that day, or the next day?*

Notes

1. "Dunce" was a word introduced into the English language by the disciples of (St) Thomas Aquinas (in the thirteenth century) to ridicule those who followed John Duns Scotus, a medieval philosopher and theologian. It has come to mean someone who is slow-witted, a dullard; in other words, stupid (actually John Dun Scotus was not stupid at all, he was a Franciscan who had studied, and lectured, at Oxford – they just did not like him).

Notes

1. ...

Chapter 6

Challenging children and children with emotional and behavioural difficulties

Argumentative and challenging behaviour in students

Argumentative and challenging student behaviours, it seems, are far more common in classrooms these days. I've worked with a number of private (independent) schools and teachers there, too, have noted a perceptible increase in more challenging behaviours. It is difficult to garner reliable, and meaningful, statistics (or even measures) in this whole area. There are frequent newspaper articles on "increases in violence" in schools (including recently in Australia – several serious knife incidents). Surveying teachers themselves – however – indicates that while extreme violence is rare (thankfully) there is a noticeable increase in 'attitude' – by this teachers mean disrespect, "rudeness", argumentativeness, resistance to reasonable teacher directions.[1] This was acknowledged in the Elton Report (1989) and seems to be a common perception among teachers. However – the perception *does* vary according to how such perceptions correlate with teacher confidence; skill; whole-school emphasis regarding behaviour policy and practice and – crucially – the nature, kind and degree of colleague support in a given school (Rogers 2002).

In one such school where I had worked as a consultant, a beginning teacher recounted how she had asked a Year 10 student "Why" she was out of her seat during work time. The young girl turned, faced the teacher with a firm "I've-got-you-sorted look" and said, "Why? If you *must* know I was just talking to my friend about borrowing a pen [sigh]". Here she ticked off the first point on her finger. "Secondly, I really don't think it's any of your business, Miss, and thirdly we pay your wages here … and I was *just* going back to my seat. OK?" The student had said all this in a quietly confident, "street-lawyer" way. I asked my colleague what she did in response, she said, she was just lost for words! "I felt stymied!"

When I've shared this account with other colleagues, more than a few have said how they feel they'd like to "maim" the student. I can understand both the feeling of loss of authority and control that some teachers might feel, and the possible temptation to slightly "maim" – at least verbally!

How would you deal with this minor out-of-seat behaviour (for it is minor disruptive behaviour)? What is more annoying here is the "secondary behaviour"; the attitude, manner and words used by the student in response to the teacher's questions (p. 17f).

It is worth pointing out, again, that an interrogative question about behaviour ("*Why* are you …?"), especially in front of the student's peers, is an invitation to a pointless discussion, or a possible "slanging match".

I've never had a student say to me "… we pay your wages here". If I ever did, my response would be an exclaimed and satisfying "Eureka!! So you're the one – You've been paying my wages, eh? I've been looking for you for a *long, long* time …!" However, a brief "I" statement with a redirection to the task at hand is, normally, more than enough to deal with this little piece of "cock-sparrow" behaviour – for example: "I'm not speaking to you rudely [or disrespectfully]. I don't expect you to speak to me rudely". Then the teacher could refocus from the student's avoidance behaviour ("I was just getting a pen") to the task at hand.

Sometimes a direct question can help: "What are you supposed to be doing now?" Of course, a pleasant, business-like and respectful tone is important.

In response to the question, "What are you doing?". I've had students say, "I don't know what I'm supposed to be doing, do I?" In this case it is enough to simply, briefly and firmly point out what they should be doing and give them some take-up time. It will be important to come back, later, to check for time on task and (also) to re-establish a working relationship with the student. It may also be helpful to have a "follow-up" session (in non-class time) to address the student's disrespect.

Such follow up is important, because what *we* perceive as disrespect (tone of voice, body language, sighing, eyes to ceiling, and so on) may not be seen so by the student. This does not excuse their behaviour, of course; they may even be unaware that they 'come across' like this. A one-to-one meeting, with some "mirroring" (p. 108f) can help make clear what we (as teacher) see, hear, feel when we perceive insouciance and disrespect.

Is there a "distribution" of challenging students in any one class?

In any classroom group, there is often a basic distribution of challenging students in proportion to those students who are more cooperative and considerate:

- 70–80 per cent of the students are probably reasonable, considerate, naturally respectful, cooperative and display basic civil behaviours – *given the chance*.
- 10–15 per cent of students are attentionally distracting, some are argumentative (at times), or can be challenging in their behaviour. Sometimes such students are exercising attention-seeking goals, in effect saying: "Hey (…) *notice me*. I'm being funny, stupid, 'cool' …"; "My calling-out, my seat-leaning, my late entrance with a body language flourish … is inviting you to *notice me, attend to me*!" And, of course, if a 5-year-old boy is rolling under a table and barking like a dog, it is difficult *not* to notice and attend simply in order to discipline him and protect the learning, and safety, rights of the other students.

  Sometimes students challenge others, particularly the teacher, through expressions of inappropriate power – a kind of game where the student, in effect, says, "I can do or say – basically – what I like and how I like and you can't stop me …"; "I'm the boss here …".
- 1–5 per cent of students display *frequent*, and often intense, patterns of disruptive behaviour. They may also present with emotional or behavioural difficulties (EBD), or behaviour disorders such as attention deficit or attention deficit hyperactive disorder (ADD/ADHD) or autism spectrum disorder (ASD).

Caveat

It is very important that in using terms like EBD, ADD or ADHD or ASD we do not easily *label* the child as an *ADD child*. The negative effect of labelling is well known in education literature. Children often conform to the expectations that adults have about them and may also view themselves as inadequate; ineffective; useless or a troublemaker *within* these labels and expectations. The term EBD, as used here, is descriptive of children's typical behaviour in a given context.

Attention deficit spectrum disorder is an increasingly diagnosed disorder in children in the UK (as in Australia and the USA). Children diagnosed with ADSD are often prescribed Ritalin or Dexamphetamine, medications that can assist with aspects of concentration, focus and impulsivity. Like any behaviour disorder, however, the positive assistance offered by medication will always need support from behaviour therapy to give some direction and guidance to a child's increased concentration or decreased impulsivity.

Corey (aged 14) had been diagnosed as ADHD and was taking four tablets of Ritalin a day. I discussed his behaviour with him and asked him if his tablets had taught him to enter the classroom without "grandstanding". He returned my smile with a knowing grin.

I then asked if the tablets had taught him to "sit in his seat without serious rocking backwards", or had taught him "to put his hand up without calling out or clicking his fingers" (I mirrored these behaviours to him; p. 108f). He grinned again.

"Nahh ...!"

"Well – do the tablets teach you to stay in your seat, focus on the learning task and give it your best shot for – say – ten minutes or so without getting up and wandering?"

"Course not – no." He was starting to "cotton-on" to what I was getting at. We discussed other aspects of behaviour such as a quieter voice in class time and supporting other students by not annoying them.

I asked him who was "in charge of Corey". "Who really drives Corey along in the minutes and hours of a day?" I used the analogy of a car and a driver. It seemed to connect. We then discussed how a driver has to be focused, has to check rear vision mirror, seatbelt, position; he has to select his gears, speed, indicator, has to decide where to go, and why, and how. We then discussed *how* he, Corey, could better (more helpfully, more thoughtfully, more cooperatively) "drive his own behaviour". From this came a behaviour plan as both "map" and "guide"/reminder. This analogy of driver/car/behaviour is one that my colleagues and I have found quite helpful in developing behaviour plans with older secondary students.

Corey still kept on with the Ritalin (although the dosage was reduced) but the behaviour plan gave him added confidence and specific focus to work on aspects of his behaviour, and the special attention he received from key teachers assisted in building his self-esteem. It was "three steps forward and one, even two, steps back" on some days, but the colleague support – across all the teachers who taught Corey – helped to give some consistency and supportive encouragement to both the teachers and Corey.

Supporting students diagnosed with ADSD[2]

When working with, and supporting, children diagnosed with ADD (or ADHD) it can help to:

- seat them near a classmate who is both a supportive and a positive role model. If table group seating is used, be sure these children sit with the quieter, less distractable children (even if they promise they will be fine if they sit next to overly motoric classmates!). At primary level teachers will sometimes utilise the support of a responsible student to act as a "learning buddy" to sit with, and support, the student with special needs.
- use visual cueing to assist student focus and attention. Seating near the front of the room (near to where the teacher engages *whole-class* teaching, learning and class dialogue) can also help. Small picture cues for work tasks (on their table) can also act as an aides-memoire (see p. 189).

- develop work schedules for key learning tasks, with set structure for work progress. It can help to have a daily progress sheet with goal based targets (even small, incremental, targets – breaking up the total requirement into time-manageable tasks). This gives a sense of time sequencing. Structure is important for children diagnosed with ADD or autism spectrum disorder; avoid giving too many choices.
- check for understanding when giving task instructions by asking the student to repeat back (correspondence training); this can be carried out in one-to-one teaching as well as class time.
- make normal learning *routines* clear; even how to utilise workspace, set out workbook(s) and analyse tasks (read twice, check "do I understand?", "do I know what is asked of me here?", "how do I get help?"). Give older students a table pencil case (pp. 10, 190) instead of a huge pencil case (full of interesting distractions). An uncluttered desk will also help. *Specifically teaching* a child (one to one at non-class time) *how* to organise desk space and work time as basic academic survival skills; *deceptively* basic. Some children need to learn these skills within one-to-one support opportunity with their teacher.
- allow time for reasonable movement by the student in class time, if only to quietly leave their work area (desk/table group) to come and check their incremental progress (every five minutes) with the teacher or teaching assistant. The teacher then gives a brief, positive feedback.
- avoid keeping such children in for extended lengths of time at recess – they (particularly) need physical activity at playtime.

Autism spectrum disorder

Increasingly in schools teachers are required to teach – and support – children diagnosed with autism spectrum disorder who will present behaviours that affect:

- their social communication and interaction
- the way they process and perceive information (particularly auditory information); sometimes referred to as a "comprehension deficit".

This, in turn, affects:

- their social *imagination* and the way they interact socially. They often find difficulty empathising with others because they may fail to perceive/understand why others feel upset, or hurt or angry. There may well be confusion and uncertainty regarding "normal" social situations, social cues and social interactions. The child diagnosed with ASD may often display speech limitations in social situations and what appears to be insensitivities and isolationist behaviours.

■ their ability to cope with, and encourage change (particularly unexpected change) may precipitate anxiety ("tantrums" in young children), withdrawal or unintended distressed even "aggressive" behaviour. Children diagnosed with ASD like predictability and structure.

■ They may well present with obsessive and inflexible patterns of speech/ interest/behaviour.

Like all diagnosed disorders, the degrees of behaviour (as those above) present within a spectrum of frequency, intensity, generality and duration. Teachers should not merely assume or *predict* a child is "autistic" if there has been no formal diagnosis because of such behaviours.

If teachers do frequently observe such behaviours they should – of course – alert (and discuss with) senior colleagues. A formal diagnosis is crucial.

In working with children diagnosed with ASD (or who present with symptomatic, undiagnosed, "ASD behaviours") it is important to:

■ build, and sustain, a calm working – and relational – environment and use a calm voice (firm, not loud or raised – children diagnosed with ASD are often *very* sensitive to loud voice levels)

■ take care in touching the child unless parent(s) have made clear how their child perceives and understands *any* touching

■ use clear, context specific, language cueing

■ have clear routines; always prepare (with the child) – in advance – for *any* changes in daily routine

■ because the child may not fully appreciate encouragement in the same way as other children, focus on the effort and application in specific – supportive – ways (rather than "great", "well done", "marvellous" ...) (see also p. 132f). Again – it is worth checking with the child's parents in terms of the child's familiar language cueing and the child's perception/understanding. It will rarely help – for example – to appeal to them with emotionally loaded cueing, e.g. trying to create a sense of "guilt", or simply displaying your anger at their behaviour. ("Come on – please be nice ...", "Be a good boy!", "Do the right thing ...")

■ have an individual behaviour plan, which can often be helpful with the more extreme aspects of social behaviour in school. An individual plan can *significantly* teach and support key social and academic behaviours (see p. 182f).

In the Bibliography I have included a section under "Autism", which lists very helpful texts and websites.

Attention-seeking behaviours

Chris, a Year 8 student, was repeatedly calling out in one of my English classes; eight, ten or even 15 times a lesson (on occasion). His calling out was sometimes masqueraded as asking a question; sometimes it was a silly comment; mostly it was "attentional-behaviour". When I believed his behaviour was affecting my right to teach *or* other students' rights to learn and participate I would firmly and briefly remind him of the rule: "Chris, we've got a rule for asking questions. Use it thanks."

He would often use such a rule reminder as an occasion to further seek attention, "But I was *only* asking a question! Is it a crime to ask a question in this class?" He would then – often – sulk.

I could easily see why other teachers found Chris's behaviour so frustrating at times.

It also doesn't help when a headteacher, who having interviewed and chatted with a child (presenting with significant attentional behaviours), then says to the teacher, "He's no problem with me – I get on with him very well". Of course! With an audience of one he's fine, but back in a classroom, or playground setting, the child's behaviour is affected by his belief that he can only belong when others are giving him lots of attention – even for disruptive behaviours.

■ *Some* attention-seeking behaviour can – in the short term – be *tactically* ignored. Infant teachers know that by not giving any verbal or non-verbal recognition we can sometimes avoid unnecessary reinforcement of the behaviour; I say *sometimes*. They – then – respond (briefly and positively) when the child is behaving appropriately; cooperatively. In this sense *tactical* ignoring and *selective* attention reinforce the same outcome. As with all teacher discipline and management there is no guarantee – no simplistic formula in any management or discipline approach.

It can help to *preface* the tactical ignoring when a student is calling out. Prefaced tactical ignoring involves the teacher giving the student a conditional direction, *then tactically ignoring* subsequent calling out behaviour: "Craig, *when* you've got your hand up without calling out [the prefacing, *conditional* direction] *then* I'll answer your question." It can help to briefly add, "Remember our class rule." The teacher then turns their eyes and attention away from the student to focus on students with their hands up … tactically ignoring any subsequent calling out.

As noted earlier (p. 100f), the skill of *tactical* ignoring in teacher behaviour is a context dependent skill. We should never ignore any behaviour that sees a child hurting others (even pinching, or so-called low-level "testosteronic bonding") or *persistently* disrupting other students' right to learn (by repeated, loud calling out; touching others' work; annoying them).

The test of any efficacy regarding tactical ignoring is the degree to which the student reduces, or stops, his disruptive behaviour. Tactical ignoring is only effective if the rest of the class takes their lead from the teacher and also ignore the disrupting student.

■ If the disruptive student gains any significant *kudos* from others in the class it will be important to briefly and firmly describe what the student is doing (in their attentional behaviour) and direct them to the appropriate behaviour: "Chris (…), you're calling out (…). Remember the class rule (…). Hands up without calling out". If the student challenges, argues or tries other diversionary tactics, the teacher will keep the focus on the primary issue or behaviour (necessary at that point).

Avoid the temptation to debate, argue or be sarcastic and score points. While repartee, and even a workable bon mot, can defuse and refocus some attentional behaviours (from upper primary age upwards) sarcasm only feeds attention-seeking and power-seeking behaviours. If the student makes silly, rude comments the teacher needs to make *that* point clear:

"That's not a helpful comment, Craig. You know that."
"That comment is rude [or …] and not acceptable here."
"We have a rule for respect. I expect you to use it."
"We don't use put-downs in our class."

In such cases a brief, firm, assertive, tone will carry the meaning.

On some occasions an immediate in-class consequence will be appropriate. If a student continues to be disruptive by, say, talking to, or annoying, students next to (or near) them, we can often use a choice/consequence statement: "If you continue to … I'll have to ask you to work somewhere else in our classroom". If they continue with the disruptive behaviour and we then direct them to move and work somewhere else (the consequence) some students prevaricate or argue: "But I'll be alright now! I will Miss, I'll be good …!!" If we have raised the consequential stakes it is important to carry the consequence through with certainty (p. 155f).

If the student refuses to move to another place in the classroom, when directed by his teacher (I've had this more than a few times over the years), rather than end up in a win/lose situation it may be preferable to give a *deferred* consequence: "If you choose not to move now and work over there I'll have to follow this up with you at recess in your own time" (p. 106f). An alternative is to use the colleague-support exit/time-out plan (p. 149f).

■ In some cases where the attention-seeking behaviour is significantly affecting the teacher's right to teach and the students' right to learn we will need to exercise the time-out consequence immediately. When directing a student from the classroom to take time out, a *calm* exit is important. Avoid any last minute grandstanding by using a loud voice or threats ("and you're going to be in detention *as well!!*").

■ If attention-seeking behaviour has occurred several times, over a few lessons, some early and thoughtful follow-up will be imperative. It is often in these longer-term (one-to-one) sessions that teachers can (more consistently) make clear to the student what he or she is doing in class and even *why*, and engage the student's understanding and cooperation (p. 106f). Such a process needs to be seen as helping the student to understand and take responsibility for his or her behaviour rather than merely using such follow-up time for yet another punishment.

In such one-to-one settings it is important that the teacher assures the student that their main concern is about the student's *behaviour*, and the effect it is having on other students' learning, and (of course) the teacher's right (and ability) to teach.

If we are uncertain or uncomfortable about pursuing a "semi-counselling" approach like this, invite another colleague to work with us. The key focus areas in such a follow-up will address the following:

– Is the student aware of their behaviour? "Are you aware of what you do in class when you call out ...?" It is important to be *specific* about the student's typical, characteristic behaviour. In response to such questions, students often shrug their shoulders, and some laugh (nervously, or because they think their behaviour *is* actually funny).

– Describe the student's disruptive behaviour, specifically and briefly (some mirroring may be helpful; p. 108f). Ask the student *what* they need to do to change the way they currently (and characteristically) behave. Point out that this behaviour is affecting others in the class; describe *how* it affects others.

– A simple, achievable agreement – or plan – may help the student have a *focus* for *personal* behaviour management. I have found that a simple, printed agreement can often help such a focus by concentrating on three things that the student needs to *stop* doing (so that others can get on with their work without having to put up with X, Y and Z behaviour), and three things they need to *start* doing to gain some success in their learning and so others can get on with their learning (without having to put up with X, Y and Z).

The three "things" are *specific*, achievable, *behaviours*. For infant age children the thing may be one "overall" behaviour such as "sitting on the mat" (this includes sitting without rolling around or touching others; and facing the front and listening with eyes and ears – and joining in with hands up …), see p. 182f.

Earlier this year I was asked to work with a difficult class of 11–12-year-olds (Year 5–6). There were several students who had been described to me as attention-seeking and power-seeking. One was described to me as "oppositionally defiant". These early, brief descriptions proved all too true.

On the way into my first lesson with the class, Kelly (I didn't know her name at that stage) started to ask me who I was, in an overly repetitive way, in a voice that seemed to say, "Look at me – look at how I'm hassling this new teacher who is going to work with us …".

Later in the first class period, she called out frequently; sometimes with her hand up, sometimes without. One feature of her calling out was the sing-song tone of voice she used. Initially, when I *tactically* ignored such behaviour she would say things like, "I'm talking to you … can't you see me?" She would sigh and turn to a classmate adding … "I'm talking to him, and he's not listening …". I could hear all this as I tactically ignored her.

Sometimes I would preface the tactical ignoring (p. 101f); sometimes I'd give a rule reminder at the onset of her calling out.

This student's behaviour irritated her regular teacher a great deal and I can understand why. As I worked with my colleague my struggle with her students – in a sense – ratified, and supported, their struggle with this student.

In their research on classroom behaviour and dynamics, Rudolf Dreikurs et al. (1982) discuss such behaviour in terms of the child's purpose in a given social context. According to Dreikurs, *behaviour is directed towards particular goals*. The general goal is to belong to the social group (in this case the classroom peers, or a small group of peers). In pursuing that goal some students (like Kelly) pursue their belonging *through* attentional behaviours. In this sense the *frequent* calling out; the silly comments; nuisance behaviours; the non-verbal sighing; rolling of eyes; and so on are not only the *cause* of the behaviour, but are also its *purpose and goal*. The goal (to gain attention or power …) is itself the cause; the active force, as it were, behind the behaviour; even if the child is unaware of what they are doing. As children get older their "private logic" may well embrace such thinking as, "I only really 'belong' when people pay lots of attention to me; when they notice me a lot".

Being aware of that purpose, that "goal", helps to explain the child's behaviour in its peer context. It is understandable that when we give undue attention to such behaviour (partly from our own frustration and partly because we are seeking to manage classroom dynamics) we also reinforce, or sometimes *over*-reinforce, the student's "attentional", or power-seeking goal.

I have worked with children who use frequent expressions of charm, cuteness or powerlessness ("I can't do the work") to gain significant and frequent adult recognition (attention). This, too, can be seen as a child trying to gain both excessive assurance and a sense of "belonging".

In the same classroom, on the same day, I noticed (how could I not) Liam making frequent hand gestures across the room, to a classmate, while I was teaching to the whole class. Several students laughed and giggled. I directed them to "face the front and listen, … Liam (…), Liam (…)!" He turned and faced me, sighing.

"You're making hand signals to your classmate." I briefly looked at his classmate. "You need to be facing this way and listening, thank you." He raised his eyes to the ceiling and folded his arms – and settled for a while. He repeated the same behaviour a little later.

This time I called his name, "Liam (…) …", and non-verbally cued him to face the front.

He was getting, if briefly, the attention he was after. I was doing my short-term best to keep attentional focus on teaching and learning while giving minimal attention to his "secondary behaviours".

Later, in the on-task phase of the lesson, I noticed he wasn't working; he was chatting to his classmate, but clearly not working. When I encouraged him back on-task he became resistant. "NO ... I don't want to do this. I hate this kind of work ...", he muttered.

I helped him refocus and gave him some take-up time, but he still refused to do the work. At times he refused to listen, or look at me when I spoke to him, or walked away while I was talking to him. This was more than attention-seeking.

It is understandable that teachers *feel* threatened, even somewhat defeated (at times) by such behaviour. I can also understand why some teachers feel they need to "show the child who is boss here". The child's displays of power may be active and vocal, or expressed in passive displays of power through non-verbal resistance. The child's private logic here, focuses on beliefs such as: "I can do what I want and others can't stop me..."; "I am going to be the boss here ..."; or "*I count* only when I can do what I want; when I call the shots ...".

When I got to know these students a little better, I decided that I would pursue an approach that Dreikurs describes as "goal-disclosure".

Disclosing a student's behavioural goal

Dreikurs et al. (1982) propose an approach designed to supportively help the student understand "why" they are behaving the way they do. This approach involves particular questions being asked to raise the student's awareness about the possible goal of their behaviours. The tone of these questions needs to be supportive and non-judgemental if they are to help the student understand their "purposeful" behaviour. This approach needs to take place in a supportive, one-to-one, context. The teacher – in question – needs to have a reasonably positive working relationship with the student to pursue this approach.

■ The first question raises the child's awareness about their specific behaviour through an open question: "Do you know why you …?" We need to be specific about the student's actual, disruptive behaviour: "Do you know why you call out many times in class …?"; "Do you know why you make frequent comments like [here the teacher recounts typical clownish, and silly, comments]?" Most students respond to such a question with a non-verbal response (a shoulder shrug, a wry frown or smile); sometimes there is a muttered, "Nope". Allow some brief reflection even if the silence is a little uncomfortable. It can also help to increase the specific shared awareness about the student's behaviour some *brief* mirroring of their distracting/disruptive behaviour (pp. 108–9).

■ The teacher then *suggests* what they think about *why* the student typically behaves the way they do: "I'd like to tell you what I think …" or "Can I suggest why you call out a lot [or butt in, and so on]?" I've never had a student say "no" to this question (though they are naturally inquisitive). A typical response – particularly in older children – is the shoulder shrug and raised-eye frown or the "knowing smile". The teacher then moves the question towards a possible reason (goal) as to *why the student typically behaves this way in class.*

■ Some suggested "goal disclosures" include:
 – "Could it be that when you call out a lot you want the class to look at you and notice you?"
 – Or, if the issue is clownish behaviour, "Could it be that when you say things like … [be specific] you want the class to look at you and laugh?"
  Dreikurs makes the point that the "disclosure" of the child's goal is meant to sound hypothetical rather than as a "judgement" ("*Could* it be …?", "I'd like to *suggest* …").
  If the student's goal is some sort of power exchange (refusal to comply with teacher requests/directions; frequent answering back in front of peers; walking

away while the teacher is talking; harassing others, including the teacher), the disclosure would focus on this aspect of the student's behaviour:[3]

– "Could it be that when you refuse to do the work you're wanting to 'show' me that you can do what you want and that I can't stop you …?" This assumes that the student *can* do the work and that their behaviour, regarding task refusal, is a display of attentional power. It further assumes that the teacher knows the student well enough and has a positive working relationship with them for them to engage in dialogue in this way.

– "Could it be that you want to do what you want, when you want – and that you believe no one can really stop you …?"

– "Could it be that you want to be the boss, call the shots …?"

■ Most students respond to a disclosure of their "goal" in non-verbal ways (as noted above): raised eyes, a slight grin, a shoulder shrug. This "recognition reflex" (as Dreikurs terms it) is often the student's assent; their acknowledgement that the teacher is "on to something here".

If the student says "no" (in response to the disclosure – "Could *it be that* …?") it can help to ask, "If that's not the reason, can you suggest why you call out lots of times [or refuse to do the work when I know you can do it …]?"

It will also help to point out to the student that they have *learned* to behave like this at school. Somewhere, sometime, somehow, they *chose* to behave this way. They *choose* to behave like this now. The teacher suggests, the student has *learned* that certain ways of behaving get them the kinds of attention, or the kinds of attentional power they seek. We might well admit to the student that we cannot *make* them learn, or (in fact) do anything. Only they can *make* themself do things. They do not, however, have the right to do *whatever* they want, *whenever* they want. They will have to face the consequences. The teacher is seeking – through this process – to engage a cooperative understanding. They are encouraging the student to learn to *change* their behaviour – and for good, worthwhile, cooperative reasons.

Teachers can work with the student to refocus attentional, power-seeking behaviours into more cooperative opportunities so that the student can gain a sense of social belonging in purposeful ways, such as in positions of responsibility (monitor roles, peer-monitoring, cross-age tutoring) – this positive role is often taken up with some enthusiasm.

■ In light of the "goal-disclosure", the teacher invites the student to work on a behaviour plan. A key feature of this plan will involve the teacher consciously noticing, and giving descriptive recognition, for cooperative attentional behaviour (see p. 132f).

■ An approach that involves the wider class group – through a whole-class discussion – can highlight (for the student) what their peers think of behaviours such as frequent interruption and clowning (and why).

In conducting such meetings it is important that we do not *name* an individual student (although no doubt particular names will be uppermost in most students' thinking!).

I have even conducted such meetings with infant-age children. The basic rules for such meetings are: "One at a time"; "We're here to discuss issues that affect us all"; "We do not put anyone (or anyone's ideas) down"; "We listen to everyone's contribution"; "If we make any decisions as a result of our meeting those decisions have to fit with our classroom behaviour agreement".

For example, there may be a decision – from the group – that students who persistently disrupt learning should have to work away from others or even face time-out (if they do not respond to a teacher reminder, or direction warning). Students (as a group) also can learn to *tactically* ignore non-physical, attentional behaviours of an individual student. This strategy is particularly effective at early years level but must be balanced by the teacher's respectful support of the student at other times (including individual behaviour plans).

Consequences like those noted above would need to be consistent with the classroom behaviour agreement, would need to *relate* to the behaviour in question and be *respectful* in their application.

Working with challenging children and children diagnosed with emotional, behavioural disorders

James (grade one) was sitting on the carpet in front of his teacher (and myself), we were about to begin morning sharing time. James started to extend his hands outwards to touch the children either side of him. As he did so he laughed very loudly. My colleague told him to "stop that" and "sit up properly". He did – for a while. He started again, my colleague warned him, "James, leave the other children alone and sit properly or I'll have to move you." I was – yet again – surprised how tolerant the other children were of James's vigorous touching and poking and loud laughing. Although it did not seem at all malicious (he seemed to derive satisfaction from the "touching") it was disruptive and (of course) unacceptable.

I whispered to my colleague to ask if I could have a word with the class (we were team-teaching). While I was "re-settling" the class James started again. I called his name; after several calls he turned to look at me frowning. I said to the class "… excuse me a moment everyone. I need to speak to James".

"James (…), James (…) I want you to look this way (…) so I know you're listening." I then hopped off my chair at the front of the room and briefly modelled appropriate sitting. … "James (…) I want you to cross your legs like this (I modelled it) (…). Hands in your lap, like this ... and eyes and ears looking this way. That's it." I resumed my seat and thanked the class for waiting and, re-engaging a class discussion, I asked them what they were doing in their maths work ... Twice I had to remind James of *how* to sit. Each time with brief, *behavioural* directions (p. 85f).

An individual behaviour plan

Later my colleague and I developed a plan for James involving the explicit teaching of sitting-on-the-mat-together-behaviour. We did this with James at lunchtime. Using a simple stick figure drawing showing James sitting like the other children (their faces and the teacher's face were shown as looking happy). Using the picture as a basic social story we identified the helping behaviours *we all use* together during whole-class teaching time.

- *Where* to sit (we later appointed a "mat-buddy" to sit with James during whole-class teaching time).
- We discussed *how* to sit (and keep your hands and feet safe).
- We explained *how* to listen with eyes and ears; hands up (without calling out if you want to share or ask a question).
- We explained *how to wait* for the teacher to call on you (when you've got your hand up and want to share ...).
- We explained how to use your "inside voice" (instead of a loud voice) when you share in whole-class teaching/learning time.

    When working with children diagnosed with ASD (particularly younger children like James) it does not help to simply tell them to "sit properly" – properly is (in a sense) too general; perhaps even "meaningless". They find a sense of security in clear, specific, direct speech and supportive routines.

- We described the behaviours (using the picture card). (See p. 188.)
- We then modelled each of the behaviours and – crucially – we encouraged James to practise each of the behaviours above. This was – in effect – his plan.

We had top-up sessions three times a week (initially) to practise and discuss how his "plan" was going. In class time we used the picture cue to *briefly* act as a visual *aide-memoire*.

The key, though, was the specificity of behaviours, the routines, the practise sessions and specific encouragement in class time (p. 132f).

The responsibility and input of the class were also very positive as James started to change his behaviour. Later we developed a similar plan for time-on-task behaviours at his table group.

This approach can work at any age-level at primary (even middle-school years), (see McPherson and Rogers 2008; Rogers, in Clough et al. 2005; Rogers 2003a).

The picture cues, the modelling and rehearsal sessions (of specific behaviours) and regular positive reinforcement can all be developed with students with symptomatic or diagnosed behaviour disorders in an *age-appropriate* approach in supportive, one-to-one teaching sessions (p. 187f).

Some teachers will respond to children with diagnosed behaviour disorders as "uniquely different" and will tolerate behaviours they would never tolerate in other students. I believe this is misguided. Even if a child has been diagnosed with ASD we should not (in my view) ignore extremes of behaviour such as "poking", "pushing", "hitting out" or disrupting children's work time or *any* aggressive behaviour.

Of course there is a range of cognitive activity and social awareness in the ASD range. However, when we effectively ignore, play down or excuse a student's disruptive or hurtful behaviour (*because* of their disorder) we effectively say to the other students that his behaviour is "OK"; that this is *so* different from other children that the normal rules and expectations do not apply – it conveys an unhelpful and unhealthy message to the class as a group. Cooperative learning, and social behaviours can be *taught* to children diagnosed with behaviour disorders (like James). They need (of course) one-to-one support for this learning (p. 187f) and that is the important key – teaching children with diagnosed behaviour disorders the academic and social skills needed to cope, manage and even enjoy day-to-day schooling (Rogers 2003a).

The concept of "challenging children" varies across schools and across a teacher's perception and experience. For one teacher, in one context, a student coming late to class is a major discipline incident. For another teacher the incident is a minor irritant and only *potentially* a discipline issue. Children diagnosed with EBD present with more serious concerns for the teacher.

There are many aspects of a child's life, temperament, home and background circumstances and environment that we have little, or no, control over; that contribute to and affect behaviour in a school context. The way some children are treated at home – dysfunctionality in the home environment; structural and generational poverty and parental long-term unemployment; lack of positive guidance; discipline; values and role models; the amount and kind of television that even very young children watch; abusive "relationships"; poor nutrition; substance abuse of parent(s) (or siblings) – are all aspects of a child's life that have an impact on the child's behaviour at school. We cannot *control* those influences, structural factors and impacting relationships in a child's home environment. It took me a while as a younger teacher to really appreciate this frustrating truth. It is also of little help to keep whingeing about these factors: "If only …".

Our emphasis and energy is better placed supporting the student, in their ongoing welfare and learning while they are with us at school. Where, and when, we can support their welfare out of school we will (particularly if the child is "at risk"). This does not mean we are unsympathetic to those factors noted earlier. Indeed, there are occasions when we can hardly imagine how some of our students cope, how they stay as sane as they do. It means we avoid:

- *blaming* home environments for the child's disruptive behaviour at school
- too easily *excusing* the child's disruptive behaviour because "he comes from a difficult home"
- too easily making the child the "victim" of what we may believe are simply *causative* pathologies; that is, "he *is this way* because he comes from a difficult home and has a dysfunctional parent, and dysfunctional siblings and … therefore he *can't really help* his behaviour or *can't really change*".

It is important to recognise that while significant disruptive, and challenging, patterns of behaviour clearly have a contribution from family dynamics, structural poverty and abuse (how could they not?) a student's disruptive behaviour at school *is also learned in context*. Negative behaviour is also reinforced when parents and teachers easily "excuse", over-service or reinforce significant patterns of disruptive and challenging behaviour. It is hard not to get impatient with such students or even get angry and shout at such students. In a kind of reinforcing, "socially cybernetic loop", adult behaviour can reinforce the child's attentional and power-seeking behaviour.

Yes, it is understandable that some teachers will shout or even yell at students who frequently roll around on the mat; who make animal noises; or who walk away while the teacher is talking to them; or call out "all the time"; or hide under tables and refuse to join in, or task-avoid and task-refuse ("It's rubbish!!"; "I hate it!!"; "Can't make me!!"; "It's shit!!"); or swear and yell at their teachers; or push and shove and hassle other children in order to get adult attention.

It is hard, as a busy teacher – with 25 *other* students – to take time to reflect on what we currently do when managing such children, or what we can do to help such children *learn* to behave more thoughtfully, positively and cooperatively. Any reflection and any workable plan for such students needs to be developed on a team basis, or even a whole-school basis.

A team approach to individual behaviour plans

The key elements of any team approach to working with students who present with EBD include the following:

■ There should be a well established time-out plan (p. 149f). There are students who can easily, even quickly, "hold a class to ransom". When a significant pattern of behaviour is affecting fundamental rights in the classroom a teacher needs *immediate* time-out support (as does the rest of the class). While we often think of the disruptive child as taking time out, the teacher (and class) also need cool-off time, and calming time, from such insistent, or even dangerous behaviour.

■ *Teacher time out*, in a crisis, can also include a senior colleague withdrawing several disruptive students from the classroom to calm and settle the rest of the students (see p. 226).

■ With very disruptive – and challenging – students we have found it helpful to "relocate" the child in another class for one or two periods a week to give the regular class teacher a breather. This "relocation" involves the child having a set time period, with set work, in another teacher's room. It is to be distinguished from time out.

■ Develop a case-supervision approach with the student. A "case-supervisor" is a teacher who works with the child one-to-one on their behaviour by developing an *individual behaviour plan*. This plan is then communicated to, and utilised by, all the colleagues who teach (or support) that student.

At primary level such case-supervision is normally conducted by the grade teacher. At secondary level "case-supervisors" are normally senior teachers who are given dedicated time-release – and who have responsibility – for working with students who present with EBD behaviours. Such teachers will be selected for their ability and skill in rapport building, communication and behaviour therapy. They also need to be colleagues who are well respected by staff and students alike (Rogers 2006b).

It is also important to consider the ethical probity of any one-to-one settings where a teacher spends some time "alone" with a student. If the student concerned is a female it is wise to appoint a female teacher as the ongoing case-supervisor, and a male case-supervisor for a male student.

Case-supervision

In working with students described (or diagnosed) as EBD, it is unhelpful to leave each teacher to come up with their own strategies and approaches. It is more effective to take a collegial approach; not blaming any one teacher that they can't cope with or manage Jason, or Troy, or Melissa.

It also won't help to blame the parents. We need their understanding and support. While this does not mean that we do not communicate an honest appraisal of a child's disruptive behaviour, it does mean that such appraisal needs a cooperative approach and not a blame profile (Rogers 2009).

When considering case supervision we begin with a *behaviour profile* of the student with contributions from all adults who work with the student in the school setting:

- A behaviour profile needs to include how *frequently* a child calls out; butts in; wanders; pushes in line; exhibits low-frustration tolerance behaviours; and so on; how *intensively* he calls out; butts in; wanders ...; and how *generally* he exhibits such frequently disruptive behaviour across all teachers and all classes. It is also important to determine if the behaviour is *durable* (all lessons, every day?) or is it more a "bad-day syndrome" pattern, occurring *some* days more than others?
- In working with such students, early intervention is crucial. As soon as a "pattern" of disruptive behaviour is clearly present (in terms of *frequency*, *generality*, *durability* and *intensity*) the senior staff will need to support teachers in developing a collegial plan. This plan will involve both structural colleague support and case-supervision. *Structural support* involves time-out plans, classroom rotation (see "relocation" above) and timetabling meetings for case-supervisors and teachers to discuss and plan.

Case-supervision involves a key teacher working with the child, one to one, on a long-term basis. The case-supervisor's role involves, in the main, developing a personal – individual – behaviour plan with the student. The case-supervisor also communicates that plan to all teachers in the team, explaining the purpose and elements of the plan, and discussing discipline, encouragement and time-out options within the plan. The case-supervisor also liaises with parents to explain how this plan will support their child's learning at school, and invites parental understanding, cooperation and support.

This individual plan emphasises key behaviours that will enable the child to improve their social interaction (and acceptance by their peers), and their on-task learning.

The plan further involves teaching and reinforcing those behaviours with the child through individualised modelling, rehearsal and encouragement. The case-supervisor *teaches* the child behaviours such as:

- how to enter the room thoughtfully (without loudness, pushing, shoving, or "grandstanding")
- going to their seat, or sitting on the carpet space (infants), without hassling others' personal space
- how to organise the workspace (table/desk) thoughtfully
- how to *focus* on a learning task, and *develop* a learning task (within a given lesson)

- how to put their hand up without calling out during whole-class teaching time and on-task time
- using partner-voice in on-task learning time
- how to better manage frustration and anger. It is the teaching of these *specific* expressions of positive behaviour that are – in effect – the student's plan. The case-supervisor's role is to discuss the child's present disruptive behaviours in light of their expected behaviour and then *teach* the student – through the plan – to be self-aware and self-monitoring within the new and required behaviours.

Key elements in developing individual behaviour management plans

Case supervision involves a dedicated, one-to-one approach with the student over time. The key elements are set out in Figure 6.1.

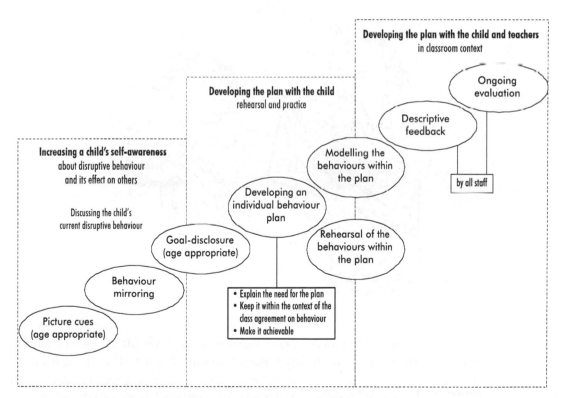

Figure 6.1 Key entry points in behaviour recovery: developing an individual behaviour management plan

■ *Picture cues* are often used in individual plans at early years and middle primary level, and with older students on a case-by-case basis. To help the student's self-awareness about their behaviour, and to enhance dialogue with the student about their behaviour the case-supervisor prepares simple drawings of the child's disruptive behaviour and also the expected, appropriate behaviour. "Have a look at this picture … *Who do you think this is, Nicky?*" Students almost always nominate the picture of the student (rolling on the mat, or calling out, or being loud …) as themselves.

The teacher then asks the child what they (the child in question) are *doing* in the picture. The teacher avoids asking the child, at this point, why they are calling out, or rolling on the carpet, and so on. In the background of this picture the teacher will have drawn (in smaller figures) other children with sad, or concerned faces and also an adult's face (the teacher) with similarly sad or concerned face to indicate social concern and disapproval.

These drawings of students being disruptive (in such plans) can be simple stick figure drawings. The student will still nominate themself as the disrupting student.

The teacher can then refer to the 'social disapproval' displayed in the picture cue (the sad or concerned faces of teacher and students), and discuss, briefly, the effect of the child's disruptive behaviour on other students and the teacher. *Mirroring* has been discussed earlier (p. 108f). The teacher *briefly* displays the child's typical distracting/disruptive behaviour and invites the student to see what their *behaviour* looks like when they call out, or push and shove or are talking loudly, or are leaning back in their seats and so on.

My colleagues and I have used "mirroring" approaches with every age group. It is important to use such an approach with the child's permission ("Do you mind if I ...?" or "I'd like to show you what it looks like when you ...", or – with older students – "Can I give you a demo? – It will be clearer if I do"). If children refuse (which happens very rarely) the teacher will utilise the picture as the focus for discussion.

As noted earlier, we need to keep any "mirroring" *brief*; physically *step away* (having shown the student what the disruptive behaviour looks like) and *refer back* to the behaviour: "*That's* what it looks like when you ...". Many boys (particularly) will laugh when teachers mirror the student's typically disruptive behaviour; that is normal (and natural!).

There are, I believe, some limits to mirroring.[4] Personally I never mirror back to a student hostile and aggressive swearing, or throwing furniture. In these cases it is enough to pick up a chair, pretend to throw and put it down. That is ample. A simulated "f" (a forceful, fricative, *sound*), without the full word, to 'illustrate' what we mean by swearing is sufficient.

It is also helpful to briefly refer to the class behaviour agreement (or specific rule) and ask, "What are you supposed to be doing when …?" This question can lead into the plan (see cartoon on previous page – the bottom picture).

- With older children (upper primary age on) *goal-disclosure* can help raise self-awareness about behaviour. The teacher will then discuss the student's disruptive behaviour in terms of their attentional or power-seeking goals (p. 179f).

- Develop the plan itself. A second picture illustrates the expected, desired, appropriate behaviour (as contrasted to the first picture).

The teacher discusses what is different in this picture. For infant and middle primary age, simple pictures keep the attentional focus in the discussion. "So, Nicky, what are you doing in *this* picture?" or "What's *different*, here, in this picture? What are you *doing* here?" The teacher then draws the discussion around to the appropriate behaviour.

Pictures (as an aide-memoire on a small postcard-sized sheet) can be used with older children, too, where appropriate to the child, age and context.

Above is a plan I developed with a Year 8 student who was frequently loud, and restless with his voice and hands (p. 189). He had a habit of clicking his knuckles, in part to get attention and, probably, in part because he was struggling with the work – an avoidance behaviour.

I had drawn a simple drawing (prior to our meeting) and we discussed his behaviour in terms of possible attention (p. 179f). He rather liked the drawing and asked me if he could have a copy. The actual plan for behaviour change involved:

– keeping his hands quiet and using them to work (with writing)

– a modified work-task – he struggled with particular subjects and we were able to negotiate some goal based learning tasks with the teachers concerned (and the heads of department)

– a small *table pencil-case*, which helped him have a less cluttered desk. Instead of a large pencil case full of bits and pieces (as well as defunct pens) we gave him a smaller pencil case to house a blue pen, a red pen, a pencil – no sharpener – and an eraser

– the (postcard-sized) drawing acted as his aide-memoire, as well as a record of his plan. He kept a copy in his school diary. Each teacher who taught him also had a copy of his plan and was encouraged to give him descriptive feed-back (privately) during the lesson, and at the end of the lesson wherever possible

– a twice weekly meeting between the case-supervisor and the student to talk about his progress with *his* plan – we always emphasise the plan as the *student's* plan.

Each teacher's role is to support and encourage the child's ownership of his responsible behaviour *within the plan.*

- It is also important that the case-supervisor *models* the behaviour expressed in the plan. In the countless one-to-one sessions my colleagues and I have had with students over the years we have sat on the floor (with infant-age children) and modelled how to have eyes and ears facing to the front of the room; we have modelled partner-voice; personal space awareness; how to say sorry; how to put your hand up without calling out; and even how to manage feelings of frustration and anger when they come.

- The case-supervisor then encourages the student to *practise* the behaviour (the plan); this involves rehearsing the behaviours several times (one-to-one with their case-supervisor).

    During such rehearsals the teacher can fine-tune aspects of behaviour such as "personal space", "hands in lap", "keep hands and feet to yourself when sitting on the mat", "partner-voice", "how to line up", "how to move through the room without annoying others" "how to get teacher help during on-task time" …

- Each teacher in the year team who teaches the student (in question) needs to be made aware of the student's plan and any special cueing, or disciplinary approaches. For example, for a student who is particularly loud, in helping the child to focus on partner-voice the case-supervisor will rehearse simple, non-verbal, reminder cues – perhaps the teacher simulating the turning down of volume. This minimises teachers having to over-use *verbal* disciplinary reminders.

    Each subject, or specialist teacher also has the same copy of the plan as the student (the visual aide-memoire). If the student is disruptive in class time, teachers are asked to positively remind the student (particularly during on-task learning time) about their plan: "Remember your plan", or even "What's your plan? What should you be doing now in your plan?" It can help as a disciplinary, *and* encouragement, focus.

- The student's behaviour is monitored, and tracked – within the plan – across the year level.

    All teachers working with the student are encouraged to give the student descriptive feedback at several points in the lesson particularly during the on-task phase of the lesson (as a typical plan will involve "time-on-task behaviours"). This encourages the student when they are behaving thoughtfully within their plan.

Such encouragement is best given "privately", or as a quiet aside, where possible (that is, out of direct hearing of others): "You remembered your plan; you used your partner-voice ...". The *descriptive* feedback focuses on what the child did (in terms of their behaviour, "their plan") that made a difference. We avoid global praise like "fantastic", "brilliant", "great", "wonderful" (p. 129f).

Sometimes a brief non-verbal cue will encourage a child back on task: a smile when the child is working within the plan; a thumbs-up; an OK sign. Such non-verbal encouragers are even appropriate in the more public, whole-class teaching settings.

■ Once (even twice) a week the case-supervisor will meet with the student to go over the plan (or any new plans), particularly focusing on: "What part of the plan is easiest [for the student] and *why*?"; "What part is hardest and *why*?" The *why* question, in this case, helps the child to be more self-reflective and increase their self-monitoring behaviour.

Plans can be adapted, developed and fine-tuned in these meetings.

Any such plan is a means to an end: the end being to help the child become more responsible, more self-regulating in respect of their behaviour as it affects others around them (including the teacher).

■ In *evaluating* the plan case-supervisors work with their collegial peers to determine if there is any positive change in frequency and intensity of disruptive behaviour; whether the student is still needing time out; and if there is any stability and generalising of the expected behaviours.

There are some students for whom no amount of one-to-one time, or behaviour therapy seems to help or affect changes in their disruptive behaviour at the school. In these cases we will have to work at alternatives to their schooling outside a mainstream school setting. No student can be allowed to continually, persistently, disrupt the learning and safety of others in a school. Alternatives to mainstream schooling in such cases are not only important for the welfare of the other children in the school; they are also important for the welfare of staff.

Inappropriate or "bad" language and swearing

In a press article on swearing recently, we were told that "90% of Britons are not offended by swearing". "The average Briton utters fourteen expletives a day ..." (One wonders how they get such an exact number?) It was – perhaps – no surprise that " ... men admitted to being the more foul-mouthed gender ...", though the article goes on to state that "83% of women" swore on a daily basis. The journalist concludes that the British are not so conservative in their public discourse (David Manchester, *Daily Mail*, 16 January 2009).

Not all "bad" language or swearing is the same. Even adults sometimes (sometimes?) swear out of frustration. Even teachers (teachers?) swear in staff rooms, in the photocopy room or after the hostile parent has finally left. Whether we like it or not, swearing, as it has been traditionally understood (or sometimes, "bad" language), is more common today in schools than in times past.

For some people swearing is even passé. Certainly in many films, books and television shows it has become a "norm" in descriptive dialogue as well as in expressions of frustration and anger.

I was discussing issues of playground behaviour with some "dinner ladies" (midday supervisors) one day and the issue of swearing cropped up, as it often does.

"What kind of swearing?", I asked.

"What do you mean?", they said, initially puzzled.

"Do the students swear at you or each other?"

"Sometimes at each other – very rarely at us", they noted.

"So, what is the most frequent kind of swearing?"

It turned out that students were using swearing ("shit", "f—ing", "a—hole") mainly in conversations, or frustration outbursts in game-playing. Should we then distinguish between "kinds" of swearing – or "bad" language? If so, why and how? Thoughtful teachers distinguish between a child who mutters, "Shit" (*sotto voce*) out of frustration and a student who swears *at* a fellow student or teacher. Some swearing is also "quietly" muttered, in passing, when the student walks past, or away from the teacher ("wanker", "a—hole", "dick-head", "bastard") – do they want us to hear such swearing? – they may well want their classmates to hear.

Swearing as hostile intent directed at another person (student or teacher) needs to be dealt with immediately by the teacher – firmly, without aggression (this only feeds the latent hostility or anger): "That language is unacceptable here. When you've calmed down we'll sort this issue out"; or "Michael (...), We don't swear *at anyone* here. Full stop." Block any argumentative appeals as to why they swore at so and so (or even why they swore at you!). Avoid pointing, gesticulating and hostile hand movements. An open, blocking hand movement helps to assert the firm voice without aggressive intent. Direct the student to take informal, or formal, cool-off time if necessary (p. 149). It is pointless asking (or demanding from) the student *reasons* why they swore (at you, the teacher, or at a fellow student). In the immediate, emotional, moment the teacher needs to communicate (and enable) calmness alongside appropriate assertion.

I have known teachers appeal to a swearing student: "Why are you swearing at me? I'm not nasty to you am I? What have I done to hurt you?" This non-assertive stance, expressed in a "please be nice to me" voice, is counter-productive and often feeds latent student attention and power.

In the immediate emotional arousal, when hostile swearing is present, it is important to keep the assertive statement brief; focus on the issue or rule (about language or respect); direct the student to take some cool-off time and follow the issue up *later* with a third party (a colleague) for support if necessary.

Younger children will need a direct, immediate rule reminder: "We don't swear like that in our class." Such behaviour may need to occasion time out in the room, or out of the room if the child is physically hostile or aggressive.

In the immediate emotional moment we avoid long explanations about *why* the language is unacceptable and resist the moral lecture, "Is that the kind of language you use at home?!" I've actually heard teachers say that *and* I've heard students reply in the affirmative.

If a student swears *sotto voce* ("on the run" as it were, "under their breath"), such swearing can sometimes be tactically ignored in the immediate, emotional, moment and followed-up later when the student has calmed down. It depends, in part, on how *sotto* the *voce* was (did we really hear a frustrated, loud, whispered "wanker"?) and in part on the audience reaction. It is often enough to say something like: "Paul," – use the child's first name because it gains some attentional focus, and personalises the adult–child discipline role – "I heard what you said. I know you're feeling annoyed (or upset). I don't speak about you like that. I don't expect you to speak about me like that." If he argues what he said was not said *to* you, quietly remind him of the rule. Then direct the child back to the task or to what he should be doing now or to cool-off time if necessary.

If we can direct the student aside for a brief chat (using similar language to above), even better. If other students have heard the muttered swearing they need to see us do something.

We can sometimes add, in the one-to-one aside, "David, I heard you swear at Paul earlier …". I've had students look puzzled here (because they don't always think what they say is swearing). I sometimes add in the swearword they used, or even write it down. "Look, I know you were uptight with Craig before [this briefly tunes in to how the student was probably feeling] but we have a class rule about respectful language …".

In a particularly challenging high school in the western suburbs of Melbourne I was teaching a Year 9 English class. As I was moving around the room (in the on-task phase of the lesson) I overheard one of the more vocal (and time-wasting) lads call a girl near him a "f—ing bitch"; just above *sotto voce*. I knew they were friends but I could hear the frustration in his voice. I went over and said something like, "Look, Adam, I heard what you said to Belinda ...". I pushed the piece of paper on which I had written down his swearing language across to him.

"I didn't say that!" He sounded annoyed.

I added, "I heard you Adam ..."

He explained, "I tell you I didn't say that. I said f— off, you bitch. I didn't say f—ing bitch!" He was upset that I'd got the words wrong not that he'd used such offensive language!

The annoying thing was that when I called them both back later (after class) to engage in some very brief reminding, Belinda seemed unfazed. She shrugged her shoulders and said, "... it's just Adam ... that's how he is ...".

Part of the challenge of addressing swearing with some students (adolescents most notably) is the "no-big-dealness" of it all. It can often help to raise the issue of swearing and offensive language more widely with the whole-class group through a classroom meeting (Rogers 2006b). Ideally class teachers should have covered the issue of interpersonal communication; mutual respect and careless, thoughtless, disrespectful and abusive language within the classroom agreement (p. 40f). A classroom meeting can *reaffirm* the issue of respectful language and reassess "how we communicate with one another here".

> Swearing, at infant level, may sometimes mean something quite different to a child's perception. One of my colleagues recounts the occasion when a 5-year-old student came up to him with a most serious look on her face and said, quietly, "Sir ... Con said the F word."
>
> "Did he Maria – really?"
>
> "Yes he did."
>
> "Are you sure?"
>
> "Yes ... the F word."
>
> The teacher thought he would check and quietly asked, "Maria ... *what* did he say?"
>
> Maria replied, with the utmost seriousness, in a whisper; "He said, he said – *stewpid!*"; and covered her mouth as if to say "sorry I had to tell you he used the F word [stewpid]"

Conversational swearing

It is not uncommon, even in primary schools, to hear "conversational swearing"; I even hear it sometimes in classrooms (and staffrooms): "Did you see that fantastic f—ing game the other f—ing day. Shit! How was the f—ing score they got, eh? The other team; they're rat shit!"

Should we ignore this kind of "swearing" in the playground? Should we relegate it to the argument of, "… that's the reality now. That's how it is today – it's just street language …"? I have heard this argument many times now – principally from non-educators. However a school is not a "street"; nor is a classroom a "street".

Ignoring such language (when we hear it on playground duty or even in the classroom as a *sotto voce* exchange) can easily send the message that we do not care how our students speak, or that such language is OK; or is even the norm (as a conversational exchange).

Of course such language is "street-language", but acceptance can easily excuse, even ratify, language norming. The issue for educators is how can we encourage our students to converse without lazy recourse to "f—ing and blinding …"?

A group of students are discussing the latest "f—ing film" they saw recently; some action-packed thriller with serious maim, gore and gratuitous … (well, *gratuitous anything* really). You can hear the descriptive qualifiers quite clearly, several yards away. It won't help if the teacher charges in moralising: "Oi!! I could hear *every* word you said!! Is that the kind of language you use at home – is it? You disgusting creatures!!"

It may well be they use such language at home, but a judgemental appeal to "home environment" goes down like a lead balloon and may, in fact, get a hostile reaction.

The issue of "conversational swearing" can be addressed by a quiet, firm, acknowledgement, followed by a rule reminder about use of language (assuming the issue of thoughtful and respectful language has been explored across the school).

Sometimes a humourous question, or aside, can give a bit of self-checking. The teacher walks over and casually greets the students.

"How's it going?"

The returned, non-verbal body language suggests, "Well, we were going kind of OK till you walked over – really." Their *actual* reply is, "OK." Do they sense their "swearing" is heard?)

The teacher leans a little towards them (as if to suggest he doesn't want others to hear) and asks a question about the "*eff*ing film" they had momentarily been discussing (without using the actual words they used). "Seen any interesting films lately beginning with 'F'?"

A couple of the students catch on with a weary smile and sigh. The teacher walks off with a pleasant "goodbye for now". Relaxed vigilance.

If some students habitually, and loudly, converse with strong swearing it is worth following up with these students at a later stage (one to one) to discuss their behaviour and engage their responsibility for the way they communicate in our school.

Most conversational swearing is an *unreflective habit*; some (of course) is peer-group, positional, posturing, "Listen to me being 'tough', 'with-it' ...", 'cool', 'just like everybody else' ...".

If the issue of conversational, or banter swearing is typically frequent (particularly at upper primary and secondary level) it can help to run classroom meetings in tutor groups (or grade classes) to raise the issue: define what is meant by inappropriate or disrespectful language and swearing; discuss how feelings are affected by what we say and how we say it; and re-address core rights and responsibilities as they impact on what we say in relationships – that words are powerful for good or ill.

If you're not confident in conducting such a meeting, or if it is outside your experience, ask a colleague to discuss, plan and conduct the meeting with you.

Most of all it is getting a balance between language probity, and usage, thoughtful discipline and education and modelling. Our own modelling (as teachers) will go a long way in demonstrating that one can communicate frustration, even anger, without resorting to the lowest, "common", language denominator.

Reflection

- We have all worked with students who procrastinate and argue ... are you aware of how you engage argumentative students – particularly when they display "secondary behaviours"?
- How aware are you of how you typically communicate with challenging students – in the heat of the moment?
- Do you *always* follow up with challenging students (say beyond time-out referral, or referral to senior or SENCO colleague)?
- How does the discussion on "attentional" and "power-seeking" behaviours help in the understanding of challenging behaviours? How does it inform your practice?
- Within the support opportunities, and mechanisms, for challenging students and students with behaviour disorders in your school, what provision is made for case-supervision as explored on pp. 184–92?
- How does the discussion on swearing (within the distinctions noted in the text) inform and shape your practice? Do you distinguish the "distinctions" or

"types" of swearing in your school? What is your school's policy regarding bad language and swearing? How do we "raise" and "discuss" this issue with students generally? And one to one?

Notes

1. In a major research study (by H. Rudolph Schaffer) the point is made that, "… the *potential* (emphasis mine) of children to recover from early environmental stresses of a quite severe and lasting nature has been underestimated in the past and that a self-righting tendency analogous to that found in physical growth can, under certain circumstances at least, be seen in psychological development too …" (2000: 8, my emphasis).

2. The literature addressing challenging behaviours, and emotional-behavioural disorders, is increasingly using terms – now – such as attention deficit *spectrum* disorder; so too, autism *spectrum* disorder. This (obviously) acknowledges degrees of symptomatic behaviour within a diagnosed behaviour disorder.

   A helpful text that addresses a wide range of related issues regarding anti-social as well as challenging behaviour, and behaviour disorders in schools is the *Handbook of Emotional and Behavioural Difficulties* (Clough et al. 2005).

   In an essay on "The influences of the school contexts and processes on violence in American schools" (2005) (by Michael Furlong et al., cited in Clough et al. 2005) the point is made that we need to distinguish between "violence" and "disruption" and the reality that "school is a place where aggressive, antisocial youth congregate …". We also need to ascertain in what ways aggression "is, at least in part, caused by the dynamics of the school" (ibid.: 123). Furlong et al. give a summary of school violence trends indicating that there has been a trend towards "decrease of weapon possession and physical fights on school campuses" (ibid.: 125).

   There are a number of strategies in place in American, British, European and Australian schools that address bullying and aggressive and antisocial behaviours. These programmes range from welfare, breakfast clubs, and social skills, to mentoring programmes for disenchanted and at-risk young men and women. Some of these programmes are explored in Clough et al. (2005).

   There is, obviously, no single – or simple – solution to addressing challenging behaviour in schools – its genesis and likely expression is affected by many factors. We do know – from the research – that supportive school environments can, and do, provide a sane, normally safe, secure local learning *community* that can support and enable at-risk students (Rogers 2006a).

   A wonderful book for those engaged in supporting young adolescent males in schools is Celia Lashlie's book *"He'll Be OK: Growing Gorgeous Boys into Good Men"* (2005) (a silver medal winner).

For a teachers' text that utilises case studies – in very practical (and often very moving) ways – see *How To Manage Children's Challenging Behaviour* (2009), ed. B. Rogers. A series of essays written by English and Australian teachers working with very challenging children and classes (www.sagepublications.com).

I would also encourage high school, and pupil-referral unit, colleagues to explore the mentoring programmes for challenging boys developed from the work of The University Luton Vauxhall Centre for the Study of Crime. A study by De Montfort University (in Leicester) found that "over 70% of young offenders who had been mentored had not committed another crime six months later" (*Independent*, 7 June 2004).

The MAP (Mentor And Peers project) has had other positive reviews. Colleagues are encouraged to check www.esv.org.uk and De Montfort University.

3. The issue of harassment of teachers by students is addressed later in Chapter 8 (pp. 229–39).

4. My colleagues and I do not use mirroring approaches with children diagnosed with ASD. Such mirroring may unhelpfully confuse or upset them. We focus on directly teaching the required, necessary behaviours. (See also pp. 108–9 and 171–3.)

Chapter 7

Managing anger
in ourselves and others

That carries anger as the flint bears fire;
who, much enforced, shows a hasty spark.
Shakespeare, *Julius Caesar* (4, iii)

Managing anger

England is full of roundabouts – or so it seems to me. On one of my trips to the UK, a few years ago, I hired a car at Heathrow airport and was beetling down towards a suburb called Basildon (and a hotel). I had a map, but I was lost. At one of the large roundabouts I sat and waited to get into the circling mass of cars. To my right an old car pulled up; and with a brief glance I noticed two young lads, both drinking large cans of lager and smoking roll-ups. The lad nearest to my right-hand window wound his window down and said, "Oi – get going alright!" Apparently he could see it was easy for me to race into the traffic throng from the cusp of this roundabout. Sitting in this new car, with cars speeding past me, I was much more cautious.

My caution seemed to really annoy them; I was closer to the entry of the round-about than they were. He called out again, "Just go; f—ing go, alright!!"

I thought their anger was disproportionate to the 20–30 seconds of caution on my part. I looked at him and shrugged (as if to say, "be fair, fellas – I'm waiting for a break in the traffic ...").

"F— you!" was the last I heard from the two lads and they shot off (having "gunned" the car) into the roundabout. But as they shot past my car they hit my right hand mirror and it did a 360° turn – Bang!

Having entered the roundabout – at last – I took a turn off to what I hoped would be Basildon. As I motored on I saw the two lads on the hard shoulder, standing looking at the damage to their car (where they had hit my mirror). I pulled over and parked about 20–25 yards in front of them, and got out (hoping I *might* get their number for potential insurance purposes ... an unwise move perhaps, but ...).

As I was "casually" examining my twisted side mirror, I noted (out of the corner of my eye) one of the lads walking towards me, with his can of lager. He looked tense; perhaps he thought I was going to create a scene. I turned side on (as casually as I could) and said (still looking as if I was examining my mirror) "You OK?"

He said, surprised, "Yeah."

"I'm glad." I replied. "Your car OK?"

"Yeah." Still surprised, even wary.

"My mirror is jammed." I didn't verbally attack him, or judge him, or blame him (notwithstanding the fact that he'd arrogantly hit the mirror although I'm sure he didn't "mean" it).

He looked at the mirror – "It's jammed!"

("Course it's bleedin' jammed!", I felt like saying). I didn't. A bit of "partial agreement", I thought might be apposite. "You're not wrong, it's jammed." I was conscious of keeping my voice calm, relaxed, not too much direct eye contact.

He seemed less tense now. I was hoping my calmness would trigger some calmness in him.

"You can fix that easy," he said.

"Can you?" I wasn't too sure.

By this time the other lad had come over to see "what was happening". I said "Hi." He grunted something. I added "I'm checking my mirror …". He also noted the "bleedin obvious".

"It's jammed …"

The other lad chipped in, "They're on a spring – you just pull it out and it goes back in the housing right. I can fix it if you like." They seemed marginally affable now. I hadn't verbally attacked them – it was as if we both had some basic human needs going at this point; we were beginning to see each other as more than a mere hindrance on the road.

He pulled at the mirror, groaned and grunted. I was hoping he wouldn't pull it out of its socket! He let go. It clanked back into place.

"Shit! Fixed it!" He seemed surprised and pleased.

Neither had admitted blame or even apologised. I didn't force it either. I looked at the fixed mirror – a few scratches on the plastic housing. No sweat!

"Good on you, fellas – thanks." They must have picked up on the Aussie accent. The first smile from the two lads.

"You an Australian?"

"Yes." I felt like singing the theme song from *Neighbours*. I didn't. "Fellas, wonder if I could ask a favour." I noticed a little tenseness (perhaps I was going to ask for their license number). "I'm trying to find a hotel in Basildon." I explained where I was seeking to go to.

"I know where that is!" He ground his ciggie on the gravel. "It's …" he started to explain.

"Could you draw me a map, fellas?"

"Nope – we'll take you there. You follow us – we'll show you where to go". I had a momentary thought they might lead me up the garden path. But no – they didn't. They went out of their way to help.

While I'd never advise stopping in such a situation, I know the situation could have been worse had I just let vent with some macho posturing.

I followed them to the hotel. As our cars parted on their different paths they bipped their car horn. I think this was their version of "we're sorry".

While there is never any guarantee that our behaviour can positively affect another's in tense situations like this I believe that it helps if we consciously calm ourselves before we seek to calm the other person, and take some thought of how we communicate with tense, frustrated or angry people.

Frustration and anger – in ourselves and others

Anger is a very powerful emotion. It can disturb, even destroy, positive working relationships between ourselves and our colleagues, and ourselves and our students.

I have seen, and heard, teachers yelling, even screaming, at individuals and whole classes as their frustration, then anger reaches boiling point. I have intervened between teachers and students when I have sensed that the teacher is a few seconds away from hitting a student or getting into a self-defeating conflict. I have seen teachers so eaten up with anger that they behave in hostile and aggressive ways to peers and students alike. Anger, however, can also validate our feelings and needs – particularly our feelings for justice –and it can help communicate those feelings and needs.

Understanding our anger

It is important to *understand* our own frustration and anger; to understand those situations, circumstances and people who lower our tolerance to frustration; to understand what we *characteristically* do in such situations, how we react and respond and manage our anger as well as seeking to help others to manage their anger. We can hardly do such reflection in the heat of the emotional moment. It is, however, worth generally reflecting on the emotion of frustration and anger in terms of our role and relationships as teachers.

Aristotle (in his *Ethics*) has taught us that "we must not forget that it is human to be painfully affected by anger and to find revenge sweet" (Thompson's translation 1969: I, 100). He is not saying we should find revenge sweet; he is talking about the human tendency expressed by the familiar (and destructive) epithet, "Don't get angry, get even". A teacher with such a view of retributive justice is doomed to a short career!

Aristotle (in his *Ethics*) goes on, "Neither are we praised or blamed for the way we feel. A man is not praised or blamed for being angry; it is for being angry in a particular way ..." (Thompson 1969: II, 63). He makes clear what we know in our more reflective moments: anger (or at least frustration) is a feeling we often *can't help*; it just comes – often when we're tired, hassled or trying to do ten things at once.

He also distinguishes between the *feeling* of frustration and anger, which we can't help or stop (like when we're in a traffic jam on the M25 and we're in a hurry and we forgot how useless a road system it is at peak times and so on) and the *behaviour* that results from our anger. He adds, "Being angry, or frightened, is something we can't help but our virtues are in a manner expressions of our will; at any rate there is an element of will in their formation" (ibid.: 81–2).

The *learned* bit in anger is what we do *when* we're angry. We have learned to get angry in certain ways; perhaps we have unhelpful habits of anger-behaviour, but we've learned these habits over time even though such learning may not be readily conscious. Aristotle goes further and argues that there is an element of "will" in our angry "behaviour". He links the exercise of our will to how helpful/unhelpful, how constructively or destructively we express our anger. Frustration and anger lie on a continuum from irritation through to outrage and even aggressive anger. It is an emotion we have to learn to live with whatever the contributing causes. The "element of will", the "expression of our will" that occasions any "virtue"[1] in what we do when we're angry.

> Anger may be produced by a variety of causes – but, however that may be, it is the man who is angry on the right occasions and with the right people at the right moment and for the right length of time who wins our commendation. (Ibid.: 127–8)

For Aristotle there is a 'rightness', an appropriateness, even a virtue in how we manage and communicate our anger. Is this a tall order? Of course! Aristotle never denies the humanity of our anger. What he is saying is that there are some fundamentals about the "rightness" of anger and how we express it.

The psychiatrist Scott-Peck makes the point that to "function successfully" in this complex world of ours we need to "possess the capacity not only to express our anger but also not to express it" (1978: 67).

We live in an age, a time, where aspects of living are affected by immediacy – instant response gratification (in food, television, perhaps even in relationships), even instant "knowledge"; well at least instant information. *Knowledge* and information are not – of course – the same thing (The World-Wide Graffiti-Board).

Frustration-tolerance is a necessary life "skill"; traffic jams; queues; the phone on-hold time; hospital emergency wards ... *Learning* how to moderate, manage and communicate our concerns, frustrations and anger is a skill. Some people may be more phlegmatic and sanguine rather than choleric ("Get out of the way you b——!! Drive properly!!"). The rest of us probably had to learn how better to manage our frustration and anger. What are some of those learnings?

We are well aware – for example – of those occasions where a verbal outburst would (in hindsight) send the right message at the wrong time and, perhaps, severely damage a relationship with a friend, colleague or student. While there are times when an immediate brief, passionate expression of anger is right, at other times it is better, wiser, says Scott-Peck, "to express it only after much deliberation and self-evaluation" (1978: 67); as when we write an angry letter.

> ## "I lost my temper!"
> A frequently used phrase expressed by adults and young persons alike is, "I just lost my temper; that's all!!" We say this, later, to explain the high arousal that occurred at the time we were angry and to explain why we expressed our anger by shouting, yelling or being nasty or vindictive (unintentionally we hope).
> It's an interesting choice of words. We don't actually "lose" our temper; we "find" it. The issue, really, is what we do when we've – very quickly – found it.

■ Anger is normal; at times it's more than normal, it is *right*. There are occasions when justice demands that we clearly, unequivocally, communicate our anger to others.

On many occasions, though, our anger is more typically the outcome of life's frustrations, irritations and what Lazarus (1981) calls "daily hassles"; or what Shakespeare (in *Hamlet*) called "the thousand natural shocks that flesh is heir to". Shakespeare wrote "natural" shocks – and who wouldn't get frustrated (even angry) at intransigent, lazy, rude or arrogant student behaviour? Why wouldn't we get angry with an insensitive, unfeeling, "ill-considered" report from an Ofsted inspector (unlike, we hope, most Ofsted reports)?

It is important to be aware of the situations, circumstances and people that lower our tolerance to frustration. The issue of "secondary behaviours" (noted in Chapter 1) is typical of an annoying, even stressful, irritant for most teachers: when students speak in sulky, pouty, insouciant tones of voice; when their body language indicates they don't care (the shrugged shoulders, the eyes to the ceiling, the drawn out sighs). Awareness helps; so does skill. We can also learn more effective ways to manage and communicate our anger and to help others when they are angry.

I've talked with young men who say they "can't help getting [aggressively] angry when ...". What they mean is that they can't help *characteristically* shouting; being immature; or mean-spirited or aggressive *when* they're angry – as if men are somehow "hard-wired" in their social biology to only get angry in loud or aggressively physical ways. Angry *behaviour* is learned. Unhelpful, self-defeating even destructive angry *thinking* and angry *behaviour* can be unlearned, and other (more helpful and appropriate and constructive) anger behaviours can be learned.

■ It is important to distinguish between anger as an emotion and the behaviour that comes from anger – particularly *impulse behaviour*. Anger is not of itself bad – how can it be? And we ought not to convey to children that they are somehow "bad" for having angry feelings or emotions, or "getting angry". As Conrad Baars points out, "it is necessary to realise that the high intensity of an emotion does not make it 'bad', even though its consequences may not be beneficial for that person or others around him" (1979: 68).

Learning to understand and guide our emotions with thought and skill will, in good part, help determine any constructive behaviour that proceeds from our anger.

■ It can be helpful to distinguish between annoyance, irritation, being "cheesed off" and frustration; and between frustration, high frustration and anger; and between anger and aggression.

Anger is at the very high end of emotional arousal. Imagine, for example, saying to a student "I'm angry that you haven't finished your homework!" or "I'm angry because you're late!" Such behaviours (in students) might merit *annoyance*, or even annoyed concern from teachers, but do they merit *anger*? If we easily, quickly and characteristically get angry over such minor issues, when we *really* need to communicate anger we lose the emotional weight (or even the moral weight) of that which we might need to appropriately get angry about. Overuse of the word *angry*, or *anger*, will tend to devalue its social, relational meaning and behavioural currency.

■ Allied to the previous point is the notion of "getting angry" on issues that matter, or issues that count. In this way students can see, and hear, the relative justice in our expressed passion and behaviour.

For example, if a supply teacher is badly treated by your class, and on your return from the flu you hear a litany of serious complaints from the head-teacher about "your class" or "your students"; this is an occasion where a clear, unambiguous communication of our anger (even disgust) is appropriate.

"I am *extremely* disappointed and angry about what I've heard from the principal today about members of our class and the way some students here behaved towards the relief teacher [name the teacher]. I cannot believe *anyone* in our class, or school, would say and do the sort of things some of you did when you ...".

In communicating our anger we need to be specific and clear about *what* we are angry *about*. Avoid using the language the students may have used – swearing or harassing language – while not shirking the inappropriate or even offensive language they used.

"I know it wasn't all of you. Those who said those things will be meeting with me, and the principal, soon (one at a time). I'm also appalled that many of you let others, *in our class*, say those disgusting things and behave in the way they did. I think of you as responsible, capable, people."

Whenever I've had to speak like this to a class (thankfully rare) it is said with passion – with a firm and *unambiguously* serious voice; the students sit quietly with a look of perceptible chagrin. I suspect they are saying "we're in *really* serious poo here"!

In a case like this it is important that the teacher makes clear that it is the behaviour that is totally unacceptable and that you (the teacher) will be "having a classroom meeting later to see if we can repair and rebuild the damage created by your behaviour yesterday".

When speaking to a *group* of students like this:
– Be specific and as brief as possible.
– Make clear that you are not angry with *all* the members of "our class".
– Do not attack them: "You pack of animals, you're no better than pigs! Yes pigs!!" Tempting as such an attack might be, that is hardly going to win their understanding and cooperation; address their *behaviour*.
– Work for some group restitution *and* an understanding that next time a supply teacher comes I expect that "We (all of us) will ...". Then develop with the class a normative "convention" about working with supply teachers.

Communicating our anger: some fundamental understandings

It is difficult, very difficult, in the heat of the moment to decide what we might do or say when we're angry. Some prior reflection, and general anger management awareness can help.

■ Briefly calm yourself before you seek to communicate to the other person *what* you are angry about and why. This sounds deceptively easy; it isn't. Take a few calming breaths, but not too deep because the other party may think you're hyperventilating! Count a few seconds in your head, then communicate what is necessary. It may be helpful, then, to take cool-off-time (withdraw) and, later, work on possible resolution. It is unproductive to try to resolve the anger-arousing issues or concepts *at the point one is feeling angry*. It is enough to briefly communicate.

Brad Bushman (Iowa State University) has suggested that mere cathartic expression of anger can increase habituation of angry or aggressive behaviours. In his study (involving some 600 volunteers) he observed that those who had practised calmness before expressing their anger were less aggressive in their expression of anger.[2]

■ Focus *briefly* on the issue, circumstance, behaviour you are angry about: "I am angry *because* you …"; "I get angry *when* …". If you are only annoyed, or irritated, use that word rather than "angry".

■ Address the issue, rather than attacking the other person. This is particularly important when addressing angry children or their parents. ("Who the hell do you think you are!! Don't you ever speak to me like that …!!").[3]

If we need to use assertive language our assertion needs to focus on the behaviour, or issue, we are angry about. We do this briefly and unambiguously: "I don't *ever* make comments about your body or clothes. I don't expect you to *ever* make comments about mine. It stops *now*!" This to a student who has made a gutless, sexist comment. The first time a student happens to use sexist, or racist language do not ignore it; address it swiftly, briefly, unambiguously and assertively.

When we are assertive we need to look the other person in the eye, (but not stand too close) and avoid the wagging, pointing, finger. Extend an open, and "blocking" hand and use a clear, firm, strong voice: "I don't swear at you. *That language is totally unacceptable here.* If you're uptight with me find another way of saying it." This to a student who has sworn at a teacher (unprovoked).

Assertive language is to be distinguished from aggressive language, as when a person says, "Who the hell do you think you are, you x!!z!!" "You made me so angry with your stupid whining …!!". In contrast, by communicating with an "I" statement we let the other person know how we feel (or are affected by) their behaviour. Our non-verbal behaviour needs to be decisive without being hostile or aggressive. We model control (of ourselves) *while* communicating our fundamental right and at the same time addressing the other person's unacceptable behaviour.

- De-escalate the voice and the residual tension quickly. We may need to raise our voice (not shout) to initiate attention and assert a point. It is important then to drop the voice to a firm, controlled, more measured tone. Children are rarely adept at de-escalating emotional arousal when a situation is very tense. We, as adults, have to take the lead.

- Having communicated our anger, some cool-off time enables both parties to calm down; perhaps even think and reflect. They are then more amenable to work for resolution.

- It is incumbent – professionally and morally – for the teacher (as adult) to initiate some repairing and rebuilding after the anger-arousing incident. Few children will come to their teachers and say, "Look, I'm sorry, sir. I've been tossing that incident around in my mind – you know when I lashed out at you and said ... well ... I'd like to repair and rebuild with you ... to re-effect that working relationship".

- As the adult – even if our anger is justified in the emotional moment – we will still need to "reach out with the olive branch" to model the repairing and rebuilding behaviour that we hope they will exercise (perhaps one day).

We need to "repair and rebuild" because it is the right thing to do. Unresolved, residual, feelings of animosity unnecessarily impair the teacher–student relationship. When we repair and rebuild we give the student the opportunity to share their feelings about the issue that led to the anger episode. Someone has to make the first move.

After cool-off time sit down with the student and:

- explain, briefly, what it was you were angry about at the time, and why
- invite the student's right of reply
- tune into their perception and feelings but refer back to the fundamental right affected by the student's behaviour
- avoid forcing the student to share their feelings. If they choose not to share how they felt, or how they are feeling now it can help to briefly suggest, "Perhaps you're feeling really annoyed about what happened the other day because or/when ...". At times it is enough that we simply communicate that no grudges are held and "we move on from here"
- discuss how "we" might handle a similar incident "next time"
- separate amicably. (See also p.106f.)

For a male teacher speaking with a female student it will be important to have a female colleague present for ethical probity.

Frustrated and angry parents

If you have ever had an angry parent storm into your classroom, or office, or try to "buttonhole" you in the playground you will know how stressful such an encounter can be. In an article in *The Times* (14 June 2008) the issue of difficult, belligerent and aggressive parents is aired: *Schools face growing problems of hostile parents*. There are parents who are hostile, who *demand*, who refuse to accept the sometimes appalling behaviour of their children. Each year I read similar articles from many countries. Fortunately the number of very hostile and aggressive parents is – generally – small though the perception is that this issue is an increasing one (Rogers 2009). Nonetheless we have to deal with them professionally and supportively.

Most parents are reasonable when they present to the school with concerns and problems relating to their children. They moderate, or curb, their feelings of frustration at what they perceive as being unfair, inappropriate or unacceptable treatment of their child.

When working with frustrated and angry parents it is crucial to acknowledge and affirm how they feel and what they (initially) perceive as "the problem". Their perception may not be the same as yours and may (in fact) be incorrect, but it is how *they* feel and perceive "things to be" at this point.

- Allow the parent some time to explain how they feel; avoid the temptation to butt in and defend the school. Allowing the parent to have their say may mean letting them "run out of steam".
- Invite the parent to sit down (it's harder to be overly physiologically angry sitting down).
- Listen first, then reflect back: "So you seem to be saying that ..."; or "As you see it ..."; "I can see you're really upset or angry about ...". So, for example, if a parent believes their child is being harassed or bullied, one should be able to acknowledge and understand parental anger as well as refocusing energy towards clarifying the actual details and *then* working towards appropriate mediation and consequences.
- Assure them (briefly) that you know they (and the school) care. "I know you care about Justin – you wouldn't be here now if you didn't care. We care too – and we are here to support your son ..."
- Be sure to have the facts as the school sees them, and invite the parent to view the problems within the school's policy and due processes.
- At times compromise may be necessary without the school making promises or commitments they can't keep, and without compromising the school's behaviour policy on rights, responsibilities, rules and consequences.

- Honesty is crucial; about how things are, what has happened and the most workable, sensible and fair options open to all "parties".
- Early support given to parents can often eliminate messy, and often inaccurate, disclosures in the public domain (gossip, the media).

Hostile and aggressive anger

I've taught with a number of colleagues over the years who have been reduced to tears by bombastic, arrogant and angry parents who bring no control to the wild, ill-formed accusations, and even threats, delivered in a barrage of four-letter words.

A colleague of mine, a principal (in Australia) had suspended a girl (Year 8) for punching another girl in the face. The victim had bad bruising around the jaw and face and a broken tooth. The principal had given the other girl a non-negotiable suspension for three days, pending an accountability conference involving some mediation and restitution with the victim of this bashing.

The morning after the girl was suspended her mother stormed into his office (bypassing the school secretary).

"What did you suspend my daughter for? Eh?! Anybody calls my daughter a slut I tell her to f—ing punch her f—ing lights out ...!!" The mother was hopping around, finger wagging and waving in the air. Droplets of saliva flashing around the office in the early morning sun.

By this time a few senior colleagues are hovering near the door ready to give moral support. "And you can all p— off!!" yelled the mother.

I asked him what he did to manage this fracas. "I know what I'd like to have said," he smiled wearily. "'No wonder your daughter is off her tree with a mother like you!! Who the hell do you think you are, storming in here yelling, screaming and abusing me you stupid ————!! Now get out of this school! Go home. Take a valium sandwich and come back if and when you calm down. And don't you ever storm in here without making an appointment! Do you understand!?' But I can't say all that can I? Tempting as it may be. If I do that I'm on the television news that night. The mother is standing there, now calm, looking seriously hard done by this cruel and heartless school. She faces the camera, dressed for the part, and says, 'You go to the school because you're concerned about your daughter. She was bullied you know – I can't repeat what she was called – and what did she get – no help at all but abuse, and from a school principal!'"

"So what did you do then?" I asked, although I'd already guessed.

"I let her 'run out of steam' as it were. She jumped around, yelled at me, 'effing and blinding'. Eventually she calmed down. I was offering no resistance. Nor did I try, at this stage, to defend what I'd done. She stood there, somewhat 'out of breath'. I asked her if she'd like to take a seat. She sat, arms folded. I said, "I can see you're really upset about Chantelle – about what's happened. I know you care about Chantelle so do we. If we talk this through, without attacking each other, we can support your daughter. After all that's why you're here. I won't yell and swear at you, Ms —. I expect you not to swear at me. Thanks. Now ..."

He then talked about the incident, getting the facts clear and straight.

"No, I'm not calling your daughter a liar, Ms —," in response to her accusation that the witness reports were from liars in contrast to her daughter's *ever so honest account*.

Eventually he got some understanding and assurance that the due process of mediation (in three days' time – after cool-off time for all) would help. He didn't 'defend' the school's policy on violence; just explained and reaffirmed it as non-negotiable and supportive to *all* parties.

It is hard to stay calm and professional in such situations, indeed sometimes the parent will fly off the handle again as the discussion of the problem challenges their view of rough justice. In these cases *continual* yelling and swearing by the angry and hostile parent is best dealt with by a firm verbal assertion: "This meeting is over. It's not working Ms —." He holds up a blocking hand. "It's not working. I've asked you to discuss this calmly. You're swearing and yelling at me. I'm not prepared to continue. Leave now; when you've had a chance to calm down please make an appointment and I'll be happy to talk with you – anytime." Show them to the door. If they refuse to leave (it happens!), it is better to leave yourself. They may harangue you all the way down the corridor, "You bastard!! You've never cared about our Chantelle. You're all a bunch of gutless ...!!"

If it is the mother haranguing you, go into the male toilet at this point (even if you're female!). "Go away – it's a male toilet" (you are tempted to yell!) Meanwhile one of your colleagues will direct her to leave or warn her that the police will have to be called. These sorts of scenarios are rare (thank goodness) but they do happen, and in most cases teachers are incredibly professional in the way they handle such incidents.

- Calm yourself before consciously helping the other person to calm down. This will include consciously unclenching fists, and presenting open body language (which is easier said than done).
- It may help to let them "run out of steam" (as it were) to aid their self-imposed calming.
- Invite them to sit down.

- Tune into how they may be feeling.
- Get to the facts (in writing) beforehand – hopefully from accurate, reliable, records.
- Give an appropriate right of reply; listen, reflect back briefly.
- Emphasise that you're there to work on the problem – not attack each other.
- Always keep the focus on the core rights and responsibilities of the school policy as it relates to the parent's complaint.
- Work on a solution (if possible) or refer to the due process that needs to be followed. The focus should move to a solution that is mutually workable wherever possible.
- Separate as amicably as possible with an assurance that the parent can ring and make another appointment if necessary.

It is crucial that the colleague who has been on the receiving end of such parent behaviour has some debriefing later that day with their peers. I've done this many times (a glass or two of workable Australian red can help). I've seen teachers unnecessarily blame themselves for the anger episode. A debriefing can allow the teacher's pent-up frustration, or anxiety, to be shared and provides the opportunity to validate their feelings and move on – hopefully learning something.

Many schools now have an internal procedural policy for managing complaining and angry parents. Such a policy needs in-servicing, reflection and review.

When the other person is angry

There are times when we have to manage a very frustrated or angry student. In a Year 8 class I taught, some years ago, a student had taken massive umbrage that I'd "taken over the class from another teacher". Within a few minutes of me being in the classroom Lisa stood up (in the front row) and in a raised voice, leaning forward, nearly shouting, she said, "What did do you have to come into our class for?! We don't need you!! This class was alright till you came!!" That was probably true! I'd come into this class as a mentor-teacher to help refocus their noisy, unfocused pattern of behaviour and now Lisa's power position was under *perceived* threat.

In such cases yelling back would be pointless (if tempting). I chose (in the emotional moment) to let her "run out of steam". In a sense this "took the wind out of her sails". A surprising and unexpected thing happened. The student next to her pulled down on Lisa's jumper and said, "At least he's listening to you!!".

While I was letting Lisa "run out of steam" (as it were) I was scanning the eyes of the other students to non-verbally communicate to them that "you are part of 'this' too – as an audience you have a part to play". Fortunately the rest of the class was "with me". Lisa sat down, folded her arms, slumped back in her seat with a frown, a pursed mouth, muttering f—s(!) The class was basically very quiet now. Some nervous laughter. I thanked the student next to her, "Thanks, Carmel". Turning to Lisa I said, "I *was* listening to you, Lisa; but I don't yell at you. I don't expect you to yell at me". I wasn't nasty; just clear, brief and assertive.

When the other person is angry, and we have a management responsibility to lead (and even "control"), we need to assist the other person to reclaim some sense of self-control. At times this may involve a dignified time-out (calm-down) option. On this occasion the student settled (if sulkily) back into her seat.

"OK, everyone" (this to the class), "the show's over." We carried on with the class discussion and the lesson. Over several sessions my colleague and I worked with the class to help them refocus how the class was (and wasn't) working and what we needed to do to change things (see p. 223f). Later I had a one-to-one chat with Lisa about the incident (with a female colleague "sitting in" p. 106f).

I also found out (later) that Lisa had an alcoholic father and that she had had run-ins with other male teachers. Having explained (to her) why I was the "new teacher", and also that I thought I understood a little of how she might be feeling about having a new teacher in the class we then discussed other ways of making one's feelings and concerns known. We made some progress.

In time Lisa and I got on reasonably well. She learned to moderate her more "bolshie" communication style and when I finished my time with her class we parted amicably, with some residual goodwill.

The rare situation – anger and aggression

There are some situations when an assertive command is necessary, as when two students are engaged in serious fighting. The sharp, brief, command "Oi! (…) Stop that! Move away *now*!" needs to make unambiguously clear that such behaviour must stop. The sharp tone is then reduced to a firm, controlled, assertive and calmer voice: "Move away (…) *now*." We'll often need to repeat the command: "Move away (…) *now*." The dropping of the voice communicates a sense of calm-ness and control and *expected* compliance. If the voice is *kept* sharp and high it can create too much arousal. If the fighting students don't move apart we will need to decide whether to physically intervene (a risky course of action). Whatever we do in a fight situation we should *always* send for a colleague (for practical sup-port and as witness) and direct the peer-audience away (often the audience are just waiting for "adult permission" to leave the fight scene in a face-saving sense).

Most schools have a policy for managing crisis situations. (See Rogers 2006a, *Behaviour Management: A Whole-School Approach*.)

In the rare circumstance where a student physically threatens a teacher (with a weapon, a chair or a fist) an assertive *command* may not be appropriate. Nor will it be appropriate to let them run out of steam!

A colleague of mine had a student walk into her high school class with a large knife. He was clearly, visibly, angry; breathing heavily, rapidly. His eyes darted around the room. He was looking for someone. My colleague knew this lad quite well; that helped. She looked him in the eyes and in a calm voice, *amazingly controlled*, said, "Ahmed (...), Ahmed (...), I know you don't want to hurt me or anyone else here. I can see you're very angry." She tuned into his feelings quickly, calmly, making a reference to herself in the situation. "I know you don't want to hurt me or anyone else here ...". She never took her eyes off him, as if by calm, sustained eye contact and the calm (reassuring) voice she could communicate calmness to him. "Put the knife over there, Ahmed. Come on. We'll go outside now and we can talk. Come on." She walked slowly, with her arm beckoning gently. He put the knife down and followed her out. Thank God.

The class was sitting in stunned silence; many students visibly shocked. By this time the principal had heard what was going on and rushed down to help. He saw the teacher walking with Ahmed towards the office area. Wisely, he too responded calmly, walking with the student and teacher towards the office. Halfway down the corridor my colleague collapsed – she fainted. She had, she said later, used "all her emotional energy up" and just collapsed. The class and teacher had some debriefing, and counselling – later. Ahmed, too, received counselling (after a formal suspension of two weeks). Apparently the knife was to scare another boy whom he had accused of stealing his girlfriend. The police were also involved at a later stage.

You may never have had, or will ever have, such an experience (I hope you don't). If you teach in EBD schools, or Pupil Referral Units or schools within prisons hopefully you will receive training for appropriate, professional, responses in crisis-management situations (including "restraint procedures"). In mainstream schools such scenarios are – fortunately – rare. Spare a thought for teachers who regularly have to manage tense, hostile, aggressive students like that of my colleague noted here.

At the end of the day I share nothing here – about anger and anger management – that I do not struggle with as a teacher, father and colleague. What I am trying to share is that *all behaviour*, particularly in more challenging contexts, has a reciprocal effect for general good or ill. These comments and understandings about anger are an attempt to engage some reflection and, hopefully, more thoughtful behaviour in our professional role as teachers.

Reflection

When did you last get angry – really angry? Reflect – just for a moment – how difficult it can be for a child to manage their anger when we – as adults – struggle with this emotion at times. We distinguish between anger (the emotion) and what we do when we're angry (the behaviour).

■ How aware are you of your characteristic anger behaviour; what do you *do* and *say* when you are very frustrated or angry?

■ It is not easy to express our feelings at times and our feelings are natural; we cannot often "help feeling a given way". How do the suggestions on "communicating our anger" enable your experience and reflection (p. 207f)?

■ Do you have an internal school policy on dealing with hostile and angry parents? How do the suggestions noted in this chapter inform that policy/practice? (It is always harder to think of "what to say/do" in the heat of the emotional moment!)

Notes

1. Virtue (in this sense) means the characteristic direction of one's moral will.
2. Y. Merroberry and S. Farrer, *Sunday Times*, 9 May 1999.
3. In the second edition of *How to Manage Children's Challenging Behaviour* (2009) my colleagues and I have devoted a chapter to exploring how we work with (and try to support), hostile and angry parents.

Chapter 8

When things get difficult: hard class, hard times

People must help one another it is nature's law.
Jean de la Fontaine (1621–95)

Your needful counsel which craves the instant use.
Shakespeare, *King Lear* (2, i)

Struggling teachers – the hard class

> A few years back I was struggling with a really hard class. I'd tried being kind, I'd tried the "power-struggle" [*sic*] approach … I'd kept kids back – even the whole class yet … I was also too proud and naive to attempt to discuss my problems with any of my colleagues who seemed to be handling things so well. (Secondary teacher, cited in Rogers 2002)

From time to time a difficult class, like this (noted above), comes our way; a class that seems to sap and drain our energy and makes *that* timetable slot, or *each* day, a struggle. In the case of the colleague speaking above it was a seemingly recalcitrant Year 7.

All that we would normally do, and more, to manage such a class, still saw my colleague struggling, halfway through Term One: residual noise levels; students frequently off-task; calling out; talking while the teacher was trying to teach; lateness – all seemed to be too annoyingly and stressfully frequent.

A class like this can shake the confidence of even experienced teachers. I've worked with teachers who have felt they are a failure because they cannot manage *this* class, *this* year. Rather than seeing the failure as the annoying natural mix of challenging students and classroom dynamics, some teachers (struggling with such a class) will tend to blame themselves.

The term "struggling teacher" should not be a simple pejorative label. When teachers experience a hard class, or several difficult to manage students, they sometimes feel that admitting that they are struggling or having a problem indicates that they are not able to cope (which is actually true but not a bad thing in itself). When teachers feel less effective (in their role) they may also feel that an admission of their struggle means they will be evaluated or judged in some way. Hopefully, this attitude is not present in your school. If a teacher perceives any opportunity for (or offer of) colleague support as having an implied judgement – or "strings attached" – it may well constrain them from asking for early, valuable and necessary support.

Colleague support is crucial when coming to terms with the management of a harder than average class.

That support, in the first instance, needs to be offered and expressed in a "no-blame" way.

Offering support

There's this ludicrous idea that when someone is really struggling we have this hands-off mentality – just in case we do, or say, the wrong thing. It's stupid really especially when we *know* they need help. (Senior teacher, cited in Rogers 2002)

The Elton Report (1989) has outlined this ambivalence about directly offered colleague support as it relates to behaviour management and discipline issues. On the one hand the offer of support may seem that one implies that a colleague is not coping; so, too, the request for support by a struggling colleague may imply (or "telegraph") that they cannot cope. So a teacher who is struggling with a hard to manage class may struggle on alone – unassisted.

Teachers have tended to stay out of each others' classrooms and not talk about their own discipline problems. Too often teachers do not seek help because it feels like an admission of incompetence and they do not offer it because it feels like accusing a colleague of incompetence. As a result, the tradition of classroom isolation persists in many schools (Elton Report 1989: 69).

This ambivalence, however, depends on how collegially supportive the school is (as a whole) and on how the school enables colleague support. Such support includes moral support as well as "structural" expressions (and forms) of support that can meet colleague needs.

"I don't have a problem with ..."

I've been in many, many meetings with colleagues to discuss issues relating to behaviour management and discipline concerns and someone will say, "but I don't have a problem with ... [a particular student or class ...]". Even if what they say is true it hardly helps a struggling teacher. What can often result from such a comment is that the colleague is engaged in negative self-rating: the struggling teacher unrealistically, unhelpfully, rates themselves against the "better" or more able colleague.

The sad thing is that the "more able" colleague who "may not [really] have a problem" may well be able to understand, support and give valuable assistance. The struggling teacher is, however, unlikely to listen when hearing that others "don't have a problem ..." (with the class they struggle with).

Tim O'Brien describes a typical scene where a teacher has had a hard time with a difficult student, comes into the staff room for a caffeine fix and bravely (and professionally) shares his or her struggle: "in the hope that empathy or advice will ensue. The response (sometimes) given is the verbal equivalent of a swift kick in the groin. 'He's alright with me ...'." Tim goes on to suggest (tongue in cheek?) that we should "ban the singular and plural versions of this morale wrecking phrase from our schools" (1998: 90).

Some teachers may say, "I don't have a problem ..." because they are anxious that if they speak up about management or discipline concerns they will be seen (or judged) to be "ineffective" or "weak" teachers; perhaps even incompetent. The masked assurance ("I don't have a problem ...") may also indicate the teacher's belief that request for support from senior colleagues may invoke offers of support with "strings attached"; and the request will be remembered in the teacher's ongoing service review. This kind of unprofessional culture tends to breed a degrading survivalism rather than professional empowerment (Rogers 2002).

Colleague support: stress and coping provision

Non-judgemental colleague support can affect stress levels and coping resources in a number of ways:

- In their research on job-related stress, Russell et al. (1987) note that social support can affect stress – even burnout – in positive, "buffering", ways.

   Job-related stress, and feelings of stress and de-personalisation, decreased as the level of *supportive* supervision increased. Individuals who have supportive collegial relationships are able to rely on others to aid and support them in dealing with stressful situations.

Schools that consciously seek to address colleague support are aware that stress *and* burnout have a relational, social causation as well as psychological causation (Rogers 2002; see also Hobfoll 1998).

- Positive support from supervisors was predictive of measures of physical and mental health (Russell et al. 1987).
- Teachers who indicate that when others (particularly senior staff) in their school acknowledge and affirm their skills and abilities there is a greater sense of personal and team accomplishment and that feelings of depersonalisation were lessened (Rogers 2002; see also Bernard 1990).
- Supportive collegiality consciously seeks to address the normative stress of day-to-day teaching by enhancing the "ecology of support" and strengthening the sense of supportive interdependency within the school.
- The degree to which a school *consciously* acknowledges colleague support as an integrating factor in a school's culture (as well as its normative work), and the degree to which a school leadership seeks to address the needs of its staff will significantly affect the *dependability* and *reliability* of ongoing support.
- The "buffering" and "coping" aspects of colleague support are enhanced when such support is given in a non-blaming, non-judgemental way; where the "ecology of support" in a given school seeks to meet colleagues' basic human needs as well as their professional needs (Rogers 2002).

In collegially supportive schools "reliable alliances" are nurtured through informal, and formal, sharing and teaming. These alliances can be informal, transitional and dyadic as well as expressed in more formal and systemic expressions such as teaming and policy imperatives.

Colleague support can:

- lessen the feelings of isolation ("I'm not alone here ..."; "It's not all my fault ..."; "I'm not totally responsible for all that happens ...")
- provide fundamental moral support – even in the many brief collegial transactions within a school day (sharing a coffee, offloading a concern, seeking reassurance about a lesson activity, or coping with the follow up of a difficult student ...)
- empower staff through the sort of teamwork that promotes committed and caring relationships among staff. Such teamwork can also increase an individual's confidence and risk-taking as they grow professionally
- provide assurance that one is on the right track (in terms of one's teaching resources, strategies, approaches, and so on)

- provide a forum, a *collegial* context, for problem sharing; problem analysis; problem solving and coping resources. This, in turn, reduces negative feelings of inadequacy (as one accesses wider resources beyond oneself)
- enable the essential stress relieving support in the management of attentional, disturbing and challenging student behaviours (Rogers 2002).

Senior administration can effect significant support to their colleagues by allowing genuine needs-analysis on those structural, organisational and role factors that contribute to stress in the workplace day-to-day: even so-called "minor" irritants like fluorescent lights not working; poor photocopier facilities; inadequate staffroom facilities; communication processes; procedures and systems (particularly unfair timetabling); broken furniture in classrooms and so on.

A stress audit, conducted each year, is a positive and practical way of legitimising genuine concerns or complaints of staff and enabling action planning to reduce the stress associated with such concerns (Rogers 2002).

Moral, structural, professional support

Colleague support can range from normative whingeing to active and constructive problem solving. Teachers need to "offload" – to whinge – to complain about individual children and classes that they find difficult. If that is all colleagues do, though, it will be of little help long-term with hard-to-manage students and hard-to-manage classes. Colleague support, in such situations, needs to be professional and "structural" in its ongoing application *as well as* giving the moral support we all need to be reassured and encouraged.

"Structural support" in this sense, refers to those dependable "forms", "processes", "procedures", "action plans" and "policies" that can be depended on by colleagues when under pressure.

Professional support refers to the way we enable our colleagues to reflect on, and appraise, their professional obligations *and needs*, in light of the aims and objectives of their role in the school.

No one *expression* of colleague support stands alone, or is sufficient in itself. All expressions of support seek to meet colleague needs. When addressing the management of a hard class, a *collegial* action plan seeks to meet colleague needs with emotional and practical support through shared action planning.

Developing a collegial action plan for re-establishing a difficult to manage class

A collegial action plan provides a forum and a process for meeting the moral, practical and professional needs of a colleague struggling with a hard to manage class, or several hard to manage students. When such a process is effected early in the cycle of concern, it can often re-engage the necessary hope, goodwill and energy of teachers and students alike.

■ This process begins with a year-level team meeting as early as possible before the hard-class issue becomes a habituated problem drifting into Term Two. Early intervention is crucial. Once a profile of *group* behaviour is clear it will be important to have a meeting with *all* the teachers who work with the class in question.

Issues to be addressed will include:
– How many (and which) students are disruptive and it what ways?
– How frequent and intense are the disruptive behaviours?
– Who are the ring leaders? – the "power-brokers"?
– Is the class "hard" to manage for all teachers who teach this group or these students? Is it hard "only" for one or a few? (Even if it is only *one* teacher struggling with a given class we still need to offer early colleague support). A typical – disconcerting – obstacle in supporting struggling teachers is the common perception that it is a sign of weakness to admit there is a significant problem with the management and leadership of a given class. The non-judgemental collegial approach, and constructive offer of support, can help minimise negative and self-defeating perceptions. In time – of course – trust invested (we hope) will be trust rewarded.

No doubt there will be some whingeing in such a meeting. This can be cathartic; up to a point. It can be healthy to affirm our common struggle and validate common feelings, as long as colleagues avoid the easy "I don't have any problems with that particular student, or class" or, conversely, blaming all the students and categorising them as "impossible to work with". Any whingeing will need to go beyond just the whingeing itself to problem analysis and shared action planning.

It is also true that *some* teachers by the way they *characteristically* treat individuals and groups contribute to the "hard class" phenomenon. At this first meeting it is important to allow some focused collegial attention to this reality. Teachers need to acknowledge (and address) their own *characteristic* behaviour may need to be addressed *as well as that of their students*.

■ Develop a year-level plan based on thoughtful year-level needs analysis utilising the questions noted above. Some of the issues that will need to be reassessed in such a plan are:

– a reassessment of how colleagues established the class group in their first meetings, including basics such as: establishment of routines like seating plans (or lack thereof); classroom entry, settling and calming; noise levels; routines for asking questions, and obtaining teacher assistance; classroom rules for behaviour and organisation for learning and so on (see Chapter 2). The way a class is initially established has a significant effect on group behaviour norms (Rogers 2006a);

– a discussion of short-term options for immediate colleague support in areas such as time-out options for provocative, and *persistently* disruptive, students or even time-out options for the teacher (see p. 226f on colleague assisted time out);

– a clarification of procedures for tracking particularly difficult students, including how colleagues currently follow-up with such students beyond classroom settings (p. 106f);

– a discussion of *any* issues of harassment of teachers (p. 229f). In developing a collegial action plan, it is essential to elicit and engage the support of senior administration.

■ Decide on possible approaches in enacting the plan. A common approach we've used – for example – is to have a classroom meeting with all the students of a given class group to discuss issues of common concern. We then use student, and teacher, feedback to develop a shared plan to re-establish the class. In this sense the students are given a degree of ownership in the re-establishment or "fresh start" process.

Classroom meetings to re-establish a difficult class

Any such meeting should address: the common behaviours of students currently causing concern to teachers and most probably causing concern to the cooperative students in the class; the rights being affected by disruptive behaviour (that is, the right to *basic respect*; the right to *learn/and teach*; the right to *feel safe* in this class group); the responsibilities being ignored by some students – at present, and what needs to happen (as a class group) to address these issues.

In a more "open" classroom meeting the teacher can direct the class focus to questions such as:

– What is working well (in our class) at this stage in our class journey?
– Why do you think such aspects of our class are working well?

– What isn't working well – and why?

If an issue or concern is too personal, or likely to cause embarrassment to the "respondent"/student, or the teacher, it can be written down (anonymously) and read by the teacher at a later stage (assure confidentiality). The last question is:

– What can we do to change things in our classroom and how?

This question addresses individual, and group, behaviour to the goal that everyone's rights are enjoyed (and protected) and we take on our individual and shared responsibilities.

When we conduct such an open classroom meeting there is always the possibility that some mean-spirited students will use such an open forum to "have a go" at the teacher. If there is any suspicion this *might* happen these questions can (and should) be asked through a questionnaire format (Rogers 2006b).

The emphasis behind such questions addresses how we (teacher and students) consciously address the positive development of a learning community: "we *all* share the same place; time; space; needs, resources here; and that is why we need to work on these concerns and issues together. We also share the same basic feelings and needs." The questionnaire gives *all* students a voice, and an appropriate right of reply.

It is crucial after such a meeting that teachers (at a later stage) give feedback to the class on their responses and work with the class on developing a shared plan for key aspects of behaviour and learning – a re-establishing and a basis for a "fresh-start" as a class.

In a re-establishment plan we refocus the class back to:

– their *core rights* and *responsibilities* (p. 42)
– the *rules* for classroom behaviours that affect those core rights and responsibilities such as the way we treat one another; the way we learn here and how we create a safe classroom/school community. A "safe" classroom always needs to address "psychological", as well as physical, safety (that is, teasing, put-downs, hassling and bullying). Some rules may need some specific focus (for example, use of shared equipment and property, movement around the room)
– the *routines* for the smooth running of the class, particularly procedural routines (Chapter 2)
– the *consequences* for affecting others' rights. These consequences will range from obvious rule reminders through to time-out options and even detention. Students need to know the consequences in advance. They also need to know that these consequences are fair and relate back to protection of our common rights (Chapter 5)

– students also need to know the positive outcomes that will flow from students supporting each other, and their teacher, within such a plan. This is a crucial feature of any "fresh start". If the meeting is simply another opportunity to growl, or moan, at the class group it will further alienate the goodwill of the majority of the class who are probably quite cooperative and – when given a chance to engage a fresh start – will support positive teacher leadership.

It is helpful to publish the essential elements of the plan on a couple of large posters with headings emphasising the central features of our "fresh start". These posters are displayed in the classroom and referred to wherever necessary. It is also important to utilise positive language wherever possible in the published outcome. The plan can also be published on A4 sheets and made available to all students.

Any such meeting, involving students, is best developed by those colleagues in the team who are both experienced and "comfortable" in conducting classroom meetings to support the struggling teacher.

- Support each other (collegially) in the initiation and development of the whole-class behaviour plan. This will include ongoing shared collegial feedback and can also include cross-class visits (in our rare non-contact time) to see how students behave in other subject areas/settings. It can even involve some elective team-teaching, observational feedback and mentoring (p. 237f).
- Have a review meeting with the colleague team a few weeks into the reestablishment phase of the plan and discuss what is working well, what isn't, and see if there are areas where fine-tuning or change is necessary. It may be helpful to look at: how the time-out referrals have operated; how individual case-supervision (of students with challenging behaviour) is affecting the class dynamic; and how teachers' perceptions about noise levels, time on task, general student motivation, enthusiasm and cooperation have changed (if at all).

Any such review may also need to include possibilities such as changing the structure and student placement in groups and even possible teacher rotation across groups. If, for example, one or two students are, effectively, holding the class to ransom, it will often be necessary to shift such students to other classes (even "enrolling" such students in classes above their year-level with set work on a regular basis). This may be necessary both for the welfare of other students as well as the teacher. While this is a somewhat difficult organisational option, it will need to be considered.

The fact that the senior administration have been a supportive part of this process will significantly affect how such an option is considered and realised.

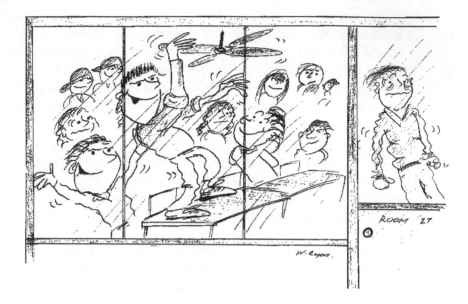

Time out for the teacher (colleague safety valve)

Walking past a classroom in the corridor one day I saw (and heard), through the corridor windows, some serious "catalytic conversion" going on: loud yelling, excited voices and raucous laughter. Looking through the window I saw a student standing on a table with his arm in an overhead rotating fan. He was laughing, his "mates" egging him on. The teacher looked quite stressed out. Should I intervene? As a senior teacher in the school if I do intervene – how?

One *short-term* supportive strategy in such a situation is for the "passing", colleague or even a colleague teaching nearby, to knock on the door and offer either to withdraw one or two students (the ringleaders), or even give the teacher an opportunity for a dignified "exit". It is particularly important that senior teacher intervention observe basic protocols of collegial dignity and respect.

- If a teacher walks past a classroom situation where a colleague is clearly struggling, rather than staring through the window with a look of implied judgement, or simply walking past, or (worse) walking in and shouting the class down, the support colleague knocks, enters and walks across to the teacher and quietly says – for example – "Excuse me, Mr Smith (...), I wonder if I could borrow one or two students?" This is "code" for "I'll take the two or three most difficult 'ringleaders' or 'power-brokers' off your hands for the rest of the class period". The teacher may feel like saying "One or two would be fine but eight would be better!"

The support colleague escorts the trouble-makers away to a time-out situation and talks through with them their inappropriate and unacceptable behaviour. A follow-through consequence may also need to be organised for the students later that day. The support colleague may even escort the students to another classroom for some "time out". This option will need to have been discussed, with colleagues, as a viable school-wide option.

This approach is preferred to a teacher walking in and shouting at the class, "Who the hell do you think you are!! I can hear you all from my office!! You pack of animals ...!! I'm sick and tired of your stupid behaviour. Just shut it – alright?! You make me sick!!" *Of course* the students may well go "*stumm*"; especially if the harangue is given by a senior teacher. While such a reaction (from the students) is understandable, it hardly helps the class teacher's self-esteem. As the senior teacher walks out – on the now quiet class – his non-verbal demeanour says, in effect, "*That's* how you deal with them." The class teacher may well feel unsupported even undermined.

■ *Teacher time out.* There are situations in the classroom where loss of control is so serious that the best short-term support we can give the teacher is time-out (for the teacher). This is what I did in the instance of the boy with his arm in the fan. I need to add his arm was in plaster; he was having a lot of "fun" using it as a brake in the fan ... and, of course, getting plenty of peer attention.

The supporting teacher knocks on the door (loudly – it needs to be loud to be heard). "Sorry to bother you, Mr Smith," with an "excuse me" to the whole class, (as he briefly scans their faces …). "There's a message for you at the office." This is code for, "Leave the classroom … I'll take over for now …". The "message" at the office is simply, "Who's got your class?"

Your colleague then has a breather, gains some re-composure and – perhaps – takes stock of what happened. The supporting teacher's action is not merely some "white-knight" routine: it is a dignified collegial option in a crisis.

The supporting teacher then meets with their colleague, later that day, to debrief and offer longer-term support. Our first thought though, in an immediate crisis, is for the emotional welfare of our colleague; followed – of course – by the safety and welfare of the students.

When we "take over" in such a situation, it is important not to convey the message to the students that the regular teacher is ineffective, or can't cope: i.e. "OK!! The *real* teacher is here *now*. The one who *has it all sorted* (unlike the teacher who has just left …").

Fortunately situations like this are rare. Any such "colleague safety-valve" support must be followed up by longer-term needs analysis and strategic planning with the supported colleague and the class (p. 222f).

There is a big difference between a testy class, or bad-day syndrome, and a class where there is a loss of control and a feeling of panic that order, purpose and focus cannot be regained by the teacher. It is one of the most unpleasant, stressful, feelings in teaching.

If you have ever had such experiences then early acknowledgement that there *is* a problem is not a sign (or symptom) of weakness; it is a professional acknowledgement that you need colleague support. I've worked with teachers who have struggled for weeks on end with such classes and end up "breaking-down":

> "I didn't want people to think I couldn't cope …"
> Well you couldn't. That's not a sin; it's a recognition that something is wrong and you need support to reassess "where?", "why?", "how?" and so on.
> "What will others think of me? Will it be a black mark against my career …?"
> Not in a supportive school …

I can understand why some teachers are reluctant to disclose their anxieties and struggles – but hopefully it shouldn't take a crisis issue like that noted here to begin a process of support.

In some situations the only long-term recourse will be to reassign the teacher to another class. This is not the most elegant solution but it may be the necessary one.

Where colleague support (including ongoing mentoring) has seen no real changes in a teacher's ability to successfully work with a class it will be necessary to re-establish the class with a new teacher. The educational welfare of the students needs to be considered as well as the welfare of the current classroom teacher.

When passing the leadership of the class group to another teacher it will be important that the "new" teacher not convey, or impute, that their previous teacher was a "failure" or was incompetent. A brief acknowledgement that it's time for *us* to move on is enough.

Harassment in the workplace

A provocative newspaper headline reads "Workplace is a war zone ...". A closer reading of that research (from the Australian Institute of Criminology), conducted among police, doctors, nurses, taxi-drivers and teachers, indicates that these professions face the greatest risk of verbal attacks and even assaults; at least teachers are last on the list! The article used a broad term, "workplace violence", to include: "injury through employer negligence, physical and verbal abuse, racial abuse, bullying, sexual harassment and even malicious gossip" (*The Age* [newspaper] 2000). The article goes on to say that "we should not countenance such behaviours as 'permissible, systematic work-related risk'" (Perore 2000). Harassment of any kind is a workplace health and safety issue – it should never be trivialised or minimised – or given the gutless "wink-wink/nudge-nudge" that it is somehow "the victim's fault"! In such a climate teachers often feel scared to speak up (scared of even losing their job because they "can't manage these kids"). Harassment, and lack of acknowledgment and support, can (and does) affect health, wellbeing and confidence. Teachers will even say they feel somehow unworthy, even "blamed"(!).

When the issue of harassment *of teachers* is raised as an issue, particularly in more "challenging" schools, there is sometimes a tacit acceptance of some expressions of hostile or verbally challenging behaviour as *only* "boys being boys" or "this is the way kids are around here", or "some classes here are just difficult", such statements may minimise or even tacitly accept what is – in effect – an acceptance of psychological harassment. Worse, if we categorise harassing behaviour as merely "disruptive behaviour" that the teacher *cannot control*, we may then – too easily – blame the teacher for the harassing behaviour of the students.

Harassment is more than merely unacceptable – it is wrong. It is an abuse of fundamental rights: the right to feel safe and the right to be treated with basic respect. Such harassing behaviours also significantly affect the right to teach and the right to learn.

Blaming the victim is not an uncommon feature of bullying/harassing students: "yeah, well she deserves it [the teacher] she's a useless teacher". This global, quick labelling then ratifies and even excuses the students' behaviour when they call out such things as, "don't listen to her", "she's rubbish", and "this is boring – boooring!!" Harassing behaviour can include the non-verbal suggestions that students use to refer to a teacher's sexual preference, or body shape, or clothing or "anything" they can pick on that will ratify and – gutlessly gratify – their exercise of power. (There has – recently – been a spate of Facebook incidents of students vilifying, harassing, teachers in "web-space" as reported on Australian television and in the press.)

I'm not talking here about "reactive student behaviour" and the occasional silly, stupid, unthinking behaviour of some students, or even the outbursts of challenging students (Chapter 6). That kind of behaviour needs to be addressed for what it is – it is not bullying. There are occasions when a teacher's behaviour sees understandable reactions from students. A teacher walks past a student's open bag on the floor, by the chair, and espies a packet of cigarettes in the bag. The teacher takes them stating, "You're *not* supposed to smoke here – I'll take *them*!!" The student's reaction is immediate, "Hey!! They're mine ... don't you f—ing touch them!" The *student's* behaviour here is not harassment; it is an understandable reaction to a piece of unthinking, unnecessary, behaviour by a teacher. What did the teacher think? Did she really think the student would just acquiesce? Did she care?

Harassment – addressing the issue

This is not an easy issue to write about. I have done so because I have observed it in some schools and have been involved in supporting colleagues to address it wherever it occurs.

- Harassment is not occasional bad-day syndrome behaviour. Some students will sometimes take the risk of "having a bit of fun" with a teacher (particularly a new teacher or a supply teacher). Most teachers recognise such behaviour for what it is; point out quickly that the student/s has gone too far and the teacher will reign it in. Such behaviour will also necessitate the teacher conducting some follow-up (p. 106f) to make the point clearly about the limits of "fun" (as the student perceives it).

Harassment involves those *intentional*, *selective* and *repeated* behaviours of an individual or a group designed to hurt or abuse their victim. Bullies 'select' people they perceive as weaker than they are (psychologically and physically weaker) and use bullying behaviour to confirm (and continue to ratify) their social power (Rogers 2006b).

■ Bullies rely on collusive acceptance of (or acquiescence) by other students in their bullying/harassing behaviour. *Collusive bullies* may not directly harass a teacher but they do silently approve of, or give a non-verbal chorus to, the bullies' behaviour. Unintended collusion can also occur when students who are afraid of the bully go silent and will not speak out in (or out of) class. Bullies accept such collusion as confirmation of their social power.

Bullies also trade in secrecy – not from their peers (they need their "collusion") but from adults. They don't want to be "found out". It is important to crack this "secrecy code" early.

■ As noted earlier, one of the problems inherent in any workplace harassment is that some teachers feel insecure about admitting that they are "having problems in a given class"; they believe that an admission that some students are "making their life hell" is a sign of their own weakness; that they can't cope; that they *should* be able to cope.

"I didn't want people to think I couldn't cope ..."; I've heard this many times – sometimes too late in the day. The point is that sometimes a teacher cannot cope with such harassing behaviour on their own; *nor should they have to*.

A more disturbing issue arises when teachers feel that if they do "speak out" about harassment then nothing (effectively) will be done; that such student behaviour will not actually be seen as harassment.

It is important to address harassment as early as possible in its cycle – to crack the "secrecy code", confront the main perpetrators and the active collusive perpetrators (where necessary) and support the victim (the teacher and perhaps other students).

If you are ever in this situation or circumstance of knowing that the behaviour you are experiencing is more than merely a disruptive class on a bad day; that you are going home disturbed, anxious or even angry about repeated disruptive or personally abusive behaviour; or you virtually hate coming to school when you have to teach a particular class, then you need to speak to a senior colleague *as early as possible* to address and confront the issue (see later).

If you are a senior colleague who senses that something is clearly wrong with a teacher's class, and suspect that harassment is a factor, it will be important to speak supportively with your colleague about your concerns and offer immediate support.

At such a meeting with a colleague it will be crucial to allay any anxiety about perceived judgement, or that in coming forward with their concerns they are a weak and ineffective teacher. A sharing of what you suspect about the class concerned (and the behaviour of some of its members) and an invitation to talk it through should lead to an early reassurance of support and the development of a plan to confront the perpetrators.

Ideally, the first incidence, or suggestions of harassment, by any students should have been nipped in the bud with an assertive comment by the teacher and immediate follow-up beyond the classroom (p. 106f). Some teachers, however, who lack assertive skills let such early behaviour go in the belief that it will go away in time. It rarely does – it needs to be confronted decisively.

Accountability conferencing

The concept of "accountability conferencing" can be utilised for any significant issue of concern that a teacher has about the way a student has behaved towards an adult (in or out of a classroom setting) – particularly here, though, it is discussed relative to harassment.

Early intervention should include the teacher directly confronting the student with their harassing behaviours. Such an intervention needs the support of a senior colleague and thoughtful prior planning. By "confronting" I mean setting aside "one-to-one" meeting time with the student (the perpetrator of the harassment), where the senior teacher (and the teacher who is the victim of such harassment) makes *clear* to the student what it is they have *specifically* been doing, saying or suggesting (or writing/texting) that constitutes the harassing/bullying behaviour. Such confrontation needs to be respectful, truthful and non-laboured. An opportunity is then given to the student to reply and account for their behaviour. And, then, give a clear assurance and commitment that such behaviour will cease.

It is crucial that the facilitator (a senior teacher) plans this meeting with the teacher concerned beforehand. It is essential to get the facts clear (and written down). The *specific* nature, frequency, occasions and context(s) of the bullying behaviour will be noted; the specific language used; the non-verbal posturing and also the behaviour of the collusive bullies. The senior colleague will also enable their colleague to think through the order of the meeting and how the different stages of the meeting might develop towards the desired outcome.

Any student who bullys others needs some collusive support of other students to applaud, to "confirm" and "consolidate" their behaviour within their peer-audience. It will also be crucial to conduct a meeting between each collusive bully and the teacher concerned.

We will need to discuss with each suspected collusive perpetrator (one at a time) – what they know about *what has been going on* with regard to the bully's behaviour with regard to the teacher who is the victim of the bullying. While collusive bullies do not regard themselves as *bullies* they need made clear that "laughing along with ..."; "goading" and "cheering" and "desk-banging" are forms of harassment that they are responsible and accountable for. They also need to give a clear *assurance* of what they will do to make these behaviours stop.

Conducting an accountability conference with a bullying student

Such a meeting can reawaken quite emotional issues and concerns for the teacher, so it will be important to discuss what they will say and how they might respond to "discounting" and "avoidance" behaviours by the student. If the perpetrator is a female student and the "victim" a male teacher it may be wise to have a female senior colleague facilitate the process (for perceived ethical probity).

- The facilitator (a senior teacher) calls a meeting between the teacher and the student (the perpetrator of the harassment). The meeting is obligatory for the perpetrator.
- At the outset of the meeting the facilitator (senior teacher) explains why this meeting has been called. The tone of the meeting is serious; formal but respectful. If the tenor of the meeting is vindictive and merely an opportunity to attack the student, it will not work for the desired outcome. Nor should the meeting suggest that "this is *just* a little chat about a few problems in class".

   "I've called this meeting between you, Troy [the student], and Ms Smith because we are really concerned about ...". Here the facilitator briefly outlines the facts that relate to the student's *behaviours*. It is not an attack on the student as a person (tempting as that might be). The facilitator makes the rules of the meeting clear. We each listen to the other without interruption; giving assurance that there will be a right of reply. The aim of the meeting is to determine what has been happening (in the classroom or wherever) and to make sure that the upholding of the rights and *responsibilities* of the individual, and of a safe, respectful classroom, are the outcome.
- The teacher who has been the recipient of this harassing behaviour is now given the opportunity to address their issues of concern about the student's behaviour, *directly* to the student. The teacher outlines the behaviours that the student has been engaged in, *briefly* and *specifically*. It will help to have the typical incidents recorded (with a copy) to refer to during this meeting. It can sometimes help if the facilitator "models" some of the non-verbal harassing

behaviour to increase clarity and understanding. This possibility needs to be discussed beforehand with the teacher concerned.

- The teacher *briefly* explains how such behaviour affects the teaching and learning in "our class ..." and how it affects "the teacher's right to respect and treatment ...". Avoid talking too much about personal feelings ("I went home last night and had eight aspirin, six Valium, and some far-too-serious Scotch and I've been tossing and turning all night. And it's all your fault ...!!"); such admissions may be unhelpful "grist to the bully's power-seeking mill!"

- The teacher points out that the behaviours detailed are *harassing/bullying behaviours* and must stop: "This behaviour (beckon to the list) has to stop so that I can get on with the job of teaching and the students in *our* class can get an with their learning ... and so that I can feel safe here and have that basic respect I seek to give to you ...".

- The facilitator then invites the student to respond and explain what they will do to "Make these behaviours stop ...". Many students (in response to the invited right of reply) will disclaim, discount or minimise their harassing behaviour: "I was only mucking about ...!"; "I was just joking ...!"; "Just having a bit of fun ...!"; "Other kids said stuff too!!"; "I wasn't the only one ...!"

The facilitator or teacher will reframe these discounting and avoidance behaviours: "Maybe you thought it was a joke, Troy, but it clearly *wasn't* for Ms Smith *because* ...";"*That* kind of joke or mucking-around is never acceptable in our school – even if half the class laughed with you ..." (and they didn't!); "Maybe you were not the only one who said and did these things ... *I'll be speaking to other students in our class too* ... At the moment I'm talking about what *you* did ... and about *your* responsibility ...". This lets the student know that the "secrecy code" will be cracked across the classroom group; one by one, as necessary. Sometimes students claim a kind of "right to silence" – refusing to speak. If they refuse to respond verbally, the facilitator can suggest to the student what they might be saying: "Perhaps you're saying in your head, Troy (because you're not speaking to us) ... perhaps you're saying that it is no big deal because you were just mucking around. It is a big deal *because* ... – it is extremely serious *because* ...". Here the facilitator reframes why such behaviour cannot be minimised, "laughed off" or excused. The tone and manner (as stated earlier) is very important; firm but respectful.

"Troy, what do you need to do *now*, and in the future to change this behaviour?" Here the teacher invites an apology and an assurance of behaviour change from the student. A brief reminder about the fundamental rights and responsibilities expected in the student's behaviour is outlined.

Some students will benefit from having a provisional plan about the specific behaviours they need to stop and the behaviours they need to start; relative to what has been happening. This provisional plan can form the basis for a discussion about behaviour change.

The key messages emphasised by the facilitator (the senior teacher) are:

■ "You own your own behaviour; nobody makes you do X, Y and Z."
■ "It's your choice every time you go into our classroom to decide whether you'll support fair rights or not."
■ "It's all about what *you choose to do* …". The facilitator will emphasise that the class/grade teacher is wanting to work these issues through with the student in a way that does not need to involve the student's parent(s) *at this stage* but does need the understanding, the accountability and cooperation of the student.

If, however, the meeting sees no appropriate response at all from the student, or sees a defiant unwillingness to acknowledge any responsibility, or accountability, the issue will need to be referred to a more formal harassment due process – within the school's harassment policy. The student will need to understand what the more formal due process will involve.

Point out, if necessary, the consequences of a refusal to acknowledge, and change, their current pattern of behaviour.

■ If the student has grudgingly (or even cooperatively) acknowledged their harassing behaviour and agreed to change, assure them there will be a review meeting (in a week's time) "to see how things are going back in your classroom [or wherever the harassing behaviour has been occurring]". This puts the student "on notice", but does so with the belief communicated that, "You can make things change … You can support the rights and responsibilities here." It is crucial to keep accurate records of the student's behaviour during that week.

  At the review meeting, if there is no change in the behaviour (during that week), formal due process will need to be entered into quickly. We should give no indication that we will continue to tolerate such behaviour. If necessary, due process may necessitate suspension and even (on some occasions) expulsion.

■ Separate amicably at the close of the meeting. Avoid any telegraphing of animosity, "pay-back" or threat. The relative success of this accountability–mediatory approach relies on early intervention; senior colleague support, thoughtful planning and teacher goodwill to work with the perpetrator to expose and confront the behaviour while inviting understanding and cooperation and necessary change in behaviour.

Special areas of focus for colleague support

Colleague support in some schools can often be incidental, based in loose (one-to-one) associations as well as more formal expressions (such as meetings and teams), there are key areas, however, where colleague support cannot be left to mere good-will or chance association.

Induction of new staff to a school

Each school has its own, unique, idiosyncratic culture and practices. A new teacher to a school can be assisted by having a "teaching buddy", to help induct even experienced teachers into a new school. Such induction is not patronising to an experienced colleague; it is the offer of support from someone who can help make sense (through their availability) of the essentials one needs to know and be aware of when starting out in a *new school* (in *this* school). It is also important to introduce and welcome the new colleague formally at assembly – to the whole school – and even to their new classes. I have been in schools where this normal, cordial, collegial convention has been ignored.

First year teachers

I have heard too many accounts of newly qualified teachers having to engage their first year of teaching, and the new culture of their first school, without focused colleague support.

- Provision needs to be made for a "mentor" – an experienced colleague – to support the new teacher during their first term. Such support will involve regularly meeting with the new teacher to discuss any concerns, as well as being available at other times. Issues such as lesson planning, classroom management and follow-up of students are typical concerns that will need to be addressed. The mentoring role may also involve in-class teaming to give the "mentee" an opportunity to observe a senior colleague's teaching practice and conversely gain supportive feedback from the mentor observing the "mentee's" classroom teaching and management (see later).
- An in-school peer-support group can be formed to act as an "emotional clearing house" (without it being a total whinge session). Such groups can be a forum for needs identification, ideas generation, problem-solving, professional development and suggested action-planning.
- A network forum with other first year teachers (across several schools) to

discuss common concerns, needs, experiences and strategies is also an extremely useful peer-support option. (Rogers 1998)

It is also important to assist first year teachers with basic essentials such as: a decent map of the school; a list of "break" times; the published discipline policy; time-out practice; detention policy; referral procedures; and playground management procedures. These "basics" are often so well entrenched in the organisational culture that senior colleagues may forget how different, even strange, the first few weeks in a new school culture can seem for a newly qualified teacher or a teacher new to that school.

Again, a "teaching buddy" can give valuable assistance in coming to terms with these fundamentals.

Supply teachers

On the law of averages, supply teachers often take over the more difficult classes for one or several days. In some classes supply teachers are treated as "fair game" by students. They will need support similar to that offered to new teachers even if such support is "only" needed for a day's teaching cover (map, break times, and so on). It can also help if a senior teacher introduces the supply teacher to the staff *and* their new classes to enhance the link between the administration and the "new" teacher. (See, particularly, *Effective Supply Teaching*, Rogers 2003b.)

Elective mentoring

Elective mentoring can provide the opportunity for a teacher to work with a trusted, supportive colleague over a period of time, providing a basis for ongoing professional reflection; review of *characteristic* teaching and behaviour leadership and exploring opportunities for skill development.

Mentoring has to be elective if a colleague is going to feel that they have some professional ownership of the support offered through such mentoring. Obviously the normative opportunity for such mentoring needs to be present in a school for colleagues to take it up as an option.

The emphasis of such mentoring needs to be seen within a supportive, professional development context rather than "struggling-teacher context". Mentoring, in this sense, does not imply a superior–inferior relationship or an implied imputation of failure in one's teaching and management practice.

Any mentoring, even with a trusted colleague, has some natural "risk" attached. Inviting a colleague to work with you, over time, particularly in a difficult class means exposing one's personal, and professional, self-esteem to another. Collegial goodwill and professional trust can minimise any perceived sense of inadequacy as both mentor and "mentee" focus on (the) common aims and needs as the basis for mentoring support.

For example, the "mentee" may be unaware of some of the factors in the classroom dynamics that their classroom management, or even their normative teaching practice, may be affecting. A key aspect of the mentor's role will be to enable a colleague's awareness of what is actually going on in their classroom. That awareness will involve supportive feedback that addresses such teacher behaviour where necessary. This supportive feedback enables *professional self-awareness* as the precursor to encouraging change. Any feedback needs to be given with conscious sensitivity to a colleague's professional self-esteem.

Before any feedback is given, however, the mentor will need to discuss the purpose of feedback, how it is likely to be given (supportively and non-judgementally) and how such feedback might be used in ongoing action-planning, particularly the development of one's teaching and management practice.

There are a number of "stages" in the ongoing professional journey of mentor and mentee. These are set out in Figure 8.1. Any mentoring will need to begin from a basis of perceived need on the mentee's part and a willingness to work in a professionally supportive way with a colleague-mentor.

Normative whingeing: "hearing" a teacher's frustration and concern

"Whingeing" can range from the occasional grizzle and moan to an ongoing state of being! At its most typical it is frustration battling with goodwill and the constraints of time. It can also be a way of bonding with another ("in the same boat … leaking, rusty, but roughly going in the same direction").

At its most basic, and fundamental, it is often a brief, transactional occurrence or chat in the corridor or staffroom, or even as we get into our car en route to partial freedom. It can enable a reframing of built-up tension, particularly through shared humour, giving a little "coping edge" or "momentary uplift" in the day. It can also ratify a view of one's struggle; "you're not the only one".

Some whingeing, though, can be ongoing, laboured and even resilient to reframing and problem-solving. When sharing with a colleague who frequently, even consistently, moans and complains it is important to:

- listen and acknowledge (first) before offering possible suggestions – *unsolicited* advice is not always well, or easily, received. Such listening is an affirmation of

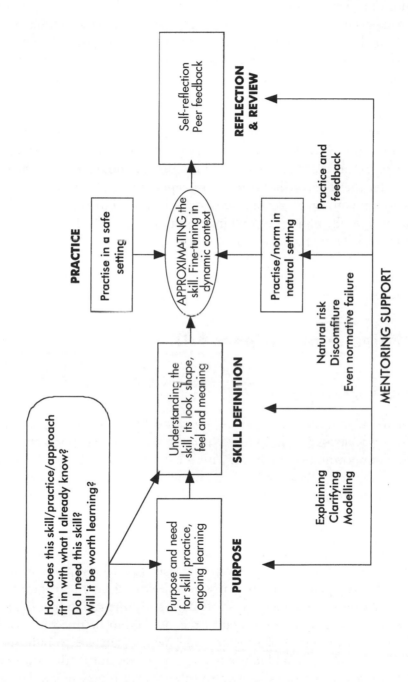

Figure 8.1 Skill development within a mentoring model

their feelings and needs; it doesn't have to validate all they are saying about a given incident or concern

■ be aware that sometimes the whingeing is enough, acting as a kind of "offloading" (even if you're the one who has been cornered for the offloading)

■ if the whingeing is a recurrent pattern, or keeps raising a recurrent theme, suggest a more focused form of support that includes some needs analysis; problem-solving; conflict-resolution (if necessary) or some kind of workable plan to address the recurrent concern

■ if whingeing descends into a destructive moaning, inaction, destructive blame or dissenting behaviour that stymies any effective change or resolution options, make it clear to the colleague what it is they are doing *through* their whingeing, and let them know that productive support will always help if the problem, issue or concern is actually confronted and addressed. Some colleagues, it seems, would rather keep whingeing about X, Y and Z than do something (anything!) about X, Y and Z.

This sort of constant whingeing behaviour can sap at the goodwill of supportive colleagues.

The mentoring process (Figure 8.1)

The particular approach

The particular mentoring model – addressed here – is one my colleagues and I utilise for behaviour leadership. It is primarily a coaching approach based in team-teaching opportunities. By being with a colleague, teaching with them – *in their class* – we can see, hear and feel the normative classroom dynamics and *characteristic* features of a teacher's behaviour leadership and teaching practice.

Problem analysis

This is aided by the mentor making early visits to the class in question. Such visits need to be well planned, particularly in respect to: how the mentor is introduced to the class (briefly); the mentor's role during team-teaching times; how any management issues might be addressed by the mentor during the course of any lesson; and any cues or signals the mentor and mentee can use to indicate when (for example) the mentor could take a management lead during the course of a lesson. I have (on many occasions) chosen to calm a disturbingly noisy class and refocus their attention during a colleague's struggle to manage whole-class behaviour. The cue for this (verbal or non-verbal) needs to be planned prior to any exercise of "direct classroom control" by the mentor. The last thing a supportive colleague needs to do is convey, publicly (to their class), that the supported colleague is an ineffective, incompetent teacher. The approach I normally use is to give a brief, verbal cue at such an appropriate time: "Excuse me, Mr Smith, do you mind if I (have a word with …) …?"

The word "mentor" comes from Homer's *Odyssey*. In this epic Greek myth, Mentor (the long-time loyal friend of Odysseus) is entrusted with the support of Odysseus' and Penelope's son, Telemachus. He carried out this role so well that the word "mentor" has come down to us today as meaning "wise advisor and guide – one who gives support, encouragement and feedback". Odysseus, king of Ithaca, was one of the heroes of the Trojan War. (The Romans named him Ulysses.)

Time-fraction

One of the organisational challenges of such mentoring is that it is labour-intensive. We need to find time (within a busy timetable) to allocate one session a week (at least) over a negotiated time frame. If we value professional development (within a mentoring model) it is possible to find and creatively use that time.

Goal setting

Mentor and "mentee" discuss and develop goals for the "mentee" to work on. These goals may include (for example) a particular approach to management (say

– establishing whole-class attention more thoughtfully or more effectively), or particular skills in the language of discipline; or even particular approaches to classroom teaching.

It is always important to remember that what seems patently obvious, and clear, to the mentor (as a "skill") may appear difficult or even confusing to the "mentee". It will be important to clarify and discuss a particular approach or skill; even practise the skill in a "safe", non-classroom, environment. It will also be important to reassure one's colleague that skill development takes time, effort and even *normative* failure; and that normative failure is OK. Any goals regarding teaching or management practice developed need to be developed collegially; they also need to be realistic, behaviourally focused, *incremental* and supported with ongoing feedback.

Feedback

For feedback to be supportive and effective it needs to focus on targeted areas; particular goals or particular skills. When giving feedback, mentor and "mentee" should focus on the present *behaviour* or the present issues observed in the natural setting of the classroom. While it is helpful to *generally* note that a certain class is particularly noisy, and difficult to settle, it also helps if the mentor *specifically* notes what they believe contributes to the noise level and restlessness (in that class); even if the mentee's behaviour (as the class teacher) is a "factor". Before any feedback session it is essential for mentor and mentee to discuss the purpose and nature of colleague feedback by mentor to mentee and vice versa.

The mentor will keep any feedback *descriptive* and be sure to focus the feedback on aspects of teacher behaviour (including discipline language). For example, one of the factors that may contribute to ineffective discipline could be frequent use by the teacher of interrogative forms of language in a management context: "*Are you* calling out ...?"; "You're not supposed to be calling out *are you*?"; "*Why* are you talking?"; "*Are you* out of your seat ...?"; "*Can you* face the front please?"; "*Haven't you* started yet?"

A teacher may be unaware of their *characteristic* language usage in discipline contexts; they may also be unaware of their non-verbal behaviour, how they "come across" to their students; they may be unaware of the interactive effect of their non-verbal behaviour; they may be unaware of how they address particular aspects of disruptive behaviour. In giving *descriptive* feedback the mentor is describing what they see, hear and perceive as a basis for shared reflection and shared action planning. Before developing any new skill repertoire a colleague will need to be aware of their current characteristic discipline/management behaviour.

Descriptive feedback, supportively and sensitively shared, enables that professional self-awareness.

Examples of the typical questions used to raise "mentee" awareness in feedback sessions are: "Were you *aware* that ...?"; "Did you *hear* yourself say ...?"; "Were you *conscious* of ...?"; "How did you *feel* when ...?"

- We should also avoid giving feedback that is too extensive or wide-ranging as it can easily dissuade or discourage a colleague. Overloaded feedback that covers too many factors about a colleague's teaching and management behaviour may make change look insurmountable. One can cope with incremental, *supported*, changes.
- Keep any feedback non-judgemental. The feedback should avoid any criticism of "personality" factors.
- Encourage, develop and affirm a colleague's skill development within and from the feedback. Professional feedback, of any kind, is most useful, valued and effective when linked to common needs, aims and objectives. My colleagues and I found the practices and skills noted in Chapters 3 and 4 (in particular) a useful framework for skill development in colleague mentoring.

Disengagement

There will need to come a time when the mentor will need to separate from the ongoing, supportive, journey with their "mentee" colleague; though occasional visits to the class are often common practice. This does not mean a lack of further support; it means the professional mentoring journey now focuses the "mentee" on *generalising* their skills and adapting their skills into their own teaching practice. A school should have its own normative opportunities for ongoing professional sharing, professional development and appraisal. Ideally, such opportunities are geared to enabling and encouraging personal and shared reflection on one's teaching and management in a spirit of professional goodwill.

Colleague support

Not all colleagues want or feel they need support from their peers; even in supportive schools. Some teachers will give support because the culture in the school makes the giving of such support easier, or perhaps because one perceives it as a personal or professional duty arising from "mutual regard" and shared perspective-taking. Within a school culture there are complex relationships that exist between personalities, structures and the demands of one's role.

Those who do give – and give unstintingly – of their time and energy to support their colleagues speak about the stress of *giving* support as well as the benefits of support enjoyed by the recipients (Rogers 2002).[1] It is important for school leadership to acknowledge these natural, creative, tensions.

Further, colleague support cannot simply be mandated. Like any feature of school culture and practice, the things that really matter cannot be mandated or forced on others (Fullan 1993; Stoll 1998; Rogers 2002). Herein lies the anomaly. Teachers generally acknowledge that they want, need and benefit from colleague support, yet a school administration cannot simply mandate that colleagues give and receive support, or that it *will* operate. This does not negate external direction, policy initiatives, and the establishing of "forms" or planned expressions of support but it does mean that what colleagues say they value and need cannot *simply* be built by policy imperative. Thoughtful procedures, plans and policies – while subject to the constraints of fallibility – can, however, be vehicles for human support and action. They can give a sense of shared purpose, dependable organisational structure, "back-up" and reciprocal interdependency. Of course such "structures" or "forms" need to be broadly and characteristically worthy of our trust. Time and usage will give the confirmation or refutation of such assurance and trust.[2]

When a school leadership seeks to address colleague support, the focus of support needs to focus on how the school, as a collegial community, can meet colleague needs. In this sense "form" always follows function. The question we always need to ask is: *does the colleague support we offer (or "plan" for) actually meet colleagues' needs?*

Collegially supportive structures, "forms", processes, opportunities, "teaming structures", and so on can be enhanced by periodic colleague review. Such a review proceeds from the affirmation that the school values mutual regard and supportive interdependency.

Needs analysis and colleague support

- How acknowledged are the individual and collective needs of colleagues at your school? In what ways are they acknowledged? What current "forms", structures, processes or policies seek to address these needs?
- Where would you regard your school, now, in terms of a general "consciousness of colleague support"? (this in part will be perceived within your current role.)
- What changes will need to be made (or are functionally able to be made) to address and seek to meet identified needs?
- What changes to current "forms", structures, plans, policies and procedures will need to be made to enable the meeting of identified needs? (Rogers 2002)

Commitment to an "ecology of support" (Rogers 2002) depends on how a community of professionals chooses to operate, and cooperate. Choices that enhance and *enable* colleague support are more likely to occur when the school culture consciously endorses, and encourages, colleague support. That kind of colleague support can only be based – fundamentally – in a sense of mutual-regard, colleague watchfulness and shared humanity.

Reflection

- If you are struggling with a difficult-to-manage class, how confident are you of obtaining colleague support? What support would you – realistically – want? Who would you seek support from? Or *expect* support from?
- If you are a senior teacher and are aware of a teacher clearly having management/discipline problems, *how would you approach them to offer support?*
- How are teachers struggling with challenging students/classes "identified" and supported in your school?
- If such teachers do not "come forward" to ask for support how do we extend/offer/process such support?
- How do you respond to the concept of short-term – immediate – support with a class losing control (p. 226f)?
- What forms/processes exist for assisting a teacher to develop a fresh start with a hard-to-manage class (p. 222f)?
- Are classroom meetings used to help refocus challenging classes? How?
- How do you respond to the definition of harassment (of teachers)? Are there any colleagues you are aware of who may be experiencing harassment from students? How is the issue of such harassment addressed in your school (pp. 230–5)?
- The behaviour leadership skills noted in Chapters 3 and 4 can provide a basis for professional review/development. In what ways could such professional development be pursued and developed in your school, your faculty, your grade team?
- What mentoring opportunities does your school offer/provide? (For first year teachers; for "buddy" systems; for coaching?)
- What feedback opportunities exist in your school (apart from summative approaches like Ofsted)?

Notes

1. In his autobiography, *Clinging to the Wreckage* (1989), John Mortimer notes that the world is divided into "nurses" and "patients" – ring a bell(?).

2. Hargreaves (1994) notes that trust can be invested in persons or processes; in the qualities and conduct of individuals, or the expertise and performance of abstract systems. It can be an outcome of meaningful face-to-face relationships or a condition of their existence (1994).

Epilogue

A cord of three strands is not quickly broken.
Ecclesiastes 4:12

No doubt, like me, you went into teaching because you believed you could make a difference to the lives of your students in their educational journey. This is a profession that takes up a good deal of our time in and out of the classroom. We also spend time outside of classroom teaching, supporting our students by sharing time and assistance, being part of special events, and keeping on top of the ever present marking and feedback. Our profession is more than a job – it is a *noblesse oblige*, and a very challenging one at that.

This book has a parallel text, beyond classroom management, discipline and effective teaching: that of colleague support. Without colleague support – reasonable, basic support – our profession is made more difficult and more stressful.

Colleague support can meet our basic needs for belonging and affiliation as well as our professional needs for affirmation, assurance, shared professional identity and supportive feedback.

From the transitional whinge and offloading to the brief assurance that we're on the right track; from the sense of shared identity through to shared teaming and appraisal, colleague support affirms and enables our coping, our morale and our professionalism.

To some of you (if you've read this far) I will have said more than enough about the sorts of management, discipline and teaching issues you face each day as a teacher; to others I will not have said enough. There is always more that can be said to qualify, extend and clarify. I hope that what I have shared has helped your *personal* reflection on your day-to-day teaching and management.

I wish you well in your teaching journey – all sanity and grace, day-to-day.

Kind regards, Bill Rogers
November, 2010 **247**

My daughter, Sarah, did this drawing when she was 11-years-old. I had been chatting with her about what I was writing on colleague support. "What's a colleague?" she had asked. I did my best to explain (my wife and I, and our oldest daughter are teachers). We chatted about colleagues (and support) she then did this drawing. The rings under the eyes show that these are teachers. She has tried to demonstrate colleague support: note the long, collegial arms!

Case studies and examples index

Glossary

Assertive behaviour   Communicating with a firm, resolute, unambiguous tone of voice and manner, matched by confident but non-aggressive body language.

Behaviour agreement   An agreed set of rules and routines that emerge from discussions with the students about behaviour and learning.

Behavioural consequences   What happens after certain behaviour; they can be an attempt to teach responsibility and accountability, for example, the teacher links a consequential outcome to a student's disruptive behaviour.

Case-supervision   This involves a key teacher working with the child, one to one, on a long-term basis. The case supervisor's role would include developing a personal, individual behaviour plan with the student, and communicating the plan to all teachers working with the student and to the student's parents.

Collegial action plan   Provides a forum and a process for meeting the moral, practical and professional needs of a colleague struggling with a hard to manage class, or several hard to manage students.

Deferred consequence   You explain what will happen if the student doesn't comply with your directed choice of behaviour, but you don't dwell on this (you move on with the lesson).

Establishment phase   The beginning of your relationship with a class, and a period when rights, rules, responsibilities, expected behaviours can be established.

Partial agreement   You might agree with the statement the student makes, but not the way they react to it.

Primary behaviour   The behaviour that is the cause of the disruption.

Relaxed vigilance   The teacher's confident, assured, firm expectations about cooperative compliance when engaged in behaviour management.

Secondary behaviour   The behaviour that contributes to the primary behaviour, for example, tone of voice, body language.

Bibliography

Autism (autism spectrum disorder)

Some very helpful resources:

- The National Autism Hotline, UK, 0845 070 4004, www.nas.org.uk
- The Centre for Social and Communication Disorders, www.patient.co.uk
- The Interact Centre, www.interactcentre.com
- Haddon, M. (2004) *The Curious Incident of the Dog in the Night-Time*. London: Vintage Random House. (A unique kind of novel about an 18-year-old with Asperger's syndrome – written by someone clearly able to see inside the mind and perceptual world of Asperger's within the context of a thoroughly good read!)
- *Martian in the Playground: Understanding the School Child with Asperger's Syndrome* (2009) London: Sage. (This should be a seminal text in schools.)
- Attwood, T.C. (2008) *The Complete Guide to Asperger's Syndrome*. London: Jessica Kingsley.
- Ben-Arich, J. and Miller, H.J. (2009) *The Educator's Guide to Teaching Students With Autism Spectrum Disorders*. Thousand Oaks, CA: Corwin Press.
- See also www.acer.edu.au/autism

Baars, C.W. (1979) *Feeling and Healing your Emotions*. Plainfield, NJ: Logos International.

Beck, A.T. (1976) *Cognitive Therapy and the Emotional Disorders*. New York: International Universities Press.

Bernard, M. (1990) *Taking the Stress out of Teaching*. Melbourne: Collins Dove.

Campbell, D. (2000) *The Mozart Effect for Children*. Sydney: Hodder.

Carr, W. (ed.) (1989) *Quality in Teaching: Arguments for a Reflective Profession*. London: Falmer.

Charles, C.M. (2005) *Building Classroom Discipline: From Models to Practice*. 8th edition. Boston, MA: Allyn and Bacon.

Clark, M. (1991) *The Quest for Grace*. Ringwood, Victoria: Penguin.

Clarke, D. and Murray, A. (eds) (1996) *Developing and Implementing a Whole-School Behaviour Policy*. London: David Fulton.

Clough, P., Garner, P., Pardeck, J.T. and Yuen, F. (eds) (2005) *Handbook of Emotional and Behavioural Difficulties*. London: Sage.

Cornett, C.E. (1986) *Learning Through Laughter: Humour in the Classroom*. Bloomington, IN: Phi Delta Kappa Educational Foundation.

Cummings, C. (1989) *Managing to Teach*. Edmonds, WA: Teaching Inc.

Denenberg, V.H. and Zarrow, M.J. (1970) "Rat pax", *Psychology Today*, 3(12): 45–7, 66–7.

Dodge, K.A. (1981) "Social competence and aggressive behaviour in children", paper presented at Midwestern Psychological Association, Detroit, Michigan, USA, May.

Dodge, K.A. (1985) "Attributional bias in aggressive children", in P.C. Kendall (ed.), *Advances in Cognitive Behavioural Research and Therapy 4*. Orlando, FL: Academic Press.

Doyle, W. (1986) "Classroom organisation and management", in M.C. Whitrock (ed.), *Handbook of Research on Teaching*. New York: Macmillan.

Dreikurs, R. (1968) *Psychology in the Classroom*. 2nd edn. New York: Harper and Row.

Dreikurs, R., Grunwald, B. and Pepper, E. (1982) *Maintaining Sanity in the Classroom*. 2nd edn. New York: Harper and Row.

Extreme situations (including restraint)

- HMSO (1974) *Health and Safety at Work Act*.
- Department for Education and Skills (2007) *School Discipline and Behaviour Policies*.
- HMSO (2005) *5 Steps to Risk Assessment*.
- Department for Education and Employment (1998) Section 550A (Education Act 1996) *The Use of Force to Control or Restrain Pupils*.
- Department of Health and Department for Education and Skills (2002) *Guidance for Restrictive Physical Interventions: How to Provide Safe Services for People with Learning Disabilities and Autism Spectrum Disorder* (Department of Health).
- Department for Education and Skills (2003) *Guidance on the Use of Restrictive Physical Interventions for Pupils with Severe Behavioural Difficulties*.
- Department for Children, Schools and Families (2007) *The Use of Force to Control or Restrain Pupils*.

Edwards, C. (1997) "RET in high school", *Rational Living*, 12: 10–12.

Edwards, C.H and Watts, V. (2008) *Classroom Discipline and Management*, 2nd Australian edn. Stafford, Queensland: John Wiley and Sons.

Ellis, A. (1977) *Anger: How to Live with it and Without it.* Melbourne: Sun Books.

Elton Report (1989) *Discipline in Schools, Report of the Committee of Inquiry.* London: HMSO.

Faber, A. and Mazlish, E. (1982) *How to Talk so Kids Will Listen and Listen so Kids Will Talk*. New York: Avon Books.

Farrell, P. and Tsakalidou, K. (1999) "Recent trends in the reintegration of pupils with emotional behavioural difficulties in the UK", *School Psychology International*, 20(4): 323–37.

Frankyl, V. (1963) *Man's Search for Meaning: An Introduction to Logotherapy*. New York: Simon and Schuster.

Fullan, M. (1993) *Change Processes: Probing the Depths of Educational Reform.* London: Falmer.

Fullan, M. and Hargreaves, A. (1991) *What's Worth Fighting For? Working Together for your School*. Toronto: Ontario Public School Teachers' Federation.

Geffner, R. and Brians, S. (1993) *Effective Teaching Approaches for ADHD Children.* Texas: ADHD Association of Texas.

Gillborn, D., Nixon, J. and Rudduck, J. (1993) *Dimensions of Discipline: Rethinking Practice in Secondary Schools*. London: HMSO.

Glasser, W. (1986) *Control Theory in Classrooms*. New York: Harper and Row.

Glasser, W. (1992) *The Quality School*. New York: HarperCollins.

Goffman, M. (1972) *The Presentation of Self in Everyday Life*. Harmondsworth: Penguin.

Green, C. and Chee, K. (1995) *Understanding ADD*. Sydney: Doubleday.

Groom, B. (2006) "Supporting the return of pupils with EBD to mainstream school from specialist provision", *Reach: Journal of Special Needs Education in Ireland*, 20(1): 61–9.

Guskey, T.R. (1986) "Staff development and the process of teacher change", *Educational Review*, 15(5): 5–12.

Hargreaves, A. (1994) "Restructuring restructuring: postmodernity and the prospects for individual change", *Journal of Education Policy*, 9(1): 47–65.

Hart, P.M. (1994) "Teacher quality of life: integrating work experiences, psychological distress and morale", *Journal of Occupational and Organisational Psychology*, 67: 109–39.

Hart, P.M., Wearing, A.J. and Conn, M. (1995) "Wisdom is a poor predictor of the relationship between discipline policy, student misbehaviour and teacher stress", *British Journal of Educational Psychology*, 1195(65): 27–48.

Hobfoll, S.E. (1998) *Stress, Culture, and Community: The Psychology and Philosophy of Stress*. New York: Plenum Press.

Howell, K. (1993) "Eligibility and need: is there a difference between being disturbed and being disturbing?", in D. Evans, M. Myhill and J. Izard (eds), *Student Behaviour Problems: Positive Initiatives and New Frontiers*. Camberwell, Victoria: ACER.

Jarman, E.C. (1992) "Management of hyperactivity: multi model interventions", *Practical Therapeutics*, August: 31–8.

Johnson, D.W. and Johnson, R.T. (1989) *Leading The Cooperative School*. Edina, MN: Interaction Book Co.

Jones, P. and Tucker, E. (eds) (1990) *Mixed Ability Teaching: Classroom Experiences in English, ESL, Mathematics and Science*. Roseberry, New South Wales: St Clair Press.

Kounin, J. (1971) *Discipline and Group Management in Classrooms*. New York: Holt, Rinehart and Winston.

Kyriacou, C. (1981) "Social support and occupational stress among school teachers", *Educational Studies*, 7: 55–60.

Kyriacou, C. (1986) *Effective Teaching in Schools*. Oxford: Basil Blackwell.

Kyriacou, C. (1991) *Essential Teaching Skills*. Oxford: Basil Blackwell.

Labi, N. (2001) "Let bullies beware", *Time Magazine*, 2 April: 45.

Lashlie, C. (2005) *"He'll Be OK: Growing Gorgeous Boys into Good Men"*. Auckland: HarperCollins.

Lazarus, R.S. (1981) "Little hassles can be hazardous to health", *Psychology Today*, July: 58–62.

Lee, C. (2004) *Preventing Bullying in Schools*. London: Sage.

Lee, C. (2007) *Resolving Behaviour Issues in Your School*. London: Sage.

Leiberman, A. (ed.) (1990) *School as Collaborative Cultures: Creating the Future Now*. London: Falmer Press.

McGrath, H. and Francey, S. (1993) *Friendly Kids, Friendly Classrooms*. Melbourne: Longman.

McInerney, D.M. and McInerney, V. (1998) *Educational Psychology – Constructing Learning*. 2nd edn. Sydney: Prentice-Hall.

McPherson, E. and Rogers, B. (2008) *Behaviour Management With Young Children: Crucial First Steps with Children 3–7 Years*. London: Sage.

Miller, A. (1996) *Pupil Behaviour and Teacher Culture*. London: Cassell.

Mortimer, J. (1984) *In Character*. London: Penguin.

Mortimer, J. (1989) *Clinging to the Wreckage*. London: Penguin.

Nias, J., Southworth, G. and Yeomans, R. (1989) *Staff Relationships in the Primary School*. London and New York: Cassell.

O'Brien, T. (1998) *Promoting Positive Behaviour*. London: David Fulton.

Ofsted (1999) *Principles Into Practice: Effective Education for Pupils with Emotional and Behavioural Difficulties.* London: Ofsted Publications.

Ofsted (2004) *Special Educational Needs and Behavioural Difficulties.* London: Ofsted Publications.

Pearce, H. (1997) "Groupwork in the classroom", unpublished notes.

Perore, S. (2000) "Workplace is a war zone", *The Age* (newspaper), 22 February: 8.

Relf, P., Hirst, R., Richardson, J. and Youdell, G. (1998) *Best Behaviour: Starting Points for Effective Behaviour Management.* Stafford: Network Educational Press.

Rickard, J. (1994) *Relaxation Activities for Children.* Melbourne: ACER Press.

Robertson, J. (1997) *Effective Classroom Control: Understanding Teacher–Pupil Relationships.* 3rd edn. London: Hodder and Stoughton.

Rogers, B. (1996) *Managing Teacher Stress.* London: Pitman.

Rogers, B. (1998) *You Know the Fair Rule and More.* London: Pitman.

Rogers, B. (2002) *"I Get By With A Little Help": Colleague Support in Schools.* London: Sage.

Rogers, B. (2003a) *Behaviour Recovery.* 2nd edn. London: Sage.

Rogers, B. (2003b) *Effective Supply Teaching.* London: Paul Chapman Publishing.

Rogers, B. (2006a) *Behaviour Management: A Whole-School Approach.* 2nd edn. London: Sage.

Rogers, B. (2006b) *Cracking the Hard Class: Strategies for Managing the Harder than Average Class.* 2nd edn. London: Sage.

Cracking the Challenging Class

The two-part DVD series (developed and filmed in a UK school) addresses the common challenges teachers face with hard-to-manage and challenging classes.

Filmed in high school classes it addresses the common issues teachers raise about challenging students and challenging classes.

Available in the UK from Books Education Conferences Ltd., Pill Farmhouse, Lostwithiel, Cornwall, PL22 0JR (Tel. 01208 872 337).

Rogers, B. (ed.) (2009) *How to Manage Children's Challenging Behaviour.* 2nd edn. London: Sage.

Rosenthal, R. and Jacobson, L.F. (1968) "Teacher expectations for the disadvantaged", *Readings from Scientific America.* San Francisco, CA: W.F. Freeman.

Russell, D.W., Altimaier, E. and Van Velzen D. (1987) "Job related stress, social support and burnout among classroom teachers", *Journal of Applied Psychology*, 72(2): 269–74.

Rutter, M., Maughan, B., Mortimer, P. and Ousten, J. (1979) *Fifteen Thousand Hours:*

Secondary Schools and their Effects on Children. London: Open Books.

Sacks, O. (1990) *Awakenings*. London: HarperCollins.

Schaffer, H.R. (2000) "The early experience assumption: past, present and future." *International Journal of Behavioural Development*, 24(1): 5–14.

Schwab, R.L. and Iwanicki, E.E. (1982) "Who are our burned out teachers?", *Educational Research Quarterly*, 7(2): 5–16.

Scott-Peck, M. (1978) *The Road Less Travelled*. London: Arrow Books.

Seligman, M. (1991) *Learned Optimism*. Sydney: Random House.

Smith, P.K. and Thompson, D. (1991) *Practical Approaches to Bullying*. London: David Fulton.

Stoll, L. (1998) "Supporting school improvement", paper presented at the OECD conference "Combating Failure at School", Christchurch, New Zealand, 1–5 February.

Tauber, R.T. (1995) *Classroom Management Theory and Practice*. 2nd edn. New York: Harcourt Brace.

Thody, A., Gray, B. and Bowden, D. (2000) *The Teacher's Survival Guide*. London: Continuum. This book contains a useful and very practical guide to Voice Management. Graham Welch's essay is very helpful for those enabling mentoring support or professional development generally.

Thompson, J.A.K. (trans.) (1969) *The Ethics of Aristotle: The Nichomachean Ethics*. London: Penguin.

Wolfgang, C.H. (1999) *Solving Discipline Problems: Methods and Models for Today's Teacher*. Boston: Allyn and Bacon.

Woodhouse, D.A., Hall, E. and Wooster, A.D. (1985) "Taking control of stress in teaching", *British Journal of Educational Psychology*, 55: 119–23.

Index

Added to a page number 'f' denotes a figure and 'n' denotes notes.

SUCCEEDING ON YOUR PRIMARY PGCE

Graham Birrell, **Helen Taylor** and **Hellen Ward**
all at Canterbury Christ Church University

Studying for a Primary Postgraduate Certificate in Education (PGCE) can be demanding, but this book will help you to succeed on this intensive and challenging course.

By showing you how to make the most of your time on the PGCE, the book encourages you to take a positive and proactive approach to your studies, and to reflect on and learn from your experiences.

This is an indispensible guide for those embarking on a Primary PGCE, and offers those considering applying for the course an invaluable insight into what to expect and how to get onto a PGCE. The advice is based on the authors' successful work with thousands of trainee teachers over many years, and there are case studies of successful students and students who struggled. This book is a lifeline for those working hard towards the ultimate goal of becoming a great teacher.

2010 • 136 pages
Cloth (978-1-84920-029-5) •£60.00
Paper (978-1-84920-030-1) •£16.99

ALSO FROM SAGE

THE COMPLETE GUIDE TO BEHAVIOUR FOR TEACHING ASSISTANTS AND SUPPORT STAFF

Chris Lee *Former Head of the School of Continuing Professional Development at the University of Plymouth*

By providing a thorough grounding in the theory behind behaviour management, followed by suggestions for successful strategies to use in the classroom, this book gives the reader the confidence to manage the challenging behaviour of children and young people in educational contexts.

Written specifically for teaching assistants and support staff, this book covers behaviour, motivation and discipline issues with their specific role and position in mind. Supported by the views and responses of current students on Foundation Degrees and those working towards HLTA status, the book reflects the difficulties, dilemmas and successes of this vital group of people working in today's classrooms.

There are three main types of teaching assistant: the discipliner; the negotiator; the counsellor. This book helps the reader to find their own behaviour management style, and their own way of working.

Chris Lee was until recently Senior Lecturer in Education and Head of the School of Continuing Professional Development at the Faculty of Education, University of Plymouth. He has taught in secondary and special schools, and continues to work with teachers on issues of bullying and behaviour management. He is now a freelance educational consultant.

November 2010 • 136 pages
Cloth (978-1-84787-583-9) •£60.00
Paper (978-1-84787-584-6) •£17.99

ALSO AVAILABLE

HOW TO MANAGE CHILDREN'S CHALLENGING BEHAVIOUR

Second Edition

Edited by **Bill Rogers** *Independent Educational Consultant, Victoria, Australia*

In this new edition of his bestselling book, Bill Rogers brings together contributions from practising teachers that suggest ways to tackle disruptive and challenging behaviour. Bill introduces and comments on each chapter, setting out key principles for behaviour leadership in the style that makes him such a popular author. There are numerous case studies drawn from practice, each showing how the teacher manages the situation and what the outcome was: these examples from practice highlight the difference teachers can make to their students' behaviour, attitude, self-esteem and peer acceptance.

Chapters look at: finding a way back from inappropriate behaviour; dealing with very challenging behaviour on a daily basis; and creating a peaceful school and developing positive practice.

Dr. Bill Rogers is an Education Consultant and author who lectures widely on behaviour management, discipline, effective teaching, stress management and teacher welfare across the UK, Australia and New Zealand. All royalties from the sale of this book are donated to the charity World Vision and their children's education programmes in South East Asia.

2009 • 208 pages
Cloth (978-1-84860-684-5) •£67.00
Paper (978-1-84860-685-2) •£21.99

ALSO AVAILABLE